THE PRICE OF WHITENESS

THE PRICE OF WHITENESS

JEWS, RACE, AND
AMERICAN IDENTITY

Eric L. Goldstein

PRINCETON UNIVERSITY PRESS

PRINCETON AND OXFORD

COPYRIGHT © 2006 BY PRINCETON UNIVERSITY PRESS
PUBLISHED BY PRINCETON UNIVERSITY PRESS, 41 WILLIAM STREET,
PRINCETON, NEW JERSEY 08540
IN THE UNITED KINGDOM: PRINCETON UNIVERSITY PRESS,
3 MARKET PLACE, WOODSTOCK, OXFORDSHIRE OX20 1SY
ALL RIGHTS RESERVED

LIBRARY OF CONGRESS CATALOGING-IN-PUBLICATION DATA

GOLDSTEIN, ERIC L.
THE PRICE OF WHITENESS : JEWS, RACE, AND AMERICAN IDENTITY /
ERIC L. GOLDSTEIN.
P. CM.
INCLUDES BIBLIOGRAPHICAL REFERENCES AND INDEX.
ISBN-13: 978-0-691-12105-5 (CLOTH : ALK. PAPER)
ISBN-10: 0-691-12105-2 (CLOTH : ALK. PAPER)
1. JEWS—UNITED STATES—IDENTITY. 2. JEWS—CULTURAL
ASSIMILATION—UNITED STATES. 3. SOCIAL INTEGRATION—UNITED STATES.
4. EUROPEAN AMERICANS—RACE IDENTITY. 5. WHITES—RACE
IDENTITY—UNITED STATES. 6. UNITED STATES—RACE RELATIONS.
7. UNITED STATES—ETHNIC ELATIONS. I. TITLE.
E184.36.E84G65   2006
305.892′4073—dc22   2005043927

BRITISH LIBRARY CATALOGING-IN-PUBLICATION DATA IS AVAILABLE.

THIS BOOK HAS BEEN COMPOSED IN SABON

PRINTED ON ACID-FREE PAPER. ∞

PUP.PRINCETON.EDU

PRINTED IN THE UNITED STATES OF AMERICA

1   3   5   7   9   10   8   6   4   2

FOR CHERYL

CONTENTS

FIGURES

ACKNOWLEDGMENTS

DURING THE research and writing of this book I have benefited from the support and assistance of many individuals and institutions. First and foremost, I owe a great debt to the teachers and mentors who have helped shape me as a scholar and have guided me in my work. Lydia Smithers and Mame Warren helped spark my interest in academic pursuits and have continued to influence me more than they will ever know. Todd M. Endelman, my adviser at the University of Michigan, has not only been a constant source of support and encouragement but also a model of scholarship, professionalism, and collegiality. Miriam Bodian, David Scobey, Regina Morantz-Sanchez, Zvi Gitelman, Anita Norich, and Andy Achenbaum all contributed to my intellectual development in important ways.

Several institutions helped fund this project by providing grants and fellowships. In the initial stages of research and writing, I benefited from the generosity of the Andrew W. Mellon Foundation, the YIVO Institute for Jewish Research, the American Jewish Archives, the Pew Program in Religion and American History at Yale University, the Charlotte Newcombe Fellowship Program at the Woodrow Wilson National Fellowship Foundation, the Memorial Foundation for Jewish Culture, and the Rackham School of Graduate Studies at the University of Michigan. Grants from the National Endowment for the Humanities and the Meyer and Rosaline Feinstein Center for American Jewish History at Temple University helped in the completion of the project. I would also like to thank Emory College, the Emory Graduate School of Arts and Sciences, and the Tam Institute for Jewish Studies at Emory University for providing support toward the publication of this book.

For their research assistance, I give my warm appreciation to the librarians and archivists at YIVO, the American Jewish Archives, the American Jewish Historical Society, Duke University Library, the Jewish Theological Seminary of America, the New York Public Library, the New York Society for Ethical Culture, the Library of Congress, the University of Chicago Library, the William Breman Jewish Heritage Museum in Atlanta, the Chicago Historical Society, and the Klau Library of the Hebrew Union College–Jewish Institute of Religion in Cincinnati. Particular thanks go to Kevin Proffitt of the American Jewish Archives, who consistently answered research requests from afar. On the home front, the dedicated librarians at Emory's Robert Woodruff Library—Marie Hansen, Jana Lonberger, Eric Nitschke, Marie Nitschke, and Tarina Rosen—have been unstinting in their willingness to help. I would also like to acknowledge the help of Daniel Soyer and Daniel Levy, who sent me research materials that proved useful during the course of the project.

I am indebted to those who generously gave of their time to read the manuscript at various stages of completion. Hasia Diner, Marc Dollinger, George Fredrickson, Jeffrey Lesser, Tony Michels, Jonathan Prude, and Jonathan Sarna all read the entire work and provided helpful comments and suggestions. I thank Mark Bauman, Joe Crespino, Gary Okihiro, Bianca Premo, and Philippe Rosenberg for reading parts of the work and for helping me through difficult spots. I offer my deep gratitude to Brigitta van Rheinberg and the entire team at Princeton Univeristy Press—Cindy Crumrine, Ellen Foos, Allison Kalett, and Clara Platter—for all they have done to shepherd me through the publication process and to transform my manuscript into a beautiful book.

Also essential to the completion of this work have been the many friends and colleagues whose support has helped sustain me over the last several years. Hasia Diner, Deborah Dash Moore, Pamela Nadell, Marc Lee Raphael, Jonathan Sarna, and Steve Whitfield have shown me exceptional kindness and offered me important opportunities to advance my career as a scholar and teacher. The members of the History Department and in the Tam Institute for Jewish Studies at Emory University have been a constant source of encouragement and intellectual ferment. Wally Adamson, Michael Berger, David Blumenthal, Jeffrey Lesser, Deborah Lipstadt, and Jamie Melton have given me critical advice and support. Karla Goldman, Benjamin Hary, Stephen Hum, Nadia Malinovich, Tony Michels, Marc Miller, Matthew Payne, Bianca Premo, Philippe Rosenberg, and Marina Rustow have provided friendship as well as scholarly insight.

Most importantly, my family helped me persevere when the process of writing seemed daunting. My children, Max Evan and Ella Ruth, have filled each day with joy and contentment. My parents, Lawrence Goldstein and Betty Goldstein have continued throughout this project to be the kind, generous, and reassuring parents they have always been. I am grateful to my father- and mother-in-law, Steven and Renee Haas, and my sister-in-law, Melissa Haas, for always helping out when I had to travel or work late. Finally, I am forever indebted to my wife, Cheryl Haas-Goldstein, without whose love, caring, and patience this book would never have been completed.

INTRODUCTION

MANY AMERICANS today, focused as they are on the basic division between whites and "peoples of color," would undoubtedly accept the judgment of the eminent African American writer James Baldwin, who claimed in 1967 that Jews' history of difference and exclusion meant little in the United States. While the Jew had suffered abroad, wrote Baldwin at the height of the civil rights movement, here his "only relevance is that he is white."[1]

Baldwin's statement underscored the dramatically different experiences America had offered to Jews and blacks. In a society where the color line played a major role in determining social status, Jews had been able to achieve a high level of success and integration by the 1960s, while African Americans were often still fighting for basic freedoms. In arguing that the color line had created a wholly welcoming, unproblematic environment for Jews in American society, however, Baldwin failed to capture the tumultuousness that had often accompanied Jews' efforts to find acceptance in a society organized around the categories of "black" and "white." Far from playing the role of undifferentiated whites, Jews held an uncertain relationship to whiteness from the late nineteenth century until the end of World War II, a period when both Jews and non-Jews spoke of the "Jewish race" and of "Hebrew blood." Although these racialized understandings of Jewishness have long been discredited among scientists and laypeople, they were very real to those who employed them during these years. As this study argues, Jews' transition from "racial" minority to part of the white mainstream was slow and freighted with difficulty, not only because native-born whites had a particularly difficult time seeing Jews as part of a unified, homogenous white population, but also because whiteness sat uneasily with many central aspects of Jewish identity.

To white Americans of the pre–World War II era, Jews were a racial conundrum, a group that could not be clearly pinned down according to the prevailing racial categories. Members of the dominant society had a long-standing investment in the notion of a clear racial dichotomy between blacks and whites, a vision that gave them a sense of unity and superiority as they faced the challenges of the nation. Despite the diverse nature of the American population and the presence of many groups that were considered distinct in a racial sense—Native Americans, Asians, Latinos and various European groups as well as African Americans—whites consistently tried to understand the racial landscape through the categories of "black" and "white." Thus, even as American racial commentators frequently spoke of Mongolians and Mexicans, Celts and Teutons, Alpines and Mediterraneans, they often struggled to suppress this unnerving complexity by marking some of these groups as good candidates for assimilation into white America and confirming others as racial outsiders by comparing them to and lumping them with African Americans.[2]

Jews, however, presented a mix of qualities that was unusual among American "racial" groups and proved particularly resistant to categorization within the black-white system. In the minds of white Americans, Jews were clearly racial outsiders in many ways, demonstrating distinctive social patterns, clustering in urban neighborhoods, concentrating in certain trades and professions, and largely marrying within their own group. At the same time, however, most Jews did not conform to the assumptions many Americans made about the lowly status of despised racial minorities. Certainly, there were poor Jews who lived in squalid conditions, especially after the massive wave of Jewish immigration from Eastern Europe began in the 1880s. But among European immigrant groups, Jews boasted an unusually high proportion of merchants and skilled workers, and they tended to rise rather quickly on the economic ladder.[3] Unlike African Americans, who were seen by whites of the nineteenth and early twentieth centuries as the epitome of a backward, preindustrial race, Jews appeared to be thoroughly implicated in the urban, industrial, capitalist order that characterized the modern "civilized" world.

Because white Americans saw Jews as racially different and yet similar to themselves in many ways, the image they attached to them tended to be much more ambivalent than the one fastened on African Americans and other more stable outsiders. Jews could be seen as contributors to progressive capitalism or as self-interested parasites; as disciplined and ambitious or as ruthlessly focused on profit. While the black-white discourse of race bolstered white Americans' sense of confidence and superiority, their image of the Jew reflected the doubts and anxieties they harbored about their own society, ultimately undermining the efficacy of their black-white worldview. During the initial decades of the century, white Americans often tried to suppress the troubling image of the Jew as they had suppressed the distinctiveness of other groups—either by comparing them to blacks or predicting their speedy assimilation into white society. Despite such efforts, however, the distinctiveness of the Jews and their failure to fit neatly within the categories of "black" and "white" continued to vex American commentators through the end of World War II.

Another factor complicating the Jews' relationship to whiteness was their own intricate means of self-definition. While the knowledge that they were considered a problematic group in the American racial schema motivated Jews to try to conform to the prevailing racial paradigm and identify themselves unambiguously as white, their ongoing commitment to a distinctive identity often cut against their attempts to claim whiteness.

These tensions emerged in two distinct situations. First, Jews faced a dilemma in determining what their proper approach should be to the nation's primary racial outsiders, African Americans. In order to allay fears that they were an unstable racial element in white society, Jews often felt the need to assert a distinguishing line between themselves and the country's black population. They hoped that by affirming the color line, they might help divert attention away from the problems raised by their own distinctiveness. Yet they often found their efforts complicated by a sense of identification with blacks and feelings of empathy for their plight. Though immigrants of many backgrounds had experienced persecution in their homelands, Jews were the group whose self-image was most thoroughly bound up with outsider status.[4] As a result, they frequently had strong misgivings about engaging in the kind of exclusivist behavior from which they had long suffered. The Jews' highly ambivalent approach to African Americans during the pre–World War II period reflected their inability to either reject or embrace the racial conventions of white America.

Second, an equally wrenching dilemma for Jews was the struggle they faced over their own racial self-definition. Having long been confined to the social margins of the Central and Eastern European societies in which they lived, Jews from those regions had come to see "apartness" as one of the most salient aspects of Jewish identity. As a result, in the American context they often defined themselves as a distinct "race," a description that captured their strong emotional connection to Jewish peoplehood. As Jews came under increasing scrutiny in American racial discourse, however, they were often torn between their commitment to Jewish racial identity and their desire to be seen as stable members of white society. Jews often tried to obscure, downplay, or tailor their racial self-understanding to conform to the needs of the larger culture, but ultimately it continued to make its claim on them as they fashioned themselves as white Americans. Thus, in multiple ways, claiming the status of "whites" in America was far from simple for Jews. It involved a complex emotional process in which conflicting desires for acceptance and distinctiveness often found no easy balance.

In detailing Jews' uneasy relationship to whiteness, this book makes clear that the history of race in America cannot be reduced to a story of black and white. It demonstrates that the black-white racial dichotomy has functioned in American history less as an accurate description of social reality than as an ideology, which has been mobilized at critical points to control a much more complex and varied social landscape. By casting light on the constant, albeit unsuccessful, effort to fit Jewishness into a black-white framework, the book reveals white Americans' anxious attempts to obscure the fissures that divided them internally, underscoring just how tenuous the notion of a stable, monolithic whiteness has been in American life.

Even as I underscore the ideological nature of the black-white divide and its insufficiency for understanding a diverse American population, however, I also recognize the power this vision of American society has had in shaping people's lives. First and foremost, African Americans have had to suffer the social consequences of an ideology that positioned them as the essential "others" of an idealized white America. My interest in this study, however, is to demonstrate the tremendous pressures Jews and similar groups were under to conform to the dominant racial paradigm, and the significant constraints that were placed on expressions of group difference by a world intent on seeing itself in terms of black and white.

In writing this book, I have drawn on two very different streams of historical scholarship. First, I have been greatly influenced by the concerns of historians working in the field of American Jewish history. Their attention to the enduring influence of Jewish identity in the United States and the ways in which Jews continually tried to balance commitments to their group and to the larger society inform much of what is presented here.[5] Despite my great debt to these scholars, however, I find that my conclusions are somewhat less sanguine than theirs about the degree to which Jews were able to synthesize American and Jewish identities. American Jewish history is often told as a story of successful adaptation and transformation, but when viewed through Jews' struggle with American racial culture, it is a story of hard choices and conflicting emotions.[6]

The second major influence on this work has been the recent literature on "whiteness" as a social construction. Here, I have found extremely helpful the groundbreaking insight that European immigrants did not automatically become white on these shores, but had to learn and claim this status as they acculturated. In the course of documenting Jews' uneasy encounter with race in America, however, I have been struck by the tendency of scholars in this field to posit a fairly uncomplicated embrace of whiteness by immigrant groups and to downplay the way in which other "racial" identities such as Irishness or Jewishness may have continued to disrupt, confound, or inflect the immigrants' understanding of themselves as white. As a result, they often leave the impression that while American racial categories were fluid and imprecise in the initial years of the various immigrant waves, such ambiguity was quickly resolved as immigrants responded to the overwhelming dominance of the black-white paradigm.[7] The experience of American Jews, however (and I believe this holds true, albeit in different ways, for other immigrant groups as well), demonstrates that whiteness was not stable and monolithic but was constantly informed and reshaped by other competing identities.[8]

The story of American Jewish racial identity also makes clear how persistent the tensions between whiteness and Jewishness have been. Even the entrance of Jews into the white mainstream did not resolve them, for the more Jews became securely integrated in white society, the more their impulses for distinctiveness emerged. By the end of the twentieth century, an increasing number of Jews were asserting their "tribal" bonds to one another and stressing their "shared history" with African Americans, revealing nagging doubts about the toll acceptance in white America had taken on their own distinctive minority identity. Instead of facing the rejection of whites who were uncertain about Jewish racial status, Jews after 1965 encountered growing rejection by African Americans, who often challenged their right to present themselves as a persecuted minority. After a century, Jews were still struggling with the constraints of the black-white dichotomy. For reasons such as these, I have chosen not to frame this book as a study of how Jews *became* white, but as one that explores how Jews *negotiated* their place in a complex racial world where Jewishness, whiteness, and blackness have all made significant claims on them. In this way, the nuances, and the competing identities that never quite disappeared, have remained a central part of the story.

Finally, this book complicates not only the dichotomous nature of American society and the monolithic understanding of whiteness; it also questions the simplistic way in which moral questions relating to whiteness are understood. Writing on whiteness almost always emphasizes the unmitigated benefits such an identity confers on the holder: power, social status, and financial rewards that are attained primarily by the exclusion of African Americans and other peoples of color.[9] American Jews' struggle with whiteness, however, suggests that the story of racial assimilation in the United States cannot be reduced to a simple morality tale. To the extent that historians of whiteness have understood the constraints and pressures placed on acculturating immigrants by American racial culture, they have brushed over these themes to assert that identifying as white was largely a matter of individual choice. "White ethnics, while they lived under conditions not of their own choosing," writes David Roediger, "by and large chose whiteness, and even struggled to be recognized as white."[10] Positing the "whitening" of immigrants as a power play from below, however, minimizes the degree to which they were pushed toward whiteness by the needs of the larger, white society. In many ways it was native-born whites, bent on preserving a stable and optimistic vision of their national culture, who had the greatest stake in seeing Jews take on the role of white Americans. Given such pressure from above, those who wished to enter the mainstream of American life were left with few alternatives. Certainly Jews, like all European immigrants, pursued whiteness; it was key to their meteoric rise to become one of the most successful American ethnic groups. But there was also a good deal of coercion involved in the process by which Jews became part of the white majority, a process that entailed significant losses as well as gains.

In documenting Jews' encounter with whiteness, the chapters that follow explore its material and social benefits but also take seriously its emotional costs. They argue that even as Jews pursued whiteness, they wrestled with its consequences and tried to preserve other cherished means of self-definition that resided uneasily within its confines. While American Jews were never forced to deny their Jewishness altogether, the ultimate loss of "race" as a term for self-description rendered inarticulate some of their deepest feelings of group solidarity and difference. Similarly, the need to identify as white made it exceedingly difficult for Jews to assert a minority consciousness in American society, something that was extremely central to many Jews' self-conception. Some Jews were able to find an outlet for these feelings by expressing empathy for African Americans or becoming involved in civil rights causes. But for most Jews, who had to work hard to preserve their own social status in the years before World War II or who have been rebuffed in the years since by those who see Jews purely as white "insiders," even these surrogate expressions of minority consciousness could be accomplished only in an inconsistent, ambivalent way. Thus, acceptance often came at a heavy price, belying the widespread notion that the pursuit of whiteness conferred only privilege. While American Jews were often buoyed by their ability to move freely in white America, their entry into that world resulted in alienation, communal breakdown, and psychic pain as surely as it produced the exhilaration of acceptance in non-Jewish society.

This book is divided into four parts. Part I ("The Jewish 'Race' in America"), consisting of a single chapter, takes us back to the last quarter of the nineteenth century, a period in which Jews remained relatively marginal to American discussions of race and therefore enjoyed a great degree of latitude in crafting a racial self-definition without bringing their status as white into question. Part II ("Jews in Black and White") focuses on the Progressive Era, a time when mounting problems of modernization and an increased desire on the part of white Americans for order and hierarchy brought the Jews under more intense racial scrutiny. In a series of three chapters, I explore how white Americans increasingly tried to fit the Jews into a black-white mold, and how Jews were pushed to struggle with their approach to African Americans and with the issue of Jewish racial self-definition as a means of defending their status as white. Part III ("Confronting Jewish Difference"), which also consists of three chapters, details how the issues first raised in the Progressive Era intensified during the interwar years as both Jews and non-Jews found themselves unable to obscure Jewish difference beneath the categories of "black" and "white." As white Americans began to refer to a distinct "Jewish Problem" in the United States, Jews found themselves caught in a seemingly irresolvable conflict between their unshakable group commitments and their desire to identify as white. Part IV ("From Old Challenges to New") consists of a final chapter that explains how Jews ultimately came to be accepted as unambiguous whites in the World War II era. It also argues that this transition was not the end of Jews' difficult encounter with the black-white dichotomy, but in many ways the beginning of a new struggle to maintain their group distinctiveness. The epilogue focuses on the contemporary period to demonstrate how many of these issues are still central in the lives of American Jews today.

PART I

THE JEWISH "RACE" IN AMERICA, 1875–1895

CHAPTER 1

"DIFFERENT BLOOD FLOWS IN OUR VEINS": RACE AND JEWISH SELF-DEFINITION IN LATE-NINETEENTH-CENTURY AMERICA

IN 1887, Solomon Schindler, rabbi of Boston's Temple Israel, delivered a Friday evening sermon to his congregation on the topic "Why Am I a Jew?" Schindler spoke of the universal task of Judaism, its superior logical foundation, and its concordance with reason in explaining why he was a follower of Jewish religious teachings. But first and foremost, he emphasized, his connection to Jewishness was a matter of "race." Despite the fact that the Jewish nation had disappeared from the earth, Schindler told his congregants, "it remains a fact that we spring from a different branch of humanity, that different blood flows in our veins, that our temperament, our tastes, our humor is different. . . . In a word, we differ [from non-Jews] in our views and in our mode of thinking in many cases as much as we differ in our features."[1]

The use of "race" as a positive means for self-description among American Jews has not been well documented by historians and, given the contemporary implications of the term, most likely comes as quite a shock to the modern reader. Even more surprising is the fact that this self-description was employed by Schindler, one of the most radical exponents of nineteenth-century Reform Judaism, a movement usually seen by scholars as having distanced itself from strong expressions of Jewish particularism in its attempt to adapt to the American setting. What Schindler's remark testifies to, however, is the pervasive use of racial language as a means for Jewish self-definition in late-nineteenth-century America, even among those most anxious to take their place in American life. By "race" nineteenth-century Jews meant something different from "ethnicity" in its present usage. Their conception of Jewish distinctiveness was one rooted not in cultural particularity but in biology, shared ancestry, and blood. Such overt racial discourse has usually been treated by modern Jewish historians as the province of antisemites, yet racial language also served as an attractive form of self-expression for Jews.[2] American Jews drew comfort from a racial self-definition because it gave them a sense of stability at a time when many familiar markers of Jewish identity were eroding. Despite its strong biological thrust, the racial definition of Jewishness did not impede Jews' identification with American society and institutions during these years. Because non-Jews of the period generally saw the "Jewish race" in a positive light and defined it as part of the white "family" of races, Jews had few reservations about defining their communal bonds in racial terms. Race, then, fit the needs of Jews to define themselves in a changing social landscape, allowing for emotional security and a degree of communal assertiveness without threatening their standing in the larger white world.

The Setting: Shifting Social Boundaries

The social conditions that promoted a racial self-definition among Jews in America did not emerge until the 1870s. Before that decade Jews preferred to describe themselves in ways that furthered their unimpeded acculturation into American life. During the nineteenth century, Jews in the United States—largely immigrants from Central Europe—enjoyed a level of inclusion unmatched at that time in any other setting. While Jews in many European countries had obtained the same rights as other citizens, their exclusion from certain national institutions often prevented them from being seen as authentic Germans, Frenchmen, or Englishmen. By contrast, America had no royal family, no established church, no landed aristocracy; its national culture was more fluid, diverse, and open to new influences. Under these circumstances, Jews felt themselves to be an integral part of American society and adopted American ways with zeal. They changed their habits of dress, their language, their dietary and leisure practices, and even their mode of worship to conform to American styles.[3] They spoke of themselves as a religious community because they felt such a description would ease their adaptation to a country that respected religious diversity. Rabbi Isaac Mayer Wise, a champion of Americanization and the emerging spokesman for the country's Jews, expressed this sentiment in 1859: "We are Jews in the synagogue and Americans everywhere."[4]

Despite the speed with which Jewish immigrants from Central Europe adapted to American customs, manners, and mores, however, these changes did not reflect a thorough integration of Jews into the intimate social circles of their non-Jewish neighbors. While Jews publicly stressed their identity as a religious group, they continued to spend their leisure hours with other Jews, marry other Jews, and express their strong social bonds through an elaborate network of communal institutions. Across the country, clubs and fraternal organizations served as focuses for Jewish social solidarity, which often proved more durable than ties to the synagogue. A historian of the Chicago Jewish community estimates that by the late nineteenth century these organizations had eclipsed the synagogue as the major institutions of Jewish life in the city.[5] For men, fraternal lodges such as B'nai B'rith, often with their own elaborate rituals, served as what historian Deborah Dash Moore has called a "secular synagogue" and became a more popular form of Jewish affiliation than the religious congregation.[6] Jewish women remained more devoted to religious observance than their male counterparts, but these pursuits remained only part of a larger sphere of activity where Jewishness was expressed in social terms.

Of course, the openness of American culture and the desire of Jews to attain a position of prestige in American life prevented their complete isolation from non-Jewish social activities. Jewish men were often welcomed in German-American athletic and singing societies and frequently joined Masonic lodges.[7] In some cities there were social clubs that catered to both Jews and non-Jews. But in general, before the 1870s Jewish immigrant men had little extensive social interaction with non-Jews, and Jewish immigrant women had almost none. Even in smaller Jewish centers, where social contact between the two groups was more common, Jews still preferred to meet non-Jews in organizations such as Atlanta's Concordia Association, where Jews formed the majority.[8] At the Los Angeles Social Club, an organization of similar composition, young Jewish women usually attended only those events at which most of the men were Jewish.[9] This pattern suggests that Jews formed their own clubs not merely as a result of social discrimination but because of an assumption by *both* Jews and non-Jews that, despite some interaction, each group would carry on separate social relations. What Max Vorspan and Lloyd Gartner have said of Los Angeles during this period seems to have been the rule for the rest of the country as well: "there was a line of social assimilation beyond which the Jews voluntarily did not go."[10]

By the 1870s, however, the line that had distinguished Jewish and non-Jewish social circles began to grow less distinct. More than a decade after immigration from Central Europe had reached its peak, Jewish immigrants and their children were beginning to attain a level of wealth and social prominence that brought them into closer contact with non-Jews. While social exclusivity did not vanish in either group, Jews and non-Jews increasingly met one another at the theater, at summer resorts, and in certain social clubs. Such interaction was further encouraged by the rise of a younger generation that no longer took the social divide between Jews and others for granted.

The blurring of social boundaries created a feeling of uncertainty and uneasiness on the part of both Jews and non-Jews. The loss of those distinctions that had given shape and definition to their lives left each group scrambling to erect new boundaries that would help provide stability in this time of change. For some non-Jews, especially those vying for upward mobility in the wake of the Civil War, social discrimination against Jews became a way of asserting their claim to membership in polite society. The late nineteenth century saw a growing number of resorts and public accommodations closed to Jews due to the demands of non-Jewish customers, while clubs, lodges, and other social and civic organizations that had once admitted Jews now began to exclude them. Citing Jewish vulgarity and "clannishness," these status-conscious non-Jews enacted restrictions to prevent what they saw as the dangerous leveling of social distinctions.[11]

For Jews, the shifting social boundaries of the period posed an even greater challenge. Despite the rise in social discrimination, the last decades of the nineteenth century brought the Jewish immigrants from Central Europe unprecedented opportunities for social integration. While these opportunities made Jews ebullient, they also raised anxieties about what borders were to remain between them and the rest of society. Much of this anxiety stemmed from the tension between Jews' impulse for integration and their desire to maintain a distinctive Jewish identity. Jews' history of persecution and social exclusion had imbued them with a strong minority consciousness that was not easily surrendered and that led them to place a high value on group survival. Since social ties were seen as the protective force that had guaranteed Jewish continuity in the past, most Jews were reluctant to break these bonds. And while others were less concerned with preserving a level of social distinctiveness, even those most anxious for integration retained an emotional attachment to the Jewish group. In 1889, the *American Hebrew* jokingly commented on the large class of Jews who could say, "But still I'm a Jew / Although it is true / There's nothing that's Jewish / I care for or do."[12] In fact, whatever their level of Jewish commitment, Jews became more self-conscious about their Jewish identity as they became increasingly immersed in a non-Jewish world.

Given their emergent sensitivity to the question of identity, American Jews were unnerved by trends during the 1870s that underscored the dangers social integration posed for Jewish cohesion. Occasionally these fears were fueled by events of spectacular force, like the "apostasy" of Felix Adler, the son of a prominent New York rabbi who left the Jewish community to form the Society of Ethical Culture in 1876.[13] More commonly, however, they focused on marriages between Jews and non-Jews, which were occurring on a small but previously unheard of scale. While the exact rate of intermarriage is unknown for this period, the increasing concern expressed in the Jewish press indicates a perception among Jews that its rise was undermining the basis of Jewish peoplehood. "In America such marriages become alarmingly numerous," complained Rabbi Bernhard Felsenthal in 1879. "The aversion against entering into family connections with non-Jews is not so strong any more as it used to be, particularly if the family is in good social and financial position."[14] The *American*

Hebrew predicted that further intermarriages would spell the end of both Judaism and the Jews. The problem, it explained, was not only religious, but also "ethnological and sociological."[15]

If alarm was voiced over intermarriage, the shapers of communal discourse—largely men—also became concerned over the increasing exposure of Jewish women to non-Jewish social circles. Before the 1870s, Jewish women had remained more isolated from social interaction with non-Jews than their husbands, fathers, and brothers, allowing men to assign them responsibility for the preservation of Jewishness in the home sphere. Although this perceived responsibility stemmed largely from Victorian gender roles, Jewish men argued that women's position as guardians of Jewish survival was central to Jewish tradition.[16] As a result, when mixed-sex forms of leisure became more popular and allowed Jewish women greater opportunities to meet those from other backgrounds, many of their male counterparts feared that they would abandon their posts.

While wives were thought to be in danger of ceding their responsibilities, Jewish men raised special concern about the vulnerability of unmarried women to the allure of assimilation and defection. "Maftir," the San Francisco correspondent of the *American Israelite*, expressed this anxiety in an 1880 letter that described the marriage of a local young woman to a non-Jew. The Jewish community had long since accustomed itself to men who married outside the community, he wrote, but "when . . . a Jewish girl links her fortune with that of a Christian, the thing looks, as yet, quite different, because it is not in style."[17] If this marriage unsettled San Francisco Jewry, an 1875 report confirmed a fear among American Jews so widespread that "few Jewish fathers or brothers, no matter how lax in their religious observances, would think of introducing a Christian gentleman to their daughters or sisters."[18] The Jewish community expressed even greater alarm three years later, when a daughter of Isaac Mayer Wise was secretly married to one of her brother's non-Jewish friends.[19] Since Jewish men had cast women as the representatives of the Jewish home, many in the community feared that the increasing social interaction of Jewish women with non-Jews threatened the ultimate dissolution of the Jews as a social unit.

Thus, the 1870s introduced a new challenge American Jews would face through the close of the century: how to articulate their attachment to Jewishness in the face of social trends they feared were eroding Jewish cohesiveness. Although religious tradition had already begun to wane in the first decades following immigration, social exclusiveness, endogamous marriage, and the concentration of women in the private sphere had all combined to keep the social boundaries between Jews and non-Jews more or less stable through the 1860s. The weakening of these practices in the socially fluid period following the Civil War necessitated a new means for Jews to mark the boundaries of Jewishness. At the same time, the rise of social discrimination made them anxious to counter accusations that they were "clannish" and hostile to fellowship with other Americans. If their concern for maintaining group boundaries increased, they still wished to continue their drive for social acceptance unabated. Under these circumstances, Jews created a rhetorical strategy that stressed their desire for distinctiveness without undermining their claim to full membership in American society. At the center of this strategy was the language of race, which served particularly well in meeting both needs.

Race as a Framework for American Jewish Identity

Jews had long been understood as a "race" in Western societies. According to Yosef Hayim Yerushalmi, racial terminology was applied to the Jews as early as the fifteenth century, when Purity of Blood Statutes were enacted in Spain to restrict Christians of Jewish descent from holding certain privileges.[20] By the mid-nineteenth century, the opposition between "Aryan" and "Semite," which had grown out of the study of philology, had become an orthodoxy of racial science in Europe.[21] In America, however, where racial theories grew in response to a history of colonization, slavery, and westward expansion, Jews did not become a primary focus of racial discourse. White Americans spoke of the Anglo-Saxon heritage that had endowed them with a talent for good government and contrasted themselves to African Americans, Native Americans, and other peoples of color.[22] But despite the national preoccupation with these groups, by the mid-nineteenth century there were also a number of European immigrant populations—mainly the Irish, Germans, and Jews—who began to be referred to in racial terms as they became more prevalent on the American scene.[23] By the 1850s, Josiah Clark Nott, one of America's leading ethnologists, characterized the Jews in explicitly racial terms and saw them as the product of pure descent from the ancient Israelites. "In obedience to an organic law of animal life," Nott and his collaborator George Gliddon observed in their *Races of Mankind* (1854), contemporary Jews exhibited "the same features which the Almighty stamped on the first Hebrew pairs created."[24]

While racial language flourished in nineteenth-century America, Jews themselves were slower than other Americans in adopting racial terminology to express their own group status. During the colonial period they had frequently referred to themselves as a "nation," a term commonly used in the early modern period to describe communities of foreign birth.[25] But in the age of the American Revolution, which extended to Jews the same rights of citizenship enjoyed by other whites, such terminology quickly became anachronistic. With American independence, "nation" took on a political meaning it had not held earlier, raising the specter of dual loyalty. As a result, religion became the preferable means of identification, and Jews began to articulate a denominational definition of Jewishness.[26] When Jews occasionally wanted to express a sense of identity beyond religion they used "nation" but qualified it, describing themselves as a "dismembered" nation, a "portable" nation, a nation "independent of every soil."[27] As long as Jews were primarily concerned with speeding their acceptance in American society, they remained guarded in using anything but the most tentative terms to describe Jewish peoplehood. But by the 1870s, when concern for their group integrity began to accompany the desire for Americanization, Jews discovered that "race," a term widely accepted in the non-Jewish world, would allow them to express their desire to maintain a distinct identity without the unwanted political connotations.

Given the American context, Jews felt confident that they could employ a racial self-description without being subjected to demonization on racial grounds. While unflattering racial caricatures of Jews were familiar in nineteenth-century America, positive racial images were at least as common.[28] Non-Jews frequently spoke in complimentary terms of the Jews "as a race," emphasizing their thrift, commercial success, and community mindedness.[29] While social discrimination, often expressed in racial terms, excluded them from certain quarters of non-Jewish society, American Jews remained confident that their racial qualities only enhanced their claims to American national identity. Underlying this confidence was the fact that despite the widespread recognition of a distinct Jewish race, Jews of the period were overwhelmingly seen as white. Unlike Europe, where questions of national belonging often turned on the distinction between Aryans and Semites, here racial commentators emphasized the distinction between whites and nonwhites and especially the line between whites and blacks. From the earliest days of the republic, the notion of an essential divide between blacks and whites had served as a master narrative, offering white Americans a clear means by which they could fortify their own self-image and imagine themselves as racially superior. Especially when social categories shifted in threatening ways, as they did in the early nineteenth century with the rise of an American working class or after the Civil War with the emancipation of the slaves, the myth of a black-white dichotomy was often marshaled to give white Americans a feeling of unity, strength, and stability. While white Americans recognized the existence of many "racial" groups in their society that did not fit easily into this binary system of categorization, this did not prevent them from viewing African Americans as a central paradigm for racial "otherness."

This, however, did not mean that all European "racial" groups were automatically or consistently accepted as white. Irish immigrants, who were vilified as a "simian race" and frequently compared to blacks before the Civil War because of the menial work they often performed, had to aggressively defend their status as white.[30] Jews, however, faced fewer challenges than the Irish in establishing their racial credentials in antebellum America. True, the strong support some Jews expressed for white supremacy and the slave system during these years betrayed a sense of insecurity about their whiteness.[31] But because Jews remained a small and rather inconspicuous group that acculturated quickly to American standards, their distinctiveness seemed to pose little threat to the established racial order. They almost never suffered the kind of racial stigmatization meted out to African Americans, and also met with consistently better treatment than the Irish, whose whiteness was questioned for much of the century. Native-born whites during this period tended to see Jews' economic success and their perceived links to "civilization" as characteristics that affirmed their membership in the dominant racial grouping. Instead of casting Jewish racial particularity as an obstacle to whiteness, most white Americans saw the survival of the Jewish "race" through the centuries as a sign that Jews exemplified white power and superiority. The Jew "was a white man," declared a midwestern journalist in 1851, and therefore a member of "the God-appointed, ruling, progressive race of humanity."[32] Similarly, although ethnologist Josiah Clark Nott saw the Jews as a remarkably uniform race, he still welcomed them as honored members of the "Great Caucasian family."[33]

As Jews integrated more thoroughly into the ranks of middle-class American society in the post–Civil War period, their status as white became even more secure. In 1874, a contributor to a leading American medical journal went so far as to describe them as "the purest, finest, and most perfect type of the Caucasian race."[34] In such an environment, Jews had maximum flexibility to assert their difference from the white mainstream. In some cases, this was done by expressing support for and identification with newly emancipated African Americans. Even in the South, Jewish spokesmen like Confederate veteran William Levy, who served as mayor of the town of Sherman, Texas, in the 1880s, did not hesitate to present himself to a black audience as "a man whose ancestors were also slaves" and to hold up the Jewish experience as a model for African Americans to follow.[35] But in general, Jews of this period focused not so much on identification with African Americans, but on stressing their own racial distinctiveness in American society. Failing to stir the kinds of fears and doubts about white strength and superiority that were often inspired by the Irish, Jews did not have to worry about the negative implications of "race" for most of the nineteenth century, allowing them to see it as a usable vehicle for self-definition.

The Uses of Race

Under the pressure of the shifting social boundaries of the 1870s, the language of race became an attractive vehicle for self-expression among American Jews and was used liberally in the weekly Jewish press, in popular novels and magazines, and in the pronouncements of Jewish leaders. The great appeal of racial language was its unique ability to capture the strong attachment of Jews to Jewish peoplehood, a feeling heightened during a time when many of the familiar markers of Jewishness were receding. Because Jews could no longer count on clear social boundaries to set them off from non-Jews, they looked to race as a transcendent means of understanding and expressing the ties that held them together as a group. In short, racial language helped them express their ongoing attachment to the social dimension of Jewishness even as the social distinctiveness of Jews began to weaken.

In similar fashion, racial language also allowed Jews to maintain their self-image as a persecuted people as they rose on the economic ladder and attained an unprecedented level of social acceptance. For Cyrus Sulzburger, editor of the *American Hebrew*, Jewish racial identity could not be understood apart from the history of Jewish oppression, which had deeply shaped the group's character and bound its members more closely together. The racial distinction between "Semite" and "Aryan" had been "more clearly marked by reason of the. . . . persecution which we have undergone," he explained. "The story of those persecutions form us a peculiar legacy which stirs the blood and touches the heart of every Hebrew in a way that it can stir none else."[36] Many Jewish commentators of the period developed this theme by arguing that Jews' experiences with persecution had imbued them with a heightened morality, a clearer sense of justice, and a greater appreciation for the suffering of others. While the "Aryan has stood for pillage," editorialized the *American Hebrew* in 1884, "the Semitic race has stood for peace."[37]

While the racial definition of Jewishness aided Jews in asserting a strong commitment to a distinctive group identity, however, it never took on the coherence of a full-fledged ideology. Instead, Jews used it selectively to meet their emotional needs without letting it interfere with their continued desire for acceptance in American society. Furthermore, when Jews did invoke race, they often employed it in ways that reflected their desire to pursue measured social integration, participate in American institutions, and rebut the charges of antisemites. Although Jews distinguished themselves from non-Jews by claiming to be more moral and peace loving, they also used such arguments in asserting the great contributions they had made to the world around them. It became a frequent practice among Jews, in fact, to credit their ancestors with laying the ethical foundations of Western civilization. The *American Hebrew* editorialized in 1884 that Jewish race purity had preserved "humanity's present system of Semitic civilization," which would fall if the Jews were to lose their separate racial identity.[38] Jews often spoke of their descent from the ancient Semites as a way of establishing the positive impact of their group on world history, and they endowed Semitics departments at universities across the country to insure proper recognition. In 1891, at the opening of the Harvard Semitic Collection, philanthropist Jacob Schiff described the Jews as "the modern representatives of the Semitic people," telling those in attendance that they "may be proud of their origin and ancestry." He hoped the study of Semitic history would help counteract the ostracism of American Jews and cause society to "better understand and acknowledge the debt it owes to the Semitic people."[39]

A practice even more popular than discussing the Semitic origins of the Jews was praising the accomplishments of prominent modern Jews and attributing their success to Jewish racial traits. In 1895, Max J. Kohler, one of the founders of the American Jewish Historical Society, wrote that the new communal interest in American Jewish history was due primarily to "race pride," which he defined as "gratification over the deeds of members of our race, present or past, purely because of our common ties of race."[40] Kohler's statement exemplifies how American Jews could at once celebrate Jewish contributions to the American way of life and attribute these contributions to a distinct Jewish racial identity. It was this reasoning that led Jewish newspapers to relentlessly hail the achievements of Jewish musicians, athletes, inventors, and philanthropists.[41] Jews employed this logic even when lauding prominent Jews in other countries. In fact, the more enmeshed in a particular national culture Jewish figures were, the more American Jews seemed to take pride in their "racial" accomplishments. Benjamin Disraeli, despite his baptism, became a favorite hero of American Jews, who saw in him an exemplar of Jewish racial traits. Emma Lazarus, in an essay in the *Century* magazine, described the British prime minister as a "brilliant Semite" who exhibited the "patient humility" and "calculating self-control" that had allowed the Jewish race to survive the centuries despite persecution.[42]

If race was used to negotiate Jews' desire to be both distinctive and American, what did a racial self-conception imply for actual social relations between Jews and non-Jews? Most significantly, a definition of Jewishness grounded in blood and ancestry often set the limit of social interaction with non-Jews at marriage. With intermarriage an increasing concern, many Jews spoke against it using the strongest racial imagery. Some popular novels by Jewish authors, for example, dramatized the importance of remaining loyal to one's race and avoiding marriage with non-Jews. In *Jewish Blood*, a novel serialized in the *American Jewess*, a monthly magazine published in Chicago during the 1890s, a Jewish man warned his son that his proposed marriage to a Catholic woman was doomed to failure because of their "dissimilarity of race." "Each [of you] represents an opposite group of the human family," the father explained, "two factions of humanity, between which there has been for centuries an irrepressible conflict; and although fractions of these conflicting human elements may be united, their union can never be wholesome, homogeneous or enduring."[43] Such potent racial arguments against intermarriage were found not only in fiction but on the editorial pages of the American Jewish press. In 1884, when leading Reform rabbis converted several women to Judaism in order for them to be married to Jews, the *American Hebrew* commenced a campaign against the "conversion farce," using race as its chief weapon. Converts, held the paper, could not be made into authentic Jews since "to be a Jew means to be of the stock of Abraham— to be of the Hebrew race."[44] In this case, fear of intermarriage led the paper to modify the traditional Jewish view, which allows conversion to Judaism, in favor of a racial argument that built a more effective barrier around Jewish identity.

In using race to keep the basic distinction between Jews and non-Jews in place, however, American Jews were prevented by a continued desire for social acceptance from carrying their conclusions too far. Some Jews worried that social intimacy with non-Jews would result in intermarriage, but most felt that racial identity could be preserved without serving as a hindrance to cordial relations and even friendships with non-Jews. Prominent B'nai B'rith leader Leo N. Levi advocated Jewish social and marital exclusiveness, but felt that for certain Jews—those who were "proud of their lineage" and committed to "bequeath[ing] an unmixed strain of Jewish blood" to their children—there was no danger in social intercourse with non-Jews. Likewise, he felt Jews should have no reservations about receiving socially those non-Jews who were respectful of the Jewish desire for group integrity and who admired Jewish virtues. Such mutual respect and recognition of innate differences, he argued, would prevent any danger of intermixture and loss of group identity.[45] Ada Robeck, a writer of short stories for middle-class Jewish women, echoed Levi's sentiments in one of her sketches of the 1890s. She presented a fictive conversation between two women—Paula Russack and Lilian Weber—who reflect on the racial qualities that distinguish them as Jew and gentile, respectively. The author suggests that they are as distinct in character as they are in physical features, Paula with her "large, dark eyes" and Lilian with her "deep blue eyes" and nose of "pure Roman shape." Yet a respect and understanding of their differences allows the women to enjoy "one of those rare and lasting friendships based on mutual affinity."[46]

Racial language proved effective not only in discouraging intermarriage and in regulating shifting social boundaries; it also allowed those who had given up affiliation with the Jewish community to retain a sense of identity as Jews. Fannie Hurst, who would later win renown as an author, grew up in St. Louis, where her family did not belong to a synagogue and where she had no Jewish friends. Her father insistently told her, however, that "Jews are both a race and a religion, and you are both."[47] Similarly, some members of the Ethical Culture Society who had formally broken ranks with the Jewish religion continued to speak of themselves as "racial Jews" and were received in Jewish circles as such.[48] In some cases, race allowed the children of intermarried couples to claim a Jewish identity even when Jewish law did not provide for such an identification. A writer for the *American Hebrew* explained how a daughter of a mixed marriage maintained loyalty to her father's faith "either through sympathy for her father or strong Jewish heredity."[49] Thus, for both the majority of American Jews who were concerned about maintaining their distinctiveness as a social entity and for those Jews whose commitments had slipped, race served as an anchor in a time of changing boundaries. It allowed Jews to stress their strong emotional attachment to the notion of Jewish difference, even as they emphasized their place in American society.

Gender and Jewish Racial Identity

While American Jews as a group found the language of race helpful in articulating their identity, there remained important differences in its implications for men and women. Because the use of racial terminology to express Jewishness was itself a product of changing relationships between the Jews and society, men and women—who experienced those relationships differently—had distinct approaches to ideas about the "Jewish race."[50]

As we have seen, because Jewish women of Central European background generally integrated more slowly than their male counterparts into non-Jewish social settings, Jewish men came to rely upon them for the preservation of Jewishness in the family and in Jewish society in general.[51] When Jewish women finally began to experience significant social integration for the first time during the 1870s, men responded by casting women's perceived obligations in racial terms, hoping to reinforce the gender roles that had helped mitigate the effects of their own incursions into the non-Jewish world. In 1888, for example, Kaufmann Kohler, a leading

Reform rabbi, described the ideal Jewish woman, like Esther, as a "savior of her race."[52] Another rabbi, Gustav Gottheil, employed biological language when he spoke of the "ruling traits of the genus Jewess," which included simplicity, modesty, charity, piety, chastity ("much in the Oriental fashion") and a special devotion to home and family.[53] Abram Isaacs, editor of the *Jewish Messenger*, held that "as the religious instincts of the Jewess are innate, and her domestic qualities strong, one may expect her to champion all that is pure, and sweet, and wholesome."[54] Interestingly, while these characteristics differ little from what was said of women in general during this period, Jewish men were anxious to find something distinctively Jewish in the behavior of Jewish women. Like the larger racial discourse of American Jewry, the rhetoric concerning the traits of Jewish women was intended to mark a distinction that was increasingly absent in social reality.

Some Jewish women found in this racialized image a source of empowerment and a basis from which they could help shape the destiny of their community. Many articles in the *American Jewess* suggest that middle-class women found racial language an attractive medium for expressing what they felt were their unique qualities and contributions. Carrie Wise, for example, in a review of Anatole Leroy-Beaulieu's *Israel among the Nations* (1895), delighted in the portrait painted by the author of the Jewish woman, who "has had a large share in the uplifting of her race," mainly through her grace, purity, and faculty for assimilating the best of non-Jewish culture.[55] But while certain racialized visions of Jewish womanhood were embraced, the *Jewess* carried other articles in which women writers expressed ambivalence about racial identity. "Characteristics of the Semitic Nations," for example, emphasized the impact of Semitic history on contemporary culture but concluded that this history has no relevance for modern Jews except for "simply the memory of our distant glory."[56] Similarly, "Race Characteristics" described "duty" as one of the most distinctive traits of the Jewess, responsible for the "close and beautiful relation existing between those of the same blood." But despite this feeling, the author concluded that this sense of duty puts too many restrictions on Jewish women and urged them to "develop your individuality above everything else."[57]

These reservations about race can be explained by the different functions racial identity performed in the lives of Jewish men and women. For men, articulating an identity grounded in race helped clarify the uncertainty about Jewish identity that sprung from their contact with the non-Jewish world. Men flocked to B'nai B'rith, a fraternal organization that stressed Jewish racial ties, because it offered the warm emotional security they often missed in their daily lives. They gained a similar security from assigning women the burden of racial perpetuation, since it re-

1. The *American Jewess*, 1895. The cover of this popular monthly magazine depicted the ideal Jewish woman as an "Oriental" racial type with dark features. (Courtesy Klau Library, Hebrew Union College–Jewish Institute of Religion, Cincinnati)

lieved them of responsibility and focused on the home as the space where racial identity would be nurtured. Thus, racial identity for men facilitated both the free pursuit of worldly affairs and the preservation of a distinct Jewish identity.

Jewish women, however, because they lagged behind men in their attainment of social integration, often found themselves in a largely Jewish world, where they had less of a need to employ a racial definition of Jewishness. Instead of easing their incursions into the wider world, racial Jewishness—as articulated by men—pointed to the home as their proper sphere and assigned them a rigid set of roles. Women who sought access to non-Jewish society felt they could gain it most effectively by employing a religious definition of Judaism, since American society justified women's entry into the public sphere by stressing the beneficial effect of their religious and moral influence. When Jewish women founded the National Council of Jewish Women (NCJW) in 1893, the organization—in contrast to the men's B'nai B'rith—stressed Jewish religious work as a vehicle for enlarging the purview of women's activities.[58]

As women began to experience a greater level of social integration, however, the gap in how a racial notion of Jewishness served men and women began to close. In defining a new place for themselves in the non-Jewish world, American Jewish women found it difficult to avoid using the terminology of race for two main reasons. First, their own experiences of domestic Judaism were ones in which the religious and social dimensions of Jewishness were not neatly distinguished. As a result, even when Jewish women spoke of their religious qualities they often employed racial terminology. Second, once exposed to the pressures of life in the non-Jewish world, women began to feel the same need as men did to reinforce increasingly indistinct boundaries between Jews and non-Jews with the language of race.

The proceedings of the NCJW's 1896 convention demonstrate how quickly racial language found its way into the public discourse of American Jewish women. In addressing the convention, for example, Sophie Axman held that Jewish women possessed a special gift for child rearing that had "preserved the autonomy of the race, and laid the foundation for the brilliant achievements which have made that people the envied of most of the world and the marvel of all."[59] Clara Block, speaking on religious schools, expressed the need to instill in students a reverence for the "moral genius" which was a "particular and peculiar gift of the Hebrew people." She termed the Jews "a race so gifted that it came into the world bringing a message for the whole world, giving it a code upon which all civilization rests."[60] Julia Richman, one of the most prominent leaders of the NCJW, regularly spoke of race and religion as complementary aspects of Jewish identity. The student who did not uphold the ethical standards of Judaism, she said, was not only a "traitor to his faith" but also a "blot upon the record of his race."[61] Richman was also a strenuous opponent of intermarriage, which she felt would undermine the distinctiveness of the Jews and the "special values" of Judaism. By keeping the "race unmixed" she hoped to keep the "religion pure."[62]

Like the characteristics ascribed to them by their male counterparts, the racial traits Jewish women claimed for themselves were often indistinct from those claimed by other American women. Nevertheless, they saw them as uniquely Jewish characteristics, marking them off from their non-Jewish neighbors. But unlike male commentators, they rejected the notion that these traits required women's restriction to the private sphere. Jewish women felt that the same qualities that had made them the protectors of Jewish racial integrity in the home also made them fit for a similar role in public affairs. The *American Jewess*, for example, was certain that the refinement of Jewish women would serve to uphold the reputation of Jews when they came into contact with non-Jews at summer resorts. "Such Jewesses [when traveling] abroad are our genuine public representatives," editorialized the magazine, "the true social saviors of our race."[63] Like the Jewish community in general, then, Jewish women were able to make race work for them. Rejecting the version of racial identity that men had ascribed to them, they chose to demonstrate, in the words of Philadelphia writer Mary Cohen, that "although Jewish women are strongly attached to their own race. . . . they are not therefore prevented from identifying themselves with the politics, social interests, and general welfare of the country in which they live."[64]

The Rabbinate and Race

As the premier leaders of American Jewry in the nineteenth century, rabbis were important shapers of the discourse on Jewish identity. But their role as intellectuals led them to approach the issue of Jewish racial identity very differently than did average Jews, who reflected little about the process of accommodation to American ways and were not as constrained by the need for ideological consistency. Most American Jews of the period turned to the language of race for emotional reasons, with little concern that it might contradict their desire to identify with American ideals or have negative repercussions for Jewish acceptance. Most American rabbis, on the other hand, were dedicated to the emerging program of Reform Judaism, which identified universal religious principles as the hallmark of Jewish identity and could not as easily accommodate a racial understanding of Jewishness.

As a result, most historians have concluded that Reform rabbis were uniformly hostile to notions of Jewish particularlism, especially those expressed in racial language. A close examination of their writings reveals, however, that they often had the same strong emotional ties to Jewish racial identity as other Jews. In fact, because Reformers ventured close to the borders of Jewish identity, they were usually more conscious than others of the barriers that separated Jews from others. A few Reform rabbis were actually able to develop ideologies that accommodated their conflicting impulses, but most found it difficult to incorporate both their universalism and a racial notion of Jewishness into a consistent worldview. Instead, the pattern was one of frequent doubt and vacillation between alternating ideologies. Ironically, in their attempt to impose order and consistency, these rabbis ended up presenting a less coherent framework for the expression of Jewish identity than did average Jews in their own pragmatic way.

Among those theologians who were able to construct a complex worldview combining both universal and "racial" definitions of Judaism was David Einhorn, known as one of the most radical of nineteenth-century Reform rabbis. Einhorn believed strongly that Jews had a mission to spread ethical monotheism, a task that required their dispersion among the nations. But he also held firmly to the view that Jewish racial purity had to be preserved in order for Jews to effectively carry out this mission. Thus, he was able to express the Jewish attachment to peoplehood by reducing it to an innate capacity for morality and religious service. "Israel has disappeared as a nation," he wrote in 1870, but "as a race with certain qualities of soul and mind which form the life-giving condition and root of its own peculiar historical mission, it has remained and will remain as such until the time when this mission shall have been fulfilled." For this reason he considered intermarriage "a nail in the coffin of the small Jewish race, with its lofty mission."[65] Einhorn's views were echoed by his son-in-law and disciple, Kaufmann Kohler, who argued in 1878 against the admission of male proselytes to Judaism who had not undergone the rite of circumcision. Since Israel's historical mission necessitated a high degree of racial purity, he explained, the requirement of circumcision should be preserved as "a wall able to prevent an inflow of impure elements." Kohler felt that non-Jews should be encouraged to embrace monotheism and live ethically but not "to become part of the Jewish community and to undertake the priestly vocation of the Jews, which is assumed [only] by birth."[66] Like his father-in-law, Kohler maintained a strict opposition to intermarriage. "Just because we belong to all nations," he wrote, "we must not lose our identity by being absorbed."[67]

What Einhorn and Kohler saw as the increasing danger to the integrity of the Jewish race, however, many rabbis saw as the fulfillment of their hopes for universal brotherhood. With the breaking down of social barriers to an extent unheard of in Europe, many Reformers felt that it was now possible for Jews and gentiles to join together in a new, universal form of Judaism shorn of its racial component. The founding of free religious societies in the 1870s and the interest in Reform Judaism shown by the Unitarian Church convinced some rabbis that non-Jews were ripe to accept Judaism as a universalized creed. Because intermarriages were becoming more frequent, these rabbis took steps to eliminate the "racial" character of Judaism and make conversion as easy as possible in hopes of winning proselytes among non-Jewish spouses. In a discussion on intermarriage in the Reform journal *Zeitgeist* in 1880, Emil G. Hirsch, the rabbi of Chicago's Sinai Temple, voiced the opinion of this school of thought by welcoming mixed marriage and opposing Kohler's racial view of Jewishness. "Indeed, we preserve no sympathy with . . . a 'physiological Judaism,' " wrote Hirsch. "Our Judaism is rooted in our conviction and not in our blood."[68]

But while these rabbis agreed to take immediate steps to universalize American Judaism, their hopes for rapprochement with Christians often gave way to disappointment and self-doubt. Some came to realize that non-Jewish clergy, despite their overtures toward Jews, had no intention of adopting a universalized Judaism or of even meeting Jews on an equal footing. Solomon H. Sonneschein, a St. Louis rabbi who had envisioned a coalescence of Reform Judaism and Unitarianism, announced in 1881 that Unitarians were not yet ready to part with their race prejudice and that Jews should maintain their group integrity until the world became more accepting of them.[69] For others, it was the intensification of European antisemitism that dampened their belief in an emerging era of interfaith comity. Responding to the way in which many Jews in Germany had been pushed by anti-Jewish sentiment into a self-effacing form of assimilation, Rabbi Adolph Moses, one of the editors of the *Zeitgeist* who had written passionately against a racial Judaism, declared in 1880 that American Jews were not ready to give up their racial characteristics.[70]

Bernhard Felsenthal, a radical Reform rabbi in Chicago, provides another example of this uncertainty. In the late 1870s, Felsenthal became convinced that with the rise in intermarriage the best solution for the survival of Judaism was as a universal religion cut loose from its racial framework. When Felix Adler founded the Society for Ethical Culture, Felsenthal pinned his hopes on the new organization as a movement capable of making Judaism into a dynamic new spiritual force that could attract those from outside the fold. In his optimism, Felsenthal heralded the call to open the doors of Judaism to proselytes by abolishing the requirement of circumcision for converts.[71] But when he came to see that Adler's movement severed any historical links with Judaism, he reversed his opinion and began to place increasing emphasis on the racial definition of the Jews. Felsenthal's conception of Jewishness continued to waver during the 1880s, but in the following decade he came to believe that the fulfillment of Israel's mission would not result from the universalization of Judaism but from the preservation of Jews as a distinct racial group. By the end of the century he had adopted an explicitly racialist ideology and become a leading Zionist figure.[72]

If few rabbis came to the same conclusions as Felsenthal, most continued to vacillate between universalism and a racial notion of Jewishness. Isaac Mayer Wise, the editor of the *American Israelite* and builder of Reform institutions like Hebrew Union College and the Union of American Hebrew Congregations, was perhaps the worst offender in this regard, often allowing spur-of-the moment political motivations to override any concern for intellectual coherence. In the 1870s, Wise felt comfortable with a racial definition of the Jews, arguing that the Jew's nationality was "in his blood, in the purity of his race, in his beliefs, in his mode of thinking and feeling."[73] As he began his career as a builder of Reform institutions, however, he increasingly stressed the religious definition of Jewishness. Yet when it suited his needs, Wise still felt free to resort to the language of race. Thus, while he argued that it was scientifically incorrect to speak of the Jews in racial terms, he nonetheless condemned Jewish social behaviors that he felt reflected badly on "the whole race."[74] Wise published regular denunciations of the race concept in the *Israelite*, but this did not keep him from reprinting articles from the general press that lauded Jewish racial characteristics.[75]

Though Wise was unusual among rabbis in his disregard for ideological consistency, most leading Reform rabbis did reassess their views on the nature of Jewishness at least once during the last three decades of the century. It was not uncommon for a rabbi to make bold pronouncements about his desire for a universalistic society and then, in moments of frustration or doubt, revert to a racial understanding of the Jews. As convener of the 1885 conference of Reform rabbis in Pittsburgh, for example, Kaufmann Kohler, under pressure from religious opponents to define a consistent set of Reform principles, reversed his long-held opposition to intermarriage and the liberal admission of converts and argued in the conference's platform that Jews were to be defined as "a religious community."[76] A decade later, however, he and David Einhorn's other son-in-law, Emil G. Hirsch, who had helped Kohler write the Pittsburgh statement and had long denied Jews' racial status, emerged as strong advocates of racial Jewishness within the Reform camp. Resurrecting Einhorn's principle that Jews' work among the nations was propelled by a racial talent for religion, Kohler argued in 1894 that "there is no other Judaism but Race Judaism."[77] The following year, Hirsch described race and religion as two mutually supporting and inseparable aspects of Jewishness, dismissing critics who argued that racial identity was the relic of an unenlightened era. "A racial Judaism is no more out of reason than is humanity itself," he wrote, "for humanity is ours by birth and physiology."[78]

Despite the fact that Kohler and Hirsch emerged at century's end as major forces within the Reform movement, few of their colleagues embraced a racial self-definition as passionately as they did. Still, in the wake of the Pittsburgh Conference, there were signs that ambivalence lurked beneath continued assertions that Jews were nothing more than a faith group. In 1886, when Solomon Sonneschein again attempted to join the Unitarians, Reform rabbis denounced him as a deserter, not out of any strong theological motives but out of a persistent, if unarticulated, commitment to the Jews as a social collective. Three years later, Reform rabbis also rejected a proposal to emphasize the purely religious nature of Jewishness by abandoning the labels "Hebrew" and "Israelite," which had long been used to describe the Jews in racial terms.[79] To be sure, there were holdouts like Rabbi Adolph Moses, who admitted that Jews had been a race, but argued that they should do everything possible to distance themselves from their racial past. At the 1894 graduation of Hebrew Union College, he even recommended changing the name of Judaism to "Yahvism" as a means of removing all traces of its past as a "racial religion."[80] By the 1890s, however, it had become apparent that most rabbis, no matter how strong their universalist commitments, could not totally suppress their attachment to a racial notion of Jewishness.

The End of an Era

Despite the wavering views of rabbinical leaders, race served most American Jews of the late nineteenth century quite successfully as a means for balancing their conflicting impulses for communal solidarity and Americanization. At a time when social boundaries were in flux, race served as a potent means for expressing cherished Jewish commitments. In addition, because the Jewish presence did not seem to pose any significant challenge to the stability of the American social order, Jews found they could express their identity in terms of race without fear of being cast as racial outsiders. If racial language had been embraced by American Jews during the nineteenth century because of the particular social circumstances they faced, however, by century's end important changes in American society and the resultant shifts in the perceptions of Jews began to alter race's efficacy as a vehicle for self-description.

As the new century approached, Americans increasingly felt the impact of massive social transformations related to industrialization, urbanization, and immigration. These changes unnerved many members of the dominant white society, who sometimes worried about their ability to meet the daunting challenges they presented. While generally white Americans were able to overcome such fears and preserve a sense of optimism in the face of change, they often began to search for ways to boost their confidence and infuse their society with a sense of order and stability. While the basic distinction between "black" and "white" had always been a major organizing principle in American racial culture, white Americans began to emphasize it with increasing force during these years because it provided them with a feeling of strength and superiority in uncertain times. This trend began in the American South, where frustrated whites responded to increasing economic turmoil and social unrest by enacting the elaborate system of racial segregation know as Jim Crow. But given the power of a color-based racial hierarchy in addressing the anxieties of Americans, it was not long before white supremacy was increasingly reinvigorated as a national cause.[81]

For Jews, this growing thirst for a clear racial hierarchy would have telling consequences. As the American Jewish population swelled to unprecedented numbers with rising immigration from Eastern Europe, Jews became linked in the popular imagination with many of the destabilizing changes Americans were confronting. Just as members of the dominant society were trying to meet these challenges with a revivified whiteness, Jews became a lightning rod for the very fears that threatened to undermine national confidence, and speculation grew about their place in the American racial order. In the late nineteenth century Jews had usually been seen as an honored part of the "Great Caucasian family," but in the changing world of the twentieth century their perceived racial peculiarities now threatened to cast them beyond the pale of whiteness.

PART II

JEWS IN BLACK AND WHITE, 1896–1918

CHAPTER 2

THE UNSTABLE OTHER: LOCATING JEWS IN
PROGRESSIVE ERA AMERCIAN RACIAL DISCOURSE

JEWS ENJOYED great flexibility in defining themselves as a "race" during the nineteenth century, largely because the notion of Jewish racial difference failed to create a significant sense of danger in American society. True, Americans saw Jews as distinctive in both a physical and moral sense, and condemnations of the Jewish "race" were not unknown. Yet in general, the small size of the Jewish population and the speed and enthusiasm with which Jews adapted to American modes of dress, language, and style gave native-born whites little reason to see them as a group whose separate existence posed a significant threat to the American social order. Unlike the Irish, who inspired fears about the decreasing independence of free white labor and were often grouped with African Americans in national discourse, Jews were rarely seen as anything other than a stable part of the white population.

As the nineteenth century drew to a close and a new century dawned, however, Jews began to register more significantly as uncertain figures in American racial discourse, indicating that they were becoming a topic of greater concern to native-born whites. During these years, "Hebrew" characters became more familiar as comic figures on the vaudeville stage, and cartoons lampooning Jews became a regular feature of mass-circulation humor magazines like *Puck* and the *Judge*.[1] In more serious periodicals, social commentators regularly discussed the effects of Jewish immigration on the future of the American population, while muckraking reporters examined the problems presented by Jewish labor, crime, and housing conditions.[2] With the aid of these media, the Jew for the first time took on an important role in the discourse on national identity and became a frequently discussed "racial" figure in American culture.

Partly, this increased notice can be explained by changing demographics. The growth of the American Jewish population from about 200,000 to over one million during the last three decades of the nineteenth century certainly contributed to increasing questions about Jews' place in America's racial constellation.[3] But much of this new interest in Jews stemmed from the way in which their distinctive history and social characteristics, particularly their concentration in cities and their involvement in trade and commerce, seemed to link them to the modern forces of industrialization, urbanization, and commercialization, issues of mounting concern to Americans of this period. More than any other distinguishable group in American society, Jews served as a symbol of the processes transforming the nation.

Because many white Americans had mixed feelings about the sweeping changes the Jews had come to represent, they found it difficult to craft a consistent image of Jewish racial character, seeing it alternately as an embodiment of their hopes for and fears of the modern world. Thus, while the image of the Jew was increasingly prominent in American racial discourse during this period, Jews were harder than most other groups to classify as either a positive or negative factor in American life. This ambivalent image was especially frustrating for native-born whites at a time when they were coming to rely even more on the traditional dichotomy between black and white, which provided a sense of order and hierarchy amidst troubling changes. Seeing the world in terms of a clear racial divide based on color allowed them to face the challenges of their times with a sense of confidence and superiority. But these feelings were often undermined by the racial image of the Jew, which brought so many uncomfortable questions about modernity to the surface. To preserve their comforting view of the world, white Americans often tried to obscure Jewish distinctiveness and to understand it within a black-white context. While these efforts were not always successful, they would have telling consequences for American Jews.

The Jew: A Mirror of American Modernity

Among the many immigrants from Southern and Eastern European who arrived on American shores between 1880 and 1924, Jews were the group most identified with the ways of the modern world. Unlike most non-Jewish immigrants, Jews had not been farmers or peasants in Europe, but had practiced trades and professions that eased their transition to the modern urban setting. Upon arrival, they did not usually head for the agricultural regions of the country, but instead remained in the largest cities, where their high concentration led many to see them as epitomizing urban life. By 1915, one out every four New Yorkers was a Jew, and in smaller metropolitan centers like Chicago, Philadelphia, Boston, and Baltimore the Jewish population hovered between 8 and 10 percent of the total.[4] Although most Jewish immigrants were skilled industrial workers, they were also disproportionately involved in commerce, as were members of the more settled community of Jews from Central Europe. As a result, entire commercial districts, like New York's East Broadway or Baxter Street, became almost synonymous with Jews. Finally, Jews were thought to represent the urban experience in their mental and physical qualities. Traits such as nervousness, intellectuality, and a lack of physical development were routinely attributed to Jews and were interpreted as the marks of urban living.[5]

The association of the Jews and modernity was not unique to America, for it was also a major theme in European discussions of Jewish character. In countries like Germany and Austria, which experienced great economic and social tensions as a result of the rise of industrial society, the Jews served as a convenient scapegoat on which all the ills of modern life could be blamed.[6] In the United States, however, there was a much more positive outlook toward these changes, preventing antisemitism from finding as fertile a field. Breakthroughs in technology, the rise in material wealth, and the emergence of mass consumerism all had a beneficial effect on broad segments of the American population, resulting in fewer tensions that might find expression in anti-Jewish sentiment. This is not to say that Americans had no negative reactions to the pressures and challenges of the modern world. By the late nineteenth century, the decline of individual and community autonomy, the increasing regimentation and mechanization of society, and the permissiveness of urban life all provoked concern, causing clergy, public officials, businessmen, and others to ponder whether industrial progress could be achieved without damaging the nation's physical and moral integrity.[7] While Americans did not abandon their optimism about the future, they could not always shake their doubts and concerns about the changes they were experiencing.[8]

Not surprisingly, Americans' ambivalent attitudes about modernity resulted in an ambivalent approach toward the Jews who symbolized its changes. Of course, attitudes about Jews were hardly uniform among Americans of different classes, regions, and political and religious viewpoints. Those most disaffected by economic and social change—poor urban dwellers, displaced agrarians, and disillusioned patricians—tended to harbor the greatest animosity toward Jews, while those who had a greater stake in these changes were more sympathetic, even laudatory.[9] Overall, however, it is difficult to classify attitudes toward the Jews according to any neat division. Although Jews were widely regarded as being racially distinct, this perceived racial difference did not always carry a negative valence. Instead, racial images of the Jew during this period presented a mixed bag: sometimes he (the image was usually male)[10] was cast as the embodiment of progressive business techniques, an exemplar of all that was good about the nation's industrial capitalist ethos. On the other hand, he was also seen as the representative of many of modernity's ills—a physical weakling, a carrier of disease, someone who placed personal gain above the "finer virtues" of polite society. In general, then, the racial discourse about the Jews, with its mix of identification and repulsion, was as varied and inconsistent as Americans' own feelings about their changing world.[11]

A prime illustration of this trend is the contradictory discourse surrounding one of the Jew's most frequently discussed traits: ambition. On the one hand, commentators lauded the unusual fortitude demonstrated by the Jew in his quest for social and economic advancement. Economist John Commons praised the Jew's hard work and his ability to plan and save for the future without expecting immediate gratification. Such ambition, he argued, was the "sure test of an individual's or race's future."[12] The *New York Journal of Commerce and Commercial Bulletin* held up the Jewish merchant as a model for all American businessmen to follow, citing the "patient continuity of effort" and "singleness of purpose" that allowed him to compete effectively against "less self-denying men."[13] Still others described the Jew as a dynamic economic force whose determination to succeed could not help but have a positive impact on his surroundings. The Jew, according to social reformer Jacob Riis, was the "yeast of any slum, if given time." Riis interpreted the Jew's willingness to live and work in the worst neighborhoods as a positive factor that would eventually help conquer urban blight and lead the city to become a thriving center. "If it will not let him go," he wrote of the slum, "it must rise with him."[14]

Even as they celebrated the Jew's ambition, however, many of the same commentators expressed the opinion that Jews had become too concerned with economic success, often neglecting health and hygiene in their quest for the dollar. Commons, who was an expert on American labor conditions, pointed to the horrendous environment of the "Jewish sweatshop," which he called the "tragic price paid by that ambitious race."[15] Riis, too, equivocated in his portrait of Jewish slum dwellers, at times arguing that their singular focus on accumulating wealth made them less, not more, likely to invest in improving their decrepit surroundings. "Money is their God," he wrote. "Life itself is of little value compared to the leanest bank account."[16] This critique of the Jew echoed the warnings Theodore Roosevelt had made to the nation in 1900, when he urged Americans to take up the "strenuous life" of physical activity and military conquest, lest their preoccupation with business interests lead to a decline in their strength and vitality. These were precisely the kinds of fears often projected in the popular culture of the day onto Jewish businessmen, who were portrayed as sacrificing physical development in their incessant pursuit of profit. An 1898 cartoon from *Puck* presented a young Jew who was the exact opposite of Roosevelt's ideal: dressed for horseback riding, he reports to his grandfather that, while on the trail, he sold his horse for fifty dollars. "Goot for you, Chakey!" responds the grandfather. "Dot vos der vay to enchoy horsepack riding!"[17]

BUSINESS AND PLEASURE.

"Ven I vos oudt horseback riding dis morning, Grandfader, I dradet dot horse
undt made feefty tollars."

"Goot for you, Chakey! Dot vos der vay to enchoy horsepack riding!"

2. "Business and Pleasure," 1898. This cartoon from the humor magazine *Puck*
portrayed the Jew as the opposite of Theodore Roosevelt's ideal American man,
who knew how to keep business and pleasure separate. (Courtesy Rare Book,
Manuscript and Special Collections Library, Duke University)

The figure of the Jew also became a foil for speculation about the grave
moral issues presented by a changing society. The most pessimistic images
cast the Jew as someone whose acquisitive nature led him to trade on the
lives of human beings. In the 1890s and early 1900s, writers, cartoonists
and even early filmmakers depicted Jews as arsonists who endangered
family and neighbors by setting insurance fires.[18] Similar was the accusa-
tion that an obsession with financial gain led the Jew to become a traf-
ficker in white slaves. While Jews did play a role in international prostitution during this period, police officials and muckraking reporters often

exaggerated the claim that they were the chief perpetrators of this crime in American cities. One of these journalists, George Kibbe Turner, asserted that among the Jewish immigrants from Eastern Europe there were "a large number of criminals who soon found that they could develop an extremely profitable business in the sale of women in New York."[19]

If such images reflected fears about the toll modern life might take on American ethical standards, there were also much more positive images of Jewish morality that suggested greater hope for the future. Jews were often depicted in the press, onstage, and in other forms of public discourse as family men, and the Jewish home was seen as a source of piety and virtue. Embedded in these images was the assumption that the Jews, who were not only the most modern of peoples but also the most ancient, had been able to preserve their age-old religious code and employ it as a moral guide in facing the challenges of modern life. Thus, while the Jewish image served as a warning in the American mind about the moral depths to which people could sink in the modern environment, it also provided a model of how they might survive modernity with their moral systems intact. Commentators spoke at length about the purity and stability of Jewish home life and distinguished it from sharp Jewish business practice. The writers who created the characters played by David Warfield and Joe Welch, the most famous "Hebrew comics" on the vaudeville stage, tempered their stereotypical portrayals of the Jewish "old clothes man" by demonstrating the warm affection he had for his wife and family.[20] Though infrequently portrayed by non-Jewish writers and spokesmen, the image of the Jewish woman was sometimes employed to demonstrate that Jewish life had a strong moral side rooted in the home and detached from the vagaries of the business world. No less a figure than Mark Twain spoke of the Jewish household as "a home in the truest sense," where "the family is knitted together by the strongest affections; its members show each other every due respect; and reverence for the elders is an inviolate law of the house."[21]

As all of these examples indicate, the image of the "Jew" in Progressive Era America was constantly in flux. If commentators were certain that the Jews were a distinct "race," they could not come to any clear decision on whether they represented a positive or negative force in American life. White Americans' faith in modernity would not let them make of the Jew an essential "other," as he often became in Europe, but neither would their nagging concerns about modern life allow them to suppress their negative views of the Jew. Thus, the Jew remained a figure of uncertainty that could not be pinned down to any clear set of racial criteria. This ambivalence not only affected the place of the Jew in American life, but also interfered with white Americans' attempt to construct a stable racial hierarchy, ultimately threatening their own claims to the power of whiteness. For until white Americans could define the Jew and the forces of modernization he represented, they could not clearly define themselves.

Jews and the Black-White Dichotomy

The racial discourse about the Jew, with its mix of identification and repulsion, stood in sharp contrast to the black-white discourse of race, which allowed white Americans to envision a society ruled by clear, hierarchical categories and gave them a binary opposite against which they could stabilize their own self-image as strong, superior, and able to meet the challenges of modern life. During this period, the exceptional efficacy of a white identity was rooted in the notion of "civilization." An evolutionary concept, civilization denoted a stage of physical and moral development more advanced than those of savagery and barbarism, which were associated in the United States with African Americans, Native Americans, and the peoples of America's newly acquired imperial colonies. The fixation on civilization and whiteness provided significant psychological benefits to members of the dominant society during this time of massive change. Understanding whiteness as a source of transcendent strength reduced their insecurity about the changes they were undergoing, and the perceived weaknesses— moral, physical, and economic—that they worried about.[22]

Despite the power that the black-white dichotomy had in shoring up the identities of white Americans, however, it could not totally soothe the sense of uncertainty and ambivalence they had about the world around them. As a result, it was never able to obscure in white American consciousness the racial discourse surrounding the Jew, which was itself a product of that uncertainty and ambivalence. The persistence of the Jewish racial image during these years reflected the extent to which white Americans of the period continued to see various European immigrant groups as racially distinct, a tendency that worked against their intensifying efforts to assert a clear racial hierarchy organized around the categories of black and white. While the discourse concerning European immigrant "races" stood in tension with the black-white understanding of race, however, these two racial systems often interacted, overlapped, and influenced one another. White Americans often tried to understand Jews and other European "racial" groups within a black-white framework as a means of suppressing the troubling uncertainty they represented. Still, they could not help but continue to see the racial terrain in the United States as far more varied and complex than could be contained within a simple dichotomy. When speaking of Jews, for example, many commentators referred to them as a distinct racial group quite apart from categories of color, often in the same breath that they tried to fit them into those categories. The key here is to see how the black-white dichotomy functioned strategically and was employed by native-born whites to obscure complexity and infuse a sense of order and confidence into the national culture.

One means of defusing the troubling ambivalence of the Jewish racial image was to liken Jews to African Americans, trying to find similarities between the two groups regardless of the social and historical differences that made comparison difficult. Because blacks and Jews rarely married outside their own communities, they were frequently grouped together in discussions about the homogeneity of the white American population. In an article exploring the declining birth rate among "civilized" peoples, a writer for the *World's Work* argued that "the Negro and the Jew are sure to gain relatively on the other races of our population."[23] Another writer for the same journal, however, felt that the purity of the American race could be preserved, since the population was still "homogeneous enough except for the Negroes and the Jews."[24] Whatever the conclusion, the underlying message was that Jews and blacks were linked together by their unassimilability in American society. Similarly, social reformers often compared Jewish social conditions to those prevailing among African Americans. Jacob Riis argued that Jews, as well as Italians, were far inferior to the "Negro" in terms of cleanliness, and were appropriately considered worse tenants.[25] Sociologist Frederick Bushee made the same observation about Jews in Boston. "There are actually streets in the West End," he wrote, "where, while Jews are moving in, negro housewives are gathering up their skirts and seeking a more spotless environment."[26]

As these examples illustrate, identifying the Jews as "uncivilized" and classing them with African Americans reduced the anxieties of white Americans concerning the impact of modernity and its ability to undermine the power of whiteness. This strategy also proved useful in soothing fears among native-born whites about their vulnerability to moral excess. The perceived link between the Jew and prostitution, for example, alarmed white Americans about the propensity of a commercial society to lose its moral compass. But if the Jew could be cast as a sexual savage similar to the stereotypical "black beast rapist," the clear line between civilized whites and savage blacks could be restored. This theme was present in 1908 when George Kibbe Turner published an expose in *McClure's Magazine* on prostitution in Chicago, a city that he called "the cheapest market of dissipation in Caucasian civilization." What had led to the downfall of white standards in Chicago, he explained, was an invasion by Jews and other "rough and hairy tribes" who had caused the city to "lapse . . . back into a condition more primitive than the jungle."[27] If Jewish "savages" were a danger to white civilization, however, their image as racially inferior brutes served as a comfortable reinforcement to the stability of American whiteness.[28]

The link between the Jew and black as sexual predators was also made during the Leo Frank Case of 1913–15, in which a Jewish factory manager in Atlanta was accused of raping and murdering a white girl. The Frank Case was one of the worst antisemitic outbursts in American history, inspired by the frustrations of southerners over the difficult process of industrialization of which Frank became a symbol. Southern men were especially disturbed during this period by the challenges that a changing economy and the increased need for women to take up factory work posed to their perceived role as protectors and sustainers of the family. Historians have missed, however, how whites sometimes tried to suppress the specific frustrations motivating their hatred of Frank by cloaking him in imagery usually reserved for blacks. Journalist and Populist leader Tom Watson attempted on a few occasions to compare Frank with African Americans accused of rape. "Every student of sociology knows," wrote Watson in early 1915, "that the black man's lust after the white woman is not much fiercer than the lust of the licentious Jew for the gentile."[29] After Frank's sentence was commuted by Georgia Governor John Slaton, Watson warned in a headline that, in the future, Jews suspected of similar crimes would not be extended the courtesy of a trial: "THE NEXT JEW WHO DOES WHAT FRANK DID IS GOING TO GET EXACTLY THE SAME THING WE GIVE TO NEGRO RAPISTS."[30] Then, on August 17, Frank was lynched by a white mob.

In only one instance did an author undertake a full-scale study intending to demonstrate the similarity between Jews and African Americans. Published in 1910 by the North Carolina minister and professor Arthur T. Abernethy, *The Jew a Negro* argued that ancient Jews had thoroughly mixed with neighboring African peoples, leaving little significant difference between the Jewish and Negro types. As the Jews migrated to more temperate climes, their skin lightened and they became successful, but their essential racial similarity to blacks remained unaltered.[31] Abernethy pointed to a number of traits frequently attributed to the modern, urban Jew and tried to link them to common stereotypes of the African American. Jews and blacks, he wrote, had little regard for the truth and no artistic taste; they were both known for their cunning and susceptibility to bribery. Reminiscent of the charges made by Watson during the Frank Case, he also claimed that Jews and blacks shared a disregard for the "regularities restricting sexual indulgences." According to Abernethy, "the Jews, like the Negroes, whom this mania often drives to crimes against womanhood, are equally abnormally full-blooded; but what the unfortunate Negro may accomplish only by brute force and crime, the Jew who is richer, artfully effects by the gentler process of blandishment, ingenuity and gold."[32] What appeared to be markers of the Jew's thorough implication in a decadent modern world, such reasoning suggested, were really just survivals of the Jew's primitive Negro past.

Drawing parallels between the character traits of African Americans and Jews could help defuse the Jew's troubling racial indeterminacy, but the surest way to try to stabilize the Jew's position along the black-white divide was to come to some definite conclusion about his physiognomy, since skin color and other physical traits were widely seen as the clearest sign of one's blackness or whiteness. Many commentators remarked on the Jew's dark hair, "sensual" lips and "animal" jaw as a way of linking him to well-known stereotypes of the African American.[33] Abernethy argued that the Jew's eyes were a mark of his black ancestry, as was "the peculiarity in the formation of the . . . . finger nails," which he called "one of the most unfailing tests of negro similarity."[34] The skin color of Jews, often described as "swarthy," was also interpreted as a sign of their connection to blacks. Major Charles E. Woodruff, an army surgeon and author of *The Effects of Tropical Light on White Men* (1905), argued that in terms of skin color, "the Semitic type is the link between the Negro and Aryan, and indeed its southern branches are called negroid." According to Woodruff, "if the Albino skin is zero as to pigmentation, and the black negro is ten, the blond Aryan would be one" and the fairest Jew a three or four.[35]

Woodruff's work demonstrated the tensions faced by American scholars and scientists who wished to make sense of multiple and shifting definitions of "race" and to restore the sense of certainty provided by a clear, hierarchical racial system based on color. As a result, much of the era's scientific literature made an attempt to elaborate new, more expansive racial systems in which the new immigrants could be measured in some way against the poles of "Negro" and "Caucasian." William Z. Ripley, whose *Races of Europe* (1899) was the most influential American work on race during the early years of the century, developed a geographical classification that divided Europeans into northern Teutons, central Alpines, and southern Mediterraneans. By creating a system that marked off those with lighter complexions in the north from those with darker complexions in the south, Ripley described the differences among Europeans in a way that satisfied white Americans' need to see race in terms of color.[36]

The Jews, who were not associated with any one geographical region, did not fit well into Ripley's schema. Yet color consciousness significantly shaped the way in which Ripley sought to uncover the story of Jewish racial origins. His initial assumption was that a more or less continuous line of descent could be established between modern Jews and the ancient Semites, whom he described as a dark-complected race with origins on the African continent. A study of Jewish skull measurements, however, suggested that Jews residing in various parts of the world were more similar in headform to their non-Jewish neighbors than to each other, dispel-

3. Is the Jew white? 1902. During the Progressive Era, white Americans who wanted to fit Jews into a black and white understanding of race sometimes compared them to African Americans. This cover of Wehman Brothers' *Hebrew Jokes* featured a Jew with protruding lips and dark, kinky hair, physical traits that were often attributed to blacks in popular culture. (Courtesy Klau Library, Hebrew Union College-Jewish Institute of Religion, Cincinnati)

ling the notion of a uniform Jewish type. According to Ripley, the great majority of Jews who lived in Europe showed signs of extensive inter-mixture with lighter European types, and had little resemblance to mod-ern-day Arabs, who were thought to retain the African traits of the an-cient Semites. Though noting that many European Jews had "full and sensual" lips, "swarthy" complexions, and dark hair and eyes, Ripley ultimately concluded that modern Jews were "more Aryan than Semitic."[37] Determined like Abernethy and Woodruff to fit the Jews into a schema organized around the categories of color, Ripley ultimately had to place the Jews closer to the white end of his racial spectrum.

Ripley's findings suggest that for some Americans, it was more logical, and perhaps more comforting, to locate Jews on the white side of the racial divide than to classify them with African Americans. This process entailed the suppression of the unsavory side of the Jewish image, making Jews a benign presence by casting them as a powerful element in the progress of white America. An argument for Jewish whiteness, for example, was embedded in a letter from a "southern lady," who chastised northerners in the pages of the *Independent* for criticizing the southern treatment of African Americans, while they themselves practiced a "much more absurd race prejudice against highly intellectual, highly polished and entirely harmless people called Jews."[38] Another southerner, Thomas Dixon, author of the *Clansman* and the *Leopard's Spots*, defended the Jews in 1905 when a number of national publications were equating the lynching of southern blacks to the massacre of Jews in Russian pogroms. Dixon considered such a comparison invalid, since he felt that blacks and Jews represented opposite polls of civilization. Jews, he wrote, were an integral part of the white population in America because they belonged to "our race." The Jew, according to Dixon, "had achieved a noble civilization" and "had his poets, prophets and kings when our Germanic ancestors were still in the woods cracking cocoanuts and hickory nuts with monkeys."[39]

In 1907, Dixon underscored his belief in the whiteness of the Jews by including a Jewish character in *The Traitor*, the third novel of his white supremacist trilogy. Focusing on the schism that had developed in the Ku Klux Klan, the novel tells of a group of renegade Klansmen who abandon their former ideals of white unity and attack a Jewish storekeeper, Sam Nicharoshinski. The "true" Klansmen, however, defend the old Jew, who is described as "a refugee from Poland [whose] instinctive sympathies had always been with the oppressed people of the South" and who had "faithfully given what influence he possessed" to their cause. When one of the Klansmen who aided him is arrested, Nicharoshinski slips him a hundred dollars and tells him: "Don't you vorry, me poy, ve'll puild a monumendt to you in de public squvare yedt!"[40]

Attempts to locate the Jews firmly within the pale of whiteness were not limited to the South. The New York Presbyterian preacher Madison C. Peters, who published his tribute to American Jewry, *Justice to the Jew*, in 1908, tried to impress upon his non-Jewish readers their essential identity with the Jews by arguing that the interpreter who sailed with

Columbus in 1492, a *converso* named Luis de Torres, was in fact "the first white man to tread the soil" of the New World.[41] In 1905, at impressive ceremonies held at Carnegie Hall to commemorate the 250th anniversary of Jewish settlement in what had become the United States, George B. McClellan, Jr., mayor of New York and the son of the well-known Civil War general, also affirmed the status of American Jews as white. In response to those non-Jews who were fearful of further immigration, McClellan argued: "We members of the Caucasian family are very much like one another, without regard to what branch of that family we may belong."[42]

Especially during the heavy years of Jewish immigration, when Jewish distinctiveness was particularly visible, most Americans would not have found an argument like McClellan's—stressing the essential similarity between Jews and native-born whites—particularly convincing. Many commentators, however, made a slightly different case, arguing not that Jews were already white, but that they were excellent prospects for assimilation into white America, since they possessed many of the positive characteristics of white society. One of the most significant attempts to argue for Jews' assimilability into white America was made by Nathaniel Shaler, the dean of Harvard's Lawrence Scientific School. In his 1904 work, *The Neighbor*, Shaler compared the "race problems" presented by the "Hebrew" and the "Negro," arguing that they were of a drastically different type. While Shaler observed that Jews, like blacks, inspired an "inter-tribal repugnance" and were distinguishable by certain physical characteristics, he nonetheless argued that they were "nearer to ourselves than the people of any other stock," and that feelings of disaffection toward Jews "should certainly be much less than that which we experience in meeting Africans or American Indians."[43] If Jews were not unambiguously white, Shaler asserted their ability to *become* white through time, training, and most importantly, physical intermixture with the surrounding American population. "We may reasonably hope," he wrote, "that they will blend in such a measure as will make a safe common element of population." His confidence in Jewish assimilation made the problems associated with the Jews seem "insignificant compared with . . . . the presence of ten millions of Negroes in this country" who, in Shaler's estimation, were "ineradicably alien" and unfit to mix with the white population.[44]

Shaler's focus on Jews as good material for white society had appeal among many Progressives, who were strong believers in the assimilatory power of American civilization. President William Howard Taft told a B'nai B'rith gathering in 1910 that he envisioned Americans—and by this he meant white Americans—"as an amalgamated race, drawing their virtues from all over the world, and making a different race from that of any one of the peoples from whom we come." To this mix, he predicted, Jews would contribute their "love of liberty and a love of the guarantees of the rights of equality" as well as a "high artistic sense."[45] Another exemplar of this view was Theodore Roosevelt, a former student of Shaler's, who became a leading spokesman for Jewish assimilability. Like Shaler, Roosevelt was convinced that Jews could "do their part in the rough, manly work" necessary to insure America's worldly dominance. But in becoming like other white Americans, Roosevelt explained, Jews would have to expand their interests beyond the business world and "develop that side of them which I might call the Maccabee or fighting Jewish type."[46] Roosevelt underscored the potential for Jews to blend into white society during the Spanish-American War, when as commander of the Rough Riders, he welcomed a number of them into the famous volunteer cavalry regiment.[47] As police commissioner in New York City, Roosevelt brought many Jews onto the police force and several years later, when he became president, he made Oscar Straus the first Jew to hold a cabinet-level position by appointing him as secretary of Commerce and Labor.[48] In all of these instances, the recruitment of Jews into public service was seen by Roosevelt as a symbolic act that affirmed the unity and stability of white America. So identified was Roosevelt with the ideology of assimilation as it applied to European immigrant groups that playwright Israel Zangwill dedicated his 1908 tribute to assimilation, *The Melting Pot*, in his honor.[49]

Another Kind of "Other"

Despite the efforts of white Americans to contain the uncertainty of the Jewish image within the categories of black and white, their ultimate ambivalence about modernity and the Jews made that impossible. Many commentators shifted back and forth between describing the Jews as a distinct racial entity and trying to obscure their particularity by categorizing them within the black-white dichotomy. Even those accounts that attempted to unambiguously classify the Jew as black or white often revealed an inordinate amount of tentativeness and required significant contortions of logic in order to make their case. Arthur Abernethy, who did not shy away from fanciful arguments and attributed countless "Negro traits" to the Jews, felt it necessary to state that "there are splendid exceptions to these characteristics—most estimable men and cultured women among the Hebrews who by their contact with humanity have acquired those finer conventionalities so pleasing to gentler society."[50] Similarly, Tom Watson was unable to sustain the notion that Leo Frank, who was known as demure and unagressive, was a Jewish version of the "black beast rapist." He ultimately charged Frank not with rape—which

4. "We . . . hope that they will blend," ca. 1906. Many Progressive Era spokesmen, like Harvard scholar Nathaniel Shaler and his eminent student, Theodore
Roosevelt, argued that the Jews were good material for the white American melting
pot. Roosevelt tried to further the assimilation of Jews by bringing them into public
service. In this portrait, Roosevelt's cabinet members, including the Jewish secretary of Labor Oscar Straus (third from left), were posed to look almost identical
to one another. (From Oscar Straus, *Under Four Administrations from Cleveland
to Taft*, 1922. Photo by Clinedinst)

he called a crime of "lustful black brutes"—but with sodomy, which he
painted as a more specifically Jewish crime reflecting the wayward direction of civilization.[51] Dixon's portrait of the Yiddish-accented supporter
of the Ku Klux Klan was equally troubled. Jewish merchants in the small-
town South, whatever their feelings about African Americans, were
hardly vocal white supremacists, as they relied upon and usually courted
the trade of African Americans.[52]

Attempts by Progressive spokesmen like Theodore Roosevelt to cast
the Jews as good candidates for assimilation into white America were also
not totally successful in defusing the anxiety surrounding the Jewish racial
image. Although talk of assimilation and racial intermixture helped some
Americans overcome their concerns about the uncertainty of Jewish racial
status, the question of Jewish assimilability remained unresolved for the
duration of the Progressive Era and beyond. Figures such as Shaler, Roosevelt, and Taft may have been convinced that Jews would assimilate, but
more doubtful opinions were expressed in the pages of *Popular Science
Monthly*, where J. G. Wilson predicted that the Jew would "continue to
be an unsolved problem long after the Pole and the Hun and Italian are
forgotten." According to Wilson, the Jew's continued tendency to marry

exclusively within his group did little to encourage the belief that he would ever achieve "the goal of complete racial amalgamation."[53] Other publications were more wavering in their predictions. The editors of *World's Work* argued that there had "not yet been time fully to test the power of free institutions to make [the Jew] an indistinguishable part of the population of the Republic."[54]

If white Americans were unable to obscure the issue of Jewish racial status by focusing on the black-white dichotomy, however, they never stopped trying in the years before World War I. Attempting to understand Jewish racial difference within a black-white framework could not soothe all of their anxieties about modernity, but it did indicate an enduring faith in their power as whites as well as a continued optimism that the United States could be the ordered society for which they longed. A noticeable trend of the Progressive Era was that despite the fact that white Americans were becoming increasingly aware of the Jew as a figure in national life, worry over the Jew's place in America's racial landscape never took on crisis proportions as it would in the 1920s and 1930s, when social critics regularly spoke about America's "Jewish Problem."

Still, Jews did pay a price for the place they held in American racial discourse during this period. Though not destined to fill the role of the essential "other" as they had often done in Europe, they faced another kind of marginalization, one that required them to disappear as a visibly distinct group in order to insure the larger society's sense of stability and self-confidence. If they failed, their critics threatened to punish their visibility by linking them to America's more stable "other," the African American. For Jews, this threat loomed not only in the words and images put forth by native-born whites, but also in the growing acceptability of anti-Jewish social discrimination.[55] Even those most sympathetic to the Jews were willing to justify Jewish entry into the mainstream of American life only by means of thorough assimilation into white society. Increasingly aware of the importance of whiteness to American national identity, as well as of their own problematic position in the country's racial schema, American Jews became preoccupied with the need to situate themselves socially as white and to find ways of defining Jewishness that did not interfere with their whiteness. Their commitment to a distinctive Jewish identity, however, would make both tasks difficult ones.

CHAPTER 3

"NOW IS THE TIME TO SHOW YOUR TRUE COLORS":
THE JEWISH APPROACH TO AFRICAN AMERICANS

B Y THE OPENING years of the twentieth century, the growing unease about Jewish racial status in the United States had become a
source of great concern for America's acculturated Jews. Although
there was little they could do to soothe the underlying social anxiety that
made them figures of uncertainty among white Americans, many Jews
hoped that they could assuage the doubts of the dominant society by affirming their place as unqualified whites. Central to this effort was demonstrating a clear social distinction between themselves and America's principal racial outsiders, African Americans.

Because most acculturated Jews had either immigrated to the United
States from Central Europe several decades earlier or were themselves
native-born Americans, they were already well aware of the importance
of the color line in American social and political life. Jews had not been
bystanders to American racial culture during the nineteenth century, having frequently taken positions on slavery and other questions regarding
the status of African Americans.[1] Yet never before had Jews' own status
depended to such a degree on their conformity to American racial standards. Until the 1890s, Jews were generally considered white no matter
how closely they observed American racial etiquette or what attitudes
they took concerning white supremacy. By contrast, their approach to
African Americans at the turn of the century held much greater potential
to affect their social status and to influence their own standing in the
American racial order.

As determined as acculturated American Jews of the early twentieth
century were to define themselves against African Americans, however,
the pursuit of this strategy sometimes raised new and difficult questions
of identity for them. As Jews tried to unambiguously identify with the
standards of white society, they often found that their self-image as Jews
complicated their reach for whiteness. A group with its own history of
persecution and an ongoing sense of "outsider status," Jews frequently
had misgivings about adopting the harsher elements of American racism.
In the post–Civil War decades, acculturating Jews had been freer to mitigate their incursions into the white world with expressions of empathy
for blacks and assertions of identification with their plight. Now pushed

to affirm their whiteness much more explicitly, they often felt torn between their impulses for inclusion and distinctiveness.

Of course, all American Jews did not experience these tensions in the same way. In the South, the sheer weight of the black-white divide made it exceptionally difficult for acculturated Jews to voice opposition to prevailing racial mores without inviting severe consequences. In the North, while acculturated Jews assiduously emphasized their whiteness as a means of assuring their social status, they enjoyed greater flexibility than their southern counterparts in expressing empathy for African Americans and opposition to antiblack measures. To make matters even more complicated, in both regions there was a growing population of recent Eastern European Jewish immigrants, whose approach to African Americans was totally different from that of more acculturated Jews. As a group still significantly removed from the pressures of social integration, the immigrants demonstrated little awareness of the need to identify as white. Thus, throughout the period before World War I, whiteness remained a highly unstable category of identity for American Jews.

Acculturated Jews in the Jim Crow South

The clear division between slaves and free whites in the antebellum South gave Jews an automatic level of social acceptance that was unparalleled in any other Western society of the period.[2] As a result, few Jews in the slave states found reason to criticize the institution of slavery. The end of the Civil War, however, altered the social profile of southern Jews, including their attitudes toward race relations. During Reconstruction, a significant migration of northern Jews, mostly recent immigrants from Central Europe, bolstered the region's Jewish population and reduced the proportion of Jews who had been thoroughly acculturated into the South's racial system. Jews also became heavily invested in the emerging business infrastructure of the New South, a role that led them to court the business of former slaves and to support the amelioration of racial tensions that might work against the growth of a new regional economy. Finally, with the removal of clear legal barriers between blacks and whites and with African Americans working toward education and self-improvement, Jews could increasingly see in the black struggle experiences that resonated with their own recent history.[3]

While southern Jews were careful to remain within the range of acceptable positions on racial issues, these factors meant that by the 1880s, it was not unusual for them to align themselves with supporters of political rights and education for blacks. Edwin W. Moise, who served as adjutant and inspector general in South Carolina, embraced the paternalistic racial attitude of the Redeemer governor, Wade Hampton, who opposed the violence and intimidation practiced by racial radicals and courted black voters.[4] In Virginia, William J. Lovenstein, a legislator who became the highest-ranking officeholder of Jewish origin in the state's history, also supported the rights of African Americans, pushing his fellow lawmakers to support health care and teacher training for blacks.[5] Black educational projects received the support of Jewish activists like Rabbi Judah Wechsler, who campaigned for a bond issue to pay for the first black school in Meridian, Mississippi, in 1888, and Samuel Ullman, who as a member of the Birmingham Board of Education advocated improved facilities for black schooling as early as 1885.[6]

Southern Jews had few qualms about expressing fairly liberal attitudes concerning African American rights during the 1880s because there was little question about their own status as white. This situation, however, began to change dramatically when economic and social upheaval, brought on by the depression of the early 1890s, devastated agricultural production in the region and threatened to undermine the entire social structure that guaranteed white privilege. The psychological impact of the depression severely damaged the confidence of southern whites, pushing them increasingly toward racial radicalism as a means of recouping their status.[7] In such an environment, Jews not only began to stand out as agents of the economic changes occurring in southern society, but as a group that did not fit neatly into the increasingly rigid definitions of black and white demanded by the emerging system of racial division.

In small part, the increasing problem Jews posed to the southern racial order was exacerbated by the stream of new immigrants arriving from Eastern Europe. Because the immigrants stood out as alien in dress and appearance, southerners often distinguished them from whites, as did the *Richmond Times* in 1893, when it reported on an altercation between a "Polish Jew and a white man."[8] In some cases, recently arrived Jews were actually confused with African Americans, and suffered attacks on the part of hostile whites who caught them in situations considered inappropriate for blacks. In Pine Bluff, Arkansas, in 1912, a recently arrived Eastern European immigrant narrowly escaped lynching because onlookers took him for a black man in the company of a white woman.[9]

But largely, Jewish racial identity became a problem not because of the new immigrants, who arrived in smaller numbers than in the North, but because southerners continued to perceive in all Jews—even the more acculturated Jews of Central European origin—distinct social, economic, and political characteristics that could be pointed to as interfering with the maintenance of clear boundaries between blacks and whites. Jewish merchants not only dealt extensively with black customers across the South, but often held a certain financial advantage over white farmers and factory workers, which was thought to undermine the preservation of white racial dominance. The relationship between Jews' economic position and southern race relations became clear in the early 1890s, when populist "white caps" destroyed Jewish shops in a number of towns in Louisiana and Mississippi. The vigilantes were white farmers who feared that the Jews were interfering with the racial balance in the area by renting land seized from white debtors to black tenants.[10] Southern Jews were shocked by the attacks, but preferred not to interpret them as antisemitic outbursts. Rabbi Max Heller, for example, wrote that the attacks did not interfere with the "perfect harmony prevailing between Jew and Gentile" in the South, where such virulent hatred was reserved for African Americans.[11]

Despite their protests to the contrary, however, a rise in such incidents drove home to southern Jews the fear that they were no longer seen as unambiguously white. By the late 1890s, Jewish political candidates in some parts of the South found it increasingly difficult to win election, just as southern politicians were calling for the political exclusion of African Americans. Jews had an exceptional record of political service in the South, with dozens of them serving as mayors, aldermen, state legislators, and members of Congress throughout the nineteenth century.[12] But as politics became more focused on the issues of racial separation, the electorate became increasingly skeptical of Jews as a group whose racial standing was ambiguous. Edwin W. Moise of South Carolina, once a prominent politician and supporter of black suffrage, was now vilified by the state's racist governor Ben Tillman as "an outsider and a member of a despised and despicable race."[13] In Atlanta, Jewish politicians fell into disfavor partly because their orientation toward business led them to oppose the prohibition of alcohol, which was seen by many southern whites as a prerequisite for effective white governance.[14] The presumption that Jewish political views differed from those of white southerners led one candidate in the Richmond municipal elections of 1893 to single out "Jews and niggers" as political troublemakers.[15]

Perhaps most devastating to southern Jews was the rise of exclusive social clubs and resorts with anti-Jewish policies. Prominent Jews had been among the original founders of the Gentleman's Driving Club in Atlanta and the Boston and Pickwick Clubs in New Orleans, but by the turn of the century, none of these organizations accepted Jewish members.[16] In states where public facilities were segregated according to color, the exclusion of Jews from clubs and hotels seemed to question their social standing as whites. The fact that many hotels and resorts in the North excluded Jews made southern Jews anxious about the spread of such policies to their region. Fear fell over southern Jewry in 1906, for example, when Bertha Rayner Frank, sister of the U. S. senator from Maryland, traveled north to Atlantic City and was denied entry to the Blenheim-

Marlborough Hotel. Editors of the Baltimore *Jewish Comment*, struck by the similarity of the new anti-Jewish measures to the racial segregation frequently practiced in their city, urged community action to prevent Jews from being put on a level "with the negro as an undesirable in places offering accommodations to the general public."[17]

In trying to rescue their position in southern society, Jews began to vehemently oppose any comparison between themselves and African Americans. Herbert T. Ezekiel, editor of Richmond's *Jewish South*, took local non-Jewish editors to task for their practice of distinguishing Jews from other whites in the newspapers when they were arrested for crimes. On one occasion, he demanded a retraction from the editor of the *Richmond Times*, which he published in his weekly magazine.[18] Sometimes the comparison in need of refutation came not from southern non-Jews but from northern Jews. After devastating attacks on African Americans by white mobs in Wilmington, North Carolina, in 1898, the Philadelphia *Jewish Exponent* published an editorial sympathetic to the black victims and likened their persecution to that experienced by Jews. Outraged by such a comparison and fearful of its social repercussions, southern Jewish editors denounced the editorial vehemently. Frank Cohen, editor of the Atlanta *Jewish Sentiment*, dismissed the *Exponent*'s comments as another example of the "deformed opinion" of northern Jews on the "negro question" in the South.[19] Ezekiel, however, took great pains to refute the comparison in his publication. "Our people, though persecuted and driven from pillar to post," he wrote, "do not possess the criminal instincts of the colored race. . . . The comparison of Jews and negroes is, we had always thought, a pastime of our Christian neighbors, and one which we, of all people, should not countenance." Providing a litany of reasons why African Americans made undesirable citizens, Ezekiel affirmed that "there is nothing in common between the two races in this section, and if a comparison holds elsewhere, either the Jews or the negroes must be very different from that they are here."[20]

The need to invalidate the comparison between Jews and African Americans remained strong in the South through the early years of the twentieth century, especially as a number of American commentators fastened on the similarities between antiblack and anti-Jewish persecution following the Eastern European pogroms of 1903 and 1905. After Booker T. Washington compared lynching and pogroms in a speech in St. Louis in 1906, the local Jewish paper, the *Modern View*, responded that he drew a "poor parallel" between African Americans, "who by carnal crimes bring their people into disrepute," and Jews, who are feared because they are "thought to be too acquisitive and too able commercially, professionally and otherwise." The paper fortified its argument by contrasting the environments under which Africans Americans and Russian Jews lived, citing the protection of a free government, the fair-minded neighbors, and the educational opportunities enjoyed by American blacks, factors that should have militated against the "ignorance and idleness that makes for criminality in the negro." The Jews in Russia, explained the editorial, suffered under an "intolerant government, a bigoted priesthood and a chained press," yet still managed to remain "peaceful, industrious, free from crime" and tenacious in their religious beliefs and practices.[21]

In attempting to affirm their whiteness by negating the comparison between themselves and African Americans, southern Jews often capitalized on the fact that their place in southern society was ambiguous, rather than totally marginal. Because southern attitudes toward Jews, like American attitudes in general, often combined admiration for Jewish accomplishments with fears about Jewish difference, Jews viewed conformity to prevailing racial mores as a strategy that had great potential to resolve their uncertain place in the southern racial constellation. They were buoyed, for example, when Thomas Dixon, one of the most virulent racists of the period, condemned the black leader Booker T. Washington for comparing Jews and African Americans in his book, *The Future of the American Negro*.[22] The New Orleans *Jewish Ledger*, one of the most prominent Jewish papers in the South, responded enthusiastically to Dixon's defense of the Jews, labeling Washington an "impudent nigger" for his comments. The paper reprinted Dixon's comments in their own columns, even embellishing them with some of their own lines, which they attributed to him: "To compare the Jew, who occupies the highest pinnacle of human superiority and intellectual attainment, with the Negro who forms the mud at its base, is something only a Negro with more than the usual vanity and impudence of his race could attempt."[23]

Dixon was not the only spokesman for white supremacy whose statements allowed southern Jews to believe that a careful policy of racial conformity could help deflect attention away from Jewish difference and confirm their status as white. In 1903, Ben Tillman, who had become the U.S. senator from South Carolina, led a campaign against the practice of appointing black postmasters in small southern towns, citing the danger white women faced from the black officials and their friends who congregated in post offices or in the general stores where they were often located. Of special significance was Tillman's objection to the appointment of a black postmistress in Indianola, Mississippi, where the post office was located in Cohen's Brooklyn Bridge Store. As Tillman told the Senate, the presence of the black postmistress had encouraged black customers to take a bold attitude toward the white customers and employees, and violent riots almost erupted among the white population of Indianola when reports circulated that an "infamous proposition and insult from a negro man [was made] to a white woman, a poor Jewess who was clerking in the same store."[24] Tillman, who ten years earlier had vilified his Jewish political opponent, Edwin W. Moise, as a racial outsider, was now defending a Jewish woman as a symbol of white womanly virtue and purity. Statements like those of Dixon and Tillman indicated to southern Jews that if they carefully observed the rules of southern race relations and did not disturb increasingly rigid racial boundaries, they could assure their place as whites, and thus their full acceptance, in southern society.

In this respect, southern Jewry offered an interesting comparison to its northern counterpart. Between 1907 and 1913, in response to the same sort of social discrimination that made southern Jews fearful of being classed with African Americans, northern Jewish leaders, headed by the prominent New York attorney Louis Marshall, lobbied for the New York Civil Rights Act, which would outlaw discrimination in public accommodations on the basis of "race, faith, creed, and color."[25] In the South, however, many observers feared that a sustained public campaign against such exclusionary policies would do nothing more than underscore Jews' status as victims of "racial discrimination" and lend credence to the comparison between Jews and African Americans. Max Heller, a New Orleans rabbi, expressed the fear characteristic of southern Jews that any law seeking to preserve Jewish rights by advocating an end to racial discrimination against blacks would "array against it . . . the whole force of prejudice against the negro."[26] Although he himself was a supporter of black rights, Heller's views were shaped by the realities of the southern racial situation, which told him that if Jews sought an end to discrimination, they would have to do it in a way that did not seriously challenge prevailing racial hierarchies.

Most southern Jews agreed with Heller that the preservation of Jewish social status relied on their conformity to southern racial standards. What remained uncertain throughout the early years of the twentieth century, however, was the *extent* to which Jews needed to embrace notions of white supremacy in order to relieve the public's doubt about their racial standing. Most Jews, for example, abstained from promoting the harshest forms of southern racism, like mob violence and lynching. Although Richmond's *Jewish South* was vigorous in asserting the whiteness of Jews, it decried lynching as a subversion of law and government that not only "defies the dignity of man" but "profanes the sanctity of human life."[27] There were at least some Jews, however, who felt the need to support such practices, including Frank Cohen, the editor of the Atlanta *Jewish Sentiment*. "The white man will rule by fair means or by foul," Cohen warned after the Wilmington Race Riot of 1898. "God Almighty never created the negro the white man's equal and even an act of Congress will not change the trend of nature or swerve the white man from his determination to retain his supremacy."[28]

If outspoken Jewish proponents of lynching remained rare, more common were southern Jewish politicians who tried to counter prejudices
against Jewish officeholding by taking up the causes of black disenfranchisement and white political dominance. In Arkansas, a state where populist politicians frequently employed anti-Jewish imagery in denouncing
"usurers" and "Rothschilds," Governor Jeff Davis and other leading
Democrats were willing to overlook the Jewishness of Adjutant General
Charles Jacobson because of his support for preserving white rule.[29]
Maryland's Jewish attorney general, Isidor Rayner, made disenfranchisement a central tenet of his political credo, arguing in 1903 that the Declaration of Independence was wrong in proclaiming that all men were created equal.[30] Later, when Rayner became a U.S. senator, he lent his
political clout to a state disenfranchisement bill championed by another
Jewish politician and one of his successors in the attorney general's office,
Isaac Lobe Straus. The bill restricting black voting rights became law in
Maryland in 1908 and was named the "Straus Amendment" after its primary author.[31]

Despite the presence of some Jews in the ranks of assertive white supremacists, however, Jews in the South generally shied away from high-
profile political engagement with racial issues. Instead, they tried to assert
their whiteness in less charged ways that simply upheld the prevailing
social and cultural distinctions between blacks and whites. In New Orleans, for example, the local Jewish paper printed dialect stories lampooning blacks and regularly reviewed blackface minstrel shows and performances of plays such as Dixon's *Clansman*, which it called a
"thrilling" exposition of "the terrible struggle of the 'Reconstruction Era'
and the frightful perils of entrusting the mastery of society to a helot
race."[32] Atlanta Jews staged their own blackface minstrel show in 1898
under the auspices of the local Hebrew Association.[33] They also tried to
emphasize their stature in the city by claiming to have produced the first
example of white womanhood in the area. By the turn of the century, local
Jews often repeated a founding myth that Caroline Haas, the daughter of
one of Atlanta's first Jewish residents, was the "first white female child"
born in the city.[34] Finally, in order to assure their own continued access
to white privilege, southern Jews also supported the system of segregated
public accommodations and neighborhoods. In Atlanta, a Jewish member
of the Carnegie Library's board was among those who voted to ban African Americans from the institution after W.E.B. Du Bois, a professor at
Atlanta University, applied for reading privileges.[35] Similarly, when Atlanta's Hebrew Benevolent Congregation sold its edifice on the corner of
Garnett and Forsythe Streets and moved into a new building, the directors
stipulated that "said Temple is never to be sold, rented to, nor to be used
by colored people."[36]

The tendency of southern Jews to uphold social and cultural distinctions between blacks and whites while generally shying away from strong support of racial violence or disenfranchisement indicates that there was a point at which their desire for social acceptance began to conflict with feelings of unease about adopting the mantle of white supremacy. As assiduously as Jews tried to conform to the strictures of southern race relations, they sometimes found themselves unable to suppress an aversion to racism that had been conditioned by the Jewish historical experience and was now becoming more manifest as they tasted a bit of the social exclusion usually reserved for blacks. Though southern Jews were often forced by social pressure to downplay these feelings, there were distinct signs during the early twentieth century of the lingering reservations some Jews had about identifying unambiguously with the southern racial system.

On rare occasion, there were extreme examples of acculturated Jews who had become totally alienated from the standards of white society. Adolph Altschul, one of several German-Jewish immigrant brothers who settled in Pine Bluff, Arkansas, and peddled in the surrounding countryside, fell in love with a former slave, Maggie Carson, and married her, apparently before such marriages became illegal in the South. He remained with her until his death and had several children, while his brothers cut off contact with him and identified exclusively with Pine Bluff's white population.[37] In Natchez, Mississippi, home to a prominent and well-integrated Jewish community that dated back to antebellum days, Charles Moritz broke the predominant Jewish pattern by establishing a "permanent alliance" (a kind of common-law marriage) with an African American woman, Dorcas Walker. While Mississippi state law prevented Moritz and Walker from marrying, and while they conformed to local racial etiquette by living separately, they remained in a life-long relationship and raised two daughters together.[38]

Much more common, however, was the way in which acculturated Jewish merchants sometimes deviated from white racial etiquette in their commercial relations with African Americans. Many Jews got their start in the southern business world by dealing with black customers and continued to court their trade even after branching out to serve a more diverse customer base. Within the confines of their own stores, southern Jewish merchants were often able to form relationships with black customers and extend courtesies to them that may have appeared unseemly in the public square. Julius Levin, a prominent lumber merchant in Alexandria, Louisiana, who began his career as a country peddler, established close ties with many of his black customers and frequently made generous donations to the African American Shiloh Baptist Church of that city. When Levin died in 1910, blacks published resolutions in his memory in the local paper as well as in their church publication, the *Louisiana Baptist*, calling him a "true friend of our race as well as to humanity."[39] Likewise, the Jewish merchants of Montgomery, Alabama, developed a strong rapport with Booker T. Washington and frequently supplied the needs of the Tuskegee Institute, which they also supported with financial contributions.[40] Occasionally, Jewish merchants went beyond discreet acts of friendship and assistance and took more public stands. Once, when Tuskegee faced the possibility of an economic boycott, Jacques Loeb, a French-born Jew who headed a large Montgomery grocery concern and was influential in local business affairs, resisted the pressure of the non-Jewish merchants and continued to supply the school with necessities until other companies agreed to do likewise.[41]

If Jewish businessmen sometimes articulated feelings of friendship and empathy for African Americans in the context of the close economic relations between the two groups, Jewish clergy, acting on their understanding of Judaism as a religion that demanded social justice, also frequently spoke up for the needs of the black community. During the first two decades of the twentieth century, a small but significant circle of southern rabbis supported African American education, opposed lynching, and worked for what they termed interracial "harmony" and cooperation. As rabbis, these men formed their opinions on the issue of race under a somewhat different set of pressures and experiences than their congregants. First, because the South had no rabbinical seminary of its own, many of the Jewish clergy who served the region either came from the North or were recent arrivals from Central or Eastern Europe. As a result, they probably had much more immediate experiences with anti-Jewish persecution than their congregants did and therefore found themselves at greater odds with the southern treatment of African Americans. Second, since Jewish religious leaders were often accorded a certain respect in the South that individual Jews may not have always received, they enjoyed a degree of latitude among non-Jews in expressing their concern for African Americans, especially when such concern was voiced in the language of ethical obligation. As a result, rabbis such as Ephraim Frisch of Pine Bluff, Arkansas, and Bernard Ehrenreich of Montgomery, Alabama, felt free to use their role as civic leaders to solicit support for black schools such as Branch Normal College and Tuskegee Institute.[42]

Finally, because rabbis saw race relations in ethical terms, they were less willing than their congregants to suppress feelings of empathy for a people who were suffering many of the same indignities Jews had historically experienced. When Alfred G. Moses assumed leadership of the Shaarei Shomayim Congregation in Mobile, Alabama, in 1901, he immediately wrote Booker T. Washington to express his interest in African American affairs. "As a preacher I feel morally bound to get at the truth," he explained, "and as a Rabbi, I have the opportunity of influencing the minds of the better class of Jewish people, as well as of the community at large."[43] Seymour Bottigsheim, the rabbi of Temple B'nai Israel of Natchez, Mississippi, ignored the concerns of some of his congregants and invited George Washington Carver to address his congregation from the pulpit.[44] In 1909, Rabbi Max Heller was denounced by some leading members of the New Orleans Jewish community when he criticized a local Christmas toy drive that provided only for white children.[45] Despite such negative responses, however, Heller continued his critique of southern racism, going so far as to draw explicit parallels between blacks and Jews, which had become a virtual taboo in southern Jewish society. Knowing his congregants' strong aversion to such comparisons, Heller forcefully told them that "the Jew, like the negro, is slandered and abused as a 'race' . . . [and] is made to suffer, the mass, for the sins of the individual." He also argued that such similarities implied a duty toward African Americans on the part of Jews, who as "men who have been steeled in the furnace of persecution . . . ought to lend an uplifting hand to the weak fellow-man."[46]

While Heller stood virtually alone among his colleagues in making direct comparisons between African Americans and Jews, the belief that such a parallel existed is no doubt what led other southern rabbis to exceed non-Jewish clergy in their support of black causes. Despite southern rabbis' fairly liberal expression of empathy for African Americans, however, their activities ultimately underscored the great care Jews had to take in defining their place in the southern racial order. Although rabbis argued for the education and "uplift" of African Americans and condemned virulent racism, they never challenged the basic structure of race relations in the South or advocated meaningful social equality for blacks. None argued for an end to segregation, or even for the protection of African Americans' right to vote and hold office. David Marx, the rabbi of Atlanta's Hebrew Benevolent Congregation, served on the commission appointed to restore order in the wake of that city's 1906 riot, but the plan for "racial harmony" proposed by the group argued that the best way to improve relations between blacks and whites was to keep African Americans away from saloons and off the streets.[47] Even Max Heller strongly supported the maintenance of the southern system of segregation. He argued that African Americans could become gentlemen, but conceded that "social equality" did not mean "social mingling." The continued separation of the races, and especially the ban on interracial unions, he felt, was a necessity if whites were to effectively bear the burden of improving the more "backward" race. "It is to the interest of both races that interbreeding of any kind should be prevented," wrote Heller in 1904. "The benevolence of the separation will appear in our efforts to lift the younger brother as speedily as possible to our own level."[48] Thus, even the most outspoken Jewish supporters of African Americans continued to uphold the basic social distinction between blacks and whites, underscoring their need to position the Jews on the white side of the racial divide.

In the age of Jim Crow, then, the status of Jews in the South was contingent on a high degree of conformity to the prevailing racial mores. With the emergence of social discrimination in the 1890s, southern Jews realized that an unambiguous assertion of their whiteness was necessary to prevent the further erosion of the unparalleled acceptance they had long enjoyed. Though Jews often had misgivings about the demands the southern racial system placed on them, they were able to express their reservations in only muted ways. To assert them more strongly would have been too disastrous for their social standing. Two decades after the rise of racial radicalism, the trial and lynching of Leo Frank underscored what could happen to southern Jews when their racial status was compromised. During Frank's 1913 trial, some non-Jewish Atlantans promoted a boycott of Jewish shops by distributing small cards that read: "Now is the time to show your true colors; to show your true American blood."[49] As southern Jews watched the trial and lynching of Frank unfold, they became more convinced than ever that the key to social acceptance lay in demonstrating *their* "true colors" as whites.

Acculturated Jews and Whiteness in the North

The social discrimination that southern Jews increasingly experienced by the end of the nineteenth century was felt with even greater force by their counterparts in the northern states. Because the North had a significantly larger Jewish population concentrated in major urban centers such as New York, Chicago, Philadelphia, and Boston, Jews there stood out much more as a group distinct from their neighbors. Since the late 1870s, Jews had faced various efforts to exclude them from resorts, clubs, and other preserves of elite society on a scale unheard of in the South, a trend that worsened significantly in the 1890s. Moreover, northern cities had received the bulk of Jewish immigrants from Eastern Europe, whose low social standing became a much more significant factor there in discrediting the position of the established Jews of Central European background. While the overriding significance of the black-white divide in the South frequently served to deflect attention away from Jewish distinctiveness, in the North Jews often bore the brunt of society's fears about shifting class boundaries, urbanization, and industrialization more directly.

Still, even though white northerners were more aware of the existence of the Jews as a distinct group, they were no less determined to understand them within the clear, hierarchical racial categories that bolstered American confidence during the Progressive Era. In fact, the great diversity of urban society in the North made native-born whites especially anxious for an overarching racial ideology that could impose a sense of order on their jumbled population. Moreover, the growing number of African Americans in the North after the turn of the century helped make the black-white divide more accessible as a barometer against which all groups could be measured. As the dominant society's discourse on the Jew revealed, native-born whites' increasing cognizance of the Jew's presence in American life only made them more determined to fit him into the categories of black and white.

The growing emphasis on black and white in the North made the acculturated Jews of the region increasingly aware of the implications of living in a society shaped by the color line. On the one hand, they worried about how their status was being threatened by comparisons to African Americans, especially in light of recent Jewish immigration from Eastern Europe. Suggestions by social reformers that the Lower East Side resembled an African jungle or that Jews were as unassimilable as blacks unnerved established Jews, who feared that their hard-won status was vanishing. On the other hand, like Jews in the South, acculturated Jews in the North were buoyed by the willingness of many in the dominant society to see them as productive white citizens and contributors to national progress. They knew, however, that only by actively confirming their place in the ordered society envisioned by white Americans could they relieve the doubts and fears about their own racial status. Thus, in ways that mirrored the experience of their southern counterparts, their stance toward African Americans became a critical part of their campaign to win acceptance in the early years of the twentieth century.

Although northern and southern Jews experienced similar pressures regarding their approach to blacks, there were some critical differences in context that shaped the ways Jews in each region attempted to secure their status as white. First, because northern Jews were generally more visible as a group than Jews in the South, they were more sensitive to the ways in which increasing racism against African Americans might also encourage similar acts against other minorities. As a result, they remained more reticent than southern Jews about the advance of racial violence, segregation, and legal restrictions against blacks. Second, despite their great desire for social inclusion, Jews in the North were more accustomed to thinking of themselves as a group apart and felt greater freedom in expressing doubts about the standards of non-Jewish society. Finally, because social barriers between blacks and whites remained less absolute in the North and humanitarian efforts on behalf of blacks were viewed more positively, northern Jews had more flexibility in expressing their empathy and support for African Americans.

In the years immediately preceding the turn of the century, Jewish opinion in the North had been quite positively disposed toward African Americans, and Jews there were much more willing than their southern counterparts to liken black oppression to their own history of suffering. In 1898, the Philadelphia *Jewish Exponent* issued an unambiguous condemnation of the antiblack riot in Wilmington, North Carolina, comparing it to similar attacks on Jews and suggesting that its readers, as members of an oppressed minority group, ought to properly express their sympathy for the plight of the victims.[50] Similar sentiments were expressed the following year when Abram L. Isaacs, the editor of the New York *Jewish Messenger*, wrote to the publisher of the *Colored American* to thank blacks for their support of Alfred Dreyfus, the Jewish captain who had recently been tried for treason in France. In a show of brotherhood, he pledged that American Jews would reciprocate by opposing the restriction of African American rights and the spread of antiblack violence in the United States.[51]

By 1900, however, growing concerns about their place in the American racial order were pushing northern Jews to reassess their approach to African Americans. That year a race riot erupted in New York's Tenderloin district, reflecting the intensified climate of hostility that had been building against the city's growing black population. Echoing sentiments expressed by northern Jews in years past, the *American Hebrew* condemned the riot as an evil similar to the "attacks made on the Jews in the benighted countries, where the ritual murder charge still perverts men." But revealing a growing need to distance Jews from African Americans, editor Philip Cowen made a point of emphasizing that while in ritual murder accusations "there is not even *one* [Jew] who is guilty," at the root of a race riot there is usually "one wicked negro" responsible for the attack. He also backed away somewhat from earlier denunciations of southern racial violence, conceding that it was inappropriate to "criticize lynching and other lawlessness below Mason and Dixon's line when such an outbreak is possible in New York City."[52] In general, the editorial betrayed a new, more reserved attitude about the treatment of blacks, suggesting that Cowen would wait to survey the direction of local racial sentiment before issuing any uncompromising opinions on the matter.

Reservations about comparing black and Jewish suffering grew among northern Jews in the ensuing years, especially after a discussion erupted in the press in 1903 about the similarities between Russian pogroms and southern lynching. In Chicago, the *Public*, a liberal journal edited by the lawyer and political activist Louis F. Post, condemned American authorities who decried Russian atrocities against Jews but failed to condemn lynching in their own country. The comparison raised an uncomfortable parallel for northern Jews, who were worried about the prospect of immigrants being classed with African Americans. In answer to the *Public*'s campaign, Solomon Solis-Cohen, a prominent Philadelphia physician and a leader of B'nai B'rith, condemned what he termed the "attempt to set up an analogy between the lynching of negroes guilty or accused of rape or murder in the United States, and the massacre of Jews in Russia." Repeating the distinction first made by the *American Hebrew* three years earlier, he argued that, unlike Russian pogroms, the lynching of blacks usually had some basis in "the unspeakable crime committed by many Negroes." In addition, because lynching had no approval from the government, Solis-Cohen saw an essential distinction between vigilante activity against an accused rapist and government-approved violence against innocent Jews. Without such government sanction, lynching was no reflection on the country's level of civilization or its ability to protest against Russian barbarism. Further, the gap in the level of civilization between Jews and African Americans, he argued, made the comparison invalid. "It is not unfair," he wrote, "to contrast the advanced stage of intellectual and moral development of the Jews in general with the limited progress that the masses of Negroes in Africa and in America have as yet had the time and opportunity to achieve."[53] Although northern Jews remained critical of lynching, in the wake of Solis-Cohen's interchange with the *Public*, they became more careful about expressing their empathy for its victims by directly comparing Jewish and black suffering.

Fears that a black-Jewish comparison might carry grave consequences were most strongly felt by northern Jews in the wake of the Leo Frank trial. Although the trial took place in Georgia, it aroused national attention, and Frank relied on extensive financial, legal, and public relations support from Jews in the North. As a result, northern Jews, who followed the case closely, became increasingly sensitized both to the danger of comparing blacks and Jews and the possibilities of deflecting antisemitism by emphasizing their whiteness.

The Frank trial was especially important for northern Jews because of the impact it had on Louis Marshall, the prominent New York attorney and Jewish communal leader who was taken on as special counsel to Frank. While on the case, Marshall supported the policy crafted by Frank's southern lawyers of trying to use the overwhelming power of the black-white divide in the South to Frank's advantage. The legal team took every opportunity to emphasize Frank's whiteness while trying to shift blame for the crime to Jim Conley, a black janitor who had also been implicated in the murder. While the lawyers believed Conley to be the true assailant, they also felt that, as a black man, he would fit the jury's preconception of a rapist and murderer, thus helping to acquit Frank. Although Marshall, who was a strong defender of black rights in the North, shied away from making racists remarks during the trial, he made race an issue in private correspondence, referring to Conley as a "degenerate negro of criminal antecedents."[54] Marshall also understood that Frank's whiteness could be accentuated only if his Jewishness was downplayed. As a result, he urged Jewish supporters of Frank not to make the trial into a "Jewish case." In a letter to Frank's friend, Morton Klein, Marshall warned that Jews "should practice self-suppression or else a serious evil might result. . . . I am satisfied that, eventually, justice will be done through the ordinary processes of the court."[55] Ultimately, Marshall's prediction was wrong, but his experience during the trial left him with the strong belief that Jews had a better chance of achieving justice by presenting themselves as undifferentiated whites rather than as Jews.

During the Frank trial, it was already apparent that northern Jews were reshaping their approach to Jewish defense work in light of the events in Georgia. The editors of northern Jewish papers who covered the Frank Case, for example, employed a strategy similar to that of Frank's lawyers in their efforts to defend the accused Jew. Although they remained reluctant to engage directly in racist remarks, they liberally reprinted anti-Conley editorials from the daily papers that used statements such as "black human animal," "depraved negro," "treacherous negro" and "negro dope fiend." Jewish editors walked a fine line in their use of anti-black imagery. "They seemed reluctant to engage in the kind of . . . racism common in the daily press," explains historian Eugene Levy, "while at the same time they keenly wanted to use all means available, including anti-black statements, in aiding Frank's cause."[56]

Efforts to protect Jewish civil rights in the North also seem to have been influenced by lessons gleaned from the Frank Case. In 1913, during the same month in which Marshall was asked to assist in Frank's trial, he and other northern Jewish leaders succeeded in having civil rights legislation passed in New York State that outlawed discrimination in public accommodations on the basis of race as well as religion. Southern Jews like Max Heller had long opposed such measures because they threatened to group Jews with blacks in the eyes of the public. As Frank's trial got underway, however, some northern Jews also began to sense the danger of placing themselves in a class with blacks in their defense efforts. Julian Morgenstern, a young Reform rabbi and professor at Hebrew Union College in Cincinnati, suggested that Jews' efforts to open hotels and restaurants to all racial minorities including blacks was a tactical blunder and cut against Americans' right to free association. "I have never invited a negro to dine with me, and probably will never do so," wrote the rabbi. "I must accord the same right to the anti-Semite to feel the same way toward the Jew." Antisemitism, Morgenstern reasoned, would fade away with "time and education," and Jews would be better poised for social acceptance if they could win it without grouping themselves with African Americans.[57] By the end of the Frank Case, Morgenstern's view was in-

5. "Get Your Tickets Now for the Minstrel Show," 1914. Minstrel shows became a regular entertainment offering of Jewish social clubs and community organizations in the early twentieth century. The show advertised here was sponsored by the Acorn Club, one of the many groups that met at the Young Men's Hebrew Association (YMHA) of New York. (Courtesy 92nd Street Y Archives)

creasingly embraced by Jewish organizational leaders. Founded four weeks after Frank's trial ended, the Anti-Defamation League of B'nai B'rith became one of the community's central agencies for combating prejudice. But notably, from the start the organization shied away from campaigning for "civil rights" as African Americans did and concentrated on improving public opinion about Jews. Even when it did support legislative action, it was careful to oppose discrimination based on "creed" but not on "race."[58]

If Jewish leaders in the North hoped to speed Jewish social acceptance by emphasizing Jews' whiteness, average Jews pursued a similar strategy in carrying out their social and cultural activities. As early as 1902, Jewish clubs in the North staged their own blackface minstrel shows, like the one hosted that year by Chicago's Standard Club, featuring a review of "coon songs" performed by two female members.[59] At the Young Men's Hebrew Association (YMHA) in New York, minstrel shows also appeared just after the turn of the century and were often held in conjunction with Purim festivities. A description of the 1904 show related how "thirty black-faced mistrels, with several stray white faces in their midst . . . gave a mighty programme, consisting of singing, joking and dancing numbers following one another in quick succession."[60] Such shows continued to be staged at the YMHA until World War I, and were often described as the most enjoyable events of the social season.[61]

Another way in which acculturated northern Jews emphasized their whiteness was by keeping their neighborhoods white. As the migration of African Americans from the South increased, some of the main residential areas occupied by Jews of Central European background became sites of racial tension. Around 1908, acculturated Jews living in West Harlem formed the Property Owners Improvement Association, which was headed by Adolph B. Rosenfield and aimed at introducing restrictive covenants to the neighborhood. In 1909, they tried to keep African Americans out of the area bounded by 90th Street, 100th Street, Riverside Drive, and Central Park West. Claiming that he was not prejudiced against African Americans, Rosenfield explained to the local press that he was trying to "remove the apprehension of the neighboring property owners, many of whom are seriously feeling the effects of their proximity" to blacks.[62] Some of Harlem's long-established Jewish merchants also resisted racial change. L. M. Blumstein, owner of the area's largest department store, founded in 1896, opposed black settlement in the neighborhood and refused to hire African Americans except as menial workers.[63]

In Chicago, Jews also participated in the movement to keep African Americans out of certain residential neighborhoods. By the second decade of twentieth century, the city's South Side, home to many Central European Jews, was quickly becoming absorbed by the emerging "Black Belt." In describing what he called the transformation of "Little Germany" into "Black Africa," Chicago judge Charles Bregstone cast the steady influx of blacks as a powerful menace. "God created the Gan-Eden [Garden of Eden] on the South Side," he wrote, "but the Devil grew jealous and brought Hell to its very edge."[64] As a result of these shifts, some of the city's most prominent Jews became interested in establishing restriction movements. Max Loeb, a Jewish member of the Board of Education and a resident of Hyde Park, suggested a plan to segregate Chicago's schools, while the city's Real Estate Board, of which Loeb and many other Jews were members, advocated a racial zoning ordinance that would segregate the entire city.[65] Following the Chicago Race Riots of 1919, the Hyde Park–Kenwood Property Owners' Association was formed to protect the South Side neighborhood from black encroachment and asserted the principle that residential segregation would prevent any further violence. Hyde Park's Jewish alderman, Ulysses S. ("U. S.") Schwartz, was a supporter of the movement and seemed particularly aware of the social stigma threatened by racial transition in the area. "Many have spent years in making a home and a happy place in which to live and bring up their children," he explained. "With an influx of the Negroes they see all this swept away and they have no place to go."[66]

As anxious as Jews were to emphasize their social status as whites, however, they were often pulled in opposing directions by the realities of Jewish life in the North. Even as they maintained a consistent pattern of distancing themselves from African Americans and affirming their superior standing, they were also driven by certain social and historical factors to sympathize with the plight of African Americans and to oppose many anti-black measures. First, some Jews were fearful that in states where African Americans had far greater freedoms than in the South, and where Jews often suffered more intense social discrimination than in other parts of the country, Jews too might suffer from any far-reaching legal effort to restrict black rights. In 1903, the *American Hebrew* criticized the Congregational minister Lyman Abbot, editor of the *Outlook*, for his support of disenfranchisement, fearing that it might lead to the limitation of rights among certain classes of whites, especially those thought to show "a falling off from the white standard."[67] Northern Jews applied the same logic in speaking out against racial violence and segregation. Days after Leo Frank's lynching, a writer for the Pittsburgh *Jewish Criterion* warned that the lynching of blacks must be stopped if Jews were to avoid a similar fate. "If yesterday a negro was lynched," he wrote, "what is to prevent a white from being lynched tomorrow? And if one white man, why not another?"[68] In 1916, when a racial segregation ordinance was enacted in St. Louis, the editor of the Chicago *Jewish Sentinel* warned of the possible threat to Jews. Once adopted, he explained, such a policy could be "easily extend to others, even those in the magic circle of the 'white races.' "[69]

A second factor that complicated northern Jews' pursuit of a white identity was their empathy for African Americans, a group whose struggle for success and freedom in many ways reminded them of their own historical experience. While acculturated Jews in the North were uneasy about direct comparisons between themselves and African Americans, most would admit that Jewish history had conditioned them to sympathize with victims of prejudice and applaud efforts at self-help. A great number of them, for example, read Booker T. Washington's autobiography, *Up from Slavery*, with at least some recognition that the Tuskegee educator's story was not too different from their own experiences. The book was read enthusiastically by many American Jews, from the Sears, Roebuck magnate Julius Rosenwald, who called it the most influential book he had ever read, to a young girl, Dorothy Fuld, who wrote to Washington for his autograph and said she hoped to meet him some day.[70] Annie Joseph Levi, a New York housewife and amateur essayist, carried on a lengthy correspondence with Washington on the possibility of writing a popular version of *Up from Slavery* for children.[71] Although they did not always clearly articulate it, all of these northern Jewish admirers of Washington seem to have recognized a similarity between the black and Jewish struggles for acceptance and self-betterment, a parallel that most southern Jews would have not allowed themselves to make.

While acculturated Jews in the North enjoyed greater leeway in expressing their empathy for and identification with African Americans, the degree to which individual Jews voiced such sentiments depended in large part on their level of social integration. As a rule, the Jews most expressive of sympathy and support for African Americans were those who had experienced a significant—even radical—degree of assimilation into American culture. For those like Felix Adler, who renounced Judaism in 1876 when he formed the New York Society for Ethical Culture, involvement in African American causes could serve as a potent means of mitigating the emotional trauma of the assimilation process. It allowed those who had escaped a Jewish social setting to express their discomfort with aspects of white, Protestant culture that they found objectionable, ultimately making it easier for them to come to terms with their new environments. Taking a benevolent attitude toward the welfare of African Americans, explained Adler in 1906, indicated "what manner of men we are, [and] how far we ourselves have progressed along the road of moral knowledge and moral development."[72] This understanding of African American philanthropy and civil rights animated many individuals who left Judaism for Ethical Culture or otherwise came to see themselves as secular humanists. Among those who followed this path were Edwin R. A. Seligman, an Ethical Culturalist who supported a plethora of black causes including Tuskegee Institute, the National Urban League, and the National Association for the Advancement of Colored People (NAACP); Henry Moskowitz, a highly acculturated—though Russian-born—social worker who headed New York's Downtown Ethical Society and helped found the NAACP; and Joel Elias Spingarn, a scholar with no formal connection to Judaism who served as the NAACP's president for over a decade.[73]

Similar motivations influenced those who remained within the fold of Judaism but took it to its most universalistic boundaries. Reform rabbis J. Leonard Levy of Pittsburgh, Joseph Krauskopf of Philadelphia, and Stephen S. Wise, founder of the Free Synagogue in New York, were among those who took a strong interest in African American education and civil rights as part of their broader commitment to the Social Gospel.[74] Both Levy and Wise shared their pulpits with Booker T. Washington during the early twentieth century, and in 1913, Krauskopf lent the use of his synagogue, Congregation Keneseth Israel, to the NAACP for the opening meeting of its national conference.[75] Like the Ethical Culturalists, this group of rabbis expressed their reservations about the racial attitudes of the non-Jewish community they hoped to embrace. Wise warned that "moral havoc" would result from the persecution of African Americans, arguing that "the white race will suffer most . . . mutilating its own moral nature and sinking to a lowered level of life."[76]

But unlike those who had severed their ties to the Jewish community, the rabbis continued to struggle with the issue of Jewish particularity, and their concern and horror over the treatment of African Americans pushed some of them to reassess the value of their own efforts at assimilation. For both Krauskopf and Wise, a greater interest in the plight of African Americans went hand in hand with an increasing interest in Zionism. When Krauskopf welcomed the NAACP to his synagogue in 1913, he spoke to them not from the perspective of a universalist Social Gospel rabbi, but as a Jew who had been moved to a new respect for Jewish peoplehood through his sympathy for the African American cause. "There is no people who can feel as deeply the purpose which has moved you to organize this body as can the Jew," Krauskopf told his black listeners. "There is no people who can understand its motives as well as we can understand them; and there is no people who can sympathize as deeply with you as we can." Arguing for a parallel between African American and Jewish experience even in the present, Krauskopf argued that "there is not a problem of yours that has not been our problem, and that is not in parts of the world our problem to-day. . . . We know the story by heart; we have good reason to know it; we are given little opportunity to forget it."[77]

Slightly different motivations characterized a third group of Jews who were especially interested in African American causes, wealthy Jewish philanthropists who became the period's most significant benefactors of black education and social service.[78] For prominent Central European Jewish families in the United States such as the Seligmans, Schiffs, Warburgs, Rosenwalds, Goldmans, and Sachses, charitable giving became a major way of defining their place in the larger society. In an age when wealth was no longer associated with virtue, donors were expected to contribute in some meaningful way to the systematic resolution of social ills.[79] By taking on the task of African American "uplift," Jews reasoned, they would be helping America solve one of its most vexing problems. "I am interested in the Negro people because I am also interested in the white people," Julius Rosenwald explained in 1910. "If we promote better citizenship among Negroes not only are they improved, but our entire citizenship is benefited."[80] This rationale led men like Jacob H. Schiff, Isaac N. Seligman, and Paul Warburg to become regular contributors to Booker T. Washington's Tuskegee Institute, and led Rosenwald to support the building of black YMCAs and southern schoolhouses.[81] And while they rarely voiced this motivation, these Jews were also moved in their efforts to aid blacks by a sense of identification with their plight. When Rosenwald announced his first major contribution toward the building of a black YMCA in Chicago, he invoked the history of Jewish persecution as a model for overcoming obstacles and encouraging African American progress.[82]

Finally, unlike the Ethical Culturalists or the Social Gospel rabbis, who saw activism on behalf of blacks as a means of mitigating their far-reaching incursions into the non-Jewish world, Jewish philanthropists remained at least somewhat concerned about their social status and its relationship to American racial categories. Although their wealth gave them a sense of security rare among Jews of the period, they still craved social acceptance from their non-Jewish counterparts. Thus, wealthy Jews saw in African American philanthropy an opportunity to deflect attention toward blacks as the main problem group in American society as they rubbed elbows with the Carnegies, Rockefellers, and other non-Jewish supporters. As a result, their efforts on behalf of African Americans remained limited to supporting causes that underscored the need for black improvement and, like Rosenwald's YMCAs, accepted the principle of segregation.[83] While several Jews were involved in the founding of the NAACP, many Jewish donors remained hesitant to make large gifts to the organization in its early years because it challenged Washington's accommodationist stance and concentrated on civil rights rather than economic and industrial "uplift."[84] While Jews like Rosenwald and Schiff were generally lauded by the black establishment, some African Americans resented what they felt was the condescension of Jewish philanthropists.[85]

Unlike these three groups of rather exceptional Jewish individuals, however, most acculturated Jews in the North remained too insecure in their status to act altruistically toward blacks in a consistent way. Instead, they usually fell into a much more ambivalent pattern, continuously asserting their social superiority as whites but expressing concern and sympathy for blacks when it did not bring their own status into question. The issue of residential segregation provides an instructive example. Jews supported neighborhood "protective" associations in New York and Chicago, but the Jewish press often found it appropriate to criticize such movements.[86] The editors of the *American Hebrew*, however, ultimately understood the dilemma faced by status-conscious Jews, who they thought would surely encourage black social advancement, education, and self-sufficiency as long as "the negro advance[d] anywhere but in their own neighborhood."[87] Many Jews who lived in transitional neighborhoods avoided the uncomfortable question of residential restriction altogether, preferring to sell their homes to African Americans and move. In this manner, they were able to fulfill their contradictory desires to put distance between themselves and the changing neighborhood *and* to avoid participating directly in the segregation effort. These dual impulses were at work in 1919, when members of Chicago's Temple Isaiah voted to

6. Julius Rosenwald, philanthropist, ca. 1912. While many Jews felt some degree
of identification with African Americans during the early-twentieth century, only
a select few were secure enough in their social status to become actively involved
in efforts to aid blacks. Philanthropist Julius Rosenwald, pictured here with
Booker T. Washington, was a generous supporter of black education. (Courtesy
Special Collections Research Center, University of Chicago Library)

relocate away from the encroaching "Black Belt" but ignored the pleas of the Hyde Park–Kenwood Association not to sell to an African American congregation.[88]

Similar contradictions could be seen in the cultural activities carried on by Central European Jews in the North. Acculturated Jews felt comfortable exploiting racial stereotypes of African Americans in their homegrown minstrel shows, but many were outraged by the appearance of D. W. Griffith's film, *Birth of a Nation*, in 1915. One Jewish woman suggested that black leaders join forces with Jewish film moguls to produce an "up-to-date story which would give the spirit of *Uncle Tom's Cabin* in a modern convincing representation of the progress and work of the negro race" and "offset the prejudicial influence" of Griffith's racist epic.[89] Rabbi Moses Gries, the organizer of a popular lecture series sponsored by the Tifereth Israel Congregation of Cleveland and attended by both Jews and non-Jews, invited the racist novelist Thomas Dixon to speak but also extended an invitation to the black educator Booker T. Washington.[90] Similarly, during the first five years of the century, as interest in race relations grew in the North, New York's Harmonie Club, the gathering spot of the Jewish elite, added the works of Dixon as well as Washington's autobiography, *Up from Slavery*, to their lending library.[91]

Finally, the cross pressures shaping Jewish attitudes can also be seen in cases where Jewish spokesmen were moved to defend the rights of African Americans, but felt the need to qualify these sentiments by reinforcing the inferior social position held by blacks. In 1906, Judah L. Magnes, rabbi of New York's flagship Reform congregation, Temple Emanuel, denounced the brutal racism of Dixon's novel, *The Clansman*, but offered in its place a paternalistic portrait of the "faithful, loyal Negro," which emphasized "his humor, his pathos, his geniality, his shrewdness, his love of his master" and his "childlike patriotism."[92] Similarly, in the wake of the Chicago race riots, Tobias Schanfarber, rabbi of one of the city's leading synagogues, condemned antiblack violence and argued for the need to improve the situation of African Americans but rejected any suggestion of social equality between blacks and whites. "We have permitted the negroes to come into our community [and] we must see to it that they be placed in proper surroundings and livable homes be given to them," he argued. "As Abraham Lincoln said, we need not associate with the negroes or permit our daughters to marry them, but we must give them an equal opportunity in the battle for life."[93]

Confronted more directly with their own status as a minority group, acculturated Jews in the North remained more ambivalent than their southern counterparts about asserting their whiteness. They generally opposed any far-reaching measures to limit black rights, fearing that they too might suffer from restrictive legislation. Free from the gravity that characterized the race question in the South, they more openly expressed the empathy for African Americans that stemmed from Jewish experiences of oppression and marginalization. But at the same time, their ongoing concern for social status led them to draw a firm line between African Americans and Jews, resisting any direct comparison and often framing expressions of goodwill with condescension and paternalism. In general, only those Jews who had achieved a high level of wealth and social prominence felt free enough to engage actively in efforts to aid African Americans.

In both the North and South, then, acculturated Jews of the Progressive Era tried hard to conform to the expectations of white society, even as their misgivings about engaging in exclusivist behavior bubbled beneath the surface. In the years before World War I, they continued to believe that by affirming the basic distinction between black and white, they could soothe the larger society's doubts about their place in the American racial order. By the 1920s, however, it would become obvious that the racial status of Jews in America was entering a new and even more uncertain phase, brought on by the larger currents of social change and instability that accompanied postwar life. Confronted with this new reality, acculturated Jews would find it increasingly difficult to contain their own doubts about the strictures American racial culture placed on them. In addition, their ongoing encounter with race would increasingly be influenced by the growing presence of Eastern European Jewish immigrants, who in the early twentieth century were just beginning to forge their own relationship with whiteness.

Eastern European Jewish Immigrants and Whiteness

Eastern European Jews, unlike their acculturated counterparts of Central European origin, remained largely resistant to embracing whiteness as a central aspect of their identity in the years before World War I. Although immigrants anxiously acquired the trappings of American culture, including an awareness of the issue of race, they did not normally experience social situations during this period that underscored the importance of whiteness as a key to social advancement, as did the more settled Jewish community. Furthermore, immigrant Jews exhibited certain social and economic particularities that made them more resistant than other immigrants groups to adopting antiblack feelings. Unlike many other immigrants who had been peasants and farmers in the Old Country, Eastern European Jews often arrived in America with experience as urban dwellers and with skills that would well suit them for trade and industrial life. The result of this special preparation was that Jews entered the occupational pool at a higher level than many of their fellow immigrants, and

rarely faced the kind of job competition with blacks experienced by others. As petty tradesmen or workers in the Jewish-dominated garment industry, they avoided a strong sense of racial "inbetweenness" based on
their patterns of work. While the Italian "pick and shovelman" or the
Slavic packinghouse worker often occupied a disquieting position between their black fellow workers and their "white" (often Irish or German) supervisors and union leaders, the circumstances of Jewish workers
during the first two decades of the twentieth century promoted a view of
the world that was divided into Jews and non-Jews rather than blacks
and whites.[94] Before 1917, there were almost no African Americans in the
garment trades; a small contingent of Italians was the only significant
group of non-Jews in the industry. While a few young African American
women found work in the shirtwaist industry at the turn of the century,
their numbers remained negligible.[95] In 1906, social worker Mary White
Ovington reported that in New York there were no black cutters or opera-
tors in the industry and no black members of the garment unions.[96]

    Similarly, immigrant Jews exhibited little fear of sharing housing or
neighborhoods with African Americans. Few blacks, for example, ventured into the heartland of Jewish settlement in lower Manhattan. Outside of heavily concentrated Jewish neighborhoods, Jews and African
Americans did frequently live in close proximity, but not as fellow tenants
competing for low-cost housing. Instead, it was the relationship between
Jewish merchant and African American customer that brought them together. Because Jews had a long history in Eastern Europe of trading
among peoples of different backgrounds, they did not resent living in an
African American neighborhood in order to make their living.[97] By the
close of the nineteenth century, there was a well-established Jewish presence in San Juan Hill, one of the largest African American neighborhoods
in New York. During the same period, Jewish immigrant peddlers were
familiar sights in rural regions of the South and Jewish petty merchants—
usually of Eastern European origin—had become ubiquitous in the segregated districts of every major southern city.[98]

    When immigrant Jews did come into contact with African Americans,
they often exhibited little consciousness of themselves as white. As merchants whose very location in black districts arose from their own marginality in non-Jewish society, they presented themselves as Jews and not as
"white men." Stories of peddlers who were on intimate terms with black
customers are common. Nathan Klawansky, who peddled through the
rural counties of southern Maryland in the 1890s, knew most of the African American residents of the region and regularly relied on them for
meals and a place to stay.[99] Dave Pearlman, who began his business career
as a peddler in southern Georgia, also accepted an invitation to spend the
night in the home of one of his black customers, although it was against

7. A Jewish merchant in black Manhattan, 1897. As new arrivals, Jewish immigrants from Eastern Europe often lived and conducted business among African Americans, a practice that demonstrated their marginality from white society and their ignorance of American racial taboos. This sketch, depicting black-Jewish commercial relations on the West Side of Manhattan, appeared in *Harper's Weekly*. (Courtesy General Research Division, New York Public Library, Astor, Lenox and Tilden Foundations)

local custom. It was on his regular visits there that he learned to speak English, and according to his own account, returned from his peddling trips speaking like a "yidische schwarzter." Despite the admonition of his brother that he keep his social distance from his black customers, Pearlman persisted in his friendliness, sharing stories of Jewish persecution in Russia with his black friends.[100] Such intimacy was also exhibited in southern towns and cities, where the trade with African Americans was largely in Jewish hands. In cities like Richmond, Norfolk, Savannah, and Atlanta, Jews ran groceries, pawnshops, secondhand stores, and saloons primarily for a black clientele.[101]

In Atlanta, the Decatur Street district, the center of the city's African American community, became the terminus for arriving Eastern European Jews.[102] Baruch Charney Vladeck, writing for the New York-based *Forverts* (Forward) in 1911, reported that the typical Jewish grocer lived in the black section of Atlanta, segregated from the white population and unaware of the importance of racial etiquette. Even though Vladeck came from New York and a Yiddish-speaking milieu, as a socialist intellectual he was more sensitive to the significance of black-Jewish proximity, and more apt to equate race and levels of "civilization," than were the Jewish grocers he described. "To make a living, the grocer must give up all of the comforts of the 'outside' civilization" and take up residence in the "old, ramshackle ruins" of the "negro neighborhood," he wrote. There, his children are "influenced by the half-wild and barbaric street life of the black." The grocer "learns the black's English, and finds himself at a very low station in life."[103]

As African American migration to New York and Chicago increased during the early twentieth century, satellites of the principal Jewish settlements developed in areas that were heavily populated by the arriving migrants. Harlem became the destination of both African Americans and Jews looking to escape their crowded downtown quarters. Although the immigrant Jews developed their own enclave in the north Manhattan neighborhood, some also settled among the African Americans and, according to Jeffrey Gurock, "showed no easily recognizable unwillingness towards living with and among blacks."[104] By 1920, over two thousand Jews lived in the north Harlem area that was dominated by African Americans, especially along the commercial streets of Fifth and Lenox Avenues.[105] Likewise, Chicago's South Side became home to many Eastern European Jews who set up pawnshops, saloons, and retail outlets along State Street and the other avenues running through the emerging "Black Belt."[106]

In some cases, the lack of a significant white identity among immigrant Jews led them to interact with African Americans in ways that other whites saw as unusual. Social worker Jane Addams observed that the immigrants at Hull House were "less conscious than the Anglo-Saxon of color distinctions," a fact she attributed to their "traditional familiarity with Carthage and Egypt." When W. E. B. Du Bois lectured at the Chicago settlement house, according to Addams, they tendered him a high level of respect "with apparently no consciousness of that race difference which color seems to accentuate so absurdly."[107] Occasionally, Jews disregarded local convention by forming romantic relationships with African Americans that sometimes resulted in marriage. In 1905, Mary Stein of Newark, New Jersey, married an African American man, Clarence Spain. Their union provoked such anger among Newark's white population that the couple barely escaped a hostile mob as they left the courthouse after the ceremony.[108] Four years later, a peddler who traveled through the South wrote to the *Forverts* regarding his intentions toward a young black woman who was one of his customers. He fell in love with her, but the strict segregation laws in the region prevented them from being seen in public together.[109]

Among the Eastern European immigrants themselves, however, marriages between blacks and Jews did not arouse significant hostility, especially when the African American spouse accepted the Jewish religion. In 1912, the black Brooklyn attorney Rufus L. Perry became a celebrity among Yiddish-speaking Jews when he converted to Judaism and was circumcised prior to his marriage to a Jewish immigrant woman, Lillian Buchacher.[110] Despite such occurrences, however, close residential proximity and a lack of white consciousness on the part of Jews did not necessarily insure smooth relations between the two groups. Jews often feared neighborhood criminals and looked down on what they considered the ignorance and rowdiness of many of their African American customers.[111] But even in these cases, they formed their opinions according to the outlooks and priorities they held as Jews, not as whites.

If immigrant Jews remained unconcerned with fitting in as whites, they nevertheless showed great interest in the American racial situation. Jewish immigrants from Eastern Europe usually knew about the history of slavery even before arriving in the United States, and often saw the emancipation of the slaves as a key event that defined the nation's democratic ideals. The works of Isaac Mayer Dick, one of the most prolific Yiddish writers in Russia through the 1880s, often featured stories of plantations and slaves and glamorized the struggle of African Americans for their freedom.[112] Such stories were immensely popular with Jewish readers in Eastern Europe because they spoke directly to their own desire to escape Russian tyranny and enjoy the fruits of American life. The Yiddish press in the United States encouraged the continuation of this glamorized view among immigrants after their arrival on these shores. The first issue of the immensely popular Yiddish weekly *Amerikaner*, established in 1904, featured an article recounting the familiar story of black slavery and emancipation.[113] But immigrant audiences remained very selective in the cultural representations of African Americans they chose to appropriate. Despite the ubiquity of racist images on the American stage, the Yiddish theater remained free of plays and musical presentations lampooning blacks. While a number of Yiddish theater productions borrowed their tunes from popular "coon songs," the racial references were exchanged for Jewish subject matter more appropriate to the interests of the Yiddish-speaking crowds.[114]

One arena where images of African Americans were frequently employed was the Jewish labor movement. For Jewish workers experiencing industrial oppression, the image of black slavery served as a powerful symbol. During this period, native-born and "old immigrant" workers frequently referred to themselves as industrial slaves, hoping to spark outrage that white workers had been lowered to a level unbefitting their race.[115] By contrast, Jewish workers enthusiastically embraced the com-

8. The Yiddish view of civilization and barbarism, 1908. Fresh from their own experiences with persecution, Jewish immigrants from Eastern Europe often critiqued American racism as harshly as they denounced czarist tyranny. This cartoon satirizing white Americans' notions of civilization (top) and barbarism (bottom) appeared in the Yiddish humor magazine *Der kibetser*. (Courtesy Dorot Jewish Division, New York Public Library, Astor, Lenox and Tilden Foundations)

parison of themselves to black slaves, taking it to mean that they, too, would win their freedom. Jewish labor organizers frequently used the comparison to encourage union resolve, and David Edelshtat, one of the first important poets of the Jewish labor movement, wrote of "*unzer brider shvartsen*" (our black brothers) who had engaged in the same struggle faced by Jewish workers to break the chains of slavery.[116]

Immigrant Jews drew another striking parallel between Jewish and African American experiences by comparing American race riots with the brutal pogroms of Eastern Europe. In 1900, during the first local racial disturbance of the century, the *Forverts* described what it called the "bloody pogroms against the negroes," which were carried out by the "white *pogromchiki*." Unlike the acculturated Central European Jews, who held the government authorities blameless for race riots, the *Forverts* indicted the police force, arguing that it failed to protect blacks and even incited the white rioters. "Had the police not wished to aid the white *pogromchiki* and [instead] aimed to protect the persecuted Negroes, as is their duty, so many Negroes would not have been wounded and the riots could have very easily been calmed," editorialized the Yiddish paper. "But the police did not do this. When a fleeing Negro ran to a policeman seeking protection, the policeman struck him with a club and dragged him off to the station house."[117]

Three years later, the same paper took great comfort when the U.S. military intervened to quell the riot at Evansville, Indiana. But despite the deviation from the Russian pattern, the paper still announced the event with the headline: "NEGRO POGROMS."[118] Importantly, this feeling of identity with African Americans was not merely part of the political agenda of the socialist *Forverts*. The sentiment was also shared by the Orthodox *Tageblat* (Jewish daily news), which criticized acculturated Central European Jews for adopting the prejudices of America. "Let us Jews understand enough of the needs and proprieties of our own position to see that an ill grace clothes the Jew who joins the ranks of the prejudiced Americans who find it to their interest to paint the negro as a born criminal. For the persecuted Jew to enhearten the persecutors of the negro is indeed despicable."[119] In Chicago, a city with a greater proportion of African Americans to Jews, the Orthodox Yiddish press also regularly compared the two groups. "In this world, among the masses," the city's *Yidisher kurier* (Jewish courier) concluded in 1912, "the Jew is treated as a Negro and the Negro as a Jew."[120]

Of course, despite the general lack of social integration that made Eastern European Jews feel free to compare themselves to African Americans, not all immigrants remained uniformly isolated from pressure to identify as white. Many of the socialist intellectuals who wrote for the Yiddish press and hoped to "enlighten" their readers by introducing them to modern culture, for example, exhibited a greater sensitivity than other immigrants to American racial categories. Often with some secular education and ties to German and American-born radicals, these intellectuals embraced the study and popularization of science, including racial hierarchies. Philip Krantz, a leader of the Jewish socialists and editor of the Yiddish socialist weekly *Arbeter tsaytung* (Worker's paper), wrote a three-volume history of civilization, *Di kulturgeshikhte* (History of culture), which employed color-based racial categories to explain the development and evolution of human societies.[121] Similarly, Abraham Cahan, who founded the *Arbeter tsaytung* along with Krantz in 1890, submitted a translation of "A Journey among the Congo Savages," popularized from an article in *Scribner's Magazine*, for the pilot issue.[122] As former immigrant radical Morris Hillquit rose to a high position in the American Socialist Party, he found himself defending the interests of white workers against what party officials called the "backward races." At the International Socialist Congresses at Amsterdam (1904) and Stuttgart (1907), Hillquit supported restrictions on the immigration of African and Asian workers. "Even if this appears to be reactionary, it is necessary if we do not want our entire labor movement to be destroyed," he explained. "Not to admit Chinese coolies and Negroes—this is a question of life and death for our labor movement."[123] Hillquit's position, however, brought him into disrepute with immigrant Jews, who overwhelmingly identified with the plight of the nonwhite immigrants.[124]

At the other end of the political spectrum, immigrant entrepreneurs who rose quickly on the economic ladder often acquired the prejudices associated with the scramble for social status. One of these "allrightniks," Meyer Jarmulowsky, made a fortune from real estate in Harlem, and by 1912 became the leader in an effort to establish a line dividing the black and white settlements in the area. As he explained to a group of black leaders he gathered to discuss the proposal, while "he did not believe in segregation on account of color, he favored the plan when vast interests were involved in the situation as today in Harlem."[125]

Those most susceptible to the desire to identify with whiteness, however, were the children of Eastern European immigrants who were either born in the United States or came of age here. In 1881, a young immigrant, Abraham Bisno, worked as an apprentice to a non-Jewish tailor whose family he lived with in Chattanooga, Tennessee. Working among non-Jews and barely able to speak English, he found antiblack prejudice a potent means of identifying with his American surroundings, and began to harass a young African American girl who also worked in the shop. "Since the atmosphere was antagonistic to negroes," he later recalled, "I think I excelled more than any other member of the family in meanness and contempt."[126] In the South, where there was less of a Jewish environment, Jews more quickly began to feel the need to identify with whiteness. Jewish schoolchildren often absorbed racial prejudices and expressed them toward black children in their neighborhoods. As Charles Rubin recalled of Atlanta, "the term 'nigger' [was] used by Jewish sons of immigrant parents with the same venom and contempt as the tem 'Zhid' was used in the old country."[127]

One of the most vivid departures from the tendency of Eastern European Jewish immigrants to identify with African Americans came with the bloody antiblack riot in Springfield, Illinois, in 1908. A day after the

פיג. 57—אַ פרוי פון דעם שטאַם אזאַנדע אָדער ניאַם־ניאַם אין אפֿריקאַ.

9. Immigrants learn about race, 1903. This anthropological sketch, depicting "a woman from the tribe of Azande or Niam-niam in Africa," was used to introduce Yiddish readers to the science of race. (From Philip Krantz, *Di kulturgeshikhte*)

Yiddish press responded to the bloodshed with its usual denunciations of the "Negro pogroms" and comparisons between antiblack and anti-Jewish violence, it was reported that a young Jewish immigrant, Abraham Reimer, was among the leaders of the mob who lynched an African American man during the unrest. Reimer, a native of Zaslov, Russia, was reported to be a ne'er-do-well who had a tattooed arm and worked as a circus performer before immigrating to the United States five years before the Springfield riot. Relocated from the New York ghetto to Birmingham, Alabama, by the Industrial Removal Office, he was said by the *Forverts* to have imbibed some of the "spirit of the South, where the life of a Negro is worthless." Reimer moved from town to town, holding a series of menial jobs until he ended up in Springfield. His participation in the riot shocked the immigrant community, and the Yiddish press denounced the initial reports of his involvement as an "antisemitic libel." But when he was released by a sympathetic chief of police along with several non-Jewish suspects, it became obvious that he had not been singled out for blame. The Jewish immigrant public had to resign themselves to the fact that given the right circumstances, the prospect of a "yidisher lyncher" was no longer unfathomable.[128]

Even in New York, center of Jewish immigrant settlement, the children of the immigrants were susceptible to the lures of racism. In 1905, Jewish youths harassed a black woman in Harlem with cries of "nigger" and "shvartze."[129] Two years later, the debating club of the Jewish Educational Alliance, an East Side settlement house, took as its topic: "Resolved, that the South would be justified in disenfranchising the Negro," with their team arguing the affirmative. "It seems incredible to me," wrote Louis Marshall to the Alliance's director upon receiving an invitation to the event, "that a body of Jews who have just emerged from virtual slavery, and who are seeking in this country the privilege of voting, which was withheld from them in the land where their ancestors have lived, should for a moment consider the propriety of arguing in favor of the disenfranchisement of any citizens of this country."[130] Morris Winchevsky, known as the "grandfather" of Jewish socialism, was equally dismayed at the enthusiasm of Jewish youth for American racism, especially when it came at the expense of an appreciation for Jewish culture. In 1915, Winchevsky bemoaned the fact that the passing of the great Yiddish writer Isaac Leib Peretz was virtually ignored by the youth of the East Side due to the excitement surrounding the defeat of the black fighter Jack Johnson to the "Great White Hope," Jim Jeffries. "If you would have taken a census," wrote Winchevsky, "you would have found that for every Jewish child in America who knew anything about Peretz, there were at least 200 who could describe in minute detail the fight between the two boxers."[131]

The powerful attraction of whiteness to the younger generation of East-ern European Jews demonstrates just how exhilarating social acceptance could be, and underscores the ultimate instability of Jewish racial identi-ties under the pull of conflicting impulses and pressures. Although the seeds of whiteness appeared among the children of the immigrants in the years before World War I, however, the real struggle of Eastern European Jews with the issue of race in America still lay ahead, in the years follow-ing World War I, when they would move to new neighborhoods, change their jobs, and begin their pursuit of middle-class respectability. Like their more acculturated counterparts of Central European background, they would often feel torn between feelings of empathy for African Americans and the desire to fit in to white society. But despite the early signs of racism among the younger generation, the strong sense of identity immigrant Jews had forged with African Americans and the experiences of persecu-tion still vivid in their minds would continue to work their influence as they increasingly came to see themselves as white Americans.

CHAPTER 4

"WHAT ARE WE?":

JEWISHNESS BETWEEN RACE AND RELIGION

ACCULTURATED JEWS of the Progressive Era largely agreed about the importance of clarifying their status as white in American society, even as many remained reticent about thoroughly adopting the dominant culture's brand of whiteness. They were far less certain, however, about the extent to which acceptance as white required them to redefine what it meant to be Jewish. For most Jews, describing themselves as a "race" did not represent a desire to dissociate themselves from the white mainstream. But as white Americans began to see Jews as a racial group with an uncertain relationship to whiteness, many Jews began to wonder whether they could continue to describe themselves in racial terms and still claim membership in the "Great Caucasian family." As a result, the question of whether Jews ought to fashion themselves as a race or merely a religious denomination became one of the most hotly debated issues of early-twentieth-century Jewish communal discourse.

The climate of tension surrounding the issue of Jewish racial self-definition in the early twentieth century stood in sharp contrast to the ease with which Jews had been able to define themselves as a race in previous decades. Before their whiteness became suspect, Jews often found in race a comforting means of self-understanding, one that provided a sense of security as they continued toward their goal of greater social integration. Now, with their place in America's racial constellation increasingly in doubt, many Jews began to question the viability of race as a means of self-description. Yet despite the increasing danger of the racial label after the turn of the century, American Jews did not part easily with their racial self-conception. While strong debate emerged among Jews during these years over the racial definition of Jewishness, what is most striking is the extent to which a broad spectrum of Jews, ranging from staunch accommodationists to devoted Zionists, were torn between a continued attachment to Jewish racial identity and the desire to be seen as white. Faced with these conflicting imperatives, most Jews of the period were unable to settle on any one clear definition of the term "Jew."

The notion that American Jews of the Progressive Era were incapable of crafting a consistent self-definition is somewhat out of step with historical accounts that point to the turn of the century as the height of a Jewish "renaissance," a period of emerging self-confidence and cultural flowering for the American Jewish community.[1] The answer to this seeming paradox is that Jews' posture of self-confidence actually masked a deep sense of insecurity. Like Americans of the Progressive Era in general, American Jews embraced optimistic language of progress and revival as a means of soothing their anxieties about change. In the face of growing concern about the problem of self-definition, Jews largely tried to downplay the contradictions between Jewishness and whiteness during this period. Despite their best efforts to control the disorder of their times, however, many American Jews remained ill at ease with the strictures placed on them by the dichotomy between blacks and whites.

The Increasing Liabilities of Race

By the end of the nineteenth century, race had become central to the way both Jews and non-Jews in the United States understood Jewish group difference, making it almost impossible to define Jewishness without resorting to racial language. As a tool for negotiating Jews' conflicting impulses for distinctiveness and inclusion, however, race began to lose its efficacy during this period. Many Jews had relied on racial language since the 1870s to stabilize what it meant to be Jewish amidst shifting social boundaries, as well as to assure their standing in the national culture by underscoring their contributions to civilization. The increasing concerns white Americans had about race, and their need to try to clarify the position of Jews in the American racial hierarchy, however, began to reveal how race could be as much an obstacle as an aid in balancing Jewish and American identities. If American images of the Jew remained ambivalent, often combining high praise with suspicion and condemnation, questions about Jewish racial status were becoming common enough to alert Jews to the ways their racial self-definition could be turned against them. Moreover, those commentators who did continue to praise Jewish racial traits—like Nathaniel Shaler, Theodore Roosevelt, and William Howard Taft—did so as a means of arguing for the physical absorption of Jews into American society. Under these circumstances, race ceased to serve as a successful vehicle to set limits on assimilation and to assert Jewish contributions to American life, as it had during the closing decades of the nineteenth century. Instead, due to white America's emergent obsession with shoring up its racial boundaries, Jewish racial particularity had become either the basis for anti-Jewish prejudice or a rationale for urging the "fusion" of Jews with non-Jewish society.

In addition to increasing pressures placed upon them by American society, Jews also found it difficult to sustain the racial self-definition as the social profile of their own community shifted dramatically. By the turn of the century, the mass immigration of Eastern European Jews made it harder for already acculturated Jews to control the way the public perceived Jewish racial difference. Not only did the new arrivals increase the visibility of Jews as a distinctive group, but they also held a much more expansive understanding of Jewishness that was not tailored to the demands of the American setting. Increasingly uncertain of their ability to protect their image or defend their group distinctiveness, a growing number of Jewish spokesmen began to avoid the subject of racial identity and encouraged Jews to abandon the well-worn practice of racial self-definition.

A dramatic decline in racial discourse among acculturated Jews was evident by the late 1890s, precisely during those years when concern about Jewish racial character was on the rise. During the Spanish-American War, when national discourse was highly focused on discussions of racial hierarchy, Isaac Mayer Wise carried on an unremitting campaign in the *American Israelite* against the notion that Jews were distinct in race from other white Americans. "Whatever the ancestral derivation of a family may be," he reasoned in 1898, "if it lived continually in the United States, its members after one or at most two generations can only be classed generically as of the American race."[2] Wise argued that the term "Anglo-Saxon"—often heard during the war—did not apply to a narrow racial type but was broad enough to encompass all those who had cast their lot with the British or Americans in their project to advance civilization. As a result, he argued, "there is no reason why a Jewish American or Englishman, whatever may have been the nationality of his parents, should hesitate to proclaim himself as of the Anglo-Saxon race."[3] If Wise's statements capture the mood of the period, even more revealing of the pressures felt by Jews at the turn of the century were the changing attitudes of spokesmen like Rabbi Emil G. Hirsh, who had been adamant in the mid-1890s that the Jews constituted a race. In the space of only a few years, Hirsh had totally reversed his position, first reverting to calling the Jews a nation and later abandoning all but religious expressions of Jewish particularity.[4]

The increasingly defensive stance taken by American Jews during this period was signified by the emergence of a new communal leadership, dominated by laymen prominent in law, business, academia, and philanthropy and characterized by a sensitivity to the political problems facing the community. While rabbis often had trouble disentangling notions of Jewish chosenness and ethical mission from Jewish race and peoplehood, these leaders knew the urgency of denying Jewish racial difference. The prominent attorneys Simon Wolf and Louis Marshall, the banker and philanthropist Jacob H. Schiff and the scholar Cyrus Adler were among those who believed that Jews ought never to articulate an identity that conflicted with the demands of American national culture, regardless of how they privately understood themselves. While in Jewish publications a leader such as Wolf sometimes continued to refer to the Jews as a race, to the non-Jewish world he carefully termed them "American citizens of Jewish faith."[5] Adler, who later collected and published the papers of his colleague Schiff, stated that the philanthropist frequently declared himself a "faith-Jew" rather than a "race-Jew," a distinction to which Adler himself also subscribed.[6] When Louis Marshall was questioned on the matter, he responded that he entirely concurred with Schiff, who regarded Judaism as "a faith, and not as a race." According to Marshall, there were, "ethnologically . . . as many types of Jews as there are countries in which they have lived," since "climate, environment, economic conditions, intermarriage, food, and a thousand other influences operate as causes of differentiation between Jews of one country and those of another." Jews, he argued, were "united by the bonds of religion and none other."[7]

Apart from a fleeting reference to intermarriage, Marshall—like Wise before him—pointed exclusively to environmental factors in arguing that American Jews no longer bore the marks of a distinct race. According to this view, Jews simply lost their racial status after living in the United States for a certain period of time. "When a man once becomes a citizen," Marshall explained, he ceases to be a "Hebrew" and his identity "becomes merged in his Americanism."[8] What is striking about these statements is the degree to which they ignored widely accepted understandings about what assimilation required of Jews. Many non-Jewish commentators classed "Hebrews" among the best candidates for Americanization, but almost all would have argued that the process necessitated thorough physical intermixture with other whites, and not merely a prolonged exposure and adaptation to the American environment.

Viewed in this light, the statements of Marshall and Wise must not be taken as a total rejection of the idea of Jewish racial particularity. Neither ever directly disputed the widespread belief in a distinct Jewish racial identity. Instead, their aim was to divert attention away from the importance of such a distinction. When Marshall argued that immigrants ceased to be "Hebrews" in America, he was not implying that they underwent some sort of miraculous physical transformation. Rather, he was arguing that racial factors marking them off as distinct in their countries of origin ceased to play a significant role once they became American citizens. Several Jewish spokesmen of the period made the similar argument that in America, the ability of Jews to be counted as white made any narrower racial identity irrelevant. In 1910, Rabbi Sigmund Hecht of Los Angeles averred that while Europeans differentiated between Aryans and Semites, in the United States these groupings were treated as insignificant subdivisions among Caucasians.[9] Wise argued similarly in 1899 that "the Caucasians form one race," adding that any effort to go beyond the "five great divisions of the human family" based on color was "rot, pure and simple."[10] While such arguments made the case that Jews were racial insiders in America, they also cut against the notion that Jews needed to be physically absorbed in order to become an integral part of white America. Ironically, by denying the significance of Jewish racial identity in America, spokesmen like Hecht, Wise, and Marshall were also trying to undermine demands for Jewish assimilation, safeguarding—albeit by a circuitous route—the very racial integrity and social solidarity that they claimed were inconsequential.

Convinced that this policy of Jewish invisibility was the best way to both avert questions about the Jews' whiteness and forestall calls for assimilation, several prominent Jewish leaders at the turn of the century embarked on campaigns to obscure all references to the Jews as a distinct race. Jewish defense agencies such as the Anti-Defamation League of B'nai B'rith, founded in 1913, took special interest in fighting racialized images of the Jew onstage, on screen, and in the literature of the period.[11] On the local level, groups like Chicago's Anti-Stage Jew Ridicule Committee, established in 1914, pressured theater owners and managers to limit "racial" portrayals of Jews and promoted legislation to restrict certain characterizations of Jews onstage. By World War I, such efforts had largely succeeded in banishing the stage Jew from the American theater.[12] Activists also tried to obscure signs of racial distinctiveness within the Jewish community, especially among the recently arrived immigrant population. At a time when cultural differences were seen to be markers of race, distinctions of dress, language, and custom all threatened to highlight Jewish racial difference. Besides encouraging general Americanization in manners and appearance, however, establishment Jews also tried to dissuade immigrants from forming "Hebrew political clubs" and "Hebrew workingmen's clubs," two common forms of immigrant organization that were though to suggest that Jews had "racial" interests different from those of other white Americans.[13]

By far, however, the most disagreeable form of immigrant organization in the eyes of acculturated Jews was the Zionist variety.[14] The focus of Zionism on Palestine—and for a short time, Uganda—as the proper home for the oppressed Jew offended the communal elite because it associated Jews with uncivilized lands. Kaufmann Kohler, for example, labeled Zionism an "oriental" movement and called it "a retreat before the foe by way of East Africa or Asia."[15] Many acculturated Jews were similarly concerned that Zionism would bring the Jews' whiteness into question. In 1903, a visiting rabbi in New Orleans delivered an anti-Zionist tirade in which he interspersed "negro dialect" with his denunciations of Zionist "cowards, traitors [and] Jew-haters."[16] Maurice Fishberg, a Russian-born physician who was employed by the communal elite at the United Hebrew Charities and was an adviser to Jacob Schiff, also tried to dissuade immigrants from Zionist activity for fear that it would link them to African Americans. "If Jewish nationalism is spread among the masses," argued Fishberg, "one may expect in short time that one will deal with Jews just as one now deals with the negro."[17]

Ultimately, despite Jewish leaders' manifold attempts to make the Jews invisible in American racial culture, their efforts were unrealistic. As long as Jews existed as a distinct group, in a social as well as religious sense, most non-Jewish Americans were unable to suppress their ambivalence about Jewish racial status. Even those who had a positive view of Jewish racial qualities were unable to see any solution short of complete racial amalgamation that would clarify the Jews' ambiguous relationship to whiteness. This, however, was a solution that most Jews were unwilling to accept. By trying to divert attention away from their perceived racial qualities rather than pursue the kind of complete physical assimilation prescribed by their non-Jewish neighbors, American Jews demonstrated that they, too, were unable to completely part with the notion of a Jewish race, despite its growing liabilities.

The Continuing Pull of Race

The difficulty American Jews had in parting with the racial self-definition stemmed from the fact that racial identity continued to have a strong emotional appeal for them. While race began to have adverse consequences for their acceptance in American society at the turn of the century, Jews remained susceptible to the use of racial language in articulating their deeply held Jewish commitments. In fact, many of the pressures pushing Jews to narrow the definition of Jewishness were also simultaneously creating increased feelings of "racial" solidarity. The immigration of Eastern European Jews, for example, sparked a complex mix of emotions among the acculturated Jewish community, creating feelings not only of embarrassment and repulsion but also of attraction and kinship. Likewise, while aspersions cast on the Jews' racial status could push them to deny their racial bonds, they could also inspire the assertion of racial pride.

Among acculturated American Jews, the group most willing to assert these feelings of racial solidarity after the turn of the century was the small but significant minority involved in the Zionist movement. In 1898, the year after the first Zionist Congress in Basel, Switzerland, Temple Emanuel's rabbi, Gustav Gottheil, his son, Columbia University professor Richard Gottheil, and Rabbi Stephen S. Wise formed the Federation of Ameri-

can Zionists (FAZ).[18] Like other acculturated Jews, they were determined
to respond to the increasingly uncertain status of their group in American
society. But unlike most other Jewish leaders, they felt they could best
promote a positive image of the Jews by highlighting, rather than obscuring, their strength and character as a race. While Zionists primarily defined the Jews as a nation, and aimed at the creation of a Jewish state in
Palestine, race emerged as an important part of their ideology. Because
they had no existing country on which to focus their energies, and even
the exact location of the future Jewish homeland remained a matter of
debate, Zionists often appealed to ties of "flesh and . . . blood" in making
the case for Jewish nationalism. In responding to arguments that Zionism
was impractical, they looked to race as a tangible, scientifically accepted
means of proving the potentiality of Jews for nation building. According
to Richard Gottheil, the founding president of the FAZ, Jews were "a race
that can do everything but fail."[19]

Although from the beginning the American Zionist movement was a
cooperative effort between native-born Jews and more recent Jewish immigrants, racial discourse was employed most frequently by the acculturated Zionists, who were more familiar with racial ideology. Since many
of the founding American Zionists were Reform rabbis, they sometimes
drew on the intellectual heritage of racial theories that had been worked
out during the previous century by David Einhorn and Bernhard Felsenthal.[20] Yet while these nineteenth-century Reformers saw race as a force
that would protect and distinguish Jews as they carried out their mission
among the nations, Zionist leaders at the beginning of the twentieth century often used it to assert and justify a degree of Jewish independence
from the non-Jewish world. Those like Rabbi Gustav Gottheil, who had
personally experienced the indignity of being turned away from an exclusive hotel, and his son Richard, who regularly witnessed anti-Jewish discrimination at Columbia University, came to believe that Jewish moral
qualities could be developed only if Jews were free from the demeaning
pressures of social conformity.[21] As the younger Gottheil explained in a
statement of Zionist principles in 1898: "With a home of his own, [the
Jew] will no longer feel himself a pariah among the nations, he will nowhere hide his own peculiarities—peculiarities to which he has a right as
much as anyone—but will see that those peculiarities carry with them a
message which will force for them the admiration of the world."[22]

During the early years of the twentieth century, racial language became
a staple of the Zionist organ, the *Maccabaean*, which published defenses
of Jewish racial identity and criticized Jewish leaders who denied the racial
component of Jewishness.[23] As a result of such outspokenness on the part
of Zionists, Jewish racial identity became a matter of great contention between them and the more accommodationist communal leaders such as

Schiff, Wolf, and Marshall. While one party saw the trumpeting of racial distinctiveness as a strategy capable of redeeming the name of the Jews, the other saw it as a practice that threatened to increase non-Jewish suspicion and uncertainty. To the Zionists, the denial of Jewish racial identity was tantamount to cringing before the gentiles. To the Jewish establishment, the racial "chauvinism" of the Zionists only added ammunition to the arsenal of the antisemites. As David Philipson, a leading Reform rabbi, declared, "race Jews" were the "feeder[s] of anti-Semitism" because by defining Jewishness in terms of blood, they "make evident that the Jew is not to be contrasted with Christian but with the Anglo-Saxon, the Teuton or the Slav!"[24] So divisive was the issue of race in the Jewish community that, by 1910, Israel Friedlaender, a historian at the Jewish Theological Seminary of America, could call it the "shibboleth according to which the various Jewish parties are distinguished from one another."[25]

Yet despite the charged nature of racial politics among American Jews, it would be a mistake to view the Jewish community as completely polarized on the issue of race. Because the denial of racial identity was often a diversionary tactic rather than a reflection of their true feelings, establishment Jews sometimes found it difficult to avoid references to the "Jewish race." Often community leaders confronted this problem in discussing their ties to the incoming Eastern European Jewish immigrants, which were hard to express in purely religious terms. When Henry Alexander, a prominent member of the Atlanta Jewish community, addressed a rally in support of Russian refugees in 1903, he reminded his audience that the new immigrants carried the "unsullied blood of priests and prophets" in their veins.[26] Likewise, when Jacob Schiff, Oscar Straus, and Cyrus Sulzburger met with Russian envoy Sergius de Witte in 1905 to press the case of Russian Jewry, they voiced concern for their "brethren-in-race."[27]

These were not the only gaps in the establishment's effort to discard "race" as a term for Jewish self-description. Even one of the longest-established institutions of the acculturated Jewish community, the Reform Movement, found it difficult to banish "race" from its lexicon. Kaufmann Kohler, who had succeeded Isaac Mayer Wise as the president of Hebrew Union College, may have objected strongly to the political version of Jewishness promoted by Zionists, but he continued throughout his career to describe Jews in racial terms. "Ethnologically, the Jews certainly represent a race, since both their religion and history ever kept them apart from the rest of the people of the country they inhabit," Kohler wrote in 1903.[28] As late as 1918, in his magisterial *Jewish Theology*, Kohler argued that "religion and race form an inseparable whole in Judaism."[29] Sharing Kohler's racial view, some of his Reform colleagues remained reluctant to bring converts into the Jewish fold, despite the official doctrine that Judaism was a universal faith.[30]

The extent to which acculturated Jews failed to live up to the purely religious definition of Jewishness forwarded by the communal elite was most obvious in their social and cultural activities. Several observers spoke of the large class of "race Jews" of Central European background who—despite all detachment from Jewish religious life—socialized mainly with Jews, insisted that their children marry Jews, and were buried in Jewish cemeteries. While Reform rabbis and communal leaders often chastised the Eastern European immigrants for organizing "Hebrew" political clubs, these organizations were also founded by "uptown" Jews.[31] Similarly, despite the efforts of Jewish activists to make Jews invisible in popular culture, acculturated Jews were not adverse to praising sympathetic stage portrayals of the Jewish "race" or lauding the accomplishments of famous "racial" Jews.[32] The *Jewish Encyclopedia*, published between 1901 and 1906 by Funk and Wagnalls and edited by a distinguished group of Jewish scholars, included innumerable entries on figures such as Benjmain Disraeli and Sarah Bernhardt, who did not practice Judaism but were seen as exemplars of Jewish racial traits. As one of the editors, Joseph Jacobs, later explained, despite the tendency of the communal elite to speak of Jews as a religious group, no one could exclude the likes of Disraeli from the "galaxy of Jewish worthies."[33]

While the most accommodationist of acculturated Jews could not totally reject the racial definition of Jewishness, a similar ambivalence characterized those on the other end of the ideological spectrum who asserted Jewish racial identity more vigorously but could not free themselves from concern for Jews' racial standing in the non-Jewish world. Zionists, who saw race as an essential building block of Jewish nationhood, were highly aware of the need to avoid casting Jews in the role of racial outsiders and, as a result, often tried to downplay the physical dimensions of race while stressing its spiritual and psychological aspects. This approach was most notably pursued by the group of "cultural Zionists" affiliated with the Jewish Theological Seminary of America, who tended to see the Jews, in historian Israel Friedaender's formulation, as a "race, or nation, whose distinguishing feature and whose reason for existence is religious."[34] Louis Brandeis, who headed the Zionist movement in the United States from 1914 to 1921, offered a more secular approach to the same problem. As he explained in one of his early Zionist addresses, Jews were held together as much by their "conscious community of sentiments, common experiences, [and] common qualities" as by their "common race."[35]

The downplaying of the physical aspects of Jewish racial identity by American Zionists went hand in hand with a policy of clarifying that Jews were still part of the white family of races despite their racial individuality. Caspar Levias, a professor at Hebrew Union College (HUC) who penned a defense of Zionism in 1899, hoped to legitimize Jewish racial particularity while also relieving doubts about the Jew's whiteness. Describing Jews as one of many "Aryan" races, he justified their continued separateness from other whites by arguing that intermarriage with non-Jews would undermine their ethical mission to the world, just as whites' civilizing mission would be undermined by intermarrying with Africans.[36] Such disclaimers were a regular feature of Zionist writings about race during the early twentieth century. "That we Jews are not a race in the sense of the black or yellow race is self-evident," wrote Max Margolis, another HUC professor active in the Zionist movement. While pointing out significant peculiarities in Jewish hair, eyes, and facial features, Margolis stressed that "if the color of skin be had in view, we belong to the whites."[37]

Ultimately, it was not easy to distinguish between acculturated Jews who feared the implications of racial language and those who persisted in using race as an emotionally satisfying means of self-definition. Differing very little in their background, lifestyle, social connections, level of religious commitment, or their concern about acceptance in white American society, both accommodationists and members of the Zionist minority felt many of the same pressures. Neither can there be any great distinction made between the success of their two strategies. The Zionists may have enjoyed a psychological advantage due to their refusal to suppress their deep attachment to the Jewish "race." The assertion of racial particularity did not serve them particularly well, however, in a society increasingly skeptical of unassimilated alien races, something the establishment leaders readily understood. Although it is impossible to explain definitively why a particular person may have chosen one path or the other, both views represented an effort to control the definition of Jewishness in a tumultuous arena where perceptions of Jewish racial difference had untold consequences for the Jewish community.[38]

Eastern European Immigrants and Race

If it is impossible to organize the positions of acculturated Jews on racial identity into neat ideological groupings, it is easier to draw a distinction between the impact of the race question on the acculturated Jewish community and its effect on the newly arrived Eastern European Jewish immigrants. While acculturated Jews, regardless of their ideological position, felt conflicting pressures and ambivalence about Jewish racial identity that arose from the challenges of assimilation, Eastern European Jewish immigrants came to the task of self-definition with an entirely different perspective. Just as they remained relatively isolated from pressures to identify with whiteness, recent immigrants did not feel the need to craft a self-definition that answered the expectations of white American society.

In fact, since immigrant Jews had only recently emerged from an atmosphere where Jewishness was an all-encompassing identity, it was not easy for them to define themselves through the use of discrete categories such as race or religion. According to sociologist Isaac B. Berkson, who studied immigrant adaptation to America, "Jewish tradition and with it the Jewish masses speak neither in terms of 'race' or 'religion.' Both of these terms are imported from the Western World and are foreign to the Jewish spirit as terms descripti[ve] of Jewishness."[39] A survey of the Yiddish press and popular literature confirms that most immigrants, even after a number of years in America, continued to speak of *dos yidishe folk* (the Jewish people) rather than *di yidishe rase* (the Jewish race).

Isolation from pressures to define themselves according to American racial categories, however, did not mean that Eastern European Jewish immigrants were insensitive to the attempts of more acculturated Jews to disassociate themselves from the newcomers by disclaiming any "racial" ties with them. When Senator Simon Guggenheim objected to the U.S. Immigration Commission's practice of categorizing incoming Jews racially as "Hebrews," Avrom Liessin, a writer for the *Forverts*, denounced the senator's argument as nothing more than an attempt to distance himself from the new immigrants. Liessin dismissed as "simply comic" Guggenheim's assertion that "Jews only differ from other peoples in matters of religion," arguing instead that the "present European Jew is surely more similar to the Asiatic Jew of 2,000 years ago than the present-day Englishmen is to the inhabitants of England of 2,000 years ago."[40] When the rabbi of Harlem's prestigious Temple Israel criticized "race Jews" among the Russian immigrants for forwarding a nonreligious definition of the Jews, immigrant journalist Bernard Richards shot back that it was the Reform rabbinate, with its lack of appreciation for Jewish blood ties, whose definition was deficient.[41] In Chicago, the *Yidisher kurier* also expressed its exasperation with prominent "theorists" who tried to argue the Jews out of existence. According to the *Kurier*, the Jewish establishment continuously engaged in "word-play," defining abstract categories such as race or nationality according to certain criteria, only to demonstrate how the Jews failed to meet them. "How would these theorists feel if in a discussion it was proved, perhaps with a little exaggerated logic, that they, the theorists, were not men?" asked the editors of the *Kurier*, to whom the deep ties between Jews were self-evident, no matter what one called them.[42]

Though most immigrant Jews were unfamiliar with the terminology of race, this was not true of the small group of intellectuals at the helm of the American Jewish labor movement. Adhering to various shades of socialism, immigrant intellectuals advocated internationalism and shunned any identification with Jewish group loyalties. "We are not Jews, we are Yiddish-speaking socialists," was their slogan.[43] The use of the immigrant's language and the organization of unions along Jewish lines were not seen as an endorsement of Jewish particularity but as temporary means through which Jews would eventually be weaned away from their specifically Jewish identity. On the other hand, socialist intellectuals were well versed in science, including racial theory, which made it hard for them to ignore contemporary wisdom about Jewish racial difference. Editor and journalist Philip Krantz, who popularized ethnology for a Yiddish-reading audience, included a discussion of the Semitic race in his book-length survey of world cultures.[44] If their scientific outlook meant that they could not deny Jewish racial identity altogether, however, socialist writers often tried to challenge its importance. In one of his propagandistic pamphlets, for example, Krantz conceded the existence of a Jewish race but cast doubt on its purity, hoping to undercut arguments for Jewish national solidarity.[45] Ultimately, however, such statements cannot be taken as total disavowals of Jewish particularism. Living in a social environment in which Jewish particularity was taken for granted, and in which the main aim was to become more American, it was very easy to embrace a universalist platform.

After the Kishineff pogrom in 1903, a growing number of Eastern European Jewish intellectuals who were moved by the tragedy began to combine their socialism with Jewish nationalism. In the United States, many of them turned to racial language to express their secular brand of Jewish identity. Yiddish writer and socialist veteran Morris Winchevsky, for example, referred to the "historical physiognomy" and "facial distinctiveness" of various racial groups, including the Jews. While America encouraged the melting down of immigrant races, wrote Winchevsky, "such national suicide would be simply impossible for us." The Jewish "race" was much stronger than others, he explained, and would not "sink into the concoction" as easily.[46] By 1909, some of these immigrants were finding encouragement for their views in the FAZ, and one of the bases of this influence was the new Yiddish Zionist organ, *Dos Yidishe folk* (The Jewish people). Bernard Richards and Abraham Goldberg, two stalwarts of the immigrant Zionist movement, contributed articles to the paper forwarding explicitly racialist views of Jewish identity.[47] Interestingly, however, because the immigrant radicals had little contact with non-Jewish society, they did not feel the same pressure to moderate their use of racial language as the more acculturated Zionists did.

All in all, Jewish immigrants from Eastern Europe, including the few who were conversant with racial terminology, remained largely untouched in the years before World War I by the pressures forcing more acculturated Jews to struggle with the concept of race and how it was applied to them. To the extent that immigrants began to seize a voice in Jewish communal affairs, however, their opinions on the racial question did have an impact on broader Jewish discussions of racial identity. Because immigrant commentators often saw the issue of Jewish self-definition in a way unclouded by the difficulties faced by more acculturated Jews, their insights sometimes served to challenge their Americanized counterparts and reveal the contradictions of American Jewish identity. But as we shall see in the next three sections, which explore some of the major issues on which discussions of Jewish racial identity focused during the early twentieth century, there was little that could help resolve the hopelessly ambivalent feelings most American Jews had about self-definition.

Intermarriage and the "Melting Pot"

Few social phenomena expressed the commitment of acculturated Jews to a racial self-understanding during the early twentieth century as did their avoidance of intermarriage.[48] Despite increasing pressure to downplay racial commitments, most Jews of this period continued, as they had in the nineteenth century, to treat marriage as a key factor in Jewish racial preservation and as the line at which social interaction with non-Jews was to be drawn. According to a study carried out in New York between 1908 and 1912, the intermarriage rate among Jews was only 1.17 percent, compared to a rate of nearly 17 percent among Italians and 33 percent among non-Jewish Germans. Only the city's African Americans had a lower rate of intermarriage than Jews.[49] As Jewish socialite Esther J. Ruskay explained, when Jews and non-Jews did intermarry during this period it "raised such a storm of criticism and disapproval for all parties concerned than any tendencies in this direction [were] kept in healthful check."[50]

The strength of opinion against intermarriage among acculturated American Jews was apparent in 1905, when the young Yiddish journalist and settlement worker Rose Pastor wed the non-Jewish millionaire John Phelps Stokes. The marriage made front-page news in New York and was hailed by the general press as a sign of universal brotherhood and a precursor to racial amalgamation. But despite the enthusiasm of the American public, Jews responded with skepticism expressed in pointed racial language. "The world at large does not care one iota whether their souls blend, or whether he is imbued with a Jewish spirit and she with a Christian spirit," editorialized the *Hebrew Standard*. In the paper's view, the Jews were not created to "blend" with other peoples. Universal brotherhood would only come if the "Jewish race was to be preserved separate and distinct," so that it could perform its religious mission to the world.[51]

While episodes like the Pastor-Stokes union remained rare, intermarriage nonetheless became a matter of frequent discussion among Jews during the early twentieth century. It was not a rise in the number of intermarriages that inspired the growing discussion, however, but the increased difficulty American Jews faced in justifying their preference for endogamy. As the Pastor-Stokes affair revealed, though Jews were generally wary of intermarriage, non-Jewish commentators often saw it as the only method by which Jews could become an integral part of white society. As a result, they usually interpreted Jewish reluctance to intermarry as a major stumbling block to the creation of a homogenous white "American race." But because most Jews were not prepared to surrender Jewish separateness to the extent of supporting intermarriage, they grew uncomfortable about the tendency of non-Jewish commentators to make national belonging conditional on biological "fusion." They especially feared that their refusal to intermarry would be seen as a form of racial "clannishness" and would be credited as a source of anti-Jewish sentiment. Jews of this period, therefore, began to reexamine the issue of intermarriage and to search for ways of reconciling their distaste for exogamy with their desire to be accepted by their non-Jewish counterparts.

In 1908 and 1909, this challenge was brought into particularly sharp focus by the appearance of a number of stage dramas dealing with the topic of intermarriage and usually forwarding the notion that it was indispensable to the building of the American nation.[52] This theme was most notably explored in *The Melting Pot*, a play written—ironically—by the Anglo-Jewish author Israel Zangwill, which first appeared before American audiences in the fall of 1908. Advertised as a "Drama of the Amalgamation of the Races," Zangwill's play detailed the marriage of David Quixano and Vera Revendal, a Jew and a non-Jew who both came to America from the Russian city of Kishineff, the scene of the worst anti-Jewish pogrom of the twentieth century. Despite the fact that the play was overly sentimental, and was criticized by the *New York Times* as "cheap and tawdry," the drama struck a chord with many Americans, even drawing praise from President Theodore Roosevelt because of its emphasis on America as the place where old prejudices would be submerged and the peoples of Europe would be unified into a new, more potent race.[53] Zangwill's play also commanded attention among American Jews, who felt compelled to respond to its suggestion that racial amalgamation was a prerequisite to becoming true Americans.

Under pressure to demonstrate that they were not trying to maintain racial boundaries between themselves and other white Americans, a few Jewish commentators, like St. Louis rabbi Samuel Sale, responded to Zangwill's play by agreeing that Jews needed to give up their strict opposition to intermarriage. To Sale, opening the doors of marriage to all those who shared Jews' moral and ethical standards was a sign of Judaism's broad humanity, while insistence on racial purity befitted only "savage tribes."[54] George Fox, a leader of B'nai B'rith, argued that Jews did them-selves a disservice in stressing the importance of race over moral character, a stance that was out of step with America's progressive values.[55] Despite such sentiments, however, the overwhelming majority of American Jews denied Zangwill's assertion that intermarriage was the only way Jews could take their full place in American society. As the play toured the country, the columns of Jewish newspapers were filled with articles and rabbis' sermons critical of the play's advocacy of intermarriage.[56] Even the liberal Cincinnati rabbi David Philipson argued that "the schools are to be the melting pot of America, and not intermarriage."[57] When a non-Jewish contributor to the *Chicago Israelite* suggested that intermarriage and absorption were the answers to the "Jewish Problem," editor Tobias Schanfarber passionately responded that such a "wholesale suicide" would be an "infamous way of ending the life of a people which has given to the world the highest conception of God and of man, and has pointed out the highest ideal of their mutual relation."[58]

Schanfarber's retort invoked long-held assumptions about Jewish racial purity and its connection to the Jewish religious mission. Yet his avoid-ance of the term "race" in favor of the less precise term "people" indicates that even the champions of endogamous marriage were increasingly feel-ing pressure to downplay their racial motivations. In fact, while most of the Jewish writers responding to Zangwill's play rejected intermarriage, many argued that their objection was based on religious, rather than ra-cial, concerns. According to this view, Jews had as much right to protect their religious integrity as groups like Quakers, Baptists, Episcopalians, and Roman Catholics, who were equally suspect of marriages out of the "faith."[59] By focusing on religion instead of race, Jews felt they could express their opposition to intermarriage without inviting the charge that they were resisting the process of assimilation. This did not mean, how-ever, that their emotional attachment to Jewish racial identity vanished. On the contrary, they discovered that the best way to serve their impulse for racial distinctiveness was to remove it as a matter of public debate by asserting the religious argument instead.

Defending endogamy on religious instead of racial grounds may have had strategic value, but religion ultimately proved a much less powerful tool than race for demarcating the boundaries between Jewish and non-Jewish societies. Once marital preferences were credited to belief and ide-ology rather than to innate physical and moral characteristics, it was not a far leap to the suggestion that liberal Jews might share religious sensibili-ties with non-Jews, making them appropriate marriage partners. Yet that was an idea many American Jews were not prepared to accept. Rabbi Mendel Silber, for example, argued that Jewish women were racially en-dowed to be "priestess[es] of the home" and could not be replaced by

ADELPHI THEATRE

SECOND BIG WEEK COMMENCING MONDAY NIGHT, JANUARY 31st

WALKER WHITESIDE   MANAGEMENT LIEBLER & CO.

IN ISRAEL ZANGWILL'S MASTERPIECE

The Melting Pot

A STORY OF THE AMALGAMATION OF THE RACES

Bearing the Indorsement of Nathan Straus, Leon Zolotkoff, E. G. Hirsch, Jacob H. Schiff, Stephen S. Wise, Tobias Schanfarber, and Other Leading Jews of America.

ISRAEL ZANGWILL

10. *The Melting Pot*, 1908. To counter the image of their group as a "clannish" racial minority, a number of "leading Jews of America" endorsed Israel Zangwill's play about the blending of immigrant heritages in America, despite their misgivings about its assimilationist message. (Courtesy *Jewish Exponent*, Philadelphia)

non-Jewish women regardless of their religious outlook.[60] When Emil G. Hirsch, the noted Chicago rabbi, delivered a sermon suggesting that marriages between like-minded Jews and non-Jews might be more successful than those between Reform and Orthodox Jews, many in the community felt he had gone too far.[61] The Yiddish and Zionist papers took special pleasure in attacking Hirsch and others who tried to reduce the question of intermarriage to a purely religious one, asserting that the Reform leadership recognized the power of Jewish racial identity, but went to ridiculous lengths to hide their true feelings and ingratiate themselves with the non-Jewish public.[62] Still, Hirsch's statements revealed how the need to conform to non-Jewish expectations weighed heavily on Jewish spokesmen, making it difficult for them to categorically reject intermarriage. This is probably why a number of "Leading Jews of America"—Hirsch, Nathan Straus, Jacob H. Schiff, Stephen S. Wise, Tobias Schanfarber, and even the Eastern European Zionist leader Leon Zolotkoff—felt it necessary to lend their names to an endorsement of Zangwill's *Melting Pot*, even though many of them disagreed with the play's main assertion.[63]

The high level of contradiction inherent in the attitudes of American Jews toward intermarriage was readily apparent in 1909, when the Central Conference of American Rabbis (CCAR) examined the topic in detail at its annual meeting. Commemorating the thirtieth anniversary of the death of David Einhorn, the gathering saw intense struggle over the pio-

neer rabbi's belief that performance of the Jewish religious mission required the preservation of racial purity.[64] Many Reform rabbis—including
HUC president Kaufmann Kohler—continued to embrace Einhorn's view,
and some exerted significant pressure for the CCAR to pass a resolution
condemning intermarriages. But there were also a growing number of
rabbis reluctant to appear as if they were publicly defending Jewish racial
exclusivity. In an attempt to solve this dilemma, conference organizers
chose two speakers, Rabbis Ephraim Feldman and Samuel Schulman,
who downplayed the Jewish desire for racial distinctiveness and argued
that Reform opposition to intermarriage was based purely on religious
grounds.[65] In the end, however, the attendees remained skeptical that this
argument could successfully deflect accusations of racial clannishness. As
a result, they refused to pass a proposed measure prohibiting rabbis from
performing intermarriages, settling instead for a weaker statement that
such unions were not viewed favorably by Jewish tradition.[66]

More than perhaps any other single issue, intermarriage provoked discussions that revealed the strong emotional attachment Jews still had to a
racial self-understanding during the early twentieth century. Whether they
were confident enough to express such sentiments or whether they felt the
need to obscure them by changing the subject to religion, Jews struggled
to stay out of the "Melting Pot," even as American society encouraged
them to cast themselves in. The challenge of intermarriage, however, would
prove to be only one of many pressures facing Jews as they attempted to
satisfy their dual impulses for integration and distinctiveness.

Protecting Jews' Legal Claim to Whiteness

The intermarriage debate threatened to cast Jews as a clannish minority
that did not desire to assimilate into white American society. As embar-
rassing as such an image may have been, however, it paled in comparison
to concerns that Jewish racial identity might adversely affect Jewish legal
status in the United States. In 1909, Jewish communal leaders became
worried over the increasing tendency of government officials to classify
Jews racially as "Hebrews." Officials never directly classified Jews as nonwhite, and referred to them in at least one government publication of the
period as a subgroup of the "Caucasian race." Yet many Jews feared that
the government's adoption of the "Hebrew" classification might be a first
step toward their eventual exclusion from the rights of white American
citizens. Not only was a congressional commission gathering racial statistics on incoming Southern and Eastern Europeans in order to bolster their
case for immigration restriction, but the Census Bureau was planning to
expand the racial classification on the 1910 census to include European

immigrant "races" such as the Jews. Even the public schools in Philadelphia began requiring students to complete questionnaires regarding their
racial background, and teachers returned the sheets to Jewish students for
correction when they identified their parents merely as "American."[67]

Among the gravest issues of government policy confronting Jewish
leaders in 1909 was the decision of the Department of Commerce and
Labor, which controlled immigration affairs, to classify Syrians as "Mongolians." Historically, the United States had limited naturalization to
"free white persons," although after the Civil War, free persons of African
descent were also made eligible. Other foreign groups who were deemed
nonwhite, however, were not admitted. The ruling that Syrians were not
white sparked fears that Jews, associated in the popular mind with Middle
Eastern peoples, would be similarly classified beyond the color line. Earlier, when anti-Japanese rioting in San Francisco sparked a movement
for the restriction of "Asiatic" immigration, the Jewish columnist George
Selikovitch joked in the *Reform Advocate* that the government might "re-
fus[e] to grant citizen-papers [to Jews] on the ground that we are of Asiatic
extraction like the Chinese and Japanese."[68] But several months later,
when court clerks in certain Western states refused naturalization to Syrians because of their "Mongolian" blood, Selikovitch was astonished to
discover that his prediction had not been far from the mark.[69] Selikovitch's fears were echoed by the Jewish communal elite. Cyrus Adler of
the American Jewish Committee wrote to his colleague Mayer Sulzburger
expressing fear that once the Syrians and Japanese had been placed beyond the pale of whiteness, "it will not be a very far step to declare the
Jews Asiatic."[70]

As a result of such fears, Jewish communal leaders launched an attack
on the government's efforts to classify Jews as a distinct race. The American Jewish Committee successfully lobbied Congress and the Census Bureau to remove the new racial category from the census forms.[71] In 1910,
Jewish leaders also began to take action to prevent a narrowing of those
eligible for naturalization. Several courts had already denied the government's assertion that Syrians and other "Asiatics" were not eligible for
citizenship because of race, but several bills appeared in Congress later
that year trying to revive the exclusionary measure. In response, a Jewish
congressman from New York, Henry Goldfogle, ushered a bill through
the House of Representatives proposing that "Asiatics who are Arme-
nians, Syrians or Jews" not be barred from becoming naturalized citizens.
While Goldfogle's intention had been merely to protect the citizenship
rights of Jews and other affected groups, Louis Marshall, the attorney
acting for the American Jewish Committee, saw the congressman's bill as
a disastrous blunder because its wording gave credence to the notion that
Jews were Asiatic and not white. In Marshall's words, the bill, if passed

by the Senate, "would place upon the statute books the objectionable suggestion that an Asiatic Jew is not a free white person [and] would also lead to the possible claim that, inasmuch as all Jews are in a sense of Asiatic origin . . . the right of Jews to become naturalized citizens has, in the past, been a matter of doubt."[72] Marshall quickly appealed to several senators to postpone action on Goldfogle's bill, arguing that that the entire matter might soon be settled by the Circuit Court of Appeals, before which he was arguing a related case on behalf of some Syrian clients. The Court unanimously accepted Marshall's argument against the restrictive definition of "free white persons," and the matter was settled without Jewish racial status becoming a matter of debate on the Senate floor.[73]

Despite their successes on the census and naturalization issues, Jewish leaders remained concerned about the policies of the Bureau of Immigration, which had seemed to spur all the various efforts to classify Jews according to race. As a result, they concentrated after 1909 on reversing the bureau's classification of Jews as "Hebrews."[74] The leader in this fight was Simon Wolf, the veteran Washington attorney who had long represented the interests of the Union of American Hebrew Congregations in the capital city.[75] Wolf had been concerned about the practice of tabulating Jews according to race ever since it was initiated in 1899 by the commissioner of Immigration, Terence V. Powderly. That year, at a conference between Jewish leaders and immigration officials at Ellis Island, Wolf urged Powderly to abandon the new classification, but failed to receive the support of the other Jewish representatives, who felt the policy was a helpful means of gathering data on incoming Jews. Wolf, however, remained wary of the racial classification of Jews and in 1903 renewed his efforts to abolish it. That year he wrote a letter of protest to Powderly's successor, Frank P. Sargent, alleging that Jews had been singled out by the Bureau of Immigration as the only religious sect registered in the immigration records. "We do not ask any favors not accorded to other faiths," wrote Wolf. "If all sects are to be registered, we certainly would not object, but if the Jew only is to be singled out, then we most decidedly protest."[76]

By turning the issue to one of religious liberty, Wolf ignored the true reason for the bureau's classification while claiming that his request was "in accordance with the spirit and genius of our American institutions."[77] When the officials replied that they classified all immigrants according to race, and that they were interested in Jews as a *racial* rather than a religious group, Wolf set out to gather written opinions on the question of Jewish racial identity from leading Jews that might be used in convincing the Bureau of Immigration to reconsider. Much to Wolf's dismay, however, many of the leaders failed to support his position, holding that the bureau was correct in counting the Jews as a distinct race.[78] In addition,

Philip Cowen, the editor of the *American Hebrew* and one of those who had been involved in the initial discussions of immigration policy with Powderly, fired off an editorial arguing that racial classification ought to be retained as a matter of pride, since the statistics reflected well on Jews and demonstrated the superiority of Jewish immigrants to their Polish and Slavic counterparts.[79] Apparently unable to gain a consensus among Jewish leaders or to create a sense of urgency concerning racial classification, Wolf remained quiet on the issue for several years.

By 1909, however, increasing fears among Jews about immigrant classification had resurrected Wolf's cause and gained him a significant following among Jewish leaders. Wolf successfully created a coalition of groups including the Union of American Hebrew Congregations, B'nai B'rith, and the American Jewish Committee to oppose the racial classification system, and enlisted a number of rabbis and prominent Jews across the country to stage rallies and speak out against it. Simon Guggenheim, scion of the wealthy Jewish industrialist family and senator from Colorado, became a strong advocate of Wolf's position in Congress.[80] In addition to such positive public support, Wolf was fortunate to enlist the services of Max J. Kohler, the son of rabbi Kaufmann Kohler and a young immigration lawyer, who had considerable experience opposing the discriminatory practices of immigration officials. Kohler prepared a detailed brief listing several reasons why the government was unjustified in classifying Jewish immigrants by race.[81] By late 1909, the campaign against Jewish racial classification had succeeded in gaining the attention of the U.S. Immigration Commission, an arm of Congress that invited Wolf, Kohler, and Judge Julian Mack of the American Jewish Committee to testify on the matter in a special session.

Despite Wolf's influential backing, his arguments utterly failed to impress the commission, which included Vermont senator William Paul Dillingham and his Massachusetts colleague, Henry Cabot Lodge, among other officials. In his opening statement, Wolf repeated his standard charge that the government was classifying Jewish immigrants by faith, which he argued was out of spirit with constitutional guarantees of religious liberty. Throughout his testimony, Wolf not only skirted the issue of Jewish racial identity—arguing, for example, that Russian persecution of Jews was purely for religious reasons—but refused to give any validity to racial distinctions among immigrants, holding that Poles should be classified as Russians and the Irish as British. Because Wolf denied racial divisions that almost all Americans took for granted, his testimony struck the commissioners as highly self-serving and selective in its treatment of the facts. When they pressed him on the issue by posing a particularly pointed question, he avoided answering by changing the subject. Ultimately, he was not able to sustain a logical argument, as was revealed

Dictionary of Races or Peoples.   **73**

Gypsy.

Auerbach says that 52 per cent of the Gypsies of Hungary are ignorant of the Romany tongue. Intermarriage with other peoples is becoming more frequent. Through loss of language, the assumption of a sedentary life, and intermarriage, Gypsies are decreasing in numbers and seem everywhere doomed to extinction by absorption.

The total population of Gypsies in the world is variously estimated at from 700,000 to 850,000, of whom three-fourths are in Europe. There are 200,000 in Roumania, 100,000 each in Hungary and the Balkan Peninsula, 50,000 each in Spain, Russia, and Servia, and 50,000 in Germany and Italy combined. The number in the British Isles is variously estimated at from 5,000 to 20,000. There are thought to be 100,000 in Asia and 25,000 in Africa. Only a few thousand are found in the Americas. They are included among "Other peoples" in immigration statistics. They are supposed to have first come to this country in the beginning of the eighteenth century. Simson says that many were banished from the British Isles to America in colonial times and that many more were sent to serve in the British army during the Revolution. He found a number of settled Gypsies in the Eastern States, and suggests that many of the keepers of small tin shops and peddlers of tin, as well as many of the fortune tellers of the great cities of the United States, are in reality of Gypsy descent.

H.

Hebrew.

HAWAIIAN or **SANDWICH ISLANDER.** An individual member of the northernmost Polynesian people subject to the United States. (See *Pacific Islander.*) Not counted among immigrants on arriving in the United States.

HAYTIAN. (See *West Indian.*)

HEBREW, JEWISH, or **ISRAELITE.** The race or people that originally spoke the Hebrew language; primarily of Semitic origin. Scattered throughout Europe, especially in Russia, yet preserving their own individuality to a marked degree. Linguistically, the nearest relatives of the ancient Hebrew are the Syriac (see *Syrian*), Assyrian, and Arabic languages of the Semitic-Hamitic family (see). The latter constitutes one of the four great divisions of the Caucasian race. While the Hebrew is not so nearly a dead language as the related Syrian, Aramaic, or the ancient Assyrian, its use in most Jewish communities is confined mainly to religious exercises. The Jews have adopted the languages of the peoples with whom they have long been associated. More speak Yiddish, called in Europe "Judeo-German," than any other language, since the largest modern population of Jews borders on eastern Germany and has been longest under German influence.

Physically the Hebrew is a mixed race, like all our immigrant races or peoples, although to a less degree than most. This has been fairly well dem-

11. *Dictionary of Races and Peoples*, 1911. The U.S. government published this handbook to help immigration officials categorize the diverse array of "racial" groups entering the country during the early twentieth century. The *Dictionary* described Jews as a "Caucasian" race, but many Jewish leaders feared that the classification of immigrants as "Hebrews" would put their whiteness into question.

when Lodge questioned him about the racial identity of the late British Prime Minister Benjamin Disraeli:

> *Senator Lodge.* . . . How would you classify Benjamin Disraeli? Was he a Jew? . . .
>
> *Mr. Wolf.* He was born of Jewish parents, and subsequently, at a certain age, was baptized.
>
> *Senator Lodge.* He was baptized as a Christian. He then ceased to be a Jew.
>
> *Mr. Wolf.* Yes; religiously he ceased to be a Jew.
>
> *Senator Lodge.* Ah! Religiously. He was very proud of the fact that he was a Jew and always spoke of himself in that way. Did the fact that he changed his religion alter his race?
>
> *Mr. Wolf.* It did not alter the fact that he was born a Jew; not at all; and I know the Jewish people throughout the world have claimed him, Heine, Boerne, and others, who were born of their blood . . . but they ceased to be Jews from the standpoint of religion.[82]

Unimpressed with the lack of consistency in Wolf's statement, the commission followed up the hearing with some research of its own, revealing that Jews in general were conflicted on the matter of racial identity. It cited the *Jewish Encyclopedia* and several other Jewish publications as confirmation of the widespread use of the term "race" among Jews for self-description. Finding Wolf and his colleagues unjustified in their objections, the commission recommended the continuation of the policy of racial classification.[83]

In the wake of the hearing, Jews sympathetic to a racial view of Jewishness denounced Wolf for what they saw as an abandonment of Jewish pride before the commission, and took advantage of his poor performance to argue that his case had no defensible foundation. One rabbi wrote to the *Jewish Exponent* of Philadelphia that Senator Lodge was a better Jew than Wolf, because he did not try to deny the existence of the Jewish race.[84] Zionists especially attacked Wolf's efforts, arguing that if anything could stimulate anti-Jewish sentiment, it was not the affirmation of racial identity but the "shifting, unmanly and undignified pretense of representatives of a people, who against fact and history, and against their own private convictions, disown the racial and national birthright."[85] Such criticisms were sufficient to dampen the enthusiasm of many of Wolf's supporters. The American Jewish Committee, for example, under pressure from some of its members, decided to take no further part in the campaign to eliminate government racial classification of the Jews.[86] Others expressed the view that while Wolf had the proper motive in trying to prevent anti-Jewish discrimination, he had gone too far in his denial of Jewish racial identity. Although a few scholars claimed that there was no Jewish race in the technical sense, wrote the *Jewish Exponent*, "the vast preponderance of Jewish opinion . . . holds to the old view that there is."[87] Even Wolf himself admitted privately that "his whole contention in this matter has been not to deny the Jews' racial affinities as much as to deny the right of the government to discriminate."[88] In the end, however, the main accomplishment of his campaign was to demonstrate the inability of Jews to reconcile their unshakable racial self-image with their desire for full acceptance in white American society.

Confronting Jewish Racial Origins

In defending endogamous marriage and opposing the government's racial classification schemes, American Jews often relied on diversionary tactics. By trying to change the topic from race to religion, they aimed to protect their status as white Americans without having to directly deny their cherished "racial affinities." As Simon Wolf's appearance before the Immigration Commission demonstrated, however, such tactics fell flat in the face of direct questions about Jewish racial identity. This was precisely the problem American Jews confronted as questions began to arise among scholars and scientists about Jewish racial origins. In clarifying their place in American life, Jews had to have a coherent explanation as to how they fit into the larger story of human racial development. Yet the story of Jewish origins to which most Jews of the period subscribed had significant potential to mark them as racial outsiders in white America.

During the nineteenth century the claim of "Semitic" origin had become something of a badge of honor for American Jews, allowing them to trace their heritage back to the dawn of civilization and take credit for laying the ethical foundations of Western society. By the early twentieth century, however, some Jews had become alarmed at the tendency of scientists, scholars, and popular commentators to attribute an African origin to the Semites. This theory was first elaborated in the United States in 1890 by Daniel G. Brinton, an archaeologist and language specialist at the University of Pennsylvania. Brinton's view quickly gained authority in scholarly circles, with even his Jewish colleague, Semitic scholar Morris Jastrow, accepting the notion that Semites had originated in Africa.[89] When race scientist William Z. Ripley published *The Races of Europe* in 1899, he adopted Brinton's view and helped spread it to a larger audience.[90]

The theories of these scholars did not, in and of themselves, cast aspersions on the racial status of modern-day Jews, whose connection to the ancient Semites was a matter of debate in academic circles. Ripley, for example, argued that modern Jews, although tied historically to the Semites, were the products of significant intermixture with Europeans and retained almost no trace of Semitic descent.[91] The linkage between Jews and Semites, however, remained strongly ingrained in the popular mind, and Jews most of all held fast to the notion of their Semitic descent.[92] Thus, despite the qualifications offered by scholars, Jews remained highly sensitive to any suggestion of a link between Africa and the Semitic past.

This sensitivity was exacerbated after the turn of the century, when Jews, ancient Israelites, and Semites were all linked to Africa with increasing frequency. Jewish readers of the *Public*, a liberal Chicago newspaper, for example, responded with anger when a writer speculated on the biblical verse concerning Moses's marriage to a "Cushite woman," arguing that the great Jewish lawgiver had "married a Negro."[93] In 1911, Charles Waldstein, an American-born Cambridge archaeologist, stormed out of the Universal Races Congress in London when he learned that the Jews were to be grouped with the African and Asiatic races in the congress's ceremonies.[94] When Jacques Faitlovich, the French-Jewish explorer, arrived in America during the same period asking for aid for the Falashas, a black African tribe he described as being of pure Jewish descent, he was rebuffed by American Jewish leaders.[95]

With the growing focus on Semites as an African racial type, some Jews began to retreat from their boastful claims of Semitic origin. Martin A. Meyer, a Reform rabbi in San Francisco and a scholar of Semitic studies, felt it necessary in 1909 to declare that American Jews shared more in common with non-Jewish Americans than they did with "the Arab of the desert, the true representative of the Semitic world of yore," or even with the Jews of the Middle East. "To be sure, the Jews who came out of the desert to settle Canaan were Semites, like the Arabs of today," wrote Meyer, "[but] the blood of Israel was rapidly diluted." Due to Jewish proselytizing among non-Jews that had been prevalent until the Middle Ages, he explained, the Jews "grafted prunings from all the peoples and cultures of the world" on to the original Semitic stock. "Today but little of that original Semitic blood will be found in the veins of any of us."[96] Another Reform rabbi, Samuel Sale, argued against the notion of Semitic descent with even greater fervor. "We may go on prating about the purity and unity of our race," wrote Sale, "but . . . we can not get away from the bald fact, based on anatomical measurements, that only about five percent of all the Jews bear the characteristic mark of their Semitic origin on their body."[97] Most American Jews, however, were not as willing as Meyer and Sale to dismiss the traditional story of Jewish origins. Even Meyer himself, while arguing against classifying Jews as Semites, could not help but speak prosaically about the "Semitic genius that gave the world the Bible" and the "Semitic soberness, a deeply rooted racial characteristic, that caused the sane and healthy development of the religion of the world today."[98] Such a romanticized view suggests that the notion of Jewish descent from the

ancient Semites retained considerable emotional attraction for Jews, including those who were working hard to discredit the connection.[99]

Though dedication to the story of Semitic origins remained strong
among many Jews, Jewish leaders did begin to see the importance of establishing their claim to whiteness scientifically. At the height of the controversy over immigrant classification in 1909, Jewish notables exchanged letters expressing concern about the increasing reliance of
government policy on the work of race scientists, whom they feared were
dangerously close to pronouncing the Jews a non-white race. While they
had confidence that they could continue to dispute the racial classification
of Jews on a political level, they were less certain of their ability to contest
the authoritative voice of racial science. As Cyrus Adler of the American
Jewish Committee wrote to his colleague Mayer Sulzburger, Jewish leaders needed to enlist the help of an anthropologist in order to get "a very
strongly worded declaration as to the practical identity of the white race,"
one that would presumably leave no doubt as to the whiteness of Jews.[100]

During the first two decades of the twentieth century, Columbia University Professor Franz Boas was the best known anthropologist of Jewish
origin in the United States. Boas shared the concern of the Jewish communal elite about racial nativism, but his preference to identify as a German
American rather than as a Jew prevented him from engaging too directly
in Jewish defense efforts during these years.[101] Instead, Boas worked to
discredit the centrality of race in evaluating human capabilities, arguing
that differences between groups—including those between blacks and
whites—were heavily influenced by environmental factors.[102] Because
these ideas contradicted the overwhelming consensus about the importance of racial differences in the United States, however, they offered little
to Jewish leaders hoping to win acceptance for their group in white
America. As a scholar who was well integrated into the non-Jewish world,
Boas could freely advance such oppositional theories. But for Jews struggling to overcome their uncertain racial status, it was much harder to
build their case for inclusion on ideas that undermined the basic assumptions of the larger society. To soothe white Americans' doubts about the
"Jewish race," they would have to affirm the basic distinction between
black and white.

The scientist who took up this challenge was Maurice Fishberg, one of
the leading scholars of Jewish physical anthropology at the turn of the
century, and the only American to devote himself significantly to such
research. Fishberg was born in the Ukrainian town of Kamenets-Podolsk
in 1872. After his arrival in the United States, he gained entry to the Medical College of New York University, graduating as a medical doctor in
1897. His first major position was as medical examiner for the United
Hebrew Charities, where he represented the interests of the communal

elite in keeping the immigrant population healthy.[103] By 1901, he had also become concerned with deflecting accusations that Jewish immigrants were prone to disease and were a menace to national health. As he became more deeply involved in such defense work, he realized he would have to tackle the larger issue of Jewish racial identity in order to answer the nativists effectively.[104] While it is unclear whether Fishberg's research on Jewish anthropology was undertaken due to a direct request by communal officials, his concerns stemmed largely from their influence, since he was both an adviser to Jacob H. Schiff and an employee, at the United Hebrew Charities, of Mayer Sulzburger's cousin Cyrus.[105]

Despite Fishberg's early realization that the race question was central to Jewish defense work, he did not part easily with the notion that Jews were an exceptionally pure racial type. After taking skull measurements on five hundred of his patients at the United Hebrew Charities, he concluded that Jews demonstrated a "homogeneity of the cranial type [that] has not been observed in any other civilized race."[106] He also accepted uncritically the notion of Jews' Semitic descent, but tried to recast the story of Jewish origins and break the well-accepted link between the Semites and Africa. Because his measurements revealed that Jews conformed mainly to the brachycephalic (or round-headed) type, he argued that the Semites must not have originated in Africa, where the dolichocephalic (or long-headed) type prevailed. Suggesting instead a theory that placed the cradle of the Semites in the "the mountainous regions of the Caucasus," Fishberg concluded that "the African origin of the ancient Hebrew, and even of the Semites generally, is not an established fact."[107]

Ultimately, however, Fishberg remained unsatisfied with his explanation of Jewish racial origins, primarily because the link between Semites and Africa was too well accepted to be dismissed so easily. After 1903, in order to find a better solution, he began to look more deeply into William Z. Ripley's argument that American and European Jews were not of pure Semitic descent, but were the products of extensive racial intermixture that had obliterated all traces of their Semitic origins. Ripley, writing in 1899, had made this assertion based on statistical data gathered by other researchers, and had not taken any anthropological measurements on Jews himself.[108] Fishberg, hoping to solve the question of Jewish origins and their relationship to Africa once and for all, set out to gather the proof he needed to substantiate Ripley's theory.

Fishberg concentrated his research in two main areas. First, he made an extensive study of Jewish pigmentation. Relying on the American racial orthodoxy that a race's coloring does not change significantly as a result of climate—that blacks cannot become white by changing their environment—he reasoned that the relatively light skin, hair, and eye color of many modern Jews precluded the possibility that they were of pure Se-

Fig. 134.
AMERICAN JEW.

Fig. 135.
AMERICAN JEWESS.

12 and 13. Jewish racial types from Maurice Fishberg, *The Jews: A Study of Race and Environment*, 1911. Fishberg, a Jewish physician and physical anthropologist, used these photographs to argue that American Jews (above) were the products of racial intermixture with white Europeans and had no meaningful connection to Jews in North Africa, who resembled the original "Semitic" type (opposite).

mitic or African descent.[109] Second, as the result of skull measurements he took at the schools of the Alliance Israélite Universelle in North Africa between 1903 and 1906, Fishberg was able to compare the cranial features of Middle Eastern Jews with those of his original sample from the United Hebrew Charities in New York. He concluded that each group was more closely related to the non-Jewish population among whom they lived than they were to each other. While the African Jews had intermingled with and taken on the qualities of their African neighbors over the centuries, the European and American Jews had mixed with and taken on the qualities of European whites. In fact, he wrote, European Jews had been so dramatically transformed through intermarriage that they retained "no relation at all" with the Semitic or African type, and could not claim Abraham, Isaac and Jacob as their physical ancestors.[110]

Given his findings that European Jews were essentially no different physically than the non-Jewish Europeans among whom they lived, Fishberg was able to argue that any minor differences in appearance or behavior had been artificially cultivated by the environment. If Jews had a distinctive posture and facial expression, engaged in certain trades and

Fig. 100.—TUNISIAN JEW.

12 and 13. *cont'd*

professions, and demonstrated other particular social traits, these were merely the results of centuries of persecution and social isolation, a theme Fishberg elaborated upon in his 1911 book, *The Jews: A Study of Race and Environment*. If this aspect of his argument resembled the approach of Franz Boas, however, Fishberg departed from Boas's model in identifying the black-white divide as the point at which environment ceased to explain group difference. Pointing to African Americans and other non-white races as groups who *did* bear immutable differences in headform and pigmentation, he was able to argue that Jews had no such traits that would keep them from assimilating into the white American population.[111] "It is clear that certain strata of the population cannot assimilate merely by adopting the language, religion, customs and habits of the dominant race," he explained in a subsequent article. "Negroes in the United States cannot be rendered white merely by speaking English [or] becoming Christians." Yet "the Jews, as whites, are by no means debarred from assimilating with their fellow men of other faiths."[112]

In denying any far-reaching racial distinctiveness and identifying Jews with other American whites, Fishberg had provided a scientific basis for the claims of Jewish leaders. Unlike other Jewish spokesmen, however, he pursued his conclusions with a rigid scientific consistency that was unable to make room for any lingering attachment to the notion of a Jewish race. In fact, because he had made the argument for the temporary, artificial nature of Jewish difference so rigorously, he discounted not only Jewish racial distinctiveness but almost every form of Jewish particularity. Given what he saw as the superficiality of Jewish difference, Fishberg anticipated the ultimate failure of Zionism and predicted that Jews would not even persist as a distinct religious denomination, but would in short time assimilate completely into the American population. "The fact that the differences between Jews and Christians are not everywhere racial, due to anatomical or physiological peculiarities, but are solely the result of the social and political environment," he wrote in the introduction to *The Jews*, "explains our optimism as regards the ultimate obliteration of all distinctions between Jews and Christians in Europe and America."[113]

By taking the denial of Jewish racial difference to its logical conclusion, Fishberg failed at satisfying the contradictory needs of American Jews, most of whom ultimately wanted to be accepted in white America without giving up their own distinctive racial identity. This failure was apparent in the almost universal condemnation the book received in Jewish circles. Zionists attacked the work most strenuously, using their organ, the *Maccabaean*, to counter Fishberg's findings with scientific data of their own.[114] One did not have to be a Zionist, however, to find Fishberg's prediction of ultimate Jewish effacement disturbing. The editor of the San Francisco *Emanu-El*, a Reform-minded journal, was bothered by Fishberg's argument that Jews were not a "race, creed or nation" but simply a "social phenomenon," a finding that exhibited a "complete lack of appreciation of the positive side of Jewish life and thought." Despite the success with which Fishberg refuted antisemitic race theories, the editor wrote, his book was "neither satisfactory nor assuring to the man who wills to be a

Jew."[115] Horace Wolf, a Reform rabbi in Chicago, scoffed at Fishberg's argument that the term "Jewish race" was a scientific misnomer. "What do we care that the laboratory masters have dubbed us in error," he asked, "so long as our lives reflect our implicit belief in the continued existence of the Jewish people?"[116]

The Fishberg episode revealed more clearly than any other the inability of American Jews to find stable, emotionally satisfying terms for self-definition in a society insistent on dividing the world into black and white. If Jews found that race was an increasing liability and threatened to lump them with nonwhites, they also found themselves unable to break the emotional commitment they had to a racial self-understanding. The result was a constant struggle with these two powerful impulses for inclusion and distinctiveness, one that led many acculturated Jews to assert their status as a religious group in public while privately clinging to a much broader racial understanding of Jewishness. In 1910, addressing the question "What Are We?" for a Jewish reading audience, historian Max Margolis summed up the collective frustration of American Jews by concluding that the Jews were "a great anomaly which cannot be classified according to accepted rules of definition."[117] In finding satisfactory terms for Jewish self-definition, complained another Jewish writer the same year, "we succeed to about the same extent as the man who sets out to square the circle or to prove that twice two are five. We have set up what has come to be a veritable system of compromises ludicrous and illogical in themselves, but useful only for the lack of something better and because they enable us to muddle through somehow."[118]

Like those non-Jewish whites who preferred to subvert the Jews' racial distinctiveness rather than come to terms with it, Jews persisted with this "system of compromises" through World War I. Despite the obstacles Jewish racial identity seemed to pose to full membership in American society, Jews, like their non-Jewish counterparts, were sufficiently buoyed by the optimism of the Progressive Era to believe that these contradictions would work themselves out in time. But as World War I ushered in a new intense period of social change, Americans became even more concerned about Jewish distinctiveness and the forces of modernity that it represented. As Jews became an increasing focus of national anxiety during the interwar years, they would have to face up to the contradictions between Jewish racial status and whiteness in ways that they had previously been able to avoid.

PART III

CONFRONTING JEWISH DIFFERENCE, 1919–1935

CHAPTER 5

RACE AND THE "JEWISH PROBLEM"

IN INTERWAR AMERICA

DESPITE RISING concerns about the uncertainty of Jewish racial status, white Americans of the Progressive Era had largely been able to keep their fears about Jewish distinctiveness in check. As vexing as the Jewish presence seemed at times, American racial discourse in the years before World War I continued to emphasize the distinctions between whites and blacks and tried to understand the place of Jews within those familiar categories. Looking back on the opening years of the century, Harold Stearns, one of the major social critics of the 1920s, expressed what was a widely held view concerning the Jews: "I thought that in a few generations they would be absorbed into the general population by intermarriage," he explained. "Whatever friction was engendered was merely temporary inconvenience."[1] In the years after the war, however, such optimism vanished as discussions of Jewish status took on a new, urgent tone. Unlike Progressive Era commentators, who either tried to subvert the troubling presence of the Jew beneath the categories of "black" and "white" or felt confident that the difficulties presented by Jewish distinctiveness would simply be worked out in time, white Americans of the interwar period were increasingly convinced that Jews represented a distinct "problem" in American life.

"The after-the-war imagination plays busily about the Jew," wrote New York rabbi Judah L. Magnes in 1920, describing the excited mood about Jewish issues. "Books, magazine articles, newspaper editorials, the talk of the man in the street, figure him as a sort of Mephistopheles of the peoples. It is the Jew, they say, who is bedeviling this distracted world."[2] A survey of the periodical press of the period confirms Magnes's claim. During the 1920s and 1930s, the Jews became the focus of dozens of exposés, symposiums, and series of articles by leading experts that were featured in magazines like the *Nation*, the *Saturday Evening Post*, *Atlantic Monthly*, and the *World Tomorrow*. The *Forum* was typical of American opinion in 1926 when it expressed the need to focus new light on the "Jewish Problem" in America. "It was once the practice of medicine to cover up a festering sore," explained the editors. "But fortunately medicine has advanced to the point where a direct attack upon the causes of the sore is practicable." So too had the time come for a "fearless airing of honest differences of opinion" on the place of the Jews in American life. "That a Jewish Question exists is a fact which nearly all sane men and women, whether Jew or Gentile, will readily admit."[3]

This new urgency concerning the Jew was a part of the larger ethos of an era in which the confidence of Victorian America withered under the challenges of postwar society. White Americans of the period, finding it increasingly difficult to muster unquestioning faith in progress, became determined to face up to the problems of modern life rather than obscure them with optimism. As they came to terms with those problems, they also stopped and took stock of the Jew as a distinct racial entity that stood apart from the categories of "black" and "white" and was in need of individual attention and analysis. As members of the dominant society became less able to smooth over their anxieties about modernity, they could no longer subvert the Jewish image that had come to represent them.

The Jew in National Life

While anxiety about modernity, and particularly the rise of an urban industrial society, was not new in the period after World War I, the postwar generation experienced a level of doubt about the future of the nation that was unprecedented in American history. Overt expressions of national doom had been limited during the early twentieth century to a handful of antimodernist patricians, but by the 1920s there was a widespread feeling among white Americans that they were living in a "botched civilization."[4] Much of this dramatic decline in self-confidence was due to the destabilizing political and social changes ushered in by the war. In exchange for the massive toll it took on American material and psychological resources, the war delivered few of the sweeping benefits it had promised. Instead of being remade in the cast of American democracy, Europe during the 1920s seemed as politically unstable as ever, threatened by the specter of Russian communism. As a result, many Americans became fearful of continuing foreign entanglements and the importation of radical political ideologies to these shores. In addition, the domestic social landscape was thrown into turmoil by disagreements about the return to prewar conditions. American labor was sorely disappointed when, at the war's conclusion, employers sought to reverse the gains made by workers during the wartime surge in production. Finally, racial and ethnic tensions flared when native-born whites sought to reassert their dominance in a society where African Americans and immigrants had benefited from wartime opportunities.[5]

Perhaps most significantly, the war represented to many native-born whites a final break with the idealized, community-based culture of their past. Not only had the conflict placed the United States in a position of world leadership from which it could not turn back, but it had also hastened the irreversible expansion of the country's burgeoning mass culture. If these feelings of insecurity and dislocation existed during the prosperous 1920s, they were experienced even more sharply during the 1930s and early 1940s, when economic depression and war loomed as threats to American life. Aside from the grave doubts that the economic crisis elicited about the viability of American capitalism, members of the dominant class also feared that the time was ripe for the overthrow of democracy by an alien political ideology, a fear exacerbated by the rise of communist and fascist governments in other parts of the world.[6]

If the changes of the 1920s and 1930s brought new doubts about modernity to the surface, however, they could not totally obscure white Americans' faith in progress. Even the most backward-looking groups, like the Ku Klux Klan, resisted change only in piecemeal fashion, ultimately accepting new ways as long as their vision of "traditional values" could be affirmed symbolically. For most members of the dominant society, the blandishments of modern culture—automobiles, movies, mass-produced goods, urban leisure—were too attractive and promising to reject.[7] Unable to suppress their sense of fear and disillusionment amidst rapid change, they were also unable and unwilling to turn back from the new social and cultural realities of their world. It is no surprise that in this time of radical ambivalence about modern life, the Jew became a focus for discussion and debate as never before.

During the 1920s and 1930s, Jews continued to be linked in American discourse with many of the features of modernity about which white Americans were ambivalent: business, urban life, intellectuality, self-interest. But during the interwar years, many new markers of modern life were added to this list. As the children and grandchildren of Eastern European Jewish immigrants became more acculturated in these years, they grew more prominent in the areas of American life associated with social change. Their heavy concentration in the cities and their overrepresentation in schools of higher learning made them leaders in many of the new intellectual and cultural movements. During the 1920s, Jews achieved great success in politics in the major urban centers, and by the Depression decade, they were conspicuous in the New Deal establishment. The interwar years saw the two largest Jewish garment unions transformed into major players in American industrial relations. Finally, and perhaps most importantly, the expansion of America's mass culture provided Jews who were often excluded from other fields with a means of advancement and a chance to help shape American discourse as writers, editors, artists, and performers, not to mention as creators of the era's two most important media, radio and motion pictures.[8] Despite accusations to the contrary, Jews were far from dominating American institutions, but because they remained a visible minority and were concentrated in pursuits that had such a great impact on American values and perceptions, it was easy for members of the dominant society to associate them with the forces of modern life.

Under these circumstances, Jews increasingly became a target for those nervous about the direction of modern American culture. In their attempt to understand why the nation was going astray from what they considered its core values, many white Americans cast the Jewish "race" as an infiltrating force, one that was powerful enough to penetrate the central institutions of American life but dedicated to its own selfish interests. This view of the Jew was articulated almost immediately after the war, when the nation was gripped by a series of red scares, and Jews were singled out by witnesses before several congressional committees as importers of revolutionary communism to these shores.[9] By the early 1920s, Jews were held responsible for a variety of the country's modern evils. The revived Ku Klux Klan, which now aimed its venom at Catholics and Jews as well as African Americans, argued that Jews engaged in unfair business practices and exploited the American working class while producing nothing in return. The Klan also charged that the Jew undermined American moral foundations by producing "lewd" motion pictures, selling immodest clothing to Christian women, and providing the public with "vile places of amusement."[10]

Significantly, such accusations played as well in the nation's major urban centers as they did in the traditionally rural bases of Klan support.[11] In fact, what most distinguished anti-Jewish sentiments during this period was that their appeal extended not only to those on the fringes of society, but to some of America's most prominent mainstream figures, like automobile tycoon Henry Ford. In a series of articles published in his newspaper, the *Dearborn Independent*, between 1920 and 1924, Ford charged the "International Jew" with a string of intrigues, from bringing the United States into World War I, to manipulating American business and finance for their own ends, to corrupting Anglo-Saxon virtues through their control of Hollywood and the music industry. Similarly, the fact that quotas and restrictions against Jews were no longer found only in exclusive clubs but also in major American institutions like Harvard University indicated just how pervasive fears about the Jew's place in society had become.[12]

The economic crisis of the 1930s only intensified these hatreds and added to the number of spokesmen who saw the Jews as a destabilizing force. Fear of "Jewish communism" became widespread, and was exacerbated by the frequent identification of Jews with New Deal economic and social policy. Additionally, after the rise of Nazi Germany and the impending threat of another war, figures of no less stature than the aviation hero Charles Lindbergh lashed out against Jews as a force they feared would propel the nation once again into world conflict.[13] During the Depression decade, urban Catholics suffering in difficult circumstances became especially active in making such accusations against Jews. Because they often lagged behind Jews in the attainment of economic mobility and saw them as competitors for political power and influence, many Catholics found Jews to be attractive symbols for the forces that seemed to control their lives. These resentments were most powerfully expressed by organizations such as the Christian Front and by the immensely popular "radio priest," Father Charles E. Coughlin, who blamed Jews for the sufferings and "persecution" of the American people.[14]

While the 1920s and 1930s represented a rising tide of fear and hostility toward the Jews, however, there was also a noticeable current of positive attitudes toward the Jews during the same period.[15] Just as white Americans expressed radically ambivalent attitudes toward their changing social and cultural environment, they were also hopelessly conflicted about the Jews they associated with those changes. While certain spokesmen bemoaned Jewish influence in government, in Hollywood, and in the music industry, significant segments of the white population still seemed willing to elect Jewish politicians to high office (including governors Herbert Lehman of New York and Henry Horner of Illinois) and to embrace the cultural contributions of Jews as expressions of quintessential Americanism.[16] In addition, as pervasive as antisemitism and antisemitic movements were during these years, they frequently had their counterparts among those who spoke out on behalf of the Jews and in favor of a more tolerant society. In the wake of the antisemitic campaign of Henry Ford's *Dearborn Independent*, several respectable journals took the billionaire car manufacturer to task for his anti-Jewish rhetoric, as did leading intellectuals and statesmen. In 1921, without any pressure from Jewish groups, social reformer and writer John Spargo organized a petition condemning Ford's efforts that was signed by an impressive array of eminent American intellectuals, clergy, and civic leaders, including former presidents Taft, Wilson, and Roosevelt.[17]

In the wake of these initial protests of Ford's antisemitism, a number of Christian and Jewish denominational bodies founded "goodwill" committees to promote interfaith cooperation. In 1927, these committees crystallized into the National Conference of Christians and Jews (NCCJ), a group led by rabbis, Christian churchmen, and several Jewish and Christian laypersons.[18] In many of places across the country that were labeled trouble spots for Jewish-gentile relations, one could find impressive efforts at interfaith cooperation. In Indiana, a stronghold of Ku Klux Klan power and influence, Jewish leaders drew support from Christian clergy, politicians, and the local press in their campaign to discredit the Klan, eventually leading to the organization's downfall in the state.[19] And in the country's major urban centers, where Catholic-Jewish tensions flared during the Depression, several Catholic leaders trumpeted the pope's official rejection of antisemitism and distanced themselves from the anti-Jewish rhetoric of radio priest Charles Coughlin.[20]

Despite the presence of a strong movement for goodwill between Jews and Christians, however, there was still not always a neat divide in America between the camps of antisemites and philosemites. Different as they were, each of these positions was shot through with ambivalence, making it impossible to say that any group of Americans was of one mind in their approach to the Jews. Henry Ford, despite his persistent attacks on Jewish "control" of American culture, claimed to think highly of some Jews and continued to court the friendship of the prominent Detroit rabbi Leo Franklin.[21] Charles Lindbergh, too, had close Jewish associates and claimed to admire the Jewish "race."[22] Despite the antisemitic rhetoric of the Ku Klux Klan, tales abound of the organization's frequent "cordiality" toward Jews in both the North and South. In certain cities, the Klan threw its support behind Jewish political candidates and sometimes extended offers of membership to Jews.[23] And if those who tended toward antisemitism were not thoroughgoing in their rejection of Jews, neither were those who promoted tolerance completely at ease with the Jewish presence in America. Although less cynical about the Jew's "subversive" influence on American society and more hopeful that relations between Jews and non-Jews could be worked out, advocates of tolerance often shared in the belief that Jews constituted a distinct "problem" for the nation. Not immune themselves from the anxieties and pressures of modern life, many of them were willing to accept at least some of the associations made between Jews and the wayward direction of American culture. In keeping with contemporary understandings of intergroup relations, most subscribed to the widely held notion that antisemitism stemmed not from irrational prejudice but from "race antipathies"—concrete differences in temperament and outlook that needed to be worked out and overcome through the elimination of group differences.[24]

The contradictions in the attitudes of both the antisemites and the proponents of tolerance suggest that ambivalence about the Jews was endemic in white American society. Ambivalence about the Jews, however, was nothing new. What distinguished the approach of white Americans in the 1920s and 1930s was the fact that few could continue to obscure the doubts about national life that ambivalence about the Jews represented. Just as they were unable to solve the quandary of their approach to American modernity, white Americans of the interwar period seemed unable to totally demonize the Jews or to satisfy themselves that Jews were in harmony with American ideals. Instead, for the first time in American history, they faced up to their disquieting inability to understand the Jews within the familiar categories of American life.

Traditionally, in times of national crisis and doubt, members of the dominant white society had been able to turn to the country's black-white racial system as a means of affirming their sense of superiority and their ability to overcome adversity. In the years before World War I, faith in the black-white dichotomy seemed to bolster their belief in progress and forestall fears about the mounting costs of modernization. By the 1920s, however, they increasingly began to lose the sense of confidence white supremacy had previously afforded. Once focused on the relationships between superior whites and inferior peoples of color, white Americans now became preoccupied with their own racial failings and the dangers faced by their civilization, themes popularized by racist thinkers like Lothrop Stoddard and Madison Grant.[25] The migration of a half million African Americans from the South to northern urban centers between 1915 and 1920 made whites' fears about the inadequacies of their racial strength and solidarity even more acute. In many cases, white Americans' particular fascination with African American culture during this period, while usually expressed in paternalistic fashion, stemmed from an underlying fear that blacks retained a strength and vitality that whites were losing.[26]

The period's tendency toward facing up to even the most unpleasant "truths" decisively shaped the way white Americans of the interwar years described and understood the racial place of Jews.[27] Most significantly, they were no longer able to contain the troubling image of the Jew within the more comforting categories of black and white. Given the mood of skepticism prevalent between the wars, the method used to suppress the Jewish image in the early twentieth century now seemed hopelessly naïve. On the one hand, there was a growing recognition that, for better or for worse, Jews and the forces of modernity they represented were an integral part of national life. As a result, American whites could no longer plausibly dismiss their connection to those forces by comparing Jews to "inferior" peoples of color. On the other hand, few white Americans retained sufficient confidence in the path of modern American life to see the Jews—the bearers of that modernity—as stable members of white society. Unable to either place Jews beyond the pale of whiteness or to fully embrace them as undifferentiated whites, whites Americans came to increasingly see the Jews as a distinct racial "problem."

Neither Black . . .

Growing recognition by white Americans that the Jews defied easy placement into the categories of black and white did not mean that the color line ceased to play a significant role in framing the "Jewish Problem" during the 1920s and 1930s. In fact, antisemites in the period between the two wars became preoccupied with understanding the relationship between Jewishness and whiteness. If they could no longer defuse the danger they saw in the Jews by likening them to African Americans, they aimed instead to study, clarify, and expose their role as an unstable element in white society.

This new focus on exposing the Jew as a problem in white America was exemplified by Henry Ford's campaign in the *Dearborn Independent*. Ford's propaganda aimed at unmasking aspects of Jewish racial difference that were thought to be dangerously masquerading as sameness. Early in the "International Jew" series, the editors of the *Independent* published the statements made by Simon Guggenheim and Simon Wolf during their campaign to remove the Jewish racial designation from the immigration and census records. According to the *Independent*, their testimony was nothing more than an attempt to conceal the true character of the American Jewish community and to keep other Americans ignorant of the number of Jewish immigrants that were daily arriving on their shores. In fact, the *Independent* argued, Jews were a "separate people, marked off from other races by very distinct characteristics, both physical and spiritual," and one need not look past the repeated statements of Jewish writers and spokesmen to prove it.[28] In a similar vein, Ford also drew attention to the Jewish practice of name changing, exposing it as another means by which Jews tried to blend in to the American mainstream while secretly retaining their racial solidarity. The worst offender in the regard, argued the paper, was Louis Marshall, who worked his way to a high station in America using an assumed "Anglo-Saxon" name and then dedicated himself to uprooting the principle that America was a "Christian nation." [29]

Thus, a persistent theme of the *Independent*'s articles was that unless Jews were made visible in white America, they would subvert all the standards of the nation for their own ends. The paper bemoaned, for example, how "Jewish dealers" had lowered American business standards and destroyed "the old way of the white man, when a man's word was as good as his bond, and when business was service and not exploitation."[30] As promoters of both Hollywood and African American jazz (labeled by the *Independent* as "Yiddish moron music"), they had contaminated American morals and tastes.[31] In some articles, more direct attention was given to the danger the Jew posed to the maintenance of white supremacy. One charged that Jewish distillery owners in the South specialized in the manufacture of alcohol known as "nigger gin," a beverage "compounded to act upon the Negro in a most vicious manner." Not only was the liquor itself said to provoke criminal activity among African Americans, but the labels on the bottles "bore lascivious suggestions and were decorated with highly indecent portraiture of white women." The account went on to suggest that as the drink caused a wave of black criminality across the South, a period of great regional strife began—all due to Jewish influence. Jews' support of black civil rights organizations and charitable causes was also singled out as part of their "Divide-Conquer-Destroy" strategy. "Their role in distributing Jewish influence is directly behind the present attitude of the Negro toward the white man," explained the article. "Look at the so-called 'Negro Welfare Societies' with their hordes of Jewish officials and patrons! Jewish influence in the South today is active in keeping up the memory of old divisions."[32]

The *Independent*'s accusations are significant in that, instead of painting the Jews as blacks or whites, they highlighted both the power Jews wielded in white society and the damage they did to it by acting in their own group interest. This theme was echoed over and over again in American discourse during the 1920s and 1930s and was typical of the era's attempt to uncover and expose the complex racial place of the Jew. Part of this process was the elaboration of new terms for the Jew, especially the increasingly popular epithet "kike." While the derivation of the term is vague, it was most likely coined by acculturated Central European Jews as a term of reproach for their less cultivated Eastern European cousins, whose surnames often ended in "ki." By the 1920s, it had attained wide currency among the non-Jewish public. "Kike" was used most often to refer to the Jews as members of a distinct race who were dangerously powerful and influential, rather than marginal, in the white world.[33]

This image of the Jew was particularly salient in discussions about Jewish college admissions that raged in the early 1920s. College students and administrators during these years frequently argued that schools were being overrun by Jews who were changing the character of the institutions and undermining white unity. Harvard, for example, had long prided itself on its unified student body, but now Jews were said to be instilling the spirit of competition by trying to demonstrate academic superiority over their non-Jewish counterparts. Among the surest signs that the Jewish college student concentrated on his own academic advancement to the exclusion of all else, according his detractors, was his avoidance of sport and recreation, which were meant to instill fellowship and shared school spirit among the students.[34]

Given such a critique, it is not surprising that protesters against Jewish influence at both Harvard and New York University (NYU), another school with a large Jewish enrollment, argued that these schools needed to be preserved as "white man's college[s]." Here the intent was not to suggest that the Jews were inferior by likening them to African Americans; Jews were referred to specifically as "kikes" in both instances. Rather, the assertion was that Jewish infidelity to the standards of whiteness was dangerous precisely *because* of the Jew's high stature in the university. At Harvard in 1922, a visiting alumnus, struck by the number of "kikes" in the Yard, was particularly alarmed at the sight of "two Jews and a negro, fraternizing." This scene, he suggested, was only one example of Jews' tendency to ignore time-honored social standards. He also charged Jews with creating a highly competitive academic environment in which "white boys" were eliminated. "Are the Overseers so lacking in genius," inquired the alumnus, "that they can't devise a way to bring Harvard back to the position it always held as a 'white man's' college?"[35] Apparently the same sort of feeling raged at NYU, where in 1923 students hung posters warning away "scurvey kikes" and admonishing university officials to "make New York University a white man's college."[36]

The notion of the Jew "infiltrating" and undermining the standards of white society soon mingled with the popular image of the Jew as communist, especially during the years of the Depression when both Jews and African Americans were conspicuous in American communist circles. This stereotype took root deeply in the South, where the threat of communist infiltration was most closely linked to fears of an African American assertion of power. In several southern states, Jewish communists—usually transplants from the North—were active in organizing black workers during the Great Depression, and became widely seen as troublemakers by local whites.[37] In 1930, David Weinberg, a Jewish tailor and active communist in Miami, was singled out by his non-Jewish neighbors for "associating with Negroes." To show their disapproval of his activities, a group of men abducted Weinberg, tarred and feathered him, and threw him from a car into a downtown intersection.[38] When attorney Samuel Leibowitz, who was not a communist but received backing from the Communist Party, defended the African American "Scottsboro nine" against charges of rape in 1931, he won the scorn of southern whites who argued that local racial standards were being threatened by "Jew money from New York."[39] In the wake of the Scottsboro case, militant southern groups like the James True Associates claimed that Jews intended to overthrow the white power structure and use African Americans as "the shock troops of the revolution."[40]

While fear was particularly strong in the South that powerful Jews would help undermine the racial balance, such feelings were also frequently expressed in the North. Meyer Levin, in his novel of Jewish life in Chicago, *The Old Bunch* (1937), portrayed the scorn with which the Irish police of the city greeted radical Jews who protested with African Americans on behalf of the Scottsboro Boys. In one scene, the police delight in humiliating Jewish activists after a demonstration, lining them up and making them kiss their African American comrades.[41] In the northern urban centers, where racial tensions often centered on the issue of housing

Strictly Kosher--Must not
APPLY HERE.

SCURVY KIKES
ARE NOT WANTED

At New York University
if they knew
their place they would
not be here

Make New York
University a White
Man's College.

14. The Jew as "kike," 1923. Beginning in the 1920s, many Americans used the epithet "kike" to convey an image of the Jew as powerful in white society but disloyal to its standards. This antisemitic broadside posted by students at New York University singled out Jews as an unstable element in the white population. (Courtesy Jacob Rader Marcus Center of the American Jewish Archives)

competition, the Jewish property owners were often labeled "sell-outs" that destroyed the integrity of white neighborhoods.[42] The willingness of Jews to rent and sell to blacks angered members of other immigrant groups—usually Irish—who, for reasons of both religion and class, often found it more difficult to move to other neighborhoods. As a result, they sometimes vilified Jews as "kike real estate bastards."[43] As Studs Lonigan, the title character in James Farrell's classic portrait of Chicago life in the 1920s, expressed it, "It's a lousy thing . . . Jews ruining a neighborhood just to make money like Judas did."[44] In New York, too, Jews often provoked the ire of non-Jewish whites who blamed them for allowing blacks to move into previously restricted areas. In 1923, Harry Bierhoff, the Jewish president of the Rox Real Estate Company in Harlem, received a letter from the Ku Klux Klan warning him not to rent apartments to African American tenants. "This is wholly un-American and is totally against our principles," the letter explained. "We ask you in a gentlemanly way to rescind your order or unpleasant things may happen."[45]

Just as popular parlance in the 1920s and 1930s recognized the "kike" to be a distinct and more powerful breed than the "nigger," implicated in white society but never embracing its standards, race scientists and popularizers of racial thought also began to develop a more precise definition of Jewish racial origins that fit this model. On the one hand, many began to realize the futility of linking the Jew, as some had done in the early twentieth century, with African origins. Only Lothrop Stoddard, writing in 1926, made the fleeting and uncharacteristic claim that "a Negro strain doubtlessly exists in Jewry" and that "to it the frizzy or wooly hair, thick lips, and prognathous jaws appearing in many Jewish individuals are probably due."[46] Instead, most writers trying to cast the Jew as a racial alien took an approach that helped account for the Jew's high station in American life and his particular standing in white society. Even Stoddard, later in the same article, ventured that a good percentage of Eastern European Jews were descended not from Africans, but from "a people known as the Khazars," a tribe of imprecise racial origin that was "probably of broad-headed Turkish stock from central Asia" and that had converted to Judaism in the Middle Ages.[47]

Stoddard borrowed this idea from Burton Hendrick, who had written an extensive study of the Jews for the *World's Work*, later published in book form. Hendrick explained Jewish power and influence by arguing that it was held mainly by the older Jewish immigrants, those of Sephardic and Central European origin, who were actually of a higher racial type than the more recently arrived immigrants from Eastern Europe. While the earlier arrivals were not racially foreign to America, he argued, the newer immigrants (whom he called "Polish Jews") posed a particular challenge to the process of absorption and assimilation. Yet Hendrick found it difficult to propose that even the newer immigrants were racial aliens on the scale of African Americans, given their white appearance, their concentration in skilled trades, and the high economic station they were achieving. Instead, he hit upon the notion that the Eastern European Jews were descended from the Khazars. Apparently, given the somewhat ambiguous racial status of the Khazars themselves, the theory gave Hendrick a way of explaining how Jews had been able to infiltrate white society, yet had also maintained their menacing racial integrity.[48]

The theory that Eastern European Jews descended from the Khazars was originally proposed by the Russian Jewish anthropologist Samuel Weissenberg in an attempt to show that Jews were deeply rooted on Russian soil, and that the cradle of Jewish civilization was the Caucasus, the same place scientists such as Johann Blumenbach had located the origins of European civilization. In 1911, Maurice Fishberg introduced this theory to the American reading public, arguing that the Khazars "made up the nucleus of the future Jewry of Eastern Europe," with the added aim of suggesting that Jews were white. Ironically, however, once the Khazar theory was available in English, it gave antisemitic writers a means of finding an alien source for Jewish racial endowments while also explaining why Jews prospered and blended in more successfully than the country's traditional racial outsiders.[49]

If anti-Jewish detractors often described Jews as dangerous infiltrators who retained their racial character even as they moved in white society, however, there was also a more optimistic strain to their thinking on the place of Jews in American life. While they often described Jews as a menace, and sometimes questioned their assimilability by referring to them as "Asiatic" or "Tatar" in race, these spokesmen were unable to give up completely on the notion that the Jews could someday assimilate into white American society. Here the American approach to the Jews was fundamentally different from that in many European countries, especially Germany. The faith that persisted in progress and modernity in the United States always furthered a degree of identification with the Jews that made it almost impossible for Americans to turn against them completely.[50]

This willingness to foresee the possible assimilation of the Jews was apparent even among some of the most antisemitic racial thinkers. Despite Lothrop Stoddard's suggestion of a strong biological link to the "Jewish ideals of exclusiveness and group-separatism," he also admitted that many Jews, especially the older immigrants from Central Europe, had rejected "the doctrine of racial exclusiveness" and considered "the possibility of assimilation with their Gentile neighbors."[51] Similarly, Burton Hendrick hinted that the alien "Polish" Jews might, to some extent, follow the example of their Sephardic and German predecessors, whose contributions to "education, science, letters, and other activities, show that there is nothing in the Jewish nature that necessarily dooms him to be forever an alien."[52]

Some critics of the Jews explained that their efforts to expose Jewish distinctiveness were merely a way to advance the assimilation process. Ford's *Dearborn Independent* denied any charges of antisemitism and argued that it was simply trying to call attention to the problems created by Jews' separate existence in America. Its efforts, claimed the paper, were not designed to persecute Jews but to help them find the proper path to assimilation. "In this land, the Jew will have to change his attitude of antagonism and dwell in peace as in a land prepared for him. Not as lord of it, by any means, but as a grateful wanderer at last come home."[53] Similarly, Harvard president Lawrence Lowell argued that his quota system was not designed to ostracize Jews but to end the practice of "Semitic segregation" and help the Jews of Harvard become a more integral part of the institution. With an unrestricted flow of Jews into the university, those already admitted would continue to cling together and resist mixing with non-Jewish students, he reasoned.[54] The key was to admit a smaller number of Jews that could be assimilated effectively. Significantly, while Lowell proposed segregating African American students in separate living quarters, he wanted Jewish students to mix with their white, non-Jewish classmates as much as possible.[55] Lowell's opinion that Jews should be assimilated, but in numbers small enough to insure a proper outcome, seems to have been widely held among Americans of the 1920s and 1930s. While the movement for immigration restriction has usually been seen as an effort to exclude "inferior" races from the United States, many proponents of restriction saw it as a means of reducing the immigrant flow to a more manageable size.[56] Charles Lindbergh expressed almost identical sentiments in 1939, while returning to New York from Europe on a cruiser loaded with Jewish refugees. "A few Jews add strength and character to a country," he wrote in his journal, "but too many create chaos."[57]

Of course, as open as such rhetoric makes these spokesmen seem to the welcoming of Jews into the white American fold, most of their efforts were directed toward the opposite goal—asserting the alienness of Jews and trying to exclude them from national life. It seems that the degree of optimism in American life that motivated these statements about Jewish assimilation was not strong enough during these years to overpower the doubts such figures had, doubts that created the constant need to expose the irritating distinctiveness of Jews and to prevent their "takeover" of American institutions. As long as this ambivalence about American life raged in their minds, Jews would continue to hold a problematic place as potential whites who were never willing to give up their renegade ways.

. . . nor White

If anti-Jewish spokesmen could no longer understand the Jews by likening them to African Americans and other peoples of color, those more friendly to the Jews could no longer cast them as undifferentiated or even easily assimilable whites. Thus, while they exhibited a more hopeful attitude about the prospect of incorporating the Jews into the white majority culture, they often shared with anti-Jewish spokesman a general belief that the Jew's combination of similarity and difference was unacceptable for the stability of American life. Even the warmest supporters of interfaith goodwill believed that the Jews required thorough assimilation as a means of resolving their uncertain status in white America.

Those who proposed liberal solutions to the pressing problems of "racial" and religious hatred in America were often motivated by the same need to face up to unpleasant "realities" that moved the more reactionary forces of the period. This usually meant giving up the naïve hope that assimilation of immigrants could be achieved swiftly with little intervention from the dominant society. While liberals generally discounted notions of racial determinism, by the 1920s they often believed that groups such as the Jews did have a strongly defined set of social and psychological characteristics that could be labeled "racial" and that needed to be addressed.[58] Many of the committees created by churches to investigate relations between Jews and non-Jews reflected this belief by focusing on the Jews' status as a separate race, as did the Home Missions Council's "committee on Hebrews." As such nomenclature suggests, despite the sympathy often expressed for Jews by liberal Christian clergy, Jewish racial status was still seen as a "problem" that needed to be solved.[59] "Those of us who are impressed by the importance of the task to demolish racial antagonism," explained newspaperman and goodwill advocate Norman Angell, "should be careful not to underestimate its difficulties, nor to misunderstand its nature. The difficulties are rooted in instincts which in some dim animal past may have been valuable to the race, but which today have become so anti-social that the future of civilisation may well depend (I think it does depend) upon our success in 'sublimating' them."[60]

As Angell's call for the "sublimation" of racial instinct indicates, liberals—much like their more conservative counterparts—saw divisions among whites as a threat to civilization. Believing that assimilation was the key to a stable, homogenous society free of discord, they saw expressions of prejudice as the primary obstacles. "Group strife," explained Protestant clergyman S. Parkes Cadman, one of the leaders of the interfaith movement, "is the rock on which every civilization has split."[61] John Spargo, organizer of the petition against Henry Ford, denounced antisemitism more as a retardant to assimilation than as an assault on Jewish character. In his 1921 book, *The Jew and American Ideals*, he argued that anti-Jewish bigotry stood in opposition to Anglo-Saxon ideals because it threatened the racial homogeneity of the nation. Antisemitism "would divide our citizenship by racial and religious barriers," he argued, while "the Americanism of Washington and Lincoln and Lee and Roosevelt would weld all into a united whole."[62]

In addition to attacking antisemitism as an obstacle to assimilation and white unity, liberal gentiles also consistently emphasized the major part that Jews themselves played in promoting their own isolation. Elmer Davis, a publicist writing as part of a "Symposium for Better Understanding," criticized Americanized Jews who "seem to feel that they are at once Americans exactly like the rest of us, and Jews wholly different from the rest of us." Such an attitude, Davis explained, helped fuel antisemitism, a force that would not die out "until the Jewishness of the average Jew means no more to him than that I am of Baptist training and British-German ancestry means to me."[63] This tendency to blame Jews, at least in part, for their own exclusion from American society was exemplified in a 1931 "study in prejudice" written by Heywood Broun and George Britt. *Christians Only*, one of the first books on antisemitism written by non-Jews, credited much of anti-Jewish feeling to the continued distinctiveness of the Jewish group itself. The "way out" of antisemitism was assimilation, declared the authors, who implored the Jews to join liberal religious movements like Humanism and Ethical Culture, intermarry, and generally attenuate their difference in American society.[64]

Such reasoning was also dominant in the popular culture of the period, which frequently disparaged Jewish opposition to intermarriage, albeit in a humorous vein, as an obstacle to good relations among white Americans. Ann Nichols's 1922 Broadway hit, *Abie's Irish Rose*, romanticized the union of an Irish-Jewish couple and trumpeted intermarriage as the solution to "racial" antagonism between white immigrant groups. Although unpopular with reviewers, the play enjoyed a record run of over five years, and inspired a number of film imitations. During the years between 1922 and 1927 alone, seventeen films featured Irish-Jewish romances, despite the fact that such unions rarely took place in real life.[65] Typical of these films was the *Cohens and the Kellys* (1926), in which two families, one Irish and one Jewish, grudgingly overcome their racial antagonism after the marriage of their children, Nannie Cohen and Terry Kelly. Offering a not-too-subtle critique of group separatism, the film lampooned the reluctant parents with racial stereotypes drawn from the vaudeville stage, while styling the intermarried children as undifferentiated white Americans.[66] One of the many sequels of the film, *The Cohens and Kellys in Africa* (1930), also emphasized the power of intermarriage

15. *The Cohens and the Kellys in Africa*, 1930. A string of plays and movies during the 1920s and 1930s used the Irish-Jewish intermarriage theme to encourage assimilation and to critique what was considered the stubborn separatism of immigrant groups. This film accentuated the link between whiteness and the racial "amalgamation" of immigrant groups by sending the reluctant Jewish and Irish in-laws on an African adventure. (Courtesy Photofest)

to whiten immigrant groups by depicting the now-united families as explorers of the "Dark Continent." Casting the two fathers as partners in a piano company, the film takes them to Africa in search of ivory where, among other adventures, they are captured by cannibals and eventually win the desired merchandise by beating a native chief on the miniature golf course.[67]

The fact that attitudes and images urging the radical assimilation of the Jews were pervasive even in the most liberal sectors of American society during the 1920s and 1930s demonstrates the general failure of theories of cultural pluralism to take root during these years. In the period immediately before World War I, a few non-Jewish intellectuals such as Randolph Bourne and John Dewey had joined Jews such as Horace Kallen in proposing pluralist definitions of American identity.[68] In the wake of the war and people's fears about the changes in American society, however, such ideas quickly lost their appeal, and the voices for pluralism became exceedingly few. In 1938, John Haynes Holmes, leader of the Community Church, New York's leading Unitarian congregation, published a book, cast in heavy racial terms, praising Jews' achievement and extolling their ability to maintain their group identity and also become American.[69] Another rare pluralist view was expressed by Rachel Davis-Du Bois, a Quaker pacifist who founded the Bureau for Inter-Cultural Education in 1934 and the following year published a booklet on Jewish life in America with the aid her colleague Emma Schweppe. Davis-Du Bois and Schweppe declared the "melting pot" theory to have failed as a model for American life, proposing instead a system in which each group could participate in national life and retain their individuality. Breaking with the dominant view, the book drew on the theories of Jewish anthropologist Franz Boas in arguing that the Jews were not a race but merely a "historical, cultural group."[70] Similarly, in 1934, Everett R. Clinchy, a Protestant clergyman who was a leader of the NCCJ, expounded his own brand of cultural pluralism which, anticipating the well-known work of sociologist Will Herberg a generation later, described Protestants, Catholics and Jews as "three equal 'culture groups,' . . . none of which was more American than the other, none of which was better than the other, and each of which had made substantive contributions to America and was destined to continue to do so." Like Davis-DuBois and Schweppe, Clinchy cast attention away from perceived racial differences and stressed only the "cultural" and religious status of these groups, demonstrating the realization of these writers that Jews would be accepted as part of a pluralist mix only when fears about their status as a separate racial group had been dismissed.[71]

Pluralism, however, never gained a wide following during these years, precisely because few Americans could part with their belief that Jewish racial characteristics presented a significant obstacle to the stability of white America. This explains, for example, why anthropologist Franz Boas, who became more interested in the question of Jewish racial identity after the rise of the Nazi regime in Germany, had little success finding allies in the scientific community to aid him in a campaign to discredit the Nazi's equation of race and character. Apart from his own students, some of whom took up the antiracist cause with zeal, those who did cooperate to a limited extent with Boas often had a hard time overcoming their image of the Jews as a group with stubbornly persistent racial qualities. Harvard anthropologist Earnest Hooten, who assisted Boas briefly in the beginning stages of his campaign against scientific racism, believed that Jews needed to "eradicate certain aggressive and other social characteristics which seem to me to account for some of their trouble" and privately shared nativist Madison Grant's distaste for "alien scum."[72] Similarly, Stanford anatomist C. H. Danforth declined to participate in the effort because he felt that "the Jewish Problem in this country is somewhat the responsibility of influential Jews themselves," who were too overzealous in their group solidarity.[73]

As long as the social anxieties of the interwar years continued to vex white Americans, Jews would continue to be seen as a distinct racial "problem" in the United States, an image that would vanish only with the great social and economic transformations of the World War II era. In the meantime, the intense social pressures of the period pushed Jews into a web of irresolvable contradictions regarding their place in American life. The mounting national concern over their racial status conveyed to them in unprecedented ways the urgency of demonstrating their solidarity with white America. At the same time, however, the period's climate of anti-Jewish hostility made them more reluctant than ever to identify with the racist standards of the dominant society. Similarly, Jews increasingly felt the need to defend what was seen as their incontestable racial difference, even as they aimed to prove that nothing in their makeup prevented them from becoming valued members of the white mainstream. Just as white Americans of the 1920s and 1930s were unable to incorporate the Jew into their vision of a stable white society, Jews would remain unable to weave these conflicting imperatives into a coherent American Jewish identity.

CHAPTER 6

"A WHITE RACE OF ANOTHER KIND"?

B Y THE 1920s, American Jewry was no longer neatly divided into camps of acculturated and immigrant Jews. The former Eastern European immigrants were increasingly adapting to American life and had begun to challenge Jews of Central European background for control of communal affairs and institutions. In addition, concerns about Jewish racial status and social acceptance that had once preoccupied only the older segment of the American Jewish community now also began to concern the more recent arrivals and their children. As the Eastern Europeans became more enmeshed in American culture, more aware of its codes and values and more anxious to find acceptance within its ranks, they began to understand—often intuitively—the social significance of whiteness and its relevance to their own lives. At a time when many white Americans considered Jewish difference a burning problem, acculturating Eastern European Jews learned that asserting their status as white could help them claim their place in American life. Although their belief in the promise of America was often shaken by the social pressures of the interwar years, they knew that whatever chance they did have for social acceptance rested on their conformity to the dominant racial paradigm.

If the Eastern Europeans began to demonstrate a greater desire to win acceptance in white America, however, they were often less willing than acculturated Jews of the early twentieth century had been to downplay a specifically Jewish approach to African Americans. Though a history of persecution and marginalization in their homelands made Eastern European Jews anxious for acceptance in America, it also made them reticent about the implications of identifying as white. In addition, Jews of this period were pushed in opposite directions by the climate of social discrimination and antisemitic propaganda, which encouraged them to emphasize their whiteness but frequently made them recoil from the racist standards of white America. Even the old-line Central European Jews, who felt the sting of American antisemitism as strongly as the Eastern Europeans did during the 1920s and 1930s, found themselves increasingly torn between their desire for acceptance and their growing distaste for white intolerance.

Jews of the interwar years wanted to believe that they could both win acceptance in white America and remain sensitive to the plight of American blacks, the synthesis that Yiddish poet I. J. Schwartz had in mind in

1925 when he described his fellow Jews as a "white race of another kind."[1] But as long as the pressures of the interwar years weighed on American Jews, they found themselves unable to resolve the basic contradictions in their approach to African Americans. At a time of such great vulnerability, they often felt pushed to adopt the racist trappings of American culture in order to relieve doubts about their own uncertain racial status. Yet as targets of hatred themselves, they found that they could not disassociate themselves from the plight of African Americans as easily as Jews had in the period before World War I. As a result, claiming their place in white America became a tumultuous, often agonizing process.

Encountering Whiteness in Interwar America

Much of the tension surrounding the Jewish encounter with whiteness during the interwar years was unleashed by the continuing acculturation of Eastern European Jews, who in the years after the war increasingly found themselves entering arenas that placed people within the categories of "black" and "white." These new experiences came primarily as members of the younger generation, many of whom were American born, began to venture beyond the familiar confines of home and family and imbibe the values and perceptions of the larger society.

For many young Jews, the neighborhood school was the first institution that helped to shape their self-consciousness as white. While the public school rarely accepted children on their own cultural terms, Jews were nonetheless enthusiastic about the training they received there because it emphasized their ability to become full Americans.[2] Schools often taught young Jews a version of American history that privileged the experience of white settlers and presented African American slaves and Native Americans as foils against which American national identity was formed. Schools rarely presented overtly racist principles; history lessons usually condemned slavery and the denial of Indian rights. Yet at the same time, textbooks of the period subtly taught students that as whites they had a greater right than peoples of color to claim the nation's founders as their forbears. One popular Americanizing text, Hermann Hagedorn's *You Are the Hope of the World*, encouraged children from immigrant households to follow in the footsteps of their predecessors, the "frontiersmen, the Indian fighters, the pioneers . . . dauntless of spirit."[3] When discussing the unfair treatment of racial minorities, Grace Turkington's *My Country* explained how "for many years *we* kept the both the Indians and the negroes from enjoying liberty" (emphasis added).[4]

"Colonial Day," a citywide pageant held in Annapolis, Maryland, in 1928 to celebrate the 220th anniversary of the city's incorporation, provides an excellent example of how Jewish schoolchildren learned to identify as white as they came to see American history as their own. Through the public schools, young Jews, mostly the children of Eastern European immigrants, participated widely in the celebration, dressing in colonial garb and helping to reenact scenes from the city's founding, like the signing of a 1652 treaty between the original white settlers and the native Susquehannock tribe. In the city's colonial mansions, whites from a variety of backgrounds re-created the lavish balls of the eighteenth-century gentry, while local African Americans were recruited to play the parts of house slaves. Participation in such events not only helped obscure the racial and cultural particularity of children from Jewish and other European immigrant backgrounds, but also allowed them to feel as if they were an integral part of white America.[5] Similar historical pageants, Thanksgiving Day celebrations, and other patriotic rituals that underscored the connection between race and American nationalism were staged by schools throughout the country during these years.[6]

The racial lessons imparted by the public school were often confirmed and expanded by Jews' encounter with mass culture. By the 1920s, the emergence of new popular forms of entertainment such as radio and movies provided immigrants and their children with a wide range of images that emphasized the centrality of the black-white divide in American life. While these media had a powerful effect on all Americanizing immigrant groups, Jews proved themselves among the most enthusiastic consumers of mass culture.[7] Young Jews had already been attuned to the racial politics of boxing since the Johnson-Jeffries match of 1915, an awareness that peaked after Jews entered the boxing profession in great numbers in the 1920s.[8] Radio shows like *Amos 'n' Andy*, a nightly serial that chronicled the adventures of two southern black migrants to the north and employed heavy stereotyping, were popular among Jewish audiences during the 1920s and 1930s.[9] Jews were first introduced to racial themes on the silver screen in 1915, when D. W. Griffith's *Birth of a Nation* premiered in the Jewish-owned nickelodeons that dotted the Jewish quarters of eastern cities.[10] By the late 1920s, Bruno Lasker, a Jewish sociologist who studied the racial attitudes of children, could write that motion pictures were one of the major means by which young Americans imbibed stereotypes of various racial and national groups.[11]

In addition to popular amusements like movies and radio, the expanding market of mass-produced consumer goods during the interwar years also helped acculturating Jews begin to understand the world in terms of "black" and "white." For Jews, participation in the country's culture of commercial abundance was a central means of claiming an American identity, and the prevalence of racial imagery in commercial culture strengthened the link between whiteness and Americanization.

16. Colonial Day, 1928. During the interwar years, the children of Eastern European Jewish immigrants learned the importance of whiteness not only in the classroom but through participation in historical pageants like this one in Annapolis, Maryland. (Courtesy Beverly Zaino)

Ads in the *Forverts* for products ranging from detergent to pancake flour offered images of African American domestics working in the homes of middle-class whites, with whom advertisers hoped the Yiddish-reading public would identify. Bringing racial icons such as Aunt Jemima (whose buckwheats were billed as an ideal replacement for latkes) within reach of immigrant readers, such advertisements helped Jews dreaming of success and mobility to understand these processes in racial terms. Ads for Old Gold Cigarettes drew on both communal pride and the popularity of the 1929 film *Whoopie* by featuring its Jewish star, Eddie Cantor, endorsing their product in blackface in the *Morgn zhurnal* (Jewish morning journal). Similarly, after the release of his hit movie, *The Singing Fool*, Al Jolson was recruited to sell Lucky Strikes to Jewish readers while donning burnt cork, telling them in their own language to "try a Lucky instead of a sweet *nasheray* [snack]."[12]

Eastern European Jews' increasing awareness of the black-white divide in American society was not only a result of the quickening pace of acculturation, but was also related to larger national shifts in racial demography. After 1915, the northern cities where most Jews lived were being transformed by the arrival of thousands of black migrants from the South. Some degree of segregation between blacks and whites had always existed in the north, but after World War I the boundaries separating these groups in the urban landscape became more distinct as whites grew fearful of the African American influx. According to a 1920 survey conducted by the Chicago Commission on Race Relations, northern cities had no Jim Crow policies in their schools or on trains and streetcars, but segregation was often practiced by owners of private enterprises like hotels, restaurants, and theaters.[13] In Chicago, the Jewish-owned Balaban and Katz movie theater chain enforced the color line not only with separate seating for blacks and whites, but by strategically placing black employees in stereotypical roles as doormen ("approaching the old southern coachman type"), maids, and washroom attendants.[14] Nowhere was the increasing importance of color distinctions more visible, however, than in residential patterns. As the number of black migrants rose to record numbers and the demand for new housing grew, whites resorted to both violence and an elaborate system of residential restrictions in order to keep African Americans out of their neighborhoods.

The growing importance of color in determining the social status of certain residential districts was not lost on Jews, who were actively involved in carving out their own spaces in the changing urban landscape. Acculturating Jews, explains historian Deborah Dash Moore, "came to accept the notion that where you lived told the world who you were."[15] As a result, they became anxious to avoid the stigma attached to living near African Americans. This concern was especially strong in older Jew-

17. Ad for Duz soap, 1927. National advertisers helped acculturating Jews see their struggle for upward social mobility in racial terms. Black domestics were frequently featured in ads in the *Forverts* and other Yiddish newspapers during the 1920s and 1930s. (Courtesy Forward Association)

ish neighborhoods, like Harlem or Chicago's Near West Side, where the homes vacated by upwardly mobile Jews allowed for the expansion of black settlement. According to Henry Roth, by 1927 the Jews of Harlem were increasingly conscious of the decline in status that an influx of non-whites had brought to their neighborhood. As Roth recalled in his fictionalized memoir, *From Bondage*, "125th Street, which had once appeared high-toned gentile, had become shabby. . . . The colored people, Negroes, they were called when they were referred to politely, slowly moved south from uptown, at the same time as Puerto Ricans settled at the other end of Harlem."[16] For Jews hoping to claim a place in the white middle class, these were precisely the types of changing neighborhoods they wished to escape.

In addition to shaping a new urban landscape defined in terms of race, the migration of African Americans to northern cities also heightened the significance of the black-white divide in the workplace. Unlike many non-Jewish immigrants from Eastern and Southern Europe who earned their living as steelworkers, meatpackers, or in other manufacturing and semi-skilled jobs, Jews working in the garment trades did not often work beside blacks, nor did they have an older, more Americanized guard of Irish, German, and Bohemian workers in their industries to sensitize them to the stigma of doing so.[17] Through the Depression, the industry remained dominated by Jewish—and to a lesser degree, Italian—immigrants, although the number of black women who worked as dressmakers rose dramatically between 1920 and 1930.[18] Yet even in the comparatively homogenous garment trades, Jews increasingly learned the connections made in American culture between work, color, and social status. Beginning in 1917, several garment manufacturers in Chicago, New York, and Philadelphia used young black women as strikebreakers and after 1920 began a concerted drive in South Chicago to recruit blacks to work in nonunion shops.[19] Until the 1930s, most of the African Americans in the garment trades remained outside the pale of organized labor, working at much lower wages and for longer hours than their Jewish and Italian coworkers, a factor that helped solidify the importance of whiteness as an element of Jewish working-class identity.

Finally, the expanding role of acculturating Jews in retail trade during the interwar period also helped immerse them in the culture of "black" and "white." While Jews in the South had long specialized in commercial dealings with African Americans, such relationships had remained less developed in the North in the years before World War I. With the large-scale migration of African Americans to the region, however, an increasing number of Jews in cities like New York, Chicago, and Detroit began to cater to the needs of the growing black population. Jews not only opened groceries, clothing stores, and pawnshops in African American neighborhoods but also ran hotels, bars, and movie houses that served an exclusively black clientele. While Jews' willingness to locate their businesses in black neighborhoods represented, to some extent, their insensitivity to American racial taboos, Jewish merchants serving black customers during the 1920s and 1930s did not remain unaware of the significance of the color line for very long.[20]

Many of the African Americans with whom Jewish merchants came into contact were fresh arrivals from the South and often had little understanding of the ways that Jews differed from other "white folks." Richard Wright, who arrived in Chicago from the South in 1916 and found one of his first jobs in a Jewish-owned grocery store, recalled how he "grossly . . . misread the motives and attitudes" of his employers, who he assumed held the same view of blacks as the white neighbors he had left behind in Alabama.[21] Yet if Jewish attitudes rarely resembled those of southern whites, interactions with customers and employees who saw the world in terms of "black" and "white" often pushed Jews toward a greater understanding of these categories. Events like the Chicago Race Riot of 1919 sensitized them to the black-white racial divide, especially since several Jews were attacked during the riot by African Americans who failed, in the heat of battle, to differentiate them from other whites.[22] Experiences as victims of crime in African American neighborhoods also led Jewish merchants to absorb many of the larger society's stereotypes about blacks and to often single them out as a special threat.[23] By the mid-1920s, most Jews who remained in African American districts did so not because they were unaware of the stigma of living and working among blacks but because their modest resources prevented them from opening shops in more "respectable" surroundings.[24]

As all of these examples suggest, Eastern European Jewish immigrants and their children were increasingly experiencing a world divided into "black" and "white" and finding it more and more difficult to remain aloof from identification with those categories. Because of the particular intensity of their own minority group consciousness, however, they often approached these new opportunities for incorporation into white America with greater ambivalence than had the acculturated community of Central European Jews earlier in the century. On the one hand, their experiences with pogroms, economic hardship, residential restrictions, and other features of life in Eastern Europe made them anxious to pursue acceptance in America. Identification with whiteness, Jews came to find, not only gave them greater chances for advancement but also allowed them to experience what it was like *not* to be the focus of national hostility and resentment. On the other hand, they also had some strong emotional reservations about acquiring the status of whites. While they desired acceptance in racial terms, it was often difficult for them to aspire to the discriminatory behavior of non-Jews, from which they themselves had often suffered. The fact that these Jews had long defined themselves against the exclusionary and sometimes violent tendencies of their non-Jewish neighbors often made them anxious to adopt a more benevolent attitude toward African Americans.

The ambivalence with which Eastern European Jews embraced whiteness during the 1920s and 1930s was not only a product of their historical
memory, but was constantly reinforced by the antisemitism and social
pressures of the interwar years. Even as Jews climbed the economic ladder
during the 1920s and 1930s and enjoyed a high level of occupational and
residential mobility, the problematic nature of their own "racial" status
left them excluded from the elite institutions of non-Jewish society. Quotas and anti-Jewish restrictions proliferated during this period, and housing patterns in major urban centers like New York revealed a higher degree of segregation between Jews and non-Jews than they had in previous
decades.[25] Jews encountered hostility not only from native-born Americans who tried to keep them out of the universities, clubs, and neighborhoods they wished to enter, but also from fellow immigrant groups. Well
into the 1940s, the borders of Jewish neighborhoods were marked by
conflict with Irish, Poles, and Lithuanians.[26] Such experiences, which were
ever present in the lives of American Jews during these years, often left
them feeling torn about their approach to American race relations. Even
at its worst, antisemitism never led most Jews to question their basic faith
in integration into American society, and could therefore make Jews work
harder to fit in, inspiring identification with the dominant racial mores.
At the same time, however, antisemitism could complicate Jews' identification with whiteness. If those living in the large Jewish enclaves of northern cities longed to be a part of the "real" America, the sheltered environment of the Jewish neighborhood, with its own versions of American
institutions, gave them space to assert alternate views of American identity. Finally, if the daily indignities of antisemitism made Jews want to
become less conspicuous as a problematic "racial" group, the antipathy
with which they viewed both elitist patricians and street roughs who
preyed on Jewish youth often made them question their desire to imitate
racist patterns of behavior.

Because the longer-settled Central European Jews were as sensitive to
the increased antisemitism of the 1920s and 1930s as their Eastern European counterparts, they too often began to question their desire to emu-
late the posture of white gentiles toward African Americans. Central European Jews remained strongly committed to their pursuit of acceptance
in white America, but the tensions of the interwar period made them decidedly more ambivalent about their relationship to whiteness. Furthermore, even though memories of European persecution were much fainter
for the Central Europeans than for the more recently arrived Eastern Europeans, memories of the murder of Leo Frank came painfully to mind
as the lynching campaign against southern blacks intensified after World
War I. Thus, while the older and newer communities of Jews had taken
starkly different approaches to the issue of race during the first two de-

cades of the twentieth century, during the 1920s and 1930s the two groups began to converge in their struggle with conflicting emotions concerning African Americans.

Between Empathy and Aspiration

The significant contradictions in the approach of Jews to African Americans in the 1920s and 1930s have often eluded historians of black-Jewish relations, many of whom have focused more intently on Jews' positive orientation toward blacks than on the pressures Jews felt to conform to the standards of white America.[27] Although it is true that an increasing number of Jews became active in the struggle for black civil rights during this period, a closer survey of Jewish social patterns and Jewish discourse about African Americans reveals that only a small minority of American Jews felt free enough from the daunting social pressures of white America to engage in consistent high-profile advocacy of black causes.

Mirroring the pattern of the early twentieth century, the most committed Jewish civil rights activists in the 1920s and 1930s came mainly from the ranks of Jews who had either carved out a role for themselves in the larger, non-Jewish world or had broken with formal Jewish affiliation altogether. Although these individuals were not totally immune from the sting of antisemitism, they all enjoyed a degree of independence from the social pressures experienced by most average Jews. The brothers Joel and Arthur Spingarn, who served successively as presidents of the NAACP, as well as Herbert Seligman, the organization's publicist, had no formal ties to the Jewish community and their status in the non-Jewish world was never seriously threatened by their somewhat obscure Jewish origins.[28] Anthropologist Franz Boas—a full professor at Columbia from 1899— helped undermine many of the scientific theories about black inferiority, but he rarely identified himself as a Jew and did not take up the problem of racial antisemitism with any regularity until the rise of the Nazi regime in Germany in the 1930s.[29] Although there were a few figures like American Jewish Committee chief Louis Marshall, who were visibly connected with Jewish affairs and also worked for organizations like the NAACP, they were generally the exception to the rule.[30] If many of the Jews who immersed themselves in civil rights activity were acting on impulses that stemmed from their background as Jews, it was actually their distance from the Jewish world that freed them to support African American causes in such visible ways.

Along with this highly assimilated group of Jewish civil rights activists, there were also others who had greater attachments to the Jewish community but felt free to express their concern and empathy for African Americans because their wealth, their particular professional circumstances, or their radical ideologies insulated them from concerns about winning the approval of non-Jews. Despite the fact that non-Jewish whites sometimes criticized the prominent Chicago philanthropist Julius Rosenwald for his kindness toward blacks, he worried little that such activities would threaten his standing as a major community builder and humanitarian.[31] Similarly, congressmen like the Lower East Side's Meyer London or Brownsville's Emanuel Celler relied on largely Jewish constituencies and felt they could speak freely in support of African American labor and against lynching without any serious repercussions from voters.[32] Finally, the radicalism of Jewish labor leaders also gave them an independence that allowed them to flout the racial conventions of most non-Jewish unions. While their Jewishness may have made them more sensitive than non-Jewish labor leaders to the plight of blacks, their socialism allowed them to resist American standards more easily than other acculturating Jews of the period.[33] As liberal activist David Pierce explained in 1925, because most Jews were too restrained by the expectations of the larger society to dedicate themselves to any consistent support of African American causes, "Negro champions among the Jews must be limited to wealthy philanthropists, members of radical labor groups and freelance intellectuals."[34]

Although omitted from Pierce's list, rabbis were also among the leading Jewish advocates of African American rights during the 1920s and 1930s, since they, too, felt little direct social pressure from non-Jews who may have objected to such sentiments. Thus, Emil G. Hirsch, rabbi of Chicago's Sinai Temple, felt free to compare the race riots in Chicago in 1919 to the pogroms in Poland, even though his congregants may have shied away from such an analogy.[35] Alexander Lyons, leader of Brooklyn's Eighth Street Temple, was a strong opponent of lynching and spoke out against it in Sabbath sermons and in the Jewish press.[36] Stephen S. Wise, a long-standing advocate for black rights who became one of the leading figures in the American rabbinate during the interwar period, was one of the principal speakers at a national conference on lynching held in New York.[37] The Reform rabbinical association, the Central Conference of American Rabbis (CCAR), resolved as a group to work for an anti-lynching law and the abolition of the poll tax in the southern states.[38] Yet even among rabbis, active support of black civil rights tended to come only from Reform leaders, many of whom were significantly involved in ecumenical work and were highly regarded in the non-Jewish world. Rabbis of the Orthodox and nascent Conservative movements were apparently not focused enough on the American social scene or were too conscious of their congregants' pursuit of social status to take a great interest in African American affairs.[39]

In order to derive a more balanced view of the Jewish approach to African Americans during the interwar years, we must look beyond this rather exceptional group of civil rights activists and philanthropists, whose experiences do not convey the complex and contradictory pressures the majority of American Jews felt concerning racial issues. Granted, we should not dismiss the significance of their efforts, because in many ways they do underscore the particular sense of identification interwar Jews often had with blacks. Measured against other groups of white Americans, Jews *were* conspicuous during the 1920s and 1930s in their sympathetic attitudes toward African Americans and in their frequent support of black causes. At the same time, however, it is critical to point out that for most American Jews of the period, these positions could not be taken in any kind of consistent manner, due to the constant pressures they faced in their fight for social acceptance. Instead, Jews largely remained torn between their empathy for blacks and their aspirations for full acceptance in white America.

By far, Jews in the South remained the segment of American Jewry most limited in expressing empathy for African Americans, even as their sense of identification with black plight became more intense in the 1920s and 1930s. Following the national pattern, a small group of Southern Jewish activists, mostly clergy and well-integrated civic leaders, began to take more visible stands in support of black causes during this period. In Atlanta, Rabbi David Marx became a founder of the Committee for Racial Cooperation and petitioned city officials to desegregate parks that were closed to blacks.[40] Reflecting the ongoing bitterness of Atlanta Jews over the lynching of Leo Frank, three socially prominent women from Marx's congregation joined the Association of Southern Women for the Prevention of Lynching.[41] When an African American was lynched in Memphis, the local rabbi, William Fineshriber, called a meeting of his congregation to denounce the violence, a gathering that would have been highly unusual just a decade earlier.[42] But even as some southern Jews intensified their efforts to aid blacks during these years, it is clear that southern Jewry as a whole remained extremely reticent to visibly differentiate themselves from their white neighbors concerning matters of race. Atlanta's *Southern Israelite* occasionally reported on the efforts of national Jewish organizations to lobby for antilynching laws, but refrained from supporting such legislation directly.[43] When northern Jewish papers strongly criticized the prevalence of lynching in the South, the *Israelite* urged them to focus instead on their own pressing social problems, like "Chicago Gangland and its wholesale butchery."[44] The paper also defended the practice of racial segregation against the criticism of northern Jewish journalists. "All white people know that there is nothing to be gained by seeking to send white children and colored to the same schools," wrote the editor in 1928. "That question has long been settled in intelligent minds."[45]

It was not only in the South, however, where Jewish empathy for African Americans vied with the need to safeguard Jewish social status. Although not as constrained as their southern counterparts by the demands of local racial etiquette, Jews of the urban north also exhibited a high degree of contradiction in their approach toward blacks. In the Jewish-dominated garment industry, where socialist labor leaders demonstrated an unusual level of commitment to the unionization of African Americans, the rank and file of Jewish workers forged a decidedly more ambivalent position. At times, Jewish members of the International Ladies' Garment Workers' Union (ILGWU) and Amalgamated Clothing Workers of America strongly supported the racial activism of their leadership and stood out among American workers in their warmth and even enthusiasm for the cause of African American labor. During the 1920s, Jewish unionists showed themselves willing to strike against employers who segregated black and white employees and denied African Americans fair treatment and equal wages.[46] In several cases, Jewish-dominated locals made the symbolic gesture of electing black workers to positions of leadership, in some instances electing African American presidents. When Frank Hall, an African American member of the Cloak Button Workers' Union in New York, was elected to the highest post in his local in 1924, the ILGWU organ *Justice* pointed to the "spirit of genuine trade union equality and absence of race feeling" such a move represented.[47] But these warm attitudes among Jews in the industry often vied with much more negative feelings concerning blacks, who could also be seen as a threat to Jewish economic advancement and job stability.

As one member of the ILGWU recalled of the 1920s, many Jewish workers greeted the entrance of blacks into the trade with pessimism, citing their willingness to work for low wages and their lack of enthusiasm for labor unions.[48] According to African American labor activist Edith Kine, even in the dressmaking and allied trades, where black women were a significant factor by the late 1920s, "they were regarded with suspicion and distrust by the white workers, in those years largely Jewish women, who looked upon the Negro girls as prospective strike breakers and as an element that would eventually degrade working conditions."[49] Occasionally, tensions between blacks and Jews boiled over, as they did in Philadelphia in 1921 when black labor was used to replace striking Jewish workers. "Bitter fighting took place between pickets and scabs," reported one source, and "scissors and pins were used freely by both sides."[50] Even when blacks were not serving as strikebreakers, relations between the two groups were not always of a high order. "Some of the white members of our organization . . . do not care to mingle with the Negro girls," reported Sidney Schiff, a Jewish member of the Dressmaker's Local 22, in a 1924 letter to *Justice*. "One Negro woman whom I know has no one with whom to exchange a syllable during the eight hours of work."[51]

This fluctuation between feelings of camaraderie and suspicion for their African American coworkers seems to have characterized the attitudes of Jewish workers in the garment industry through the mid-1930s. When Charles Franklin investigated the treatment of blacks in various labor unions in New York in 1935, he found Jewish-dominated unions like the ILGWU to be exceptionally liberal in their treatment of black workers. Yet while managers of various locals generally revealed a commitment to the union's official ideology of racial harmony, their occasional references to blacks as "naturally lazy and unthrifty" or as potential strikebreakers revealed the ongoing feelings of ambivalence they harbored.[52] Significantly, racial liberalism within the unions only reached its high point after a large number of Jews began to leave the industry in favor of more lucrative white-collar jobs and the organization of blacks became more critical to the union's effectiveness and stability. The remaining Jewish garment workers, most of them highly skilled, were of sufficiently high status within the industry that they had little to fear from the presence of blacks in their midst.[53]

The way in which concern for their own status prevented Jews from taking consistently liberal positions toward African Americans during the 1920s and 1930s was also apparent in their drive for new and better housing during these years. Jews often expressed a strong distaste for housing discrimination because of their history with residential restrictions in Eastern Europe and their awareness that many exclusive neighborhoods in the United States enforced anti-Jewish covenants. In the early 1920s, one Jewish landlord interviewed by sociologist Louis Wirth defended his policy of renting to African Americans, arguing that "we Jews ought to be the last ones to hold a prejudice against another race after all we've been through."[54] Another Chicagoan drew an even more explicit parallel between black and Jewish history in stating his opposition to residential restriction. "What has segregation done for the Jews?" he asked, invoking examples of the medieval Jewish ghettos and the Pale of Settlement in Russia. "It curtailed their rise, depriving them of an opportunity to develop, and I foresee the same result in the new segregation movement, and therefore deem it a great public evil and moral issue."[55]

But while Jews expressed such sentiments freely, they were not always warm to the prospect of having African American neighbors and often did what they could to avoid close residential proximity to blacks. Among those most desperate to assert their standing as white, violent conflict with blacks was not unknown. Poor working-class Jews in Brooklyn's Brownsville section, for example, saw arriving blacks as a threat to the status of their neighborhood, which most of them could not afford to leave. Between 1925 and 1927, at least three riots broke out in Brownsville between African Americans and Jews, leading one community leader to denounce blacks as members of a "downtrodden, confused race" who had disturbed the beauty and respectability of the district.[56] Elsewhere, Jews expressed their fear of neighborhood change by joining restriction movements. In Harlem, Jewish real estate owners participated in the effort to prevent the spread of blacks below 110th Street, while Jews living on the West Side of Manhattan were among the leaders of the Property Owners of Washington Heights, a group that proposed restrictive covenants to exclude "people of African descent or of the Negro race or blood" from their neighborhood.[57] In Chicago during the 1920s, Jews in Hyde Park and Woodlawn continued the restrictionist activities carried on by Jewish residents there during the previous decade.[58]

Reflecting the tensions that characterized the Jewish approach to housing restriction, many of those who participated in restriction movements did so with significant discomfort. One Harlem landlord, Harry Bierhoff, initially supported the effort to curtail black settlement in the area, but after the Ku Klux Klan warned him not to rent to blacks, he declared himself a firm believer in the right of all people to live where they wanted.[59] Driven by similar feelings of inner conflict, Jewish landlords involved in the restriction movement often went to great lengths to deny any racist motivations. Harlem landlords had long contended that their interest in containing black settlement was not a matter of race hatred but of economics.[60] In 1926, Jews involved in the Property Owners Association of Washington Heights argued that theirs was "not an effort at race discrimination but a matter of preserving present values and making possible the enjoyment of increased value when the new subway is completed."[61]

In general, however, most Jews of the period demonstrated their ambivalence about housing issues by moving away from changing neighborhoods rather than staying and fighting to maintain them as white. When the Abramson family, depicted in Meyer Levin's *The Old Bunch*, begins speculating about how "niggers" will ruin Chicago's Lawndale neighborhood, they do not speak of preventing the influx but of relocating to the north side of town, "where the better class of people were moving."[62] Moving allowed Jews to escape the poor conditions and social stigma they feared would accompany incoming African Americans, but it also allowed them to avoid the moral dilemmas presented by involvement in violent clashes or restrictionist activity. This response to neighborhood change marked Jews off sharply from the Irish and other—mainly Catholic—immigrant groups, who frequently resorted to violence in responding to neighborhood change. The Jews' approach can be explained in part by their greater economic mobility, which made it easier for them to leave, and by the fact that Jewish religious institutions, unlike Catholic churches, were not tied to a particular parish and could therefore be readily transplanted to new locations. But flight from changing neighborhoods was also motivated by the desire of Jews to escape the particularly wrenching emotional dilemmas posed by the other alternatives.[63]

If Jews' response to neighborhood change demonstrated their contradictory and uneven approach to African Americans during the 1920s and 1930s, nowhere did their sentiments combine in such paradoxical ways as in the field of popular culture. Few immigrant groups embraced popular music, film, sports, and other forms of mass entertainment as enthusiastically as the Jews, who saw them as major vehicles for claiming their status as white Americans.[64] Yet popular media and leisure activities also provided them with a comparatively free and flexible arena in which they could express empathy for African Americans and their strong affinity for black culture.

Not surprisingly, it was in Yiddish that the most assertive statements of identification with African Americans were made during the 1920s and 1930s. In their own language, unintelligible to a non-Jewish audience, Jewish writers could afford to express their deeply held emotional identification with blacks. Writers of the Yiddish press, many of whom had radical leanings and a significant level of secular education, were usually cognizant of the social issues of the "outside" world, yet sheltered from significant pressure to conform to prevailing American attitudes. As a result, the Yiddish press not only championed black rights but also showed its enthusiasm for what was considered a spiritual kinship between blacks and Jews. This enthusiasm was evident in 1927, when Carl Laemmle, the Jewish owner of Universal Studios, presented a film version of *Uncle Tom's Cabin*. The Yiddish press ran special advertisements for the production, emphasizing the deep interest they felt Jews would take in it. "WHEN A PEOPLE IS FREED FROM SLAVERY," proclaimed a notice in the *Forverts*, "the most profound joy grows in the hearts of the Jewish people, because to the present day we cannot forget our own slavery in Egypt."[65]

The tendency to emphasize the bonds of empathy between Jews and African Americans was not only reflected in the press but in Yiddish poetry and belles lettres of the period. The poet Berish Weinstein, for example, a member of the "Introspectivist" school of Yiddish writers, authored a number of poems exploring themes like life in the rural "Negro village," the migration to Harlem, and the plight of African American workers.[66] Yiddish writers were particularly attracted to the subject of lynching, which not only inspired poems by Weinstein, but several short stories by

Joseph Opatoshu.[67] According to the literary critic Isaac Rontch, almost all of the Yiddish authors who flourished in America between the wars focused at least some of their writings on African Americans. The Yiddish writer, explained Rontch, "himself a child of an oppressed people, is forever on the alert to hear and sense the ever-present protest of the Negro against his white discriminator."[68]

As strongly as Yiddish authors asserted their identification with blacks, however, it is also important to see their writings as part of larger constellation of Jewish cultural expressions that often combined empathy for African Americans with the desire to identify as white. Essential here is the fact that by the 1920s, the Yiddish press served as only one source of news and entertainment for acculturating Jews, who were increasingly becoming focused on English-language media. As a result, the Yiddish press took on the role of trying to supplement, and often counteract, the more mainstream values Jews were exposed to through other forms of mass culture. Yiddish sources often expressed an uncharacteristic empathy for African Americans because they were trying to mitigate what was perceived as the cultural loss associated with Jews' identification with the white mainstream. It was this tendency, no doubt, that led the Yiddish press to downplay the demeaning use of blackface minstrelsy in its coverage of *The Jazz Singer* (1927) and instead to emphasize the cultural affinity between blacks and Jews suggested by Al Jolson's performance as the son of a cantor who—in the words of the *Forverts*—"knows how to sing the songs of the most cruelly wronged people in the world's history."[69]

To take the *Forverts*' interpretation as the final word on *The Jazz Singer*, however, is to miss the striking ambivalence embedded in the landmark film. From the time Jolson's character, Jack Robin (né Jakie Rabinowitz), leaves behind his provincial Jewish world to become a performer who sings "mammy" songs in blackface, race emerges as a central element in his larger struggle with the forces of assimilation and loyalty to his Jewish past. While Jolson's blackface scenes employ the racist stereotypes of the day, they also suggest the powerful emotional identification of acculturating Jews with African Americans. Becoming a blackface performer is what propels Jack Robin out of his Jewish "ghetto" and into the white world of American show business, but his ability to use the black mask to express "Jewish" emotions—such as the pain he feels over the rift with his traditionalist father—gives minstrelsy a double utility for him.

This reading of the *Jazz Singer* seems to confirm the suggestion of writer Ronald Sanders that Jewish performers often used blackface as a way of expressing emotions that they did not feel comfortable expressing as Jews. In this scenario, the use of blackface obscured the performer's Jewishness and, through the use of heavy stereotype, focused the audience's attention on the black-white divide. But at the same time, blackface made the African American subject available as a surrogate for Jewish expression, combining, albeit uneasily, what Sanders calls an "element of longing admiration" with the racist elements of the performance.[70] It is significant that many of the Jews who made use of African American stereotypes—performers like Jolson and Fanny Brice—started their careers as Jewish "racial" comedians and turned to black material as their heightened desire for acceptance made it increasingly difficult for them to express themselves through the elaboration of Jewish "types."[71] Blackface allowed them to address the conflicting emotions that grew out of this dilemma.

Other forms of Jewish cultural expression also combined the elements of antiblack racism and identification with African Americans that were present in blackface. Many Jewish musicians during the 1920s and 1930s strongly identified with African American music, even as they tried to avoid too close an association with it. Irving Berlin got his start in the early part of the century writing "coon songs" and ragtime classics like "Alexander's Ragtime Band," but by the 1920s he tried to obscure his debt to black culture by asserting that "our popular songwriters are not negroes but of pure white blood . . . many of Russian ancestry."[72] Similarly, critic Abraham Roback argued that Jewish musicians had not simply adopted black musical culture wholesale, but had introduced a "note of restraint" into the "wild gyrations of the original jazz."[73] Jewish sports figures were also pulled between a sense of identification with their black counterparts and the need to assert their status as white. In the field of boxing, African Americans and Jews had very parallel experiences in trying to win respect for the "toughness" and ability of their groups.[74] Consciousness of these similarities, however, often led Jews to waver in their approach to black opponents. Benny Leonard, perhaps the most famous Jewish boxer of the period, broke with the tradition of excluding African Americans from contention for the heavyweight championship and agreed to face "all comers, regardless of race, color or creed."[75] But in 1930, Al Singer, the Jewish lightweight champion of the world, fell back on the sport's racial exclusivity when he refused a match with the well-known Afro-Cuban boxer, Kid Chocolate.[76]

This ambivalent approach to black culture was exemplified not only by actors, musicians, and sports figures of Jewish origin, but also by the young Jewish consumers of popular media and entertainment. As memoir literature reveals, cultural excursions into black America often gave young Jews of the period a sense of freedom and individuality that they were lacking in their day-to-day attempts to fit into the white mainstream. Many were drawn to the assertiveness and eroticism of the "race records" that were mass produced beginning in the 1920s, and some, like the young Kate Simon, were driven by their curiosity to seek out the nightclubs and dance halls of Harlem and other black neighborhoods in the urban North.

If Simon was attracted by the lures of Harlem, however, she quickly abandoned her "slumming" adventure when struck with fear over the danger and inappropriateness of a possible liaison with an African American man.[77] The "slumming" escapades of the young Chicago Jews depicted in Meyer Levin's *The Old Bunch* were also wrought with contradiction. The young men described by Levin relished the explicit lyrics of "race records" and sought out sexual experiences with African American women, but they referred to their conquests as "dark meat" and discussed them in the most racially demeaning terms.[78] Thus, while "slumming" in black neighborhoods offered Jewish youth an opportunity to escape from the demanding pressures of conformity they experienced in their everyday lives, it also provided ways of underscoring their status as white.

Similar contradictions were apparent in the homegrown cultural media of American Jews. English-language publications of the Jewish community regularly lauded black cultural achievements, but also included humorous sketches and dialect stories that exploited African American stereotypes. These were regularly featured not only in southern papers like the newsletter of Atlanta's Jewish Progressive Club, which printed items such as "Darky Philosophy" and "Mammy Tale," but also in nationally distributed journals such as the *B'nai B'rith Magazine*, which ran a series of jokes lampooning blacks during the 1920s.[79] Some of the same publications that regularly decried lynching and praised black artistic endeavors also used degrading terms such as "darky" to refer to African Americans.[80]

In addition to Jewish publications, the stages of Jewish community centers also presented strongly contradictory images of African Americans. In Atlanta, organizations such as the Jewish Progressive Club and the local chapter of Hadassah staged regular minstrel shows that drew record crowds.[81] Minstrel shows were also featured, albeit less frequently, at the Chicago Hebrew Institute, a youth and recreation center that founded its own "minstrel organization" in 1916.[82] But programs such as these were presented alongside other musical and theatrical events that indicated a strong admiration for black culture and the willingness of Jews to stretch the lines of segregation practiced by most white social clubs and organizations. The Jewish People's Institute (JPI), the successor to the Chicago Hebrew Institute, regularly hosted black musical acts and in 1932 featured their own version of Eugene O'Neill's *Emperor Jones*, in which the well-known African American actor Jack Smith starred alongside members of the JPI's own dramatic troupe. By the mid-1930s, even Atlanta's Jewish Progressive Club hosted black groups like Noble Sissle's Orchestra, who were given a warm reception uncharacteristic of the southern environment.[83]

18. Jews blacking up, 1925. This minstrel show was sponsored by the Atlanta chapter of Hadassah and was held at the city's Jewish Progressive Club. While Jews of Eastern European background saw minstrelsy as an avenue to Americanization, they also frequently embraced black culture as a temporary escape from the pressures of conformity in white America. (Courtesy Ida Pearle and Joseph Cuba Archives of the Breman Museum, Atlanta)

The Depression Years

While complex social pressures pushed American Jews to adopt a contradictory stance toward African Americans throughout the interwar period, the years of the Great Depression produced some particularly intense manifestations of Jewish ambivalence toward blacks that deserve special analysis. While Jews generally weathered the economic crisis better than most other Americans, fears about economic insecurity combined with concern over a new and more virulent strain of antisemitism that emerged in the 1930s.[84] Especially with the rise of the Nazi regime in Germany in 1933, American Jews began to worry that profascist groups in the United States might succeed in spreading Hitler's worldview among the American public. Although the anti-Jewish rhetoric of the period relied on a set of images and assumptions quite different from those employed against blacks, many American Jews came to increasingly identify with African Americans as a group that shared with them the experience of racial ostracism from the white American mainstream. In 1934, Jacob Weinstein, a Reform rabbi and a leader of the American Civil Liberties Union, argued that white Americans saw both blacks and Jews as political agitators and "tar[red] them with the same brush." The rabbi also suggested that the rise of racial antisemitism in Germany had allowed Jews to see an increasing number of parallels between their own group's experience and that of African Americans. "The recent lynchings in the South and the legislation passed against Jews in Germany," he wrote, "resurrect the[se] . . . parallels from the limbo of historical curiosity and make them the models for the actual happenings of our day."[85] Ultimately, however, the developments during the 1930s put American Jews in an increasingly difficult position, encouraging a heightened sense of Jewish identification with blacks but also pushing them to secure their uncertain position as whites.

The stresses of the Depression Era led to an unprecedented degree of discontent among Jews, sometimes making them more willing than before to question the basic tenets of American life. Because increasing economic deprivation was accompanied by a rising tide of antisemitism, many Jews began to question the country's system of social relations in addition to the soundness of its economic structure. This sense of alienation was most forcefully expressed by the large number of Jews who joined the radical movements that flourished in Depression-era Jewish neighborhoods. While Jewish radicals addressed the problem of antisemitism by refusing to draw lines between people of various "national" backgrounds and stressing the universalism of their goals, they also focused on the plight of African Americans and usually demonstrated a greater sensitivity than their non-Jewish comrades to the problem of antiblack racism.

For Jewish radicals who usually restricted their activities to Jewish arenas, black rights was one of the major issues that could draw them out to participate in political agitation in the non-Jewish world. This was dramatically displayed in 1934 when David Dubinsky, the socialist president of the ILGWU, ordered a walkout at the union's convention after discovering that the hotel where the meeting was taking place had refused to accommodate black delegates.[86] Irving Howe recalled how, as a member of the Young People's Socialist League, he and his friends would make a rare trip outside of the Bronx in order to distribute leaflets on 125th Street and Lenox Avenue in Harlem.[87] In fact, during the Depression, hundreds of young Jews not only made temporary sojourns in black neighborhoods, but many left behind their provincial Jewish settings altogether to work full time as communist agitators and labor organizers in the American South, as well as in major black urban centers like Harlem and Chicago's South Side. In locations such as these, they organized protests, rent strikes, and consumer boycotts, helped blacks find employment, and taught them the principles of radicalism. In Harlem, Jewish communist women played a particularly important role as teachers in the public schools, where they fought to improve conditions, secure textbooks of equal quality to those used in white neighborhoods, and introduce African American history into the curriculum.[88]

Although only a minority of Jews officially joined the Communist or Socialist Parties, the success and influence of these movements during the Depression indicated that many Jews shared the feelings of discontent they expressed, including their opposition to America's increasingly anti-black and antisemitic climate. Even in the mainstream Jewish press there was a growing recognition that Depression Era Jews and blacks faced many of the same problems and shared many enemies. "By now it must be fairly clear to Jews that their position as a minority group parallels that of the Negro," explained the *American Hebrew* in 1934. "These hatreds go hand in hand, as we have seen in the case of the Ku Klux Klan, and to remain apathetic to hatred of the Negro is to encourage hatred of the Jew." Linking the plight of blacks and Jews in a way few Jewish organs had previously been willing to do, the *Hebrew* argued forcefully that "there can be no consistent fight against race hatred unless that fight is carried out against all forms of racial animosity."[89]

The growing feeling among American Jews that their fate was intimately linked with that of African Americans was expressed most vocally in Jewish support for the Scottsboro Boys, the nine black Alabama youths who faced false charges of rape between 1931 and 1935. Propelled by an increasing tendency among Jews to see antiblack racism and antisemitism as emanating from the same sources, Jewish support for the "Scottsboro Nine" flowed from every segment of the Jewish community, from radical to conservative, Yiddish speaking to Americanized. According to Hasia Diner, no other topic concerning African Americans laid a greater claim on the Jewish imagination or received more attention in the Jewish press during these years than did the Scottsboro trial.[90]

Yet despite the increasing sense of identification many Jews began to feel with African Americans in the 1930s, most American Jews remained fearful of being placed in the same category with blacks as racial outsiders.[91] Writer Alfred Kazin recalled how the insecurities brought on by the Depression made Jews, especially poorer ones, nervous about their racial standing. Kazin, the son of a house painter who grew up in the working-class Brooklyn neighborhood of Brownsville, described the "strange, embarrassed resentment" that bubbled to the surface in his home when African Americans began to move to nearby Livonia Avenue and started competing with local Jews, including Kazin's father, for work. "They were moving nearer and nearer," he recalled hearing at the dinner table. "They were invading our neighborhood."[92] Often this kind of fear and anger was expressed by Jews whose financial reverses had denied them the kind of mobility that would formerly have allowed them to move away from areas of expanding black settlement. Similarly, Jewish mer-

19. "Justice in the South," 1927. Jewish radicals like cartoonist William Groper, who published this graphic image in the Yiddish communist press, became passionate critics of racial injustice in interwar America. During the Great Depression, Jewish communists and socialists focused even more intently on the problem of antiblack racism, and found widespread support for their views among discontented American Jews. (From William Groper, *Di goldene medine*, courtesy Klau Library, Hebrew Union College–Jewish Institute of Religion, Cincinnati)

chants who served black areas became increasingly stigmatized during the Depression. In fact, the number of Jews operating such establishments increased during this period as higher rents and the decline in the retail trade forced them out of more "respectable" neighborhoods. The combination of Jewish merchants trapped at the lowest level of the retail trade and black customers struggling for survival often created tension between Jewish merchants and their black customers, leading to a steady erosion of their long-standing relationship. By the mid-1930s, clashes between the two groups—usually verbal but sometimes involving physical confrontation—became increasingly common.[93]

One of the most vivid signs of how the insecurity of the Depression pushed Jews to assert their whiteness was the rise of so-called "slave markets" in urban Jewish neighborhoods. Frustrated in their drive for social status by the economic crisis, lower-middle-class Jewish women in New York City began to take increasing advantage of the ready availability of black domestic labor at cheap prices. According to one account, many of these housewives who had "dreamed of the luxury of a maid, found opportunity staring her in the face in the form of Negro women pressed to the wall by poverty, starvation and discrimination."[94] By the early 1930s, the Bronx especially became known as the site of many street corner "slave markets," the largest of them being located at 167th Street and Jerome Avenue in the western part of the borough and on Simpson and Westchester Avenues in the eastern section. Here, Jewish housewives would bargain with black women for their services, offering between fifteen and thirty-five cents an hour.[95] According to St. Clair Drake and Horace Cayton, who studied black life in Chicago during the Depression, such "slave markets" were also a fixture on the street corners of that city's West Side.[96]

Because the pressures of the Depression Era pulled Jews in opposing directions on the issue of African Americans so intensely, it is not surprising that the treatment of blacks became a source of conflict between different segments of the Jewish community. Many Jewish communists, particularly those who affiliated with the English-speaking branch of the Communist Party, had ostensibly broken their ties with the Jewish community in favor of a class-based, universalist view of the world. Nevertheless, they consistently revealed the Jewish roots of their antiracist activities by attacking nonradical Jews for racist attitudes they deemed inappropriate to Jewish historical sensibility. "I have no sympathy for the upper class Jew who wails about discrimination at Harvard or at high class hotels, because all of them unite in discrimination against the Negro," wrote Michael Gold in the Communist journal *Liberator*. "Many who got the same sort of treatment in Russia now hand it back to the Negro."[97] Jewish communists in Harlem frequently led local African Americans in rent strikes against Jewish landlords and participated in the commercial boycotts against Jewish merchants. At the same time, many Jews criticized the communists for inciting blacks against them.[98] The internecine struggle of Jews over the treatment of blacks was even apparent in the landscape of Jewish settlement in the Bronx. While middle-class Jewish housewives were bargaining for African American domestic servants in the "slave markets" in the middle-class sections of the borough, Jewish communists who belonged to the International Workers Order defiantly built one of the city's first racially integrated cooperative housing projects nearby, creating a community, according to one account, where the black children spoke better Yiddish than their Jewish playmates.[99]

Jewish communists, however, did not reserve their sharp criticism for Jewish merchants and other "bourgeois" Jews but also attacked Jewish socialists and leaders of the major Jewish unions for their attitudes toward African Americans.[100] Even within their own ranks, Jewish communists demonstrated an almost obsessive need to root out the most minor expressions of racism. Staging what they called "white chauvinism trials," they "convicted" their own Jewish members who were caught uttering racist statements or who refused to participate in party work in African American neighborhoods. In 1932, at a trial organized by the Brownsville section of the Communist Party and held at the Brownsville Labor Lyceum, a member was charged with mentioning to one of his comrades that he did not want his daughter to marry an African American. Israel Amter, who served as the prosecutor for the trial, expressed particular indignation that "the defendant, a Jew, who had suffered in Czarist Russia, should be the bearer of ideas that helped the capitalists of America to enslave a people which constituted a majority of the population of the Black Belt."[101]

The divide between communist and noncommunist Jews over racial matters demonstrated how the pressures of the Depression could work in strongly contradictory ways. These tensions, however, did not always divide Jews into such clear camps but resulted instead in widespread ambivalence that permeated all segments of the Jewish community. In the Reform Movement, which by the 1930s included a mixture of old-line Central European Jews and a vanguard of Americanized Eastern Europeans, there were often conflicts about the extent to which clergy should insert themselves into the nation's debate about black rights. Some rabbis, like Edward Israel of Baltimore's Temple Har Sinai, were frustrated by their congregants' reluctance to oppose racial discrimination. A vocal opponent of lynching in his state, Israel saw a direct link between his Jewishness and his dedication to the African American cause. "To me, these matters have not been mere humanitarian sentiment," he wrote in 1936. "I have felt that Negro and Jew face so many kindred problems that I was, in a sense, fighting my own battle in fighting his." But within his own congregation, one of the most socially prominent Reform temples in the country, Israel dealt with persistent objections to his activism, based on the fear, as one member articulated it, that such a stance "tended to associate Negro and Jew in the public mind." In one case, only a personal appeal from the rabbi prevented Har Sinai's board of governors from participating in a segregation pact in the temple's neighborhood.[102]

A flashpoint of tension within the Reform Movement came in 1933, when Temple Beth Or of Montgomery, Alabama, dismissed Rabbi Benjamin Goldstein for what they considered his overzealous efforts on behalf of the Scottsboro Boys. While the fear of inflaming southern prejudice toward Jews made the congregation's position predictable, what was less expected was the way the case divided members of the Reform Movement's national rabbinical organization, the CCAR. The CCAR had built a strong record of supporting racial justice, one that it continued to uphold during the years of the Depression. In its approach to the Goldstein case, however, the CCAR demonstrated how a concern for Jewish social status could complicate its liberal approach to the issue of African American rights. When the CCAR appointed Rabbi Morris Newfield of Memphis, himself a racial liberal, to investigate Goldstein's dismissal, the resulting report whitewashed the matter by claiming that the congregation's dissatisfaction stemmed from a dispute over the rabbi's religious views and not his civil rights activism. When Baltimore rabbi Edward Israel pressed for a review of the case, the CCAR failed to support him. Although committed to the cause of racial justice, the organization was unwilling to pursue these goals when it feared that a southern Jewish community might be placed at risk.[103]

Heightened ambivalence about racial matters during the Depression years was not only apparent within more liberal quarters such as the CCAR but also permeated the actions and attitudes of average Jews who were struggling with economic hardship and antisemitism. If many Bronx Jews found that hiring black domestic workers at exploitative rates could boost their feeling of social superiority, others found the spectacle of Jewish women bargaining for domestic servants at "slave markets" gravely disturbing. Kate Simon recalled the horror with which she saw black women sold to the highest bidder in front of Bronx Woolworth stores during those years. Such a display, she recalled, "made me painfully sorrowful and ashamed that I could not alter anything, nor scream and yell and protest effectively . . . After a few moments I would run from the shameful scenes."[104] Some leaders of the Jewish community apparently were also unnerved by exploitative conditions in the Bronx. Carl Ruthven Offord, who dramatized the events surrounding the "slave markets" in *The White Face*, described the efforts of a New York rabbi and other Jewish activists to establish hiring halls where prices would be regulated and African American domestics would be guaranteed a decent wage. Offord even suggested that many of the Jewish women who hired black domestics at the "slave markets" were themselves uneasy with the implications of the relationship and often tried to assure themselves that they were not taking advantage of their employees. "I didn't treat you badly, did I?" inquired one of the Jewish characters with urgent concern after her maid failed to show up for work. "Tell me, did I treat you badly?" In Chicago, at least two-thirds of the domestic servants interviewed by

Drake and Cayton stated that although Jews generally paid less than other employers, they often took greater care to treat such employees with personal kindness.[105]

By the mid-1930s, Jewish angst concerning the relationship between African Americans and Jews had reached crisis proportions. In 1935, after an extensive boycott of local stores that refused to hire blacks, a major riot broke out in Harlem during which African Americans damaged over two hundred Jewish-owned businesses. Over the next three years in both New York and Chicago, radical African American spokesmen began casting the Jews as exploiters of the black population, often arguing through impromptu newspapers and street corner orations that they possessed the worst qualities of American whites. Jews responded to the eruption of anti-Jewish rhetoric in America's major black centers with intense shock and dismay. While many Jews expressed concern over the antisemitic tenor of the events, there was also a palpable discomfort with the notion that Jews—who had suffered themselves under the ban of both economic and "racial" persecution—could be accused of oppressing African Americans by these very same means. Jewish community officials, like those in Chicago, met with black leaders to find ways of soothing the relationship between their two groups and to try to dispel the notion that Jews had treated African Americans unfairly. Meanwhile, rifts in the Jewish community widened as liberal Jews criticized the activities of the Harlem merchants, and writers for the Yiddish press blamed communist agitators for inciting African Americans against innocent Jewish store owners.[106]

The events of 1935 to 1938 marked the peak of Jews' struggle with the contradictory forces that shaped their stance toward African Americans during the interwar years. While the emerging black critique of Jews certainly overstated their responsibility for the suffering of African Americans during the Depression years, it did point out the degree to which many Jews had become complicit in the larger white power structure. This was an uncomfortable reality for many Jews, who had been pushed toward greater assertions of whiteness even as the intolerance of the Depression Era made them more attuned the evils of American racism. Despite their desire to find social acceptance while also preserving a distinctive minority sensibility, most Jews of this period found that these two goals could not be easily harmonized. As long as Jewish social acceptance depended on a high degree of conformity to the standards of white America, Jews could not totally realize Schwartz's vision of becoming a "white race of another kind."

CHAPTER 7

WRESTLING WITH RACIAL JEWISHNESS

IN 1922, at the height of the controversy over Jewish admissions to
Harvard, Maurice Stern, a Jewish alumnus of the school, wrote to
American Jewish Committee chief Louis Marshall to give his opinion
on how Jewish leaders ought to approach the matter. Stern was convinced
that Jews faced a new type of problem in the Harvard case that had to be
answered in a new way. The time had passed when Jews could simply
brush off antisemitism by claiming that "religious" discrimination had no
place in American life. Stern told Marshall that he, like many acculturated
Jews, was used to describing himself as "an American who professes the
Jewish faith and worships in a Jewish way." But Jews now had to admit
that something deeper than religious prejudice was at work at Harvard,
where professors and administrators suggested the problem was one of
"race" rather than religion. American Jews, Stern explained, needed to
tackle the matter head on, finally answering the difficult questions about
the nature of Jewishness they had long preferred to evade.[1]

Stern's letter to Marshall demonstrates the degree to which Jewish racial distinctiveness had come to be seen by American Jews of the interwar
period as a "fact" that they could no longer avoid or deny. During this
era of "terrible honesty," when even liberal spokesmen saw the Jews as a
problematic group in American society, Jews had little hope of deflecting
attention away from their status as a distinct "race." Rather, they often
confronted the "racial" character of Jewishness more directly during
these years, discussing it, analyzing it, and interpreting it in the same stark
terms as did the non-Jewish public. Fueled by the increased frequency
with which white Americans placed Jewish group status under a micro-
scope, Jewish racial consciousness was also encouraged by the changing
emotional needs of Jews themselves. As Eastern European Jews and their
children became the dominant element in American Jewish life, they
proved less willing than their Central European counterparts to use religion as a stand-in for their broader Jewish commitments. Moreover, the
mounting sense of social isolation experienced by Jews of both Central
and Eastern European background during the 1920s and 1930s made
race particularly appealing to both groups as a vehicle for redeeming their
sullied image in American society. Just as Jews began to insist on a more
distinctive approach to African Americans, they also asserted their own
racial distinctiveness with increasing vigor.

The growing tendency of American Jews to describe themselves in racial terms during the 1920s and 1930s, however, was also accompanied by new efforts to justify and legitimize their perceived racial difference. Because American Jews were increasingly native born, they were more conscious than ever of the need to present their group status in ways that did not put their whiteness into question. Unable to deny what was widely seen as the "truth" of Jewish racial difference, Jews during this period tried feverishly to recast the meaning of "race" as it applied to them, highlighting what they felt were their most positive attributes and clearly distinguishing their group character from that of African Americans. A few Jews even began to speak of Jewish "ethnicity" instead of "race," a semantic shift they hoped would make members of the larger society more willing to accept Jews as both white and different. As persistently as Jews attempted to soothe white Americans' fears about Jewish distinctiveness however, they were often stymied by the ongoing social pressures of the period, which only intensified during the Great Depression. Despite Jews' best efforts, the dominant society remained resistant to pluralist arguments and continued to label Jewish distinctiveness as an obstacle to the maintenance of an orderly and homogenous white population. While to some extent these pressures were blunted by the social isolation in which Jews lived, ultimately the period was characterized more by tension and uncertainty than by the ability to craft a neat synthesis between Jewish and American identity.

The Revival of Jewish Racial Identity

The first American Jews to demonstrate the enlivened Jewish racial consciousness of the interwar period were the immigrants from Eastern Europe and their children, whose multifaceted conception of Jewishness was well served by racial language. Because of their relative social isolation from the non-Jewish world, the immigrants had not had much use for racial language in the years before World War I. They defended the racial definition of Jewishness only as a means of responding to the insult they perceived from more acculturated Jews, who in denying race, were also trying to distance themselves from the newcomers. But once they began to experience greater contact with the world outside their neighborhoods— through schools, jobs, and mass culture—they became increasingly cognizant of their position in American life and began to require a means of defining their relationship to non-Jewish society. Because their interactions with the non-Jewish world were still heavily mediated by a strong sense of Jewish particularism, nurtured both by their history and the anti-semitism of the interwar years, Eastern European Jews found it almost impossible to define Jewishness in purely religious terms or to deny their Jewishness altogether. Echoing the rhetoric of the day, the Chicago *Yidisher kurier* argued that the ties of blood between Jews were a "reality" whether Jews liked it or not, and no amount of abstract theorizing or wordplay could obscure that "fact." "To judge from . . . the attitude of even the most liberal and radical-minded Jews to the problem of Judaism," the Orthodox paper editorialized, "one must say that the very basis of the Jewish reality is Jewish blood."[2] Echoing these sentiments from the other end of the ideology spectrum, a writer for the Chicago edition of the socialist *Forverts* argued: "Judaism is in our blood. Even the least religious among us is Jewish to the core."[3]

If the Eastern Europeans' greater minority consciousness led them to describe themselves in terms of race as they acculturated, the events of the post–World War I era allowed them to assert this definition of Jewishness within the larger Jewish community and to challenge the long-standing policy of establishment leaders to deny Jewish racial identity. The Jewish refugee problem in Europe, the diplomatic effort to secure national rights for Jews abroad, and the issuance of the Balfour Declaration by Great Britain all placed matters on the American Jewish agenda that could not be addressed without recognizing a group status for Jews that went far beyond religion. To address these issues, Eastern European Jews founded the American Jewish Congress and the American Jewish Joint Distribution Committee, organizations with which the older Central European establishment reluctantly cooperated. Despite their hesitancy about the Zionist orientation of the younger set of activists, leaders like Louis Marshall were now more comfortable describing the Jews as a "racial or ethnical" minority, believing that this terminology in no way legitimized their status as a nation in the political sense. Even the radical Reform rabbi David Philipson, who had been a strong opponent of the racial definition of Jewishness since the nineteenth century, resorted to calling the Jews a race as an *alternative* to recognizing them as a nationality. Thus, while Jews continued to wrangle over their status as a *nation*, there was increasing agreement, even among bitter opponents on the national question, that the existence of a Jewish "race" was incontestable.[4]

The widening agreement on a racial definition of the Jews in the 1920s, however, was not due solely to the urgency created by wartime events or to the rising influence of the Eastern Europeans. The most important factor influencing the changes in Jewish self-definition during this period was the larger society's increasing attention to the so-called Jewish Problem. If non-Jews were no longer able to suppress their concerns about the place of the Jew in American life, Jews too were convinced by the growing rift between themselves and non-Jews that they had to face up to the "reality" of Jewish difference. The dramatic rise in antisemitism during the in-

terwar years, not to mention the flood of articles, symposiums, and debates on the status of the "Jewish race," made it almost impossible for
Jews to argue, as many had during the Progressive Era, that they were a
denominational group similar to Methodists or Episcopalians. In fact,
Jews began to feel that a denial of racial identity not only prevented them
from addressing the problem of antisemitism adequately, but could play
into the hands of those like Henry Ford who accused Jews of trying to
conceal their true nature. The kind of evasion practiced by Simon Wolf
in his work against Jewish immigrant classification, Jews were convinced,
would no longer suffice. The failure of B'nai B'rith's Anti-Defamation
League to alter its tactics in the face of the Ford debacle, for example, led
to its decline as an important force in the community and earned it the
criticism that it was "ridiculous both in name and fact."[5] This type of
realization also led the American Jewish Committee, formerly the champion of Jewish unobtrusiveness, to begin referring in their annual reports
to the problem of "racial intolerance" in addition to the obstacle of "religious prejudice."[6]

   In addition to influencing the arena of communal politics, this new
"realism" in regard to Jewish racial identity was expressed in the popular
literature of the period, which abounded with tales of Jews who had embarked earnestly on the road to integration and intermarriage, only to
discover that Jewish racial identity was inescapable. Milton Waldman's
The Disinherited (1929) was fairly typical of this genre, with its account
of a man whose Jewish heritage finally overpowers him, causing a rift with
his wife and children, who were raised as Protestants.[7] Anzia Yezierska's
Salome of the Tenements (1923) told a similar story. Based loosely on the
failed marriage of Yezierska's friend Rose Pastor to millionaire John
Phelps Stokes, as well as Yezierska's own failed love affair with Columbia
professor John Dewey, it cast doubt on the notion that the "oriental" Jew
could ever truly come into perfect harmony with the Anglo-Saxon.[8] In
Leah Morton's autobiographical novel, *I Am a Woman and a Jew* (1926),
her increasing consciousness of "race" did not necessitate a repudiation
of her ties to the non-Jewish world. Morton had left behind her Jewish
milieu, only to achieve a greater awareness of her "racial" origins as she
came into contact with the non-Jewish world. While neither leaving her
husband nor trying to make her children into Jews, she came to the conclusion that "what every Jew is and does is something which must, indeed,
belong to his people; that no other people living have our particular quality, which is not individual, but racial."[9]

   The popularity of such novels indicates that these sentiments had a
strong resonance with Jewish readers. Significantly, the National Council
of Jewish Women (NCJW), which had traditionally shied away from any
discussion of Jewish racial identity during the early twentieth century,

now recommended novels such as these to its members as important explorations of pressing Jewish concerns.[10] The fact that the NCJW also
sponsored study groups on topics such as "Anti-Semitism" and the "Racial and National Status of Jewry" suggests that Jews were becoming as
interested as non-Jews in clarifying, examining, and understanding the
"true" nature of Jewish difference.[11] This growing sense of "realism" was
summed up by the editors of Atlanta's *Southern Israelite* in 1928: "To us
it seems a useless effort for Jews to deny their Jewishness. . . . The blood
of four thousand or even a paltry three thousand years can not be drained
out or thinned appreciably in a generation or two."[12] In addition, an identity rooted in "race" had particular psychological benefits for American
Jews of this period. More than any other term for self-definition, "race"
provided a feeling of community and connection to other Jews, something
that they sorely needed in times of great tension and uncertainty. As Irwin
Edman, a philosophy professor at Columbia University, explained, racial
self-definition enabled the Jew "imaginatively, at least, to discover an un-
dying current vitalizing him with the common warmth of his racial fellows
in this and past generations."[13] Finally, racial rhetoric could be used effectively by American Jews to respond to attacks on their group character
and to recoup the sense of honor, dignity, and belonging denied to them
by the outside world.

Despite the emerging consensus among Jews that they did in fact constitute a distinct racial group, not all Jews were of one mind on how best to
approach the topic of racial identity, and some entertained great ambivalence about the meaning of race as it applied to them. Unlike the late
nineteenth century, when American Jews were able to use race to serve
their emotional needs without having to worry significantly about negative repercussions, the 1920s and 1930s presented a climate of hostility
in which race might easily be turned against them. In a period when public
discourse stressed the importance of racial homogeneity and often singled
out the Jew as a stubborn obstacle to the stability of whiteness, Jews could
not help but be reticent about their racial status. These concerns touched
average Jews in direct ways, since their access to higher education, employment, and associational life might be jeopardized by the notion that
they disturbed the unity and homogeneity of the white American population. In addition, incidents like the blood libel accusations made in Massena, New York, in 1928, or the false charges of murder brought against
the Jewish soldier Robert Rosenbluth in 1921, which Jewish leaders
feared would develop into an American Dreyfus Affair, seemed to suggest
that the rise of a European-style antisemitism was not impossible in
America, a fear exacerbated by the proliferation of Nazi sympathizers
during the 1930s.[14] Even as such events encouraged feelings of racial solidarity among Jews, they also inspired great fear about racial status. Thus,

rather than helping them to clarify their place in American society, the predominance of racial discourse left Jews of the period caught between a series of uncomfortable alternatives, wondering how they could respond to antisemites and argue against calls for assimilation without backing into agreement with those who would demonize them.

Race's Double Edge

Given the uncertain implications of Jewish racial identity during the 1920s and 1930s, it is not surprising that the use of racial language among Jews varied greatly depending on social status and ideological position. As in the years before the war, Zionists stood out as the group most likely to assert a strongly racial view of Jewish identity. This was especially true of the Zionist leadership that emerged in the wake of Louis Brandeis's departure from the Zionist Executive in 1921. The newcomers, Eastern European in background, were headed by Louis Lipsky and favored a view of Jewish identity starkly different from the Americanized Zionism of Brandeis and his followers. Zionist historian Yonathan Shapiro calls the Lipsky Zionists "chauvinists" who forwarded a Jewish version of "hundred percent" nationalism and were suspicious of those, like Brandeis, who had tried to downplay the tensions between Jewishness and Americanism.[15] Their distaste for Brandeis's approach, as well as their tendency to absorb the racial rhetoric of the period, was exemplified by their description of the Americanized Zionists as the "Nordic opposition."[16] The new Zionist administration drove out older leaders like Samuel Untermeyer, whose son married a non-Jew, and even criticized Rabbi Stephen S. Wise, one of the founders of the Federation of American Zionists, for his overtures to the non-Jewish community. In Lipsky's view, the old guard had refused "to become part of the race and associate themselves with our problems."[17]

In popularizing its strongly racialized view of Jewishness, the Zionist movement relied on some gifted spokesmen, like the Rumanian-born, British-educated writer and lecturer Maurice Samuel. In a series of *J'accuse* books published in rapid succession during the 1920s and 1930s, Samuel responded to non-Jews who saw assimilation as the solution to the "Jewish Problem" by explaining that "the primal difference between gentile and Jew" was a permanent feature of American life. "We can not climb out of ourselves," he wrote in his 1924 treatise, *You Gentiles.* "The complete and permanent reconciliation of your way of life with ours is beyond that limit."[18] A second major writer to come out of the Zionist camp during this period was Ludwig Lewisohn, an academic and critic who had embraced Christianity before an unsettling encounter with antisemitism sparked a reawakening of his Jewish consciousness. His 1926 autobiography, *Up Stream*, served as a mea culpa for his assimilationist youth and described the process of coming to terms with his "Semitic" origins.[19] In subsequent years, Lewisohn became an active Zionist and published a series of works attacking American culture in terms comparable to Samuel's pointed rhetoric, condemning what he called the "Puritan barbarism" of the United States and advising Jews not to try and "ape the Nordic unsuccessfully," but to remain true to their own "essential Jewishness."[20]

Men like Samuel and Lewisohn represented one extreme of the American Jewish approach to racial identity, a position of unusual racial assertiveness that stemmed from severe feelings of alienation and rejection from non-Jewish society. There were, however, those at the opposite extreme, who accepted the "fact" of Jewish racial identity but whose success at integrating into the non-Jewish world made them extremely leery of accentuating Jewish racial particularity. Labor activist Bertha Wallerstein, writing in the *Nation*, implored Jews to struggle for their rights as "human beings without making a whole romance of the race." Wallerstein argued that the "jingo Jew" whose motto was "Right or wrong, my race!" was "as rampantly Semitic as the Ku Klux Klan is Nordic."[21] One of the strongest critics of Jewish racial assertiveness during these years was Walter Lippmann, a prominent journalist who condemned what he saw as Jews' aggressive tendency toward self-segregation. Contacted by officials at Harvard for his opinion on the issue of Jewish admissions there, Lippmann replied that he "did not regard Jews as innocent victims." Jews, he wrote, perpetuated many "disturbing social habits" that were the result of "tribal inbreeding." Lippmann argued that limiting the number of Jewish students was the only way to insure the breakdown of Jewish racial distinctiveness and encourage "fusion" between Jews and non-Jews.[22]

The insistence that Jews made more of their racial origins than they needed to was especially common among a certain class of Jewish doctors and psychologists, who spoke of a Jewish obsession with racial differences that edged on psychosis. Dr. Walter Berán Wolfe, a Vienna-born psychologist practicing in New York, argued that this hyperawareness of difference was a "neurotic manisfestation" that interfered with the Jew taking his place in non-Jewish society. "The sooner the Jew realizes that being a Jew is neither a special privilege nor a special disgrace," wrote Wolfe, "the sooner will he prepare his rightful place in the fellowship of mankind."[23] Writer Samuel Ornitz lampooned the views of some of New York's assimilationist psychologists through the character of Dr. Lionel Crane (né Lazarus Cohen), whose views on Jewish identity were presented in Ornitz's novel of American Jewish life, *Haunch, Paunch, and Jowl* (1923). As the founder of the field of "race psycopathology," Crane believed the Jews suffered from a severe case of "racial paranoia," and implored them to "let intermarriage bring in the saving tonic of new blood."[24] Though somewhat fanciful, Crane's views were not too different from those of flesh-and-blood doctors like Wolfe or New York physician Maurice Fishberg. Speaking before the International Eugenics Conference in 1921, Fishberg argued that intermarriage between Jews and non-Jews would not only solve the problem of social friction but would produce a mix of racial qualities that would prove "a benefit to white humanity."[25]

While the critiques of Jewish separatism made by cosmopolitan intellectuals and the staunchly racialist polemics of the Zionist leadership often made headlines, neither of these extreme positions were taken up consistently by a large number of American Jews. Few Jews of the 1920s and 1930s had integrated sufficiently into non-Jewish social settings to see Jewish distinctiveness in as negative a light as did Walter Lippmann. On the other hand, few Jews felt as pessimistic about the chances of winning inclusion in American life as did Lipsky, Samuel, or Lewisohn, whose extreme views were atypical even among Zionists. Instead, the more common response of American Jews during this period was to try to define race in ways that were not as dissonant with American identity while at the same time asserting a more pluralistic vision of American nationalism that was accepting of diversity, at least in regard to European "racial" groups. Advancing such oppositional definitions of race and national identity was an uphill battle, but ironically, the relative social isolation in which many interwar American Jews lived provided them with some space to pursue this goal on their own terms.

In trying to transvalue the meaning of race, American Jews frequently turned to the well-established practice of lauding Jewish racial accomplishments, highlighting the ways Jewish racial distinctiveness contributed to the upbuilding of America rather than to its instability. While Jewish newspapers had long made a habit of praising the accomplishments of Jews and crediting them to superior racial traits, in the climate of the interwar years this practice became a virtual cottage industry among American Jews. Weekly publications like the *American Hebrew* and the *Jewish Tribune* published regular features documenting Jewish talent in fields including art, athletics, politics, music, drama, and scholarship.[26] Even entire books were written to advance the case for Jewish racial achievement, such as Gdal Saleski's *Famous Musicians of a Wandering Race* (1928) and Mac Davis's *They All Are Jews: From Moses to Einstein* (1937).[27] Saleski, a New York composer, not only claimed Jewish preeminence in music, but argued that "the bloodstream of the Jew courses through the spiritual veins of every major art that modern civilization has risen to honor."[28] This claim was given vivid illustration in Davis's popu-

20. *From Moses to Einstein*, 1937. Mac Davis's popular book lauded Jewish contributions to civilization, typifying Jews' efforts during this period to create a positive racial self-image that might counter antisemitic claims.

lar volume, which presented sixty biographical sketches documenting the Jew's "immense" contributions to civilization as "soldier, statesman, explorer, pugilist, poet, scientist, rabbi, actress, [and] business man."[29]

Jews were happy to catalogue their achievements in almost any field of endeavor, but they often concentrated on areas in which antisemites had made particular claims of Jewish deficiency. The heavy emphasis on Jewish contributions to the arts, for example, was a means of contradicting the claims of Henry Ford and like-minded commentators that the Jew worked only for his own benefit and was a corrupter of the white man's culture. While Ford emphasized the Jew's role in tearing down artistic and cultural standards, Jews portrayed themselves as masters of the classics. Viewed by the writers of the *Jewish Tribune*, popular musicians like George Gershwin were not purveyors of what Ford called "Yiddish moron music," but experts at giving form and meaning to the "shapeless and chaotic" music of African Americans.[30] Jewish achievement in athletics was a particularly important focus for Jews attempting to prove the value of their group, primarily because antisemitic imagery often cast the Jew as weak, reliant on the labor of others, and too preoccupied with self-advancement to excel as team players. Harold Riegelman, a national leader of the Zeta Beta Tau fraternity, responded to these stereotypes by proposing a policy of "race appreciation" for Jewish college men called "Pro-Semitism," by which they were to "associate themselves as Jews . . . continuously and persistently, by their sportsmanship on the athletic field," as well as by demonstrating good social posture and a dedication to community service.[31] In turn, the Jewish press lauded those like University of Michigan football star Benny Friedman, whom the *American Hebrew* called a symbol of "character, intrinsic merit and pleasing deportment" on the field.[32] In both college and professional sports, Jewish athletes were highly aware of their role as redeemers of the Jewish racial image, and made the connection between athletic achievement and Jewish character whenever possible. When the half-Jewish Maxie Baer won the world boxing title in 1934, he dubbed himself the "first bona fide heavyweight champion of the Hebrew race."[33]

Interpreting Jewish racial distinctiveness as a positive force in American society also gave Jews a means to defend their widespread preference for endogamous marriage. Here, too, Jewish spokesmen relied on arguments that had been pioneered in previous eras, like David Einhorn's assertion that racial purity was required for Jews to perform their moral and ethical mission in the world. But now such claims were applied with much more vigor and unanimity. Chicago's Yiddish-language *Forverts* cited no less an authority than Charles W. Eliot, the former president of Harvard, in arguing that the Jew's great contributions to civilization would be lost through the process of intermarriage. In a similar vein, Dr. Nathan Krass, the rabbi of New York's elite Reform congregation, Temple Emanuel, predicted that intermarriage would lead to a decline in the "superiority of Jewish genius" and the distinctive "psychic heritage" of the Jew, which had always been nurtured by keeping out "foreign blood."[34] While the Reform rabbinate had, on the whole, been squeamish about offering anything other than religious reasons for opposing intermarriage during the early twentieth century, by 1922 even Julian Morgenstern, the president of Hebrew Union College, rejected the notion that Jews' identity as a distinct racial group in any way threatened American society. "We may continue to be Jews by race as well as by religion and steadfastly oppose intermarriage," he wrote, "and yet feel as assured that our Americanism is not affected thereby in the least."[35]

Aside from trying to turn their incontestable racial difference into a positive good, a second strategy pursued by American Jews during the 1920s and 1930s was to argue that there were more and less severe kinds of racial difference, and that Jewish difference was of the latter, more benign type. Drawing on the era's popular interest in psychology, Jews frequently argued that their racial distinctiveness lay in a particular mindset or "genius," while trying to ignore the popular wisdom that visible biological characteristics marked them off from other whites.[36] Even Maurice Samuel, who occasionally referred to himself and his colleagues as "biological Zionists," spoke almost exclusively of the "moral" and "mental" traits that constituted the Jewish "life-force."[37] By distinguishing between the "biological" and the "psychic" meaning of race, Jewish writers and spokesmen attempted to reassure non-Jews that the physical distinction between blacks and whites was still the most basic racial fault line in American society. In this schema, Jews preserved a means of speaking of themselves as different, but argued that they were little more than a variety or subgroup of the white race. In 1923, when Jewish scholar Max Margolis published a series called "The Truth About the Jew" in the *B'nai B'rith News*, he was adamant that physically, "the Jew is a white man."[38] An editorial in the same publication agreed, but explained that Jews could still be called a race because they "possess a specific Jewish 'personality' [and] stand for a particular attitude of life."[39] A similar line of argument was employed by Chicago's *Yidisher kurier*. "The raciality of the colored man is much more expressive than that of the Jewish, because we belong to the white race," the editors of the Orthodox daily argued. "Psychologically, however, our raciality is as striking and as expressive as is biologically the raciality of the colored man."[40]

Yet even though Jews tried hard to reinterpret the concept of race and assert a positive image of themselves that soothed fears about their place in white America, the intensified antisemitism of the 1920s and 1930s often interfered with their ability to find an easy synthesis between a separate racial identity and white Americanism. Because they could not fully control their image in American society, Jews often found themselves caught between a desire to defend the reputation of their "race" and a fear of opening the door to further attack. Even in this period of intensified racial consciousness, the knowledge that race could cut two ways meant that many American Jews remained uncertain when to forward their prideful version of racial identity and when to retreat into a more defensive position. Ultimately, their confidence that they could unhinge American thinking on Jewish racial difference was often tinged by feelings of fear and uncertainty.

The American Jewish Committee's approach to defense work during this period illustrates this point well. On the one hand, by the 1920s even committee leaders like Louis Marshall, who had strongly opposed the racial definition of the Jews during the early twentieth century, began to incorporate pointed racial language into his defense efforts. When an Iowa judge belittled a Jewish defendant with an attack on "the race of Israel," Marshall sent him a letter informing him of the many "distinguished Jews on the bench who are the sons of the ancient race to which I belong."[41] Similarly, when asked to broker the settlement of a libel suit against Henry Ford in 1927, Marshall informed the automobile magnate that he would help only because "there flows in my veins the blood of ancestors who were inured to suffering and nevertheless remained steadfast in their trust in God." The "spirit of forgiveness," Marshall wrote to Ford, "is a Jewish trait."[42] But even as Marshall made such statements, he remained highly sensitive to the dangers of asserting Jewish racial particularity too strongly and never fully steered his organization away from its old tactics. Throughout the 1920s, despite the committee's growing resolve to respond to acts of "racial intolerance" head on, annual bulletins routinely downplayed the growing climate of hostility by reporting a "continuing decline of anti-Jewish propaganda."[43] His own aggressive jabs at antisemites notwithstanding, Marshall wrote to various Jews advising them against inflammatory activities such as an anti-Ford boycott or a libel suit filed in the name of a Jewish agency or institution, urging them instead to respond to antisemitism through channels that allowed Jews to remain invisible.[44]

The career of Isaac Landman, a Reform rabbi who served as editor of the *American Hebrew* and was a moving spirit behind the founding of the National Conference of Christians and Jews, presents an even greater case of ambivalence about Jewish racial status. As editor of the *Hebrew*, Landman oversaw the publication of an endless stream of articles which trumpeted Jewish "genius" in almost every field of endeavor. While avoiding explicit endorsement of Jewish racial distinctiveness in his own writings, he did suggest that Jews had a unique psychological profile that made them excel in "unselfish service to the nation and the world."[45] Landman also believed that spreading news about Jews' unique contributions to civilization was an important tool in the fight against antisemitism.[46] At the same time, however, he was highly sensitive to any assertion of Jewish racial distinctiveness that could be seen as interfering with an eventual reconciliation between Jews and non-Jews, which was one of his ardent goals. Landman protested the "political and racial propaganda" disseminated by Zionist activists, and he harshly criticized the social habits of Jews, which he saw as an obstacle to Jewish-Christian fellowship. "When we make public exhibitions of ourselves, load ourselves down with diamonds and furs . . . and persist in telling the world at the tops of our voices that we are Jews," Landman argued, "we are . . . guilty of creating race feeling."[47]

Landman's ability to shift from proud assertions of Jewish achievement to strong critiques of Jewish racial separatism demonstrates how Jews of the interwar period, like many groups experiencing intense social criticism and pressure to assimilate, could sometimes accept and internalize the very stereotypes they were trying to fight.[48] The intertwining of Jewish pride and expressions of self-hatred was particularly apparent on college campuses, where students felt the pressure of social discrimination much more directly than did other Jews. As Marianne Sanua has explained, members of Jewish college fraternities often sought to build up the image of the Jewish "race," but frequently fell into the trap of persecuting fellow Jews who they felt gave the group a bad name. While undertaking their own aggressive programs to win recognition for Jewish students in campus life and on the athletic field, members of these groups regularly blackballed applicants who were considered "greasy" Jews or "kikes."[49] Both on the college campus and beyond, Jewish men during this period sometimes tried to deflect unflattering racial images onto their female counterparts, depicting them as physically unattractive, socially inept, and overly concerned with material wealth.[50]

Of all anti-Jewish stereotypes, those concerning Jewish appearance were the ones Jews internalized the most. Many Jewish youth seemed to accept the notion that physical traits recognizable as "Jewish" were not desirable. In a fiction piece written for Atlanta's *Southern Israelite* in 1929, Nina Kaye presented an ideal type in the character of Allan Parker, a "blond broad-shouldered Jew" who was able to pass as a non-Jew in school and was singled out by a science teacher as a perfect specimen of the Nordic race.[51] By contrast, Parker's classmate Julius Lipschutz, a "short, dark-haired Jew," represented the stigma carried by those with recognizably Jewish features. According to student Dorothy Linder, Jewish women applying to Vassar College in the 1920s assiduously avoided profile shots when posing for their application photos, hoping to hide their noses. Jewish women, Lindner argued, "simply do not meet the modern standard of beauty" which was set by the "blond American girl."[52]

By the 1920s, Jews who were particularly concerned about their appearance could take advantage of the increasing availability of plastic surgery, which had been perfected by doctors working on the faces and bodies of wounded soldiers during World War I. For the few who could afford it, the procedure promised to help them shed the unwanted encumbrances of Jewish racial identity. Among those who took advantage of the new technique was the entertainer Fannie Brice (née Borach), whose widely publicized nose job in 1922 inspired writer Dorothy Parker to remark that Brice had "cut off her nose to spite her race."[53] Jews like Brice, who sought to efface what they saw as unseemly Jewish physical traits, were not necessarily radical assimilationists, nor did they hope to sever their ties with Jewishness. Brice, in fact, was adamant in expressing Jewish pride and rejected the notion that her nose job was a repudiation of her Jewish identity. While her motives remain unclear, she was apparently trying to avoid being consistently cast by producers as a Jewish "type." Like most Jews of the period, she felt torn between the positive and negative aspects of an identity rooted in race.

An Appeal to Culture

Given the pressures of interwar life, most American Jews were unable to transform race into a consistently positive means of self-definition, even as they faced up to what was widely seen as the "reality" of Jewish racial difference. Yet a small number of Jewish scholars, removed somewhat from the daily struggle for acceptance and the anxieties it provoked, felt empowered to do what most Jews of the period could not: find a stable middle ground between racial distinctiveness and white Americanism. Confident in their ability to employ the tools of modern social science and encouraged by supportive working environments, these scholars set out to craft new definitions of group difference that they hoped would affirm the place of Jews in American life. Initially, their work argued for pluralism among European immigrant groups without challenging the notion of a separate Jewish race. Eventually, however, their focus on pluralism pushed them to begin speaking of "culture" as a category distinct from biology and referring to the Jews as an "ethnic group" rather than a "race." While these ideas were slow to catch on beyond intellectual circles in the period before World War II, they were nonetheless critical developments that would ultimately help reshape the basic categories of group life in America.

The American Jew perhaps best known for advancing the notion of cultural pluralism in American life was Horace Kallen, who was born in Silesia to Russian-Jewish parents and educated at Harvard and Oxford. A philosopher by training, Kallen devoted himself mainly to problems of social thought and was one of the founding faculty members of the New School for Social Research in New York.[54] Although Kallen is remembered as the ideologue of "cultural" pluralism, however, he was slow in coming to a view of Jewish identity rooted in culture instead of race. In fact, most of his writings before the 1930s used the language of race and discussed European immigrant groups in terms of their "hereditary instincts" rather than in terms of a nonracial "culture."[55] According to Kallen's earliest writings, the Jews were a relatively pure race innately endowed with a capacity for what he called "Hebraism," a moral code not only responsible for the age-old record of Jewish achievement but also for the ideals of the Puritan founders of America. Thus, the preservation of Jewish racial instincts, according to Kallen, did not conflict with American national identity, but—along with the nurturing of other immigrant racial heritages—was essential to it.[56]

If Kallen challenged long-held beliefs about the need for immigrant "races" to give up their separate existence in order to become American, he also tried to reduce the stigma attached to groups like the Jews by arguing that European immigrants had a much different relationship to American culture than did peoples of color. As early as 1906, in an article for the Zionist organ *Maccabaean*, Kallen argued that the Jews were a white race, dismissing the popular claim that the ancient Semites were of African descent and instead ascribing to them the Asian origin claimed by other Europeans.[57] Similarly, in the system of cultural pluralism that he first advocated in 1915 and that was popularized after the war, Kallen relied on the notion that the whiteness of European immigrant groups made them potential contributors to American society rather than a racial threat. According to Kallen, America could become "an orchestration of mankind" by perfecting the "cooperative harmonies of European civilization." But his orchestra did not include African Americans, whom he relegated to a footnote in his proposal. "I do not discuss the influence of the negro," he wrote. "This is at once too considerable and too recondite in its processes for casual mention. It requires separate analysis."[58] While Kallen was sympathetic to African American causes and deplored antiblack racism, he nonetheless felt that, as whites, European groups had a more natural relationship to American identity, and he put that claim to use in his effort to legitimize the separate existence of "racial" groups like the Jews.

But while Kallen tried to transvalue the meaning of "race" as it applied to Jews, there were also a number of scholars beginning to question the very concept of race as it applied to European immigrant groups and to innovate new terms for explaining Jewish group difference. The initial impetus for such work came from Franz Boas, the Columbia University anthropologist whose scholarship had long suggested that culture had little to do with innate biological characteristics. Boas's work was no doubt influenced by his Jewish origins, and he attracted a large number of Jewish students who were also anxious to uproot the notion that the Jews were an alien element in American society. But while the ideas of the Boas school were followed with interest in the Jewish community, they had little direct influence on definitions of Jewish group difference because they failed to address the desire of most American Jews for continued group survival. If Boas and his students argued against a racial basis to Jewish identity, they did so from the perspective of Jewish intellectuals trying to fit into to the non-Jewish academic world, hoping to convince Americans that there were no real barriers to Jewish assimilation. As a result, the greatest impact of Boas's ideas on the Jewish community came through scholars who, although influenced by his work, shared the impulse of average Jews for the continuation of Jewish particularity in America.[59]

One of the first Jewish scholars to suggest a cultural—rather than a racial—basis for Jewish identity was Julius Drachsler, whose *Democracy and Assimilation* appeared in 1920.[60] Drachsler, a native of Austria-Hungary who came to the United States as a child, received a doctorate in sociology from Columbia University and became one of the most prominent social scientists studying the Jewish community in the 1920s, working at Smith College, the City University of New York, and the School for Jewish Communal Work.[61] Drachsler began his research on the assimilation of immigrant groups believing—like most scholars of his day—that group characteristics were rooted in racial difference. Defining intermarriage as the only meaningful form of assimilation, he studied the marriage records of New York City as a means of determining whether "fusion" between various segments of the immigrant population was possible and how quickly it was occurring.[62] By the time he published his findings, however, Drachsler had ceased to see biological fusion as the only path to Americanization. Having proven that New Yorkers of different immigrant backgrounds were in fact marrying one another, he determined that while a serious gulf existed between "peoples of divergent races, such as the white and the black or the white and the yellow," there were few serious barriers between the various European groups, which he referred to as "varieties of the same race."[63] As a result, instead of advocating intermarriage as a necessary prerequisite to Americanization, Drachsler argued that the whiteness of immigrant groups precluded the need for biological fusion. Like Kallen, he advocated a pluralist vision of American life, in which the perpetuation of immigrant culture was legitimized by emphasizing the shared whiteness of European peoples. But unlike Kallen, Drachsler was inching closer to the notion that "immigrant peoples" differed from "races" and that "cultural heritage," not biology, was their defining characteristic.[64]

If Drachsler was struggling to articulate Jewish difference in terms of culture rather than race, such a definition was made more explicit by Isaac Berkson, an American-born scholar who approached the issue from the perspective of the field of Jewish education. In his *Theories of Americanization* (1920), Berkson drew on the thought of his mentor Israel Friedlaender, a Jewish historian and leading Zionist, in arguing that Jews could be true Americans and also develop a rich cultural life rooted in Hebrew language and literature and a Jewish spiritual home in Palestine. But unlike Friedlaender, who understood Jewishness in strongly racial terms, Berkson sharply distinguished between race and culture, and argued that Jews' whiteness made any narrower racial identity irrelevant.[65] Citing anthropologist Franz Boas, Berkson wrote that a person's racial background had little impact on mental or moral characteristics, and in the case of the "white races," the "fact of racial origin . . . means nothing."[66] To emphasize the secure claim Jews held to whiteness, he reminded his readers that "in all likelihood, the first white man to tread the soil of the New World was a Jew," and that many Jews could claim to be "native in any sense that the term might be used of white men in America."[67] By defining Jews as racially identical to other white Americans and distinct only in their culture, Berkson claimed to have found the key to harmonizing American and Jewish identity. Seeing Jewishness in terms of culture, not race, wrote Berkson, reveals "a way of retaining loyalty both to the cultural life of the ethnic group and to the life of the total group in all its aspects."[68]

While the ideas proposed by Drachsler and Berkson were a radical departure from previous notions of Jewish group identity, they quickly caught on in Jewish intellectual circles. Chief among the proponents of the new cultural definition of Jewishness were those associated with the *Menorah Journal*, organ of the Intercollegiate Menorah Association. For the *Journal*, the notion of Jewish culture detached from race was an about-face from its previous attitude. Under the influence of Horace Kallen, one of the ideologues of the Menorah movement, the *Journal*, from its first issue in 1915, had pursued its exploration of "Jewish culture and ideals" while clinging to a strongly racial understanding of Jewishness. But during the 1920s and 1930s, Kallen began to shift his focus away from race, writing that Jews were a composite of several racial types, and that the tie that bound them together was that of "historical culture."[69] Emphasizing the Jews' whiteness was an issue of great concern to Kallen, and it was also a way for the collegiate members of the Menorah Association to secure their place in the American academy, which was often questioned on racial grounds. This explains why a syllabus issued by the Menorah movement on the subject "The Jew in the Modern World," encouraged students to contrast Polish antisemitism with the "negro problem in America" and the "Japanese problem in California."[70] Thus, it is not surprising that the *Menorah Journal* became one of the primary voices supporting the cultural definition of Jewishness and regularly published articles that undermined the notion of Jewish racial identity.[71]

One frequent contributor to the *Menorah Journal*, soon to take his place as a leading intellectual force in American Jewry, played a special role in the development of a cultural, nonracial definition of Jewishness. Mordecai M. Kaplan, a Lithuanian-born rabbi who had also pursued advanced studies in sociology at Columbia University, published several articles in the *Journal* during the late 1910s and 1920s in which he described Judaism as a "civilization," encompassing not only religious beliefs but also "history, literature, language, social organization, folk sanctions, standards of conduct, social and spiritual ideals, [and] esthetic values."[72] During the same period, Kaplan helped found the Jewish Center, a New York congregation designed to embody these many aspects of Jewish expression. While he advocated a broad definition of Jewishness, however, Kaplan also emphasized the concordance of Jewish and American civilizations, and the ability of American Jews to participate in both without conflict. Though historians have emphasized how Kaplan parted with the supernatural elements of Judaism and rejected the idea of Jewish chosenness, none have examined his break with a racial understanding of Jewishness.[73]

In his earliest writings, Kaplan described the Jews as a relatively pure race, and in a circular for the Jewish Center in 1918, he underscored the need for recreation facilities in the synagogue complex by explaining that "our racial vigor depends upon having sound souls in sound bodies."[74] But in his *Menorah Journal* articles, which culminated in the publication of *Judaism as a Civilization* in 1934, Kaplan moved toward a rejection of Jewish racial identity.[75] Just as a strictly religious definition of Jewishness was invalid, wrote Kaplan, "the attempt on the part of the Jews to pass [themselves] off as a distinct race, that is, as a branch of mankind which has been endogamous for a long period and has developed distinct traits, is equally anomalous."[76] For Kaplan, the racial definition, grounded as it was in physical characteristics, was incapable of expressing the values of the Jewish people and their goals for the future. Here he drew on the example of African Americans, whom he saw as lacking the sense of unity and purpose he desired for the Jews. "The colored people constitute a race in a far truer and deeper sense than the Jews," he argued, "yet some of its members would give half their lives to be absorbed by the whites. There is nothing in the concept of physical or historical race to give the slightest hint of the institutions Jews intend to establish, or objectives and ideals they mean to pursue."[77] Here, in one of the most influential Jewish books of its generation, Kaplan makes an important link between Jewish culture and whiteness. In Kaplan's formulation, Jews possessed cultural ideals that would make them valuable contributors to American society, while African Americans remained limited by physical traits that represented their continued marginalization.

Despite the increasing popularity of a cultural or "ethnic" definition of Jewish identity in intellectual circles, the notion of a Jewishness rooted in culture and not race failed to win a large following among American Jews in the years before World War II. While the work of Kallen, Drachsler, Berkson, and Kaplan, as well as the platform of the *Menorah Journal*, seemed to reflect the widespread desire of American Jews to reconcile their particularist urges with the requirements of white Americanism, many had trouble adopting the "ethnic" definition because it was so out of step with prevailing notions of group difference. The scholars who promoted theories of ethnic pluralism felt confident that their ideas were supported by scientific facts, but most Jews continued to be guided by the language and concepts that had the greatest currency in popular discourse. Despite the drawbacks of "race," no other term conveyed the depth of emotional attachment Jews had to their group, or offered the same degree of power and legitimacy in responding to the non-Jewish world. To defend their honor in the often hostile atmosphere of the interwar years, Jews needed to use terms that were as potent as the racist charges made against them. It was for this reason, explained American Jewish Congress leader Joseph Tenenbaum in 1934, that the racial view of Jewishness was as dear to most Zionists as it was to nativist thinkers like Madison Grant. "To take away from Jews the privilege of being counted as a separate race," he explained, "would seem almost as insulting to the Jewish nationalists as it would sound blasphemous to the ears of the anti-Jewish racialists."[78]

One did not have to be a Zionist, however, to resent the denial of Jewish racial identity. When Alexander Goldenweiser, a student of Franz Boas, described the Jewish race as "nothing more than a state of mind" at a conference of Jewish social workers, one of the attendees reminded him of the "positive fact" that "in actual life and experience . . . the Jew is segregated because of his seeming racial characteristics" and should not be discouraged from defending those traits.[79] Newspaper columnist George Sokolsky echoed this point in 1935, explaining that no matter how hard scholars tried to uproot the race concept using scientific means, the daily social and political realities facing most Jews told them that "race does exist."[80] Until society at large ceased to recognize the existence of a Jewish race, it would remain impossible for most Jews themselves to do so.

The Limits of Racial Rhetoric

The ongoing social pressure and antisemitism that prevented the cultural or "ethnic" version of Jewishness from finding widespread acceptance among Jews only intensified in the mid-1930s. Paradoxically, while the climate of social exclusion meant that many American Jews were unable to break away from a racial self-understanding during these years, it also left Jews increasingly divided about how strongly they ought to assert their racial distinctiveness. In addition to insecurity stemming from their own experiences with Depression-era hostility, Jews in America were also struggling with the implications of events in Germany after 1933, paying particularly close attention to the series of racial laws promulgated by Hitler's new government. While such actions seemed to demand a defense of Jewish racial character, they also raised Jews' concerns about the ultimate danger of pressing racial arguments too far.

In the early years of Nazi rule in Germany, many American Jews responded to the Nazi assault on the "Jewish race" with intensified expressions of racial pride. In 1933, Yiddish journalist and political activist David Goldblatt answered Nazi claims with an English-language treatise comparing Jews' racial traits favorably with those of the "Aryans" so idealized in Hitler's racial worldview. "The Aryans may talk peace but they never show that they mean it," wrote Goldblatt. "War is in their blood and their frame of mind tends toward restlessness, whilst the Jews, the children of shepherd ancestry and singers of heavenly majesty, find their highest inspiration in a world of peace."[81] The following year, Rabbi Stephen S. Wise expressed similar sentiments while speaking before the National Association for the Advancement of Colored People. "I confess that I am a little prouder than I was a year ago that I am a Semite, prouder and happier than ever that there is not a drop of Aryan blood in my veins," Wise told his audience. "I am ready to match the record of the Jews, the record of contributions of Jews to civilization, with the record of Aryanism."[82] Such sentiments were not limited to a few headstrong spokesmen. When the national Jewish fraternal order, B'nai B'rith, cooperated with the New York–based social and educational club, the Judaeans, to sponsor a community-wide forum on Nazi racial dogmas, the program not only attacked the "Aryan myth" but presented a full survey of the "sources of Jewish greatness."[83] The American Jewish press, too, was rife during these years with racial language designed to counter Nazi claims. The *American Jewish World* tried to emphasize how Jewish achievement in sports undermined Nazi theories of Jewish racial weakness by labeling its sports column "Semitic Sports Slants."[84] And in a survey of Jewish participation in the American theater, the same magazine postulated the absolute decline of the drama world if Broadway ever "went Aryan."[85]

Yet if some American Jews were pushed by events in Nazi Germany toward an intensified racial rhetoric, others became more reticent about making proud assertions of racial identity. The fact that anti-Jewish racial policies could take root in "civilized" Germany made many American Jews fear that similar measures might emerge in America as well. As anti-semitism continued to rise in United States during the 1930s, profascist elements who openly declared their sympathy with the German cause were increasingly conspicuous. As a result, a small but growing chorus of Jews began to inveigh against the boastful statements made by spokesmen such as Goldblatt and Wise and to denounce any Jewish actions that might give credence to anti-Jewish racism. Jewish playwright Elmer Rice expressed concern that an aggressive racial posture would alienate those non-Jews willing to speak out against antisemitism, convincing them that the Jews had no desire to integrate into the white mainstream.[86] Some Jews opposed a boycott of German goods, fearing that such a move would bolster the racist image of Jewish economic control and confirm the claims of German-Americans that the "Jewish race" had "declared war" on their fatherland.[87] And while racial enthusiasts like Stephen S. Wise were pushing for the establishment of a World Jewish Congress to respond to the Nazi threat, accommodationists like Reform leader Julian Morgenstern warned against such expressions of "racial nationalism," pointing to their "effect as a boomerang, as a weapon which may in turn be used with deadly effect against the Jew when the all too sensitive and suspicious world shall begin to react to this growing Jewish consciousness."[88] Despite the aggressive racial claims often made by the American Jewish press, there, too, some reticence was evident. During the same period in which the *American Hebrew* often published tributes to Jewish racial accomplishment, it also editorialized that "race consciousness is nothing but the attempt of a ruling class, whether in America or Germany, to divide potential opposition to its policies by pitting one section of the population against another."[89] The press lauded the boxing hero Maxie Baer's defeat of the German heavyweight Max Schmeling as a "huge joke at the expense of Herr Hitler," but ultimately concluded that "race generalizations are absolutely absurd."[90]

What is striking about Jewish ambivalence concerning racial identity during the 1930s is that American Jews wavered on *how strenuously* to assert Jewish racial distinctiveness, but rarely on the question of *whether* they were distinct in race. In general, those who denied the racial character of Jewishness continued to be limited to a small circle of intellectuals, who had little influence on the direction of Jewish communal discourse. Even Cyrus Adler, the Semitic scholar who assumed the presidency of the

American Jewish Committee after the death of Louis Marshall in 1929, failed to influence the attitudes of most American Jews when he argued in the mid-1930s that "anthropologically, biologically and ethnologically" there was no justification for the notion of a Jewish race.[91] Ultimately, despite growing fears about how race might be used against them, few American Jews could part with a racial self-understanding during these years. At the same time, however, the disagreements about racial assertiveness that emerged during the 1930s indicated that Jews were becoming more and more limited in their ability to use racial language to serve their needs. Only with the dramatic social shifts of the World War II era would they begin to discover new alternatives.

PART IV
FROM OLD CHALLENGES TO NEW, 1936–1950

CHAPTER 8

WORLD WAR II AND THE TRANSFORMATION

OF JEWISH RACIAL IDENTITY

A T THE height of the Depression, Jews in America could scarcely have been more torn about their place in the American racial system. A growing sense of insecurity heightened their identification with blacks even as it pushed them toward whiteness. Increasing attacks from hostile forces intensified their feelings of "racial" pride and solidarity while also underscoring the danger of being seen as distinct in race. With white Americans both demanding the assimilation of the Jews and setting up social barriers that prevented their entry into the white mainstream, there seemed to be little hope that these disturbing tensions would soon disappear.

Yet amid the trials of the 1930s, forces were at work that would ultimately transform the position of American Jews, bringing them much more firmly into the fold of white Americans. Seeking the support of minorities in advancing his New Deal agenda, President Franklin D. Roosevelt increasingly promoted an inclusive nationalism that embraced Jews and other immigrants as productive participants in the national culture. Like his predecessor and cousin, Theodore Roosevelt, he brought many Jews into public service and even admitted some to his small circle of trusted advisers.[1] While there was a significant backlash to the administration's overtures toward Jews, by the war years there were also an increasing number of non-Jewish Americans who were influenced by the government's vision and were ready to take immediate steps to admit Jews and other immigrants into the white mainstream. As economic recovery and military successes transformed the United States into a much more hopeful nation during the 1940s and Jews began to vanish as a symbol of social anxiety, this tendency toward greater inclusiveness took hold among white Americans more generally.

In important ways, this dramatic transition relieved the debilitating social pressures Jews had long experienced as unstable members of America's racial culture. For the first time since the nineteenth century, many Jews felt free to voice empathy and support for African Americans without fear that it would bring their whiteness into question. The shifts of the 1940s also made it easier for Jewish leaders and scholars to promote a new definition of Jewish group difference rooted in "ethnicity," a concept that had failed to catch on among Jews as long as they remained victims of "racial" hatred. Yet the acceptance of Jews as unambiguous whites did not totally resolve the dilemmas of asserting a distinctive identity in a society organized around the categories of "black" and "white." If Jews grew more comfortable embracing racial liberalism, their ongoing desire for acceptance in the non-Jewish world sometimes pushed them to retreat from liberal positions. Even when they did voice concern and support for blacks, they were often unable to assert the specifically Jewish motivations for their posture. Similarly, while their incorporation into white America lessened the stigma attached to Jewish difference, Jews ultimately found the new "ethnic" definition of Jewishness unviable. Unable to satisfy either the emotional needs of Jews, who often continued to think of themselves in racial terms, or meet the expectations of non-Jews, who assumed that postwar Jewishness would fade into a denominational identity, the language of "ethnicity" receded as quickly as it had arisen. Thus, rather than helping them to achieve a satisfying synthesis of American and Jewish identities in the postwar period, Jews' long-awaited entry into the white mainstream often left them vacillating between forms of self-expression acceptable to the larger white society and more particularistic commitments that could not be comfortably expressed in public.

White Americans All

The notion of a "Jewish Problem" had remained strong in both the conservative and liberal streams of American racial discourse during the 1930s. But during the closing years of the decade, some of the dramatic social and political changes that grew out of the Depression and Roosevelt's New Deal helped legitimize a different, less menacing view of the Jewish place in national life. As both Catholic and Jewish immigrants became a larger and more politically mobilized part of the electorate during these years, Roosevelt began to rely on them more significantly as a base of support for his New Deal agenda. Aside from the Jews he had tapped as political advisers, he forged close relationships with Jewish figures ranging from Rabbi Stephen S. Wise, who was active in social reform movements, to Sidney Hillman, the leader of Jewish-dominated Amalgamated Clothing Workers of America.[2] Out of these increasing ties came a greater willingness to redefine American nationalism in ways that did not question the status of Jews and other immigrant groups as a stable part of white society. As Roosevelt approached his second term in office, he began to express the view that immigrant groups had become "fully American" and that they no longer presented the thorny problems of assimilation and adjustment that many whites had worried about since the

1920s.[3] During his reelection campaign of 1936, Roosevelt strongly asserted the notion that immigrants were an asset, rather than a threat, to American life, going so far as to suggest that "in some cases the newer citizens have discharged their obligations to us better than we have discharged our obligations to them."[4]

Roosevelt's vision of a more expansive white America that included Jews and other immigrant groups, however, did not go unchallenged by conservative forces. His political opponents, like Representative Martin J. Dies of Texas, chair of the House Special Committee on Un-American Activities, saw the growing ties between Jews and the Roosevelt Administration as a dangerous development that threatened the integrity of the nation. He frequently charged Jews with being communist sympathizers, taking particularly sharp aim at those who favored civil rights for African Americans.[5] During the late 1930s and 1940s, Senator Theodore Bilbo and Congressman John Rankin, both of Mississippi, regularly blamed "New York Jews" for the liberal social and racial policies of the New Deal and attacked Jewish congressmen who supported labor reform and desegregation.[6] Painting Jews as a subversive force in American race relations, Rankin argued that Connecticut congressman Herman Koppelman's proposal for desegregation in the nation's capital would encourage black men to attack white women.[7] The image of the Jews as a group that put its own interests over those of white America found particular expression after 1939, when conservatives pointed to Jewish influence as the force pushing the Roosevelt Administration toward war in Europe. This view was expressed by radio priest Charles Coughlin, who helped popularize it among urban Catholics, as well as by profascist groups like the William Pelley's Silver Shirts and Gerald Winrod's Defenders of the Christian Faith. Even more respected figures, like American icon Charles Lindbergh, joined in such rhetoric under the aegis of the America First Committee, one of the most vocal of antiwar organizations. After the United States entered the war, antisemitism continued to increase, reaching what historian Leonard Dinnerstein has called its "high tide."[8]

Yet even as the war provided a context for increased antisemitism, it also set the scene for a stronger assertion of Roosevelt's inclusive nationalism. Success in war demanded unity, and Roosevelt and his administration resolved to fight against intergroup hostilities that might threaten the cohesion of American fighting forces or jeopardize efforts on the homefront. The government was particularly concerned that the Germans or their domestic sympathizers would try to weaken American resolve by disseminating propaganda designed to inflame racial hatreds. As a result, it took strong action against racist agitators, charging many with undermining the war effort and espousing an enemy ideology. In 1942, profascists Pelley and Winrod were investigated for sedition and their publications were shut down. The same year, government officials put strong pressure on the Catholic Church to silence Father Coughlin, who ceased to broadcast his sermons under the threat of suspension from church leaders.[9]

In addition to the suppression of racist publications and spokesmen, the government also engaged in a vigorous propaganda campaign, which promoted its goal of unity by defining the American values of tolerance and equality as the antithesis of Nazi racism. The roots of these efforts stretched back to the immediate prewar years, when the U.S. Office of Education, already fearing the deleterious effect of fascist propaganda in the United States, initiated a series of radio broadcasts entitled "Americans All . . . Immigrants All." After the entry of the United States into the war, propaganda denouncing racial hatred as "un-American" became a centerpiece of efforts to mobilize the home front and was disseminated widely by the newly formed Office of War Information (OWI), not only on the airwaves but also through pamphlets, posters, films, and even comic books.[10]

As the fight against racial discrimination became identified with the war aims, some government agencies took steps to discard the terminology of "race" as it applied to European immigrant groups. The Immigration and Naturalization Service (INS), for example, created new forms for naturalization in 1940 that recorded European immigrants' race as "white" rather than employing the narrower racial designations traditionally used in the immigration records. New arrivals from Europe continued to be classified on ships' manifests according to the old "List of Races and Peoples" until the 1950s, but in 1943 a special exception was made for Jews, who ceased to be written down as "Hebrews." Apparently, repeated requests by Jewish organizations and the desire to distance government classification schemes from those used by the Nazis pushed the INS commissioner, Earl H. Harrison, to finally reconsider the decades-old policy, which he now described as arbitrary and without foundation in American law.[11]

The tolerance campaigns of the World War II era often decried discrimination in the broadest terms, condemning racism against African Americans as well as against those of various immigrant backgrounds. In practice, however, by offering a much greater degree of incorporation to Jews and other European groups than to blacks, the government's wartime policies had the effect of redrawing American racial boundaries rather than erasing them altogether. Ultimately, the Roosevelt Administration believed that domestic stability would best be achieved by consolidating immigrants into the "white" population and by reestablishing the clear division between blacks and whites that had been in doubt in American society for several decades. This process of stabilizing the black-white divide was most evident in the organization of American military forces, where blacks and Asians were segregated into their own units while Jews,

Italians, and Irish were assigned to "white" units along with men whose families had been in the United States for generations.[12] The existence of a Pacific warfront where the Japanese enemy was defined as a nonwhite racial menace also gave credence to the notion of a unified white American fighting force.[13] More than any other wartime development, the thorough integration of Jews and Catholics into the American military helped cement the public's view of these groups as unambiguously white.

Although they were never embraced universally by the American public, the government's attempts to both counter prejudice and stabilize racial boundaries helped relieve much anxiety about the place of Jews in national life. This shift was apparent in the growing authority with which liberal intellectuals were able to dispel the notion of a distinct Jewish "race" and introduce new concepts concerning group difference within American culture during these years. Though anthropologist Franz Boas had been unsuccessful in rallying the scientific community to discredit Nazi racial theory in the mid-1930s, by 1938 he was able to convince the American Anthropological Society to pass a resolution stating that the terms "Aryan" and "Semite" had "no racial significance whatsoever," and were useful only in identifying linguistic groups.[14] By the early 1940s, anthropological theories that questioned the applicability of the term "race" to European groups were popularized in book form, and certain titles, like Ruth Benedict's *Races of Mankind* and Ashley Montagu's *Man's Most Dangerous Myth*, became bestsellers. As the term "race" came to be applied more exclusively to peoples of color, concepts like "ethnicity," pioneered by Jewish scholars in the 1920s to refer to European descent groups, were finally introduced more broadly to the American public. When sociologists W. Lloyd Warner and Leo Srole contributed a volume on immigrant adjustment to the acclaimed "Yankee City" series in 1945, they distinguished sharply between nonwhite "racial" groups and white "ethnic" groups. While ethnic groups may carry "a divergent set of cultural traits which are evaluated by the host society as inferior," they explained, "racial groups are divergent biologically rather than culturally."[15] These changes in terminology were not only discernible in the writings of liberal intellectuals. In public opinion polls carried out just after the war, less than half of Americans surveyed still identified the Jews as a race, a sharp decline from the prewar tendency.[16]

The inclusive nationalism of the Roosevelt Administration, the integration of Jews into the U.S. military, and the spread of new theories about the difference between "race" and "ethnicity" all paved the way for Jews to gain acceptance as American whites during the war years. Yet ultimately, it was not until the Allied victory ushered in a new period of optimism and social stability that the Jew ceased to operate as a significant symbol of social anxiety. Despite the somewhat gradual pace of Jewish incorporation into white America, however, Jews themselves responded enthusiastically to the increased climate of acceptance from the beginning. Having experienced more than four decades of uncertainty about their place in America's racial culture, Jews of the late 1930s and 1940s were exhilarated by the promise of integration represented by these liberal forces. Despite the persistence of antisemitism during the war years, the willingness of an increasing number of white Americans to oppose anti-Jewish sentiments and declare them antithetical to the nation's values inspired great optimism among American Jews that they would finally be able to achieve unconditional recognition as full members of the dominant society.

If the events of World War II helped to diminish concern about the far-reaching racial characteristics of Jews and offered them a significant level of incorporation into white America, however, these changes did not reflect a growing comfort with Jewish group separatism. Popular discourse of the 1940s may have transformed the perceived "racial" differences of immigrant groups into "ethnic" ones and parted with references to Jews as a distinct "problem" that needed solving, but in granting ethnics equal rights and opportunities, explains historian Gary Gerstle, promoters of tolerance still "hoped to pull them out of their parochial ethnic worlds and into a cosmopolitan American society."[17] This meant that as Jews integrated into the white mainstream, they were expected to keep expressions of group difference at a level that would not offend the sense of unity and homogeneity from which whites of the postwar era drew their confidence and stability.[18] Yet because white society welcomed them with the language of tolerance and equality, Jews were not always aware of just how exacting the requirements of life in white America would be.

The Rise of Jewish Racial Liberalism

As long as Jewish racial status had remained problematic in American culture, Jews faced continual dilemmas about how to assert their whiteness without adopting forms of white racism that sat uneasily with their own self-image as a persecuted people. But as white Americans' fears about the racial status of Jews began to recede, so did much of the tension surrounding the Jewish approach toward African Americans. In fact, for many Jews pursuing social acceptance during this period, whiteness and racial liberalism often became two mutually supporting aspects of their emerging identities.

The improving image of the Jews among white Americans was not the only factor that helped ease them into a comfortable white identity. Also critical was the way in which the changing social climate of the period created new possibilities for defining how "whiteness" might be expressed. While Roosevelt's social policies did not offer blacks the same degree of incorporation into national life that they extended to Jews and other European immigrant groups, the administration did devote considerable effort to ending various forms of racial discrimination and improving conditions for the black working class, goals that many Jews had long shared. Through their support of these measures, and more generally through their overwhelming affiliation with the Democratic Party, American Jews could for the first time claim an unambiguous role in the white mainstream while also pursuing a liberal approach to racial issues. Jews also embraced this liberal version of whiteness by participating in the wartime discourse that condemned all forms of racism and bigotry as "un-American." With the defeat of racial hatred identified as one of the war aims, Jews felt confident that they could oppose antiblack measures in the name of American principles without making their specifically Jewish motivations public. As a result, they were able to satisfy the emotional need they often had to distance themselves from white racism and yet avoid the stigma of associating themselves too directly with African Americans and their plight.

The letters and memoirs of Jewish servicemen provide some of the earliest examples of how wartime Jews explained their opposition to racism by invoking American ideals without calling attention to their Jewishness or singling themselves out in any way from the white mainstream. Writing home in 1944, Manny Kruppin of Los Angeles complained that the racism of some of his fellow soldiers showed an ignorance of "what we are fighting for and what some of our boys are dying for." He expressed his hope that "these petty grievances are forgotten and we all concentrate on our common enemy—fascism—and eradicate it forever."[19] A soldier who submitted his wartime memoirs to a competition sponsored by the YIVO Institute argued that Jews' role as "citizens" required them to promote "tolerance and mutual understanding" and help find solutions to "the questions of prejudice and discrimination against the colored people, Mexicans and other minority groups."[20] Morris Palansky of Chicago expressed his belief in a 1943 letter that the fight against Hitler demanded similar action against the persecution of blacks at home. Defeating the "breeders of chauvinism and fascism" in America, he explained, went "hand and hand with their defeat abroad."[21]

At home, too, American Jews condemned racism against blacks by invoking broad American principles rather than specifically Jewish rationales. The National Council of Jewish Women, which began to oppose discrimination against a number of American racial minorities during the war years, explained its interest in these causes by stating that "the problem of discrimination is the problem of every American."[22] To link their antiracist attitudes more firmly to the nation's fight against Germany, Jews often compared domestic racism to Nazism. When important hearings meant to address discrimination in railroad employment were canceled due to pressure from southern congressmen, Brooklyn's *Jewish Examiner* argued that Hitler, while losing the military campaign, could "take comfort in this triumph of fascism on the American domestic front." The paper urged the southerners to address the paradox of "fighting against the detestable Nazi doctrine of race superiority overseas while they fight for the right to keep it alive on these shores."[23] In the final years of the war, the Greensboro, North Carolina, *American Jewish Times* took aim at the racism of Senator Theodore Bilbo and Congressman John Rankin, calling them the "Shame of Mississippi" for their "un-American spirit." Public opinion should be mobilized to force such men out of office, argued the paper, lest the United States "allow the Nazis and other kindred spirits to laugh up their sleeves at our democracy."[24]

Ultimately, this new civic discourse, which allowed Jews to speak with the authority of full Americans while also condemning all forms of racial discrimination as "un-American" and antidemocratic, was embraced by the major Jewish defense agencies in the United States, including the American Jewish Committee, the American Jewish Congress, and the Anti-Defamation League of B'nai B'rith. In the years following World War II, these agencies often shifted their focus away from the narrow defense of Jewish interests and instead set their sights on more "generalized" forms of prejudice.[25] New York State Supreme Court Judge Meier Steinbrink, who assumed the national chairmanship of the Anti-Defamation League in the immediate postwar period, explained: "as Jewish agencies we will be concerned not so much with protecting the position of the Jews as with expanding the business of democracy so that all who live in America shall enjoy equally of the rights, obligations, and opportunities which America offers."[26] In theory, the fight against "generalized prejudice" was meant to attack intolerance against all minorities rather than focusing specifically on the plight of any one group. Yet because African Americans remained the most visible outsiders in American society and Jews were quickly becoming indistinct among white Americans, these campaigns often had the effect of highlighting the black-white divide while obscuring Jewish distinctiveness. This approach to civil rights was also taken up by the leading unions in the garment industry, which still had a strong Jewish leadership in the 1940s despite a decline in the number of Jewish members. While the International Ladies' Garment Workers' Union had long fought for the rights of Jewish workers, its tolerance campaigns of the 1940s decried bigotry and racism in ways that cast Americans as blacks and whites and made Jewishness invisible. Such activism allowed Jews to identify vicariously with the civil rights' struggle

21. "The Defense of Equal Rights," 1947. Racial liberalism gave many Jews of the World War II era a means to express their empathy for African Americans while downplaying their own role as victims of "racial" hatred. In this publicity sketch for the International Ladies' Garment Workers' Union, Jews become undifferentiated whites as they join with blacks to fight bigotry and intolerance. (From Max Danish, *The Story of the ILGWU*. Sketch by Bernard Seaman)

of blacks without putting into question the strides they had made toward acceptance as unambiguous whites.[27]

There were, however, exceptions to the way Jewish discourse tended to obscure the particular investment Jews had in battling racism during this period. During the war years, the raw emotions concerning Jewish persecution in Europe and the ongoing pressures of domestic antisemitism sometimes pushed Jews to be more explicit about their reasons for opposing antiblack racism and occasionally led them to make direct comparisons between themselves and African Americans. In 1941, just before America's entry into the conflict, Rabbi Alexander Goode, who later become a symbol of interfaith cooperation as an army chaplain who died in service along with three non-Jewish colleagues, spoke of the "jim crow" policies endured by Europe's Jews and used the history of Jewish persecution to argue against the segregation of African Americans in his hometown of Washington, D.C.[28] Similarly, when a grand jury in New York's Kings County Court handed down a presentment tinged with antiblack racism, the Brooklyn *Jewish Examiner* argued that "no one is in a better position to sympathize with and understand its harsh unfairness than Jews."[29] These statements, however, were deviations from the general wartime practice of keeping the Jewish motivations for antiracist attitudes submerged, a trend that became even more pronounced as Jews made strides toward greater social integration in the postwar period. Jews did continue to compare antiblack racism with Nazi policies during the immediate postwar years, but in doing so they generally described Nazi racism not as a specifically Jewish travail but as a synonym for bigotry or hatred more generally. Since Nazism was widely seen as antithetical to "American values," Jewish commentators could describe white attackers of African Americans as "perfect Hitler material" or compare Jim Crow policies with the racism of the "brownshirts" without ever directly acknowledging the links they were making between blacks and Jews.[30] Rather than explicitly positioning themselves as a minority group like African Americans, Jews generally used blacks and black causes as surrogates for concerns that had become less immediate in their own lives, but to which they retained a strong emotional connection.

As racial liberalism began to permeate the discourse and institutions of the American Jewish community, Jews of the war years and the immediate postwar period also began to express their new approach to African Americans through the consumption of popular culture. Whereas the Jewish encounter with black culture during the 1920s and 1930s had revealed intense ambivalence, and often combined longing admiration with a defensive racism, by the 1940s Jews seem to have evolved a more confident cultural style that gave them access to black culture without fear that it would stigmatize them as outsiders. Countless memoirs record the fascination of Jewish youth of these years with African American jazz artists, whose performances in nightclubs and dance halls they would often attend. Many young Jews accorded these musicians the status of cultural icons, speaking of them with a reverence that stands in marked contrast to the mixed emotions Jewish youth had expressed about black culture just a decade earlier. Jews of this period often found that jazz could give them the sense of freedom and individuality they desired in white America without threatening their newfound status in that society. As historian Lawrence Levine recalled of his youth during this period, "through these jazz musicians we not only found art that touched us, we also saw the possibility of functioning in the outside society while retaining our individual and ethnic personas."[31]

The increasing ease with which Jews expressed their respect and admiration for black musicians mirrored a similar development in their approach to African American sports figures. Jewish men of the 1920s and 1930s had often become involved in sports as a means of countering antisemitic stereotypes, using athletic competition to demonstrate the strength and talent of the "Jewish race" and to win approval from the dominant society. As Jews of the 1940s felt less pressure to prove themselves in the ring and on the playing field, however, they often began to rally around the rising generation of African American athletes who were coming to take their place as participants in professional athletics and whose struggle for recognition seemed to recall their own experiences.[32] After Jackie Robinson broke the color barrier in major league baseball in 1947 and paved the way for the entry of other black players into the national game, the *American Hebrew* expressed its pleasure that "America's unrealized ideal of equality" was "becoming a reality in the sports world."[33] Similarly, Jews of this period often saw the African American heavyweight Joe Louis as a successor to Jewish boxing greats such as Barney Ross and Benny Leonard.[34] They also took pride in the fact that Louis's Jewish manager, Mike Jacobs, played an important role in the black fighter's rise to prominence, thereby delivering a "terrific blow," as the *Hebrew* explained, not only to those who "wanted a white man to maintain the legend of white supremacy" but to the entire "theory of race supremacy" in general.[35] As had happened in the realm of civil rights, African Americans had largely become an emotional surrogate for concerns that were no longer primary in the experience of American Jews themselves.

If the social transformation of the World War II era made it possible for many Jews to assert a racial liberalism that did not threaten their status as white in American society, these developments did not succeed in totally solving the tensions and contradictions embedded in the American Jewish approach to African Americans. Instead, two significant problems continued to complicate Jews' attempts to synthesize their Jewish and white identities. First, although Jews were finding a comfortable niche in American politics and life, they generally remained more liberal than most other white Americans, from whom they continued to seek gestures of social acceptance. As a result, they sometimes continued to feel pushed in opposite directions by the social pressures encountered in their new settings. According to Deborah Dash Moore, Jewish soldiers entering basic training at the beginning of the war sometimes acceded to the antiblack racism of their comrades in order to avoid calling unwanted attention to themselves. In Fort Benning, Georgia, Howard Sachs was shocked when one of his fellow trainees punched a black man who didn't move off the sidewalk fast enough for him to pass. Yet as a Jew trying to establish his own credentials in a new arena, he felt he was in no position to object to such behavior.[36]

During the postwar years, the most obvious example of an ongoing struggle among Jews over their approach to African Americans was in the South. Southern Jews, unlike their counterparts in most other regions, generally shied away from visible support for black civil rights, fearing such a stance would incur the wrath of white neighbors. Although some southern Jews like Atlanta rabbi Jacob Rothschild and Jackson, Mississippi, rabbi Perry Nussbaum did make common cause with African Americans, others like Georgia politician Charles Bloch and South Carolina legislator Sol Blatt strongly supported the segregationist status quo.[37] Ultimately, while most Southern Jews seem to have had a greater degree of empathy for African Americans than did their gentile counterparts, most were too fearful of negative social consequences to express such feelings openly. In a few cases, Jewish businessmen in small southern towns were sufficiently moved by feelings of insecurity and duress to join the local "white citizens councils," which actively opposed integration. "Faced with social ostracism, economic boycott and the occasional death threat," explains historian Clive Webb, "they had little alternative."[38] As civil rights activity heated up in the South, a few "quiet voices" worked diligently for social change, but by and large the sympathies of the Jewish community for blacks remained muted by a climate of fear.[39]

Northern Jews, too, sometimes found themselves constrained in their support of civil rights by a desire to continue their strides toward social acceptance. When their support of civil rights brought them into conflict with powerful white elites or when residential proximity to African Americans threatened their social status, they often retreated from their policy of racial liberalism and supported the path that best facilitated their continued integration into the white mainstream.[40] In the years directly following the war, for example, tensions continued to emerge in changing urban neighborhoods concerning the questions of racial proximity and succession. In 1949, about fifty-five thousand Jews remained in Chicago's Lawndale district, where they lived alongside a population of ten thousand African Americans. Despite the avoidance of racial violence and the foundation of a "citizen's council"—not to be confused with its southern counterparts—that worked to ensure good race relations, community officials reported that "the vast majority of Jews in the area have a tremendous resentment towards the new residents."[41] In addition, Lawndale organizations like the Jewish People's Institute (JPI) became embroiled in controversy over whether local African Americans should be allowed to use the pool, attend the day camp, or attend the evening dances frequented by local Jewish youth. On one occasion a radical group invited several African Americans to a dance at the JPI, much to the dismay of some of the other Jewish attendees. While affirming their commitment to a policy of nondiscrimination and democracy in an official statement, leaders of the JPI expressed concerns that if they admitted blacks to their events in any large numbers, "the vast majority of . . . Jewish membership would promptly withdraw."[42]

Such tensions failed to dissipate as Jews left behind urban neighborhoods for more suburban locations. While a panoply of national Jewish organizations like the American Jewish Committee, the American Jewish Congress, B'nai B'rith, the Jewish War Veterans, and the Jewish Labor Committee all supported legislation against housing restriction, many

Jewish suburbanites found themselves in the somewhat uncomfortable position of supporting neighborhood covenants. The Jewish developer William Levitt, who built model "Levittown" communities in New Jersey and Pennsylvania during the mid-1950s, refused to integrate his communities until he was forced to do so by the courts in 1960. Levitt argued that "as a Jew and a humane man he sympathized with the plight of struggling minorities," but that because "most whites prefer not to live in mixed communities," he could not be expected to undertake such a "vast social experiment" as building integrated suburbs. Levitt faced pressure from Jewish groups, but according to sociologist Herbert Gans, Jews whose own social status was endangered by the threat of proximity to African Americans often shared the developers' ambivalent view. "I don't want Negroes in Levittown, and I don't want Jews associated with interracial attempts," explained one Jewish Levittowner. As a Jew, however, the same individual refused to picket against impending integration, explaining that "we are a minority, too."[43] Although Jews' success in the postwar world helped them assert a more consistent support of black rights than had been possible in the 1920s and 1930s, such examples illustrate how their racial liberalism could give way under the ongoing pressures of integration.[44]

If their commitment to liberal values was sometimes challenged by their continued drive for social acceptance, Jews also encountered a second stumbling block in trying to synthesize their Jewish and white identities: the ultimate inability of racial liberalism to convey the full distinctiveness of Jewish concerns. True, many Jews felt racial liberalism to be a natural outgrowth of their own history as a persecuted people, and they devoted their community institutions to its cause. But the tendency of Jews during this period to cast their opposition to racism as an outgrowth of "American values" and to downplay the specifically Jewish motivations for such views reflected the constraints placed on them by their entrance into white society. Racial liberalism and intergroup relations work often served their identity needs as they sought greater inclusion in white America, but over the long run these commitments failed to provide the sense of particularity Jews once felt among America's constellation of "racial" groups. As we shall see, while incorporation into white America allowed Jews to put a difficult period of antisemitism behind them, it also severely limited their ability to articulate an identity as a group apart.

The Retreat of Jewish Racial Identity

In the mid-1930s, Jews had struggled with the limits of an identity rooted in race, often pushed by growing antisemitism toward strong defenses of their racial character but worried that they might further endanger their position with such separatist rhetoric. As wartime culture increasingly allowed Jews to position themselves as unambiguous whites, however, they no longer felt compelled to appeal to racial pride in answering the charges of their critics. At a time when the government was signaling its disapproval of antisemitism and the U.S. Office of Education was sponsoring programs recognizing the contributions of groups like Jews to American life, it became increasingly clear to Jews that they could condemn the actions of their enemies by invoking the principles of Americanism, rather than engaging in risky debates about their own racial qualities. In many ways, the goal of fighting antisemitism was pursued through the same universalized discourse that Jews used to oppose racism of all kinds. In condemning "race prejudice" as "un-American," Jews were able to answer their accusers while drawing only minimal attention to themselves. As Jewish defense agencies began during the war years to carry on campaigns against "generalized prejudice" and to label all forms of racism as the antithesis of American democracy, the need for defensive assertions of Jewish racial identity vanished.

A willingness to put aside strong expressions of racial pride during the war years, however, did not mean that American Jews wished to obscure their group distinctiveness altogether. Buoyed by what they saw as the ability to finally meld their Jewish identity with white Americanism, several Jewish community leaders of the war years—mainly rabbis—set out to popularize a new version of group identity more suited to the changing social circumstances. In a number of books and pamphlets issued between the late 1930s and the end of the war, these writers began to forward a new cultural or "ethnic" brand of Jewishness similar to that first suggested by Jewish scholars in the 1920s and early 1930s. Unlike the more technical, academic treatises produced by Horace Kallen, Julius Drachsler, Isaac Berkson, and Mordecai Kaplan, however, arguments for an ethnic Jewishness during this period were usually written in a popular style and intended for broad circulation.

One of the leading proponents of the ethnic definition of Jewishness during these years was Lee Levinger, a Reform rabbi from Wilmington, Delaware, who had studied the history and causes of American antisemitism as a graduate student at the University of Pennsylvania during the 1920s. In 1936, Levinger argued in a book about antisemitism that the Jews' common traits were "social, religious and national" rather than racial, and were a product of "social heredity, which we ordinarily call tradition."[45] Sensing the opportunity to bring these views to a wider audience during the war years, he collaborated with James Waterman Wise, the son of Rabbi Stephen S. Wise, to issue *Mr. Smith Meets Mr. Cohen* (1940), a book intended to promote better understanding between Jews

and non-Jews. Although Wise had previously asserted a racial understanding of Jewishness, he and Levinger now argued unambiguously that the
Jew was not distinct in race, but was "a member of a recognizable minority
group—set apart by his religion, language, nationality, [and] other characteristics."[46] By 1945, Conservative rabbi Milton Steinberg, in his *Partisan
Guide to the Jewish Problem*, proposed the term "people" as a more suit-
able label for the Jewish group than race. "A people is a body of persons
who partake together in a social past and its heritage, a present and its
problems, a future and its aspirations," explained Steinberg. While peoplehood was "marked by a sense of kinship and shared interests," however, it differed significantly from race. " 'Race' as applied to humans,"
he wrote, "is the analogue of 'breed' in reference to animals . . . [and] is
altogether inapplicable to Jewry."[47] Another popular book of the period,
written by Reform rabbi Roland B. Gittelsohn for use in high school
classes and Jewish youth groups, presented a number of new alternatives
to the racial definition, including "civilization," "community," "people,"
and "cultural group."[48]

In their efforts to advance this new "ethnic" version of Jewishness and
discredit the notion of a "Jewish race" among Jews, popularizers were
aided by the increasing association of racial language with the Nazi regime. Although Jews had rarely if ever advanced a view of Jewish racial
distinctiveness as absolute as the one the Nazis proposed, Levinger and
his colleagues made the argument that embracing a racial definition of
Jewishness was tantamount to accepting Nazi racial dogmas. In 1936,
Levinger used such logic to dismiss a racial view of group identity as nothing more than "a device to bolster up anti-Semitism or other types of national or group hatred." Condemning the racial generalizations made by
Jews as strongly as those made by non-Jews, he argued that the chauvinis-
tic views of writers such as Maurice Samuel and David Goldblatt were
nothing more a reversal of the Nazi race theories.[49] A similar emphasis
was made in 1943 by Gittelsohn, who was still willing to argue that Jews
were "in some ways" a race, but was certain to "distinguish clearly between our use of that word and Hitler's use of it." According to Gittelsohn,
Hitler relied on the notion that races were relatively pure and thus could
be easily placed in categories of superior and inferior. "That is why we
Jews, if we use the word race in describing ourselves, must be careful to
say 'a race in some respects' or 'to some extent a race.' "[50]

While the comparison to Nazi racial dogmas was an effective tool in
discrediting a racial view of Jewishness, spokesmen for Jewish ethnicity
also based their arguments on the growing American consensus that the
only true racial distinctions were those based on color. Such reasoning
was featured in a booklet distributed in 1939 by the Anti-Defamation
League for use in its "Fireside Discussion Group," a popular home-study

course aimed at educating Jews about "the many problems confronting World Jewry." To support its assertion of Jewish whiteness, the guide strained to downplay race among the elements contributing to Jewish identity. "Scientifically and correctly speaking, there are three great races in the world: the black, yellow and white," the guide explained. "Within the white race all the sub-races have long since been mixed and we Jews are part of the general admixture." Environmental influences, however "made us a distinctive type, and a common spiritual culture has made us a conscious unity. Approximately a race, definitely a type, and consciously a unity, we are an historic people."[51]

The broad acceptance of this view was made clear in 1943 when the YIVO Institute for Jewish Research in New York surveyed prominent academics of Jewish origin on the perennial issue of whether Jews should be classified as "Hebrews" in U.S. immigration records. Most of the respondents suggested that the term "ethnic group" be substituted for race, which they felt should only be used in reference to peoples of color. "Any subdivisions smaller than White (or Caucasian), Negro, Mongolian are objectionable to me," wrote University of Chicago sociologist Louis Wirth. "I think these categories are sufficient for the human race." Max Schoen, a psychologist and educator from the Carnegie Institute of Technology, echoed the sentiments of many of those surveyed when he wrote that "the term 'race' other than *white, black*, etc., is now utterly meaningless."[52] Schoen's statement captured the tenor of American Jewish discourse on both the scholarly and popular levels. By the war's end in 1945, it was exceedingly rare for Jews to still refer to themselves as a "race."

Although Jewish racial identity was increasingly refashioned as "ethnicity" during the late 1930s and 1940s, this semantic shift failed to provide a complete solution to the tensions embedded in American Jewish identity. Significantly, the disappearance of "race" as a term for self-definition among American Jews by 1945 did not necessarily mean that Jews ceased to think of themselves in racial terms. The tendency of ethnic promoters to use multiple, somewhat vague terms ("people," "civilization," "community") for Jewish difference without settling on any one clear description signified the difficulty they had in filling the gap left by the disappearance of "race." The imprecision with which they sometimes differentiated the new concepts of group status from the old (Jews remained "in some respects a race" or "approximately a race") suggests that the change in terminology was not accompanied by a significant change in the way Jews understood what made them different. Ironically, in some ways the older racial definition ended up having greater utility than the newer ethnic understanding of Jewishness for Jews poised on the brink of social acceptance. The ethnic definition stressed a set of shared cultural practices and an interest in things like Jewish art, literature, and music.

THESE ARE JEWS

Danny Kaye, American actor.   Israeli children.

22. "These Are Jews," 1953. Nathan Ausubel's popular *Pictorial History of the Jewish People* depicted its subjects as stemming from a variety of races, reflecting the tendency of postwar Jews to move away from references to the "Jewish race." Some wartime Jewish spokesmen tried to popularize a new "ethnic" identity among American Jews, but by the 1950s it was the religious version of Jewishness that flourished the most in public discourse.

Yet American Jews hoping to make significant strides toward social integration were much more focused on emulating the cultural patterns of their non-Jewish neighbors than on developing their own distinctive cultural repertoire. As they pursued integration, they were often drawn to a more primordial understanding of Jewishness that had little to do with actual behavior but which privileged blood ties and gave them a sense of connectedness as social boundaries changed.

Signs of a lingering attachment to "race" can be seen in the cultural production of American Jews during the war years and in the period following. The urge to trumpet the achievements of fellow Jews, for example, remained intact even after the language of race had disappeared in Jewish circles. Several books published in the 1940s hailed the talents of Jews as fighters and praised their bravery on the battlefield, even though they scrupulously avoided any overt reference to racial traits.[53] Similarly, in his 1944 treatment of antisemitism, *Must Men Hate?* longtime Anti-Defamation League president Sigmund Livingston argued the notion of a separate Jewish race while at the same time engaging in a classic racial apologetic. Starting with the premises that "there is no Aryan, or German, blood and there is no Semitic, or Jewish, blood," Livingston went on to tout the Jews' special "contributions to civilization," even including a list of seven hundred of the world's most accomplished Jews in the back as an appendix. The list employed a purely racial definition of Jewishness, in which the ancestry of the contributor, rather than the substance of his or her accomplishments, is what made them Jewish. In fact, because Livingston's goal was to show how Jewish traits had helped make Jews contributors to the larger society, those involved in specifically Jewish activities—rabbis, communal leaders, Hebrew and Yiddish authors—were excluded.[54] Similar works, like Mac Davis's *Jews at a Glance*, which offered a "gallery of Jewish greatness and achievement," appeared as late as 1956.[55] The tendency, even at this late date, to define Jews as a group bound by unique qualities and ancestral ties rather than by particular cultural markers suggests that the rise of "ethnicity" did not represent a thoroughgoing reconceptualization of Jewish identity. Instead, it was largely a linguistic strategy designed to recast their continued attachment to a racial self-understanding in terms more acceptable to the non-Jewish world.

The new ethnic definition of Jewishness not only failed to satisfy the emotional needs of many Jews, but also fell short of the expectations of non-Jewish society that Jews would suppress all but religious expressions of group difference as they integrated. While wartime culture had helped distinguish ethnicity from race, it did not necessarily see ethnic difference as a value in and of itself that was worth preserving. On the contrary, during the war years and in the postwar period, white Americans often saw the continued social and cultural separatism of groups like Jews as a divisive and "ethnocentric" force.[56] Religion, however, was seen as an acceptable form of group cohesion that did not threaten the image of a white America bound together by shared values. During the war, for example, the army promoted the notion of a common "Judeo-Christian tradition" and encouraged white military personnel to organize into faith groups.[57] By the 1950s, American popular culture—including the emerging medium of television—avoided celebrations of ethnic distinctiveness but valorized *religious* pluralism. As Will Herberg explained in his now-classic treatment of the period, *Protestant-Catholic-Jew* (1955), religion rather than ethnicity was the primary means through which groups like Jews could stake an equal claim to "The American Way of Life." Self-identification in ethnic terms, he wrote, was a "sign of incomplete integration." Any ethnic group that "becomes permanent and self-perpetuating and resists cultural assimilation . . . would be confronted with the same problems and difficulties as face the Negroes and men and women of Oriental ancestry in this country."[58]

All of these factors undermined the viability of a new "ethnic" identity for American Jews in the years following the war. Instead of creating the neat synthesis between Jewish particularism and white Americanism envisioned by ethnic promoters, Jews often defined themselves publicly as a religious group while privately pursuing Jewishness as a tribal phenomenon. If they sought to become undifferentiated Americans on the

23. Protestant, Catholic, Jew . . . and Negro, 1942. The U.S. military encouraged members of various European descent groups to cast their identities in religious instead of racial terms during World War II. African Americans, who remained segregated in the armed forces, however, continued to stand in distinction to white Protestants, Catholics, and Jews. Here, in a photo taken by the Office of War Information, army chaplains from the three white religious groupings greet an African American colleague. (Courtesy Library of Congress, Prints and Photographs Division)

suburban frontier, they often restricted their most intimate contacts to other Jews. They gathered primarily in synagogues, but usually to socialize rather than to pray. In fact, a strong preference for friendship and marriage within the Jewish group remained among the most salient features of Jewish life.[59] Rhetorically, American Jews of the period tended to interpret the Jewish experience by drawing out its broad, humanistic implications. More often than not they described the Holocaust as an event of universal moral significance rather than as a particularist tragedy and frequently spoke of Israel as a land of religious and democratic values rather than as an anchor for Jewish group consciousness.[60] But despite the religious and universalistic turn of American Jewish discourse in the postwar period, at bottom it was still the basic commitment to Jewish social identity and peoplehood—once articulated in the language of "race"—that animated most Jews. Thus, despite the great strides of social acceptance Jews had made in the postwar years, they often remained unable to square their own self-image with the slot American society had provided for them.

As the experience of Jews in postwar America made clear, achieving the status of whites had not resolved their uneasy relationship to American racial culture. Racial liberalism had failed to totally solve the sense of tension between Jews' desire for both integration and distinctiveness, just as ethnic and religious definitions of Jewishness failed to bridge the gap between their intense group consciousness and the demands of white society. Still, for most Jews of the period, these contradictions never became a matter of excessive concern or worry. As long as their primary goal was further integration, Jews did not generally feel the need to loudly assert their strong group consciousness. Most were perfectly happy to describe themselves as a religious community even as they privately functioned as much more. And while Jews sometimes retreated from their policy of racial liberalism, it remained intact often enough to give Jews the vicarious sense of difference they desired as they continued their drive for inclusion in white America. By the mid-1960s, however, communal priorities began to shift. As the consensus politics of the postwar years collapsed, and the emergence of black nationalist movements redefined whiteness in ways that made Jews increasingly uncomfortable, Jews began to feel the need to assert their group distinctiveness more strongly. This urge only grew during the ensuing decades, when Jews began to worry about the erosion of Jewish social ties and rising rates of assimilation and intermarriage. In responding to these challenges, however, they would have to confront the ways in which their embrace of whiteness had circumscribed their expressions of group distinctiveness.

EPILOGUE

JEWS, WHITENESS, AND "TRIBALISM"
IN MULTICULTURAL AMERICA

When you feel like the only kid in town without a Christmas tree,
Here's a list of people who are Jewish, just like you and me:
David Lee Roth lights the menorah,
So do James Caan, Kirk Douglas, and the late Dinah Shore-ah.
Guess who eats together at the Carnegie Deli?
Bowzer from Sha-na-na, and Arthur Fonzerelli.
Paul Newman's half Jewish; Goldie Hawn's half too,
Put them together—what a fine lookin' Jew!
—Adam Sandler, "The Chanukah Song" (1995)

AS A CONTRIBUTION to the Christmas episode of the weekly variety show *Saturday Night Live* in 1995, comedian Adam Sandler performed what he considered a "throwaway bit" aimed at providing a Chanukah song for Jewish children who felt left out of holiday festivities. Unexpectedly, however, "The Chanukah Song" became an overnight sensation, receiving generous airtime on the radio and quickly achieving the status of well-known novelty songs like "Rudolph the Red Nosed Reindeer" and "Jingle Bell Rock." Over the next several years, Sandler issued two updated versions of the song and parlayed its popularity into an animated movie, *Eight Crazy Nights*, the first Chanukah film ever to be distributed by a Hollywood studio. While the film received poor reviews, the song that inspired it has remained a holiday classic, nowhere more revered than among American Jews. Becoming the "I Have a Little Dreidel" of the twenty-first century, it has been performed widely at community celebrations, parodied by Jewish day school students, and was even sung by Jewish cadets at the United States Military Academy when a Jewish activities center opened there in 1999.[1] In fact, when Sandler performed "The Chanukah Song III" during a special guest appearance on *Saturday Night Live* in 2001, he was joined onstage by twenty-two members of the "East Coast Drei-Dels," a youth choir from the Sid Jacobson Jewish Community Center on Long Island.[2] By that time, Sandler had already been named one of the top two "Jewish heroes" in a national survey of Jewish schoolchildren, placing him, according to one report, "behind Jerry Seinfeld but ahead of Howard Stern and God, who placed fourth."[3] Older fans also accorded Sandler high status in the Jewish pantheon. In 2002, Joshua Eagle, the twenty-seven-year-old managing editor of the internet media organization *Jewish Family and Life*, told a reporter from *USA Today* that "for many Jewish people my age, Adam Sandler is a hero."[4] Jewish college students proclaimed him "one of the most important contemporary Jewish commentators" in the pages of the Jewish student journal *New Voices*, while among certain groups of young Jewish women, Sandler was reputed to be a "Jewish love God."[5]

Both the success of the recording and the admiration Sandler drew from Jewish listeners across the country suggested that the song had hit on some of the most important issues of identity confronting American Jews at the turn of the twenty-first century. J. Hoberman, an arts critic who often writes on Jewish themes for the *Village Voice*, argued in a 2001 cover story on Sandler that "The Chanukah Song" struck a chord with Jewish listeners because it asserted Jewishness in a public way that had never been attempted before by Jewish performers. Unlike earlier, self-deprecating comics like Mickey Katz and Allen Sherman, Sandler was not afraid to engage in "open cultural narcissism," undermining the assimilationist paradigm of American Jewish popular culture by fishing inconspicuous Jews like Kirk Douglas, Dinah Shore, and William Shatner out of the Hollywood melting pot.[6] Supporting Hoberman's thesis, David Wild, a contributing editor at *Rolling Stone* magazine, argued that what people loved about "The Chanukah Song" was its "outing" of Jews who had submerged their Jewish identities in their quest for success and acceptance.[7] Indeed, Sandler seemed to take special pleasure in unmasking the Jewishness of those celebrities least likely to be identified as Jewish by the casual observer, with the song's humor relying on incongruous images of white-bread characters like *Star Trek's* Captain Kirk, 1950s greasers like *Happy Day's* Fonzie, or rock stars like David Lee Roth performing Jewish rituals and engaging in ethnically marked behavior. "Melissa Gilbert and Michael Landon never mix meat with dairy," Sandler avers in one of the later versions of the song. "Maybe they shoulda called that show *Little Kosher House on the Prarie*."[8]

Hoberman and Wild seem on the mark with their argument that Sandler's dramatic shift away from a more guarded approach to Jewish self-fashioning in the United States is what seems to have won him such an enthusiastic following among American Jews. Yet in thinking that Sandler's lyrics *only* betray Jewish separatism, they have missed the other side of the equation. In fact, even as Sandler "outs" much of Hollywood as Jewish, he also takes pride in his cast of characters *precisely because* they have achieved such success in entering the inner circle of white American society. The song clearly celebrates Jews' status as racial *insiders* in

America, holding them up as the antithesis of notorious racial villains like O. J. Simpson (and in a subsequent version, Osama bin Laden), even as it undermines the Hollywood illusion that makes Jewish celebrities into undifferentiated whites. In fact, the original song's reference to Simpson ("O. J. Simpson—not a Jew. But guess who is? Hall-of-famer Rod Carew—he converted") performs a double move: it marks off Jews clearly from "unsavory" blacks like Simpson, while drawing links between Jews and "good" African Americans like Carew, whom Sandler incorrectly identifies as a convert to Judaism.[9] The song, therefore, embodies a host of mixed emotions about the place of Jews as insiders and outsiders, as white and as distinct in American culture. Given its tremendous popularity, one can safely conclude that this ambivalence is shared by its Jewish listeners, who are tickled by their ability to successfully "pass" in white America, but at the same time harbor a burning desire to show that they are different.

In many ways, a song as riddled with tensions as Sandler's is a fitting anthem for contemporary American Jewry. Exhilarated, on the one hand, with the possibility of achieving success and acceptance of a kind unimaginable even twenty years ago, some are also afraid that the Jews may cease to exist as a distinct group. As a result, many Jews fret over the chances for "Jewish survival," aware of the costs of assimilation even as they pursue it.[10] As Jews achieve further and further integration, breaking down social boundaries and marrying non-Jews in record numbers, the concern for preserving Jewish distinctiveness pervades all aspects of Jewish communal activity. Synagogues and Jewish federations scramble for ways to instill group identity in the younger generation and try to stem the tide of intermarriage. And despite their high level of economic and social integration, Jews discuss, read about, and memorialize the Holocaust with zeal as a means of keeping their sense of difference from non-Jews alive.[11] Far from having been eliminated by Jews' increasing integration into white America, the tensions and conflicting impulses of American Jewish identity have only been accentuated. Like Sandler, many American Jews want to have it both ways.

Much has changed since 1945, when Jews still worried that their Jewishness might keep them from being accepted as full members of white society. Today, many Jews fear that their thorough implication in that society may sever some of their strongest ties to Jewishness. Jews no longer have the language of "race" to express these deep attachments, but instead rely on the echoes of Jewish racial identity, a discourse of "tribalism," which gives voice to the feelings of loss Jews are experiencing in a world resistant to seeing them as a group apart. In addition, Jews have turned to the African American community in unprecedented ways in order to validate their own minority consciousness, a move that reflects their growing discomfort as white Americans. But like their renewed attempts at asserting Jewish "tribalism," their desire to see themselves as part of the multicultural rainbow of minority groups has met with resistance in a society fundamentally shaped by the categories of black and white. The origins of these contemporary trends are located in the "ethnic revival" of the 1960s and 1970s. Volumes could be written on the identity transformations of that period alone; what follows is meant only to summarize those events so that we may proceed to a fuller discussion of Jewish identity today.

From Conformity to "Revival"

Throughout the 1950s and during the first half of the 1960s, American Jews largely maintained the integrationist approach to self-definition and the policy of racial liberalism that they had forged during the World War II era. Even though they frequently maintained a deep attachment to Jewish peoplehood and continued to foster strong social ties within their group, most Jews of the Cold War era publicly conformed to the larger society's expectation that they would define themselves as a religious community. Jews often looked to racial liberalism as a surrogate for expressing ethnic distinctiveness, since it allowed them to identify as part of the white mainstream's political culture without making them feel as if they had abandoned their legacy as a persecuted minority group. But here, too, strong pressures of conformity limited assertions of group distinctiveness. Jews often retreated from liberal stances when social pressures intervened, and even when they expressed liberal values, they rarely felt comfortable asserting the specifically Jewish motivations that pushed them toward such views. While there certainly were Jewish civil rights activists like Rabbis Abraham Joshua Heschel and Arthur Lelyveld who highlighted their Jewishness as a motivating factor, most Jews engaged significantly as protestors or volunteers for civil rights work before the mid-1960s positioned themselves as white liberals fighting for a society in which racial and ethnic origins would become irrelevant, even if Jewish commitments *had* played some role in their involvement.[12]

Not until the mid-1960s did the American Jewish approach to group identity and racial politics begin to change under the influence of two important social shifts. First, Jews had succeeded in achieving a high level of integration into white, middle-class society, and no longer worried as much about the need to fit in. In fact, during these years the drive for integration began to give way to very different concerns, ones that stressed the need for greater Jewish distinctiveness in American life. As historian Marc Dollinger explains, the collapse of consensus politics during these years and the legitimization of a number of new identity-based movements focusing on women and minorities lessened pressures on American Jews to downplay their Jewishness. Over the next few decades, Jews began to express a growing impatience with the constraints of liberal universalism and exhibit a tendency to turn away from classical liberalism toward a more group-centered political agenda.[13]

Second, the rise of black nationalism posed some serious challenges to Jews' conception of American life and their understanding of minority group dynamics. Jews' postwar liberalism was built on the assumption that integration was the key to the realization of a pluralistic, democratic society, not only for themselves but for African Americans and other racial and ethnic minorities as well. In fact, even if they did not always live up to their own liberal vision, many Jews supported the abstract notion of black integration because it made their own entrance into the ranks of white society morally tenable, signifying that they were becoming part of a pluralist, rather than an exclusivist, social order. This vision was important enough to Jews' own self-perception that when social pressures sometimes pushed them to abandon liberal stances on race, they usually tried to rationalize their behavior or blame forces beyond their control in order to avoid the stinging realization that they, too, were now part of the white elite. As Nat Hentoff suggested in 1969, seeing themselves as part of an oppressive white majority was like seeing themselves as *goyim* (non-Jews), a self-image that was "exceedingly difficult" for Jews with memories of the prewar years to accept.[14] This, however, was precisely what black nationalists were suggesting: integration was no longer an option for African Americans because Jews, along with all American whites, were part of an inherently racist power structure.

The emerging outlook of black nationalists was particularly troubling to Jews because it came just at the moment when they felt a growing need to see themselves as different from the bulk of white Americans. True, Jews' impressive economic mobility and their high degree of integration into universities, neighborhoods, professions and other central institutions of American life made it hard for them to claim the status of an "oppressed minority" in anything other than a faint historical sense. Yet the more distant they became from their minority social status, the more Jews felt the need to highlight their difference from white society.

In the years that followed the emergence of black nationalism in the mid-1960s, young Jewish activists, many of whom had been active in the struggle for black civil rights, decided that the renewal of their *own* cultural traditions and the highlighting of their *own* ethnic distinctiveness was the only way to attain the sense of difference they desired. Organized loosely as the Jewish Renewal Movement, they reaffirmed Jews' role as an oppressed minority by creating a campaign to aid Soviet Jewry and by rallying in support of an embattled Israel during the 1967 Six Day War. They also accentuated their difference from mainstream America by creating alternatives to the staid, middle-class, suburban synagogue. Foremost among these was Havurat Shalom, a cooperative community established in 1968 in Somerville, Massachusetts, where young Jews engaged in creative worship, studied Jewish texts, and participated in other activities designed to underscore the distinctiveness of Jewish tradition.[15] Activists issued a string of new publications, such as *Response* magazine and the landmark *Jewish Catalog*, where the ideals of the new movement were expressed and elaborated upon.[16] In such venues, these young Jews often distanced themselves from their civil rights pasts as a means of placing Jewish concerns more front and center. "The Jew can be an ally of the black liberation movement and he should be," wrote M. J. Rosenberg in the landmark anthology, *Jewish Radicalism* (1973). "But first he must find himself." While Rosenberg argued that "the black is America's Jew and a common fight can be waged," he stressed that it must not be waged "at the expense of our own pride."[17]

While a major force in the emergence of an enlivened Jewish consciousness during the 1960s and 1970s, members of the Jewish Renewal Movement were not alone in their new assertion of ethnic identity. The influence of black nationalism and the thirst for self-assertion that came with increased integration had affected a much larger segment of the American Jewish community, just as these trends had touched a number of European descent groups that were embarking on their own path to "ethnic revival."[18] Jews of all backgrounds and classes were drawn into the celebration of ethnic difference as the movement on behalf of Soviet Jewry, the heightened use of ritual and creativity in Jewish worship, the reinvigoration of American Zionism, and a new trend toward Jewish day schools all took hold. Productions like *Fiddler on the Roof*—which appeared on Broadway in 1964 and as a film in 1971—and books like Irving Howe's *World of Our Fathers*, published in 1976, gave Jews new visibility in the arts and popular culture.[19] Even the rise of the radical Jewish Defense League (JDL), made up mostly of lower- and middle-class Orthodox youth who were frustrated by the path of "establishment Jewry," grew out of the ethnic revival. Its members were likewise motivated by the strides of black nationalism. "If Shirley Chisholm can walk around saying black problems come first for blacks—Beautiful! Right on!" declared JDL leader Meir Kahane. "Black problems *do* come first for blacks . . . [and] Jewish problems must come first for Jews."[20]

Despite the affirmation of "difference" that characterized the movement for ethnic revival, the large majority of Jews (with the possible exception of the the ultranationalist JDL) did not see the adoption of cultural nationalism as a total disengagement from the process of integration into white

America. For many, it was a way to rescue the liberal paradigm of integration, to make it viable in the same way that racial liberalism had made it viable: by affirming the pluralist nature of American democracy. With their own sense of ethnic difference affirmed or perhaps even augmented, Jews could continue on the path of integration with little fear that they were complicit in the misdeeds of an exclusionary society. And despite their parting of the ways with black nationalists, Jews retained sufficient ties with some of the less militant elements of the civil rights movement to retain the hope of an integrationist solution to the African American struggle. New Jewish organizations like Jews for Urban Justice, as well as older Jewish agencies like the American Jewish Committee, the American Jewish Congress, and the Anti-Defamation League of B'nai B'rith, all continued to pursue civil rights activism under a Jewish umbrella.[21]

Yet the persistent integrationism of most Jews also led to frustration and conflict with African Americans who did not share their view of the country's future. Among a small but growing number of Jews, black nationalists and the African Americans who followed their lead became the focus of critique as the enemies of integrationist liberalism. To this group, the anger of blacks at white America seemed misguided, not "rational," and the black nationalist tactics of sometimes using racial and ethnic slurs and even violence to assert themselves seemed like a betrayal of the liberal principles that had allowed Jews to enter the ranks of the white mainstream.[22] Ironically, because these Jews wanted to see themselves as having risen from a disadvantaged "outsider" background and were uncomfortable with the notion that they had been aided by white privilege, they were insensitive to ways in which African Americans had been denied many of the integrationist opportunities Jews had been afforded. Their narrative of immigrant success underscored the country's pluralist roots and the ability of the common person to get ahead, suggesting that groups like blacks had only themselves to blame for their failure to succeed. Although born from a desire to assert their difference from the white power structure, the ethnic revival became for some Jews (as well as for some other ethnics) the vehicle for a new, conservative politics that denigrated blacks and affirmed their own membership in the white mainstream, even as it highlighted their distinctiveness.[23]

While this conservative critique of African Americans took hold among a small but vocal group of Jewish intellectuals, and also found fertile ground among the minority of disaffected working-class Jews who felt threatened by new African American claims to entitlement, most American Jews imbibed it only piecemeal.[24] If the discourse of "ethnic revival" often drew invidious distinctions between blacks and Jews, the persistent tendency of Jews to compare themselves to African Americans and to borrow language from black liberation movements demonstrated how torn they were by their twin desires to be "insiders" and "outsiders" in American culture. In the movement for Soviet Jewry, where nearly one-third of the student leaders had graduated from the ranks of civil rights activism, the terminology of black struggle was palpable as a model for their own efforts to free their oppressed brothers and sisters. Long-distance treks to protest venues, for example, became know as "freedom rides."[25] In one of the earliest handbooks of the Student Struggle for Soviet Jewry, student leader Jacob Birnbaum reminded America's Jewish youth that "if injustice cannot be condoned in Selma, U.S.A., neither must it be overlooked in Kiev, U.S.S.R."[26] In sometimes subtle and sometimes explicit ways, the language and style of black movements found their way into Jewish ritual, Jewish education, Zionist work, and many other aspects of the Jewish "revival." The increased popularity of curly hair among young Jews and the wearing of brightly colored knit yarmulkes (skull caps) by young Jewish men mimicked the appearance of Afros and the wearing of dashikis among blacks.[27] Even the right-wing JDL, which had little sympathy for the political demands of African Americans, modeled themselves explicitly after black nationalist groups, developing an organizational structure and group discipline that consciously emulated that of the Black Panthers. Often called the "Jewish Panthers" by friends and enemies alike, the JDL adopted slogans like "Jewish Is Beautiful," rallied to the chant of "free them now," and even made and exploded a bomb according the design of a Black Panther manual.[28]

These persistent nods to black movements reflected that despite the efforts of the Jewish revival to find a niche in American life for Jewish distinctiveness, ultimately the nation's understanding of "difference" was conceived of in terms of "black" and "white," a pattern Jews had difficulty fitting into. In the remaining years of the twentieth century, Jews would find that it was even harder to assert their difference from the rest of white America. As black self-assertion became more powerful, and the black-white paradigm of group difference was reinforced by American law through many of the social programs and civil rights statutes of Lyndon Johnson's Great Society, Jews found fewer and fewer means of claiming a status different from the majority of privileged whites. Their continued efforts to claim such a status, coupled with African Americans' new resolve to preserve the dichotomy between black and white, would quickly lead to a new era of acrimony between blacks and Jews.

African Americans and Jews in a "Multicultural" Age

The growing tension between African Americans and Jews that emerged after 1965 is often described as the end of a historic "alliance" between these groups, but "alliance" is not the best term to describe the relationship as it had existed before that time. True, both Jewish individuals and organizations often aided African American causes and fought for black rights. Yet the relationship was characterized by several factors that are not normally associated with an "alliance." First, the Jewish approach to African Americans was anything but monolithic, and those who took bold stands in favor of black education and civil rights constituted only a small minority of American Jews. For most average Jews, empathy for African Americans was usually tempered by the need to further their own acceptance in white America. While on the whole there was probably more cooperation and less tension between blacks and Jews than between blacks and any other European immigrant group, Jewish behavior toward blacks was never consistent enough so as to constitute an "alliance."

Second, Jews enjoyed all of the basic rights of citizenship and were not subject to most of the disabilities imposed by law and by society on African Americans. The term "alliance" suggests mutual cooperation toward a common goal, yet the social positions of African Americans and Jews were very different, and while there was much acculturating Jews could do to aid African Americans, there was usually very little African Americans could do to aid Jews. Finally, although African Americans and Jews frequently discussed one another and in many ways accorded each other a special symbolic status, the difference between black and Jewish social power meant that these discussions were not always conducted on a level playing field. Cultural historian Jeff Melnick has suggested that because Jews had greater power to construct and guide the discourse about "black-Jewish relations," it was not really a conversation between two equal partners—one that would suggest the existence of an "alliance"—but was primarily a way for Jews to negotiate some of their own important questions of identity.[29] Hasia Diner, the first major historian of black-Jewish relations, has observed something similar of early-twentieth-century Jews: "they used black people to construct their own identity in the United States."[30]

If Jews largely controlled the discourse of black-Jewish relations before 1965, however, African Americans began to assume significant control over it in the years following, or have at least been increasingly able to respond to the Jewish version of intergroup "relations" in ways that mattered to the Jews. Jews' narrative of black-Jewish relations suggested that there were special ties between the groups, and situated Jewish support for the black struggle as a marker of Jews' own minority sensibility. For African Americans, however, especially after black nationalism began to make inroads in the mid-1960s, the Jewish narrative of black-Jewish relations interfered with their desire to draw a firm line between blacks and whites, and their ability to assign clear moral values to the actions of both groups. As a result, many African Americans began to craft a new narrative, which lumped Jews together with other whites and was skeptical of their true desire to help blacks. Jews resisted the black nationalist assertion that American society was inherently racist, hoping to preserve their minority sensibility even as they became part of white America. Yet for African Americans, the Jewish desire to straddle the black-white divide undermined the very basis of their quest for integrity and clarity. These competing visions are what underlay the last three and a half decades of conflict and tension between blacks and Jews.

The event that marked the shift to this new era was the fight over control of the schools in the Ocean Hill–Brownsville school district of Brooklyn in 1968. A conflict between the primarily Jewish teachers and the largely African American community, it demonstrated how two different visions of black-Jewish relations and race relations in general could pit blacks and Jews against one another. The teachers envisioned an integrationist approach, where they would cooperate in increasing community control of the school. Many members of the African American community, however, felt that the white members of the teaching staff and administration needed to be replaced totally, to make way for a more autonomous and self-consciously black school district. Tensions erupted when antisemitic leaflets began to circulate in the community, and an antisemitic poem, written by one of the schoolchildren, was read on the radio by a black teacher. While the Jewish teachers saw the elements of Black Power activism within the district as "politically regressive and . . . illiberal" and saw themselves as victims of racist attacks, the community largely saw *them* as the racist power structure.[31] The conflict encapsulated the way that Jewish and African American visions of American group life were totally at odds with one another.

Even before the Ocean Hill–Brownsville debacle, which brought the issue of black-Jewish conflict into the national spotlight, prominent black intellectuals like James Baldwin and Harold Cruse had already begun to develop a new critique of American Jewish identity. In an essay first published in the *New York Times Magazine* in 1967, Baldwin, a leading African American writer, struck at the heart of Jews' desire to consider themselves a minority group in the United States. African Americans did not wish "to be told by an American Jew that his suffering is as great as the American Negro's suffering," he argued. "It isn't, and one knows that it isn't from the very tone in which he assures you that it is."[32] Employing a number of autobiographical incidents concerning Jews he had known growing up in Harlem, Baldwin said that these Jews had acted no differently than other whites, and had certainly not shied away from exploiting African Americans. If Jews were truly an oppressed minority, he inferred, they would not be able to retain their liberal faith in America as a land of opportunity and inclusion. "Very few Americans, and this includes very few Jews," wrote Baldwin, "have the courage to recognize that the America of which they dream and boast is the America in which the Negro lives."[33] Ultimately, by claiming a status similar to blacks, Jews were blinding themselves to the true nature of American society, where privilege was determined by the stark racial lines of black and white. "The Jew profits from his status in American and he must expect the Negroes to distrust him for it," Baldwin explained. "In the American context, the most ironical thing about Negro Anti-Semitism is that the Negro is really condemning the Jew for having become an American white man."[34]

Cruse, whose *Crisis of the Negro Intellectual* had been issued the same year as Baldwin's article, was one of the leading black spokesmen against integration, arguing that blacks ought to strive instead for social, cultural, and even political autonomy in the United States. A former communist, Cruse had felt hindered during his activist years by Jewish fellow party members who pushed him to pursue the same integrationist path they had followed and were intolerant of his tendency to assert black distinctiveness.[35] Out of these experiences, Cruse developed a biting critique of American Jews as one of the principal obstacles to the achievement of black autonomy. He saw their attempts to work out their own identity issues through involvement in black causes, their tendency to offer themselves as a model for blacks, and their efforts to promote black integration all as meddlesome interventions in black politics and as attempts to keep blacks from controlling their own destiny. Jews were "a white group who have realized the 'American Dream,'" wrote Cruse in a subsequent article, which appeared in one of the first anthologies on black-Jewish relations. "As such, whatever qualms or fears they may or may not entertain concerning their future is a problem for them to settle with other whites with whom they share political, economic and cultural power."[36]

Despite discussions between black and Jewish intellectuals and community leaders that have gone on continuously in the decades since the Ocean Hill–Brownsville conflict, little has shaken either group from understanding minority identity and race relations primarily through the prism of their own social and psychological needs. Most Jews, for example, have steadfastly held to the integrationist paradigm and rejected group entitlements, opposing programs like affirmative action, especially when they include use of specific racial quotas. In 1977, three of the leading American Jewish organizations—the American Jewish Committee, the American Jewish Congress and the Anti-Defamation League of B'nai B'rith—submitted friends-of-the-court briefs in support of the case of Allan Bakke, a white student who was denied admission to medical school at the University of California at Davis. The Jewish establishment supported Bakke not only because the notion of ethnic and racial quotas cut against their classical liberal ideology of integration, but because it also held the potential to harm Jewish applicants to colleges and universities, thereby limiting the continued success of American Jews.[37]

With few exceptions, Jews' responses to African American concerns have also demonstrated their unwillingness to engage with the critique offered by spokesmen like Baldwin and Cruse, which argued that problems between blacks and Jews stemmed from the complicity of Jews in the white power structure. Because such a vision strongly contradicts the desire of many Jews to understand themselves as different, they have often preferred to see the root of the problem between the two groups as one of "black antisemitism." In making this case, they point to the actions of black activists during the Ocean Hill–Brownsville controversy as well to more recent statements by extremists like Leonard Jeffries, a professor and former chair of Black Studies at the City College of New York, and Louis Farrakhan, leader of the Nation of Islam, who have charged Jews with everything from controlling the slave trade to manipulating the United States government.[38]

Yet if many Jews have ignored the black critique of them as members of the white elite, so too have African Americans frequently dismissed Jews' protestations that their identities are far more complex and their minority sensibilities more intact than blacks often allow. While Jews focus inordinate attention on figures like Farrakhan, many African American spokesmen and women seem unaware that without reproducing the odious antisemitism of the Nation of Islam leader, they often replicate the simplistic dichotomies he employs when he casts Jews as the whitest of all whites. Significantly, while stressing the black-white dichotomy has traditionally been the tendency of whites who aimed to preserve their own racial self-image, today it is increasingly becoming the role of African Americans, whose post–civil rights politics have tended to focus on the assertion of racial identity and have frequently invested them in the notion of a clear moral distinction between blacks and whites. This shift is especially important because, as historian George Sanchez explains, even as African Americans remain materially and socially disadvantaged in many ways, they are taking on an ever increasing role as shapers of the dominant discourse of American national identity.[39]

One of the central vehicles for the increased role of African Americans in shaping American definitions of "difference" is the contemporary discourse of "multiculturalism," which has assumed a prominent place in the discussions of racial and ethnic group dynamics in the academy and in public policy as well as in more popular venues. Because multiculturalism is supported by multiple constituencies with wide-ranging needs and viewpoints, it has remained ill-defined. Theoretically, it was guided by the desire of its adherents to replace the notion of a single dominant culture with cultural diversity of the widest type. Yet in some of its most powerful incarnations, multiculturalism often privileges certain kinds of diversity over others. Historian David Hollinger has described multiculturalism's vision of diversity as an "ethno-racial pentagon," which divides the American population into the categories of African American, Asian American, Euro-American, Indigenous, and Latino, but does not legitimize any divisions beyond these five.[40] Frequently, however, multiculturalist discourse has reduced diversity even further, attempting to maintain the basic bipolar definition of race by drawing the most vital distinctions between whites, who comprise the Euro-American category, and "peoples of color," who comprise the other four categories. In the wake of multiculturalism, even the term "ethnicity," which had been widely used to refer to the descendants of European immigrant groups in place of "race" in the years after World War II, is now largely applied to nonwhite groups. And some Latino and Asian American spokesmen complain about the way in which all nonwhites are often subsumed into the black category, reifying black and white as the only two legitimate categories of racial and ethnic difference in American life.[41]

In such a framework, assertions or claims of Jewish difference are often met with hostility, skepticism, and the charge that they simply do not carry the political or moral weight of identities organized around color.[42] Although there are certainly other visions of multiculturalism that do not collapse the entire spectrum of racial and ethnic diversity into such a stark dichotomy, in many ways the movement has facilitated the widespread dissemination and popularization of the black nationalist belief in the primacy of the black-white divide. Ironically, in an atmosphere that purports to value and encourage "difference," Jews are stymied, as they have been since the beginning of the twentieth century, by the tendency of American culture to make blackness and whiteness *the* critical categories of group life.

The growing authority of these ideas has meant that the critique once limited to a small group of ideologically committed black nationalists now informs most major interactions between blacks and Jews. In December 1995, for example, violence erupted on 125th Street in New York's Harlem as the result of a dispute between African American residents and a Jewish store owner who was labeled a white intruder in the predominantly black business district. Protesters targeted Freddy's Fashion Mart when its Jewish owner, Fred Harari, attempted to evict a black subtenant, an African immigrant who ran a record store on the premises. Although according to interviews conducted with local residents, Harari employed a racial and ethnic mix—whites, blacks, Puerto Ricans, Guyanese—protesters cast him as a usurper of black economic control of the neighborhood. At one of the protest meetings, Morris Powell, head of a local vendor's group, denounced Harari as a "cracker"—a term of reproach for southern whites—and dismissed any lingering notion that he might be different from other whites by emphasizing that "a cracker is a cracker is a cracker."[43] Reverend Al Sharpton, who was accused of inciting the crowd with inflammatory rhetoric, told the protesters not to "stand by and allow them to move this brother so that some white interloper can expand his business on 125th Street."[44] At different moments, protesters shifted between these antiwhite slurs and antisemitic ones such as "Jewish bloodsucker," suggesting that they were aware of Harari's Jewishness, but found it more comforting to obscure that distinctiveness beneath a blanket denunciation of white oppression.[45] The protesters, many of whom had intimate knowledge of the neighborhood, must also have known about the racial diversity of the store's employees.[46] Certainly this was known by one of the protesters, who eventually walked into the store and shot four of the employees before lighting the building on fire and killing seven others. Yet even after this tragedy, protesters continued to paint the incident as a black-white conflict, a characterization that allowed them to view it with a certain moral clarity. In many ways, this strategy resembled the way that whites at the turn of the twentieth century often tried to obscure the particularity of Jews by casting them as either black or white, thus shoring up their own identities. Here, black protesters fastened onto the black-white dichotomy as a means of shoring up their identities as victims of racial persecution seeking redress from white persecutors.

This reductionist view has not only been asserted in urban protests, but also by leaders of national black organizations and by leading figures in popular culture. In an appearance on the Oprah Winfrey Show meant to further black-Jewish dialogue, Benjamin Hooks, who headed the NAACP during the late 1970s and 1980s, responded to Jewish claims of minority status by saying, "I look here and I don't see a group of blacks and Jews, I see black people and white people."[47] Similar sentiments surfaced as part of a long-running critique by prominent African American director Spike Lee and other black media commentators, who questioned the propriety of Stephen Spielberg's production of two films dealing with the black experience, *The Color Purple* (1985) and *Amistad* (1997). As with the 1995 protests outside Freddy's Fashion Mart, spokesmen like Lee and *Washington Post* columnist Courtland Milloy were highly aware of Spielberg's Jewishness, and wished to make clear that any feelings of minority status on the part of a Jew did not make him eligible to impinge on the black experience, which they felt should remain the artistic property of black filmmakers. Here, too, the commentators underscored Spielberg's Jewishness one moment, only to cast him as an undifferentiated white the next. "[If] I wanted to do a film about Golda Meir," Lee asserted on *Nightline* in 1997, "I could tell you that film would not get made."[48] On another occasion, however, Lee argued that "nobody can make films about white suburbia better than Stephen Spielberg."[49] Similarly, Milloy argued that *Amistad* "did not come close to doing for African Americans and the Middle Passage what Spielberg's *Schindler's List* did for Jews and the Holocaust." Then putting Spielberg's Jewishness aside, he charged him with making a film "about how two white guys . . . come to the rescue of some Africans bound for slavery."[50]

More than thirty-five years after black nationalists began to assert their separatist vision, African Americans and Jews still retain very different views of what "minority status" means in American life. For many blacks today, even those quite distant from the legacy of black nationalist movements, the black-white divide is the inviolable boundary that separates the privileged from the oppressed. Jews' dual insistence on integration and distinctiveness, however, has posed a challenge to African Americans, and has been the root of much of the conflict between the two groups. Yet despite the increasing power of African Americans in shaping American discourse about difference, Jews have clung to their particularist commitments.

The Contested "Tribalism" of American Jews

If Jewish particularism was loudly—if sometimes ambivalently—asserted during the "ethnic revival" of the 1960s and 1970s, changing social and political factors have made the assertion of Jewish ethnic distinctiveness an even more complex matter since the 1980s. Whereas in 1970 many Jews were still concerned about their social status and worried about college admissions and job security, today Jews are among the most secure economically and socially of any white Americans. In business, the professions, politics, entertainment, and many other fields, their status is no longer an issue. With Jews holding the presidencies of many of the Ivy League schools that once limited their entry, there are few if any doors that are not open to them.

This heightened level of acceptance has complicated expressions of ethnic solidarity, or the echoes of Jewish racial identity that scholars Steven M. Cohen and Arnold Eisen call "tribalism," among American Jews.[51] On the one hand, Jews' elevated social position has made it easier for them to express feelings of ethnic particularity that they may have shied away from in previous decades. To a certain extent, the greater acceptability of ethnic and racial difference ushered in first by the ethnic revival of the 1960s and 1970s and later by multiculturalism allows Jews to assert distinctiveness with less fear that they will be labeled outsiders. On the other hand, Jews' rapid social advance has put some stumbling blocks in the way of ethnic assertiveness. Jews' growing web of social attachments to non-Jews (including an intermarriage rate exceeding 50 percent) has not only reduced the social exclusivity of the Jewish community, but has also made many Jews more reticent about strong statements of Jewish difference, lest they alienate a close friend or family member. Moreover, while multiculturalism has increased the society's tolerance for "difference," that tolerance is sometimes equivocal when it comes to Jews and other European ethnic groups. These groups are often treated as members of the white, privileged majority, and assertions to the contrary are often treated as attempts to deny their complicity in the preservation of America's system of racial bias.

Ultimately, it is hard to trace either an unchecked pattern of "tribalist" assertiveness or a steady decline of "tribalist" sensibility among contemporary American Jews. Cohen and Eisen report that "tribalism" is being expressed more freely, but that because of the growing interconnections between Jewish and non-Jewish social worlds, Jews are increasingly careful about "choosing certain spaces and times to express it," and even then there are often "lingering hesitations, anxieties and misgivings."[52] One might say that the two phenomena—growing ethnic assertiveness and a declining ethnic cohesiveness—are actually two sides of the same coin. Tribalism functions much like Jewish appeals to "race" did during the nineteenth century, giving contemporary Jews a tool for selectively shoring up a Jewish identity that is increasingly in doubt. "Throughout all the de-racializing stages of twentieth-century social thought, Jews have continued to invoke blood logic as a way of defining and maintaining group identity," writes historian Susan Glenn. "It is one of the ironies of modern Jewish history that concepts of tribalism based on blood and race have persisted not only in spite of but also because of the experience of assimilation."[53]

Glenn's observation about the paradox of "blood logic" increasing in appeal as the process of assimilation takes hold and Cohen and Eisen's argument about the selective ways in which American Jews invoke tribalism today are both confirmed by the approaches of contemporary Jews to some of the issues that drove debate and discussion on Jewish racial status in the early twentieth century. Take, for example, the issue of government racial classification of the Jews. In a dramatic reversal of the doctrine of Simon Wolf and the American Jewish establishment of that day, contemporary Jewish leaders, as well as many Jewish individuals, have increasingly called for Jews to be recognized, and in their minds legitimized, as a distinct group under American law. This move stems in part from the frustration of Jews who feel that government classification schemes make them an invisible part of the white population and interfere with their efforts to hold on to a distinctive "minority" identity. But the trend toward seeking official recognition in legal cases, government records, and in other official matters suggests that, in contrast to Wolf's era, there are now very few liabilities attached to such an ethnic or racial classification. In the prewar period, Jewish leaders feared government classification schemes that might put data about Jews in hands of immigrantion restrictionists or those who might limit Jewish access to important sectors of society. Since the passage of the civil rights legislation and social programs of Johnson's Great Society, however, racial statistics are in some measure the key for various groups to receive federal protection and entitlements, while few of the prewar concerns remain.

The first significant effort of American Jews to gain recognition as a distinct group under American law came in 1987 with the case of *Shaare Tefila Congregation v. Cobb*, in which the Shaare Tefila Congregation of Silver Spring, Maryland, sued to have vandals charged with a civil rights violation for defacing the synagogue with swastikas and other racist graffiti. Lower courts held that because Jews were not a "racial" group like African Americans, they were precluded from protection under laws that prevented discrimination on the basis of race.[54] The U.S. Supreme Court, however, reversed the dismissal and found that Shaare Tefila Congregation did have the right to civil rights protection under the law, since Jews had been considered a race in the nineteenth century, when the Thirteenth Amendment, on which the civil rights laws were based, was written. The high court's ruling was revolutionary, but the written opinion left the meaning of "racial and ethnic minority" vague, giving no clear test by which a group like Jews might qualify as a "race" under civil rights statutes. As a result, Jewish plaintiffs had to continue to fight for protection from "racial" discrimination in the lower courts. The issue was dealt with tangentially in a number of cases, but the federal courts made no significant ruling concerning the status of Jews under the civil rights statutes until 2002, when the U.S. Court of Appeals in New York's Second Circuit ruled that Yankel Rosenbaum, a yeshiva student stabbed during the 1991 Crown Heights riots, had been denied federal civil rights as a Jew, even though he was white and his alleged attacker, Lemrick Nelson, was black.[55]

Shaare Tefila v. Cobb and *Unites States v. Nelson* made legislative history with their extension of federal civil rights protection to Jews, but the cases were even more noteworthy for the reversal in Jewish communal opinion that they represented. When the Shaare Tefila case first emerged, all of the major Jewish defense agencies were reluctant to support the efforts of the congregation, asserting their historic position, as the National Jewish Community Relations Council did, that "there ought not to be the suggestion that the Jewish community in any way gives sanction to the notion that Jews constitute a race."[56] As the case went through the courts, however, it gained support from the Jewish establishment, and by the time it reached the Supreme Court, both the American Jewish Committee and the Anti-Defamation League of B'nai B'rith had signed on to the effort, submitting strong amicus curae (friends-of-the-court) briefs in favor of the notion that Jews ought to be protected from "racial" discrimination. In the Nelson case, the support from Jewish organizations was even greater, with a coalition of groups including the American Jewish Congress, the American Jewish Committee, the Anti-Defamation League of B'nai B'rith, and the leaders of the Orthodox, Conservative, Reform, and Reconstructionist Movements all submitting briefs to answer the argument put forth by Nelson's lawyers that Rosenbaum, as a white person, was not entitled to specific civil rights protection from racial discrimination. While none of the organizations believed that Jews actually constituted a "race" in any scientific sense, there was a strong feeling that the Jewish group should be recognized and protected by law as groups like African Americans were. Ultimately, they were willing to accept the terminology of "race" because it was the only language available in American law that could bring Jews under the umbrella of civil rights protection. For the first time in their history, American Jews were not trying to prevent the government from categorizing them as a "race," but were fighting to be recognized in the eyes of the government as a distinct group deserving protection from "racial" discrimination. Although Nelson's conviction was later thrown out by the Court of Appeals on a matter related to jury selection, the court upheld the ability of civil rights laws to be applied to Jews, a ruling Marc Stern, an attorney for the American Jewish Congress, called "a very big silver lining."[57]

The increasing resolve of some American Jews, and most of the leading Jewish organizations, to break the tendency of the government to obscure Jewishness beneath the categories of "black" and "white" was also clear in discussions among Jews of the 2000 census. The census figured prominently in discussions about race and racial identity in the media because of its effort to rectify some of the vexing problems posed by the government's rigid racial categorization. For the first time in the history of the census, it allowed people to identify as "biracial" and "multiracial" rather than forcing them to choose only one of the traditional racial categories. If this flexibility satisfied the growing chorus of voices that decried the older system of racial classification, however, many Jews were frustrated by their inability to self-identify as anything other than "white." Robert Tabak of Philadelphia's Balch Institute for Ethnic Studies, for example, pointed out that while the Census Bureau had mailed out a certain number of "long form" census schedules that allowed the recipient to fill in a blank with an ethnic or racial designation of their choice, the bureau guidelines mandated that only certain designations would actually be tabulated. Apparently, while some European ethnic groups were included in the list, the bureau seems to have taken the path prescribed by Wolf over ninety years earlier and omitted Jews because they were perceived as a religious group. Thus, explained Tabak, "you can self-identify as Irish, Ukrainian, Albanian, Nigerian, French-Canadian, Hmong, Chinese—but not as a Jew."[58]

The absence of a Jewish category on the census, however, did not stop many Jews from "writing in" Jewish as an alternative to the options listed. As Tabak explained, if he had received the long form, he would have written in "Jew" anyway.[59] Tabak was not alone in his sentiment. In a discussion of the controversy on the academic listserv H-Ethnic, Sharon Vance of the University of Pennsylvania reported that she put in "Jew" under ethnic origin, as well as under the "race" question that appeared on both the long and short form schedules.[60] A more popular manifestation of this trend in 2000 was the editorial of the *Forward*, one of the largest circulation national Jewish publications, which argued that the racial question on the census should be seen more as an inquiry into "what group you want to be counted in, rather than some kind of biological fact." The paper asked its readership to "consider doing what more than one member of our *redaktzia* [editorial board] has done: checking the box 'some other race' and writing in the word 'Jew.'"[61] Anecdotal evidence suggests that many American Jews in recent years have grown impatient not only with census schedules that allow them to identify only as "white," but with a host of other governmental and nongovernmental forms that do not provide Jews with a means of identifying as they wish. "I think about this every time I'm filling in some form that asks me to check a racial category," explains David Holzel, who has written for the *Atlanta Jewish Times* and other Jewish publications. "Which pigeon hole do I prefer? White? Black? I often check 'Other.' But when I write 'Jew' in the blank space provided, it sits there hesitantly, as if it has less right to be there than the scientific designations on the line above."[62]

In responding to the issue of government racial classification, Jews have voiced their grievances about being classed as undifferentiated whites with little fear that their assertions of distinctiveness might backfire and damage Jewish social status. By contrast, they have been more reticent in their discussions of another topic related to Jewish tribalism, the study of Jewish genetics. While many Jews see genetic research on their group as a positive effort that will both deliver tangible benefits and bolster feelings of Jewish "connectedness," many also fear that the endeavor might stigmatize Jews as a deviant genetic population.

Since the 1970s, physicians have been increasingly aware of genetic disorders such as Tay-Sachs Disease among Jewish populations. By the 1980s and 1990s, however, Jews—especially Ashkenazic Jews, who make up about 90 percent of the American Jewish population—had become a major focus for genetic research, partly because of the disproportionate number of Jewish physicians who found their own community a convenient vehicle for study and because Jews, as a comparatively endogamous group, provide desirable conditions for the testing of genetic theories. During these decades, researchers identified no fewer than thirty different genetic mutations present in the Ashkenazic Jewish population, mutations that are linked to diseases such as breast, colon, prostate and ovarian cancers, as well as to emotional disorders like schizophrenia, manic depression, and autism.[63] Despite repeated disclaimers by researchers that Jews are not necessarily any more susceptible to these diseases than other segments of the population, the growing interest in Jewish genetics has tended to revive the notion that Jews are a group united by biological ties, an idea that had been largely discredited among scientists since World War II.

In recent years genetic research has taken a new turn, not just using the Jews as a sample population for medical research, but focusing expressly on finding the origins of the Jews as a group. In 1997, Michael Hammer, a professor at the University of Arizona in Tucson, along with the Candian-born Israeli researcher Karl Skorecki led a team that traced distinctive markings appearing with high frequency on the Y chromosomes of Jews who self-identified as *kohanim*, members of the Jewish priestly family descended from the biblical Aaron.[64] Hammer and Skorecki not only identified distinctive genetic markers on the *kohanim*'s DNA but were also able to analyze gene mutations in the samples, which suggested that the group's common ancestor had lived some time between 650 and 1180 B.C.E., dates consistent with the period in which Aaron would have lived. Thus, the researchers were able to furnish scientific data supporting the tradition that contemporary Jews are the direct biological descendants of the ancient Israelites. In a second study, Hammer established these findings more firmly by demonstrating a high correlation of DNA markers on the Y chromosomes of Jewish men living in widely variant geographical regions. As journalist Hillel Halkin summarized the findings: "Male Jews of Russian and Polish ancestry have a Y-chromosome profile more like that of male Moroccan, Kurdish, and Iraqi Jews than like that of Russian and Polish non-Jews; male Jews of Yemenite ancestry are closer to Jews from Rome than to Muslims from Yemen."[65] The results of these studies were startling in their implications, for they overturned generations of research by anthropologists like Maurice Fishberg, who had argued in 1911 that Jews had intermarried to such an extent with local populations over the centuries so as to render their biological connection to the ancient Israelites nearly meaningless.[66]

The American Jewish response to these genetic research projects has been mixed. In the case of the medical studies, both the scientists who undertake the research and the Jews who cooperate as subjects often do so at least partly out of an emotional attachment to Jewish peoplehood. Bert Vogelstein, a Johns Hopkins oncologist who has researched the genetic roots of colon cancer among Ashkenazim, describes the population that he studies as "my family" and credits his Jewishness and knowledge of Jewish people as factors that allowed him to make key discoveries.[67] Another Hopkins physician, Ann Pulver, chose to investigate schizoprenia and manic depression among Jews because she considered the research "a great advantage to the Jewish community."[68] As for the Jews who get tested or cooperate in the research, many have described their participation as a "mitzvah," an act of mutual responsibility that all Jews share for the welfare of the group. In many locations, Jews have not only streamed in to be tested for various "Jewish" genetic disorders, but have also put their financial and organizational resources behind research that will help better understand the biological component of Jewishness.[69]

If research on Jewish genetic diseases has inspired a sense of Jewish group feeling, work on the genetic history of the Jewish people has been an even greater rallying point. Especially at a time when Jewish social solidarity seems threatened by intermarriage, the notion of a biological dimension to Jewishness gives at least some Jews a sense of group stability and continuity, much as it has done in the past. "For some people," explains science writer David Olson, who has studied the Jewish genetic experiments, "the information provided by a test of genetic ancestry can provide a powerful sense of connectedness."[70] Laurie Zoloth-Dorfman, director of the Jewish Studies Program at San Francisco State University, has argued that the findings of genetic researchers like Hammer and Skorecki have provided Jews with as powerful a symbol as the Western Wall. "I think the [Y chromosome research] does the same thing genetically," she told a reporter from *Science News*. "It's a tangible, embodied moment of connection to our past."[71] Scorecki and Hammer have also commented on the way their research has bolstered feelings of Jewish continuity by providing a biological foundation for a long-standing cultural tradition. "It's a beautiful example," said Hammer, "of how father-to-son transmission of two things, one genetic and one cultural, gives you the same picture."[72] The research has indeed created a wave of interest among Jews, many of whom have sought to be tested to see if they carry the marker on their DNA. Family Tree DNA, a commercial DNA testing service founded by Houston real estate developer Bennett Greenspan, performs a "Cohanim test" and will even match Jewish genealogists whose genetic profiles suggest they may have shared ancestry.[73] Guided by a similar fascination with Jewish genetic origins, a group of Orthodox American Jews in Israel have established a "Kohanim Center" in Jerusalem that seeks to gather a worldwide registry of Jews of priestly lineage and touts the purity of Jewish descent from the "Ancient Hebrews" on its Web site. "Your family heritage is ancient and unique," the site explains, telling visitors they are members of "The Tribe That Never Got Lost!"[74]

In other quarters, however, Jews have expressed skepticism and fear concerning the growing focus on Jewish genetics. While Jews have been targeted for studies because they presented a convenient, easily identifiable population for research, media reports describing the discovery of Jewish genetic markers have often made it seem as if Jews suffer from a disproportionate number of genetic mutations that distinguish them from an otherwise healthy population. This has made many worry that Jews might be stigmatized as physically weak and as carriers of disease, stereotypes that have often plagued them in the past.[75] "We are getting a bad reputation," complained medical ethicist Moshe Tendler of Yeshiva University in a 1998 interview. "All the bad genes you talk about are Jewish genes."[76] Tendler became one of many community leaders and rabbis who began to warn fellow Jews in the late 1990s to avoid genetic testing until there were greater assurances that the data would not be misused. In 1996, similar concerns led a coalition of Jewish community organizations in Boston to refuse to cooperate with that city's Dana-Farber Cancer Institute, which wanted to study a breast cancer gene said to occur with great frequency among Ashkenazim.[77]

Responses of this type were often informed by the lessons of the Holocaust. For many Jews, memories of Nazi racial antisemitism are not so distant as to assuage fears that genetic data might be misused in similar fashion in the future. Some Jewish physicians, like Robert Pollack, a professor of Biological Sciences at Columbia University, have warned of the dangers of "biological Judaism," arguing that Nazi racial science stands as a warning to Jews to be wary of the new genetic research.[78] While geneticists Hammer and Skorecki stopped far short of claiming that Jews have wholly distinctive genetic characteristics that could be called "racial," many of their findings were popularized in ways that suggested a uniform Jewish genetic heritage. That assumption, Pollack infers, could only lead to trouble for American Jews. Apparently, many American Jews agree with him, since a pilot telephone survey conducted in the Baltimore–Washington, D.C. area revealed that 62.4 percent of Jewish respondents are "very concerned about potential discrimination and anti-Semitism" that Jewish genetic research might cause.[79] All in all, despite the enthusiasm of many Jews about genetic research's emphasis on the deep ties they shared with one another, their overall ambivalence about being in the genetic spotlight demonstrates how they readily embrace "tribalism" only when it carries few social costs. In cases where a "tribal" identity threatens to stigmatize them in the dominant culture, feelings of group "con-

24. Genetic testing brochure for Jews, 2002. In recent years, many Jews have expressed ambivalence about the trend toward testing for "Jewish" genetic diseases. This testing brochure appeals to Jews' mixed emotions, asserting the idea that they share a genetic heritage while also depicting them as a diverse group that defies easy categorization as a "race."

nectedness" have to vie with an often greater concern for continued integration and acceptance.

This tension has been especially palpable in discussions of one of the thorniest of issues surrounding Jewish "tribalism"—that of intermarriage between Jews and non-Jews, which, more than any other question, highlights the dilemmas American Jews face regarding self-definition in the twenty-first century. In the minds of many Jews, no other trend in Jewish life threatens to undermine the solidarity of the Jews as a social unit like intermarriage, but at the same time Jews feel that a strict insistence on endogamy cuts against some of the basic values of equality and free association that have been central to their liberal integrationist ethic.

In 1990, the compilers of the National Jewish Population Survey found that 52 percent of American Jews who had married in the previous five years had chosen non-Jewish spouses.[80] While this indicated that most American Jews no longer drew the line of social assimilation at marriage with non-Jews, it also provoked a flurry of community mobilization that showed just how worried many American Jews were about the impact of the new trend. In short time, the fight to counter intermarriage became the driving force behind a renewed commitment to Jewish religious education, youth activities, Jewish summer camps, and the support of Jewish life on college campuses, all of which were seen as ways of guaranteeing that young Jews would find Jewish spouses. In addition to bolstering these traditional tools for enhancing Jewish identity and commitment, Jewish communal institutions also began to develop new and innovative ways to stem the tide of intermarriage. Philanthropists poured millions of dollars into programs that would send unaffiliated college-aged Jews to Israel for identity-enhancing tours. New Jewish community centers aimed specifically at the populations thought to be most vulnerable to drift and defection were endowed. Jewish singles events and dating services were organized on a scale never before seen.

Yet despite this flood of activity devoted to stemming the tide of exogamy, there is also evidence that many American Jews feel extremely circumscribed in articulating a defensible opposition to intermarriage, especially when in conversation with the non-Jewish world. As members of a group that has argued for decades for equality, acceptance, and the openness of American life, many Jews feel uncomfortable defending exclusivity in their own marriage practices. In fact, some cannot defend them at all. Student activists like Mik Moore, a writer for the Jewish Student Press Service, often see a particular problem with Jewish opposition to intermarriage because the campus world in which they operate is especially inhospitable to any sort of racial or ethnic exclusivity. "During the civil rights struggle of the 1960s, many of our parents protested separatist ideologies," wrote Moore in an article aimed at other Jewish students.

"Today, some Jews find their mouths repeating segregationist ratio-nales."[81] Philip Weiss, a Jewish *New York Observer* columnist writing for a general audience, argued in 2000 that the rhetoric of much of the Jewish organizational establishment on the issue of intermarriage re-flected a "xenophobia and disdain" for non-Jews that "border[ed] on racism." The use of the term "mixed marriage" by many Jewish spokesmen, wrote Weiss, "seems oddly reminiscent of southern whites' concern with miscegenation."[82]

This trend became clear during the presidential election in 2000, when, after George W. Bush was criticized for visiting Bob Jones University, a South Carolina school that prohibited interracial dating by its students, critics began to inquire whether Joseph Lieberman, the Democratic Par-ty's nominee for vice president and an Orthodox Jew, was opposed to marriages between Jews and non-Jews. In a radio interview with talk-show host Don Imus, Lieberman was asked whether Judaism banned "inter-racial or inter-religious marriage," to which he answered "no." Trying to finesse the question, Lieberman explained that Jews have tradi-tionally married among themselves, just as Christians have, "to keep the faith going."[83] Although several Orthodox rabbis publicly corrected Lie-berman, holding that Judaism clearly does ban the practice of intermar-riage, Lieberman's answer was politically correct enough to avert a Bob Jones–like public relations catastrophe and satisfy most Jewish loyalists. The incident did show, however, the tremendous pressure Jews face when discussing their stance on intermarriage in public. Even those who criti-cized Lieberman's statements, like Agudath Israel of America spokesman Rabbi Avi Shafran, made certain to emphasize—as Lieberman did—that the opposition of Jews to intermarrige is purely religious, and "has noth-ing to do with race."[84]

Television has also been a powerful indicator of the pressures facing Jews to accept intermarriage as a normal and healthy part of integration into American society. "So pervasive has been intermarriage and inter-dating on television that it has been virtually impossible to find a Jewish couple anywhere on screen," explains Joyce Antler, an expert on Jewish media images.[85] In the 1970s, when Jewish characters were still rarely featured on television, one might have expected to find shows like *Bridget Loves Bernie*, *Rhoda*, and *Welcome Back, Kotter*, all of which featured intermarried couples. But today, when Jewish characters abound, the prevalence of intermarriage on television has not dimin-ished. Television relationships between Jews and non-Jews over the past several years have included Ann Kelsey and Stuart Markowitz on *L.A. Law*, Fran Fine and Maxwell Sheffield on *The Nanny*, Jamie and Paul Buckman on *Mad About You*, and Dharma Finkelstein and Greg Mont-gomery on *Dharma and Greg*, among others.[86] According to Stephen

Bayme, who directs the American Jewish Committee's communal affairs department, "while the rate of intermarriage in the American Jewish Community is, at the most, about 50 percent, the television intermarriage rate is almost 100 percent."[87]

Another interesting piece of statistical data about attitudes toward intermarriage emerged from the American Jewish Committee's 2000 Survey of Jewish Opinion, where half of those surveyed agreed that "it is racist to oppose Jewish-gentile marriages" and more than half disagreed with the statement, "It would pain me if my child married a gentile." While one might expect to see such disavowals of Jewish particularism expressed by Jews in non-Jewish settings, what was most surprising about the Survey of Jewish Opinion is that Jews were answering in this way to the questions of a Jewish community organization. One possible explanation is suggested by scholars Stephen M. Cohen and Arnold Eisen, who found in their own studies of American Jews that most of their study population answered survey questions very reticently and were less likely to shed the insecurities they felt as a result of outside pressures than they were when speaking in a more personal, one-on-one interview setting. Thus, even though the Survey of Jewish Opinion was Jewish-sponsored, the answers may be at least in part a product of the respondents' desire to offer answers that are acceptable to the larger, non-Jewish world.[88] Another possibility lies in the way the questions were asked. As Cohen and Eisen's research suggests, had the respondents been asked if they *preferred* their child to marry a Jew (rather than if they would be *pained*), the great majority would have said "yes."[89] The key is seeing how the underlying attachment to tribalism is kept in check in the case of intermarriage by a stronger desire to see one's children happy and successful in their environment.

What is clear, however, is that many American Jewish attitudes toward intermarriage are complex and often combine a strong commitment to Jewish group distinctiveness with a reluctance to condemn unions between Jews and non-Jews. Even those who intermarry express somewhat contradictory viewpoints. This contemporary struggle is captured well by writer Lisa Schiffman, who recounts the feelings of ambivalence she experienced when searching for a rabbi to marry her and her non-Jewish boyfriend. Although she had decided to marry someone of another background, Schiffman explained that she "didn't want to be married by a non-Jew," but "by someone with the same heritage, the same bloodline, the same olive skin and prominent nose and outsider status as myself."[90] Such statements indicate that far from having been eliminated by Jews' increasing integration, the tensions and conflicting impulses of American Jewish identity have only been accentuated.

The End of Whiteness?

When taken together with the assertion of a tribal identity by Jews in the cases of government racial classification and, to a lesser degree, Jewish genetic research, it is clear that the figures on perceptions of intermarriage from the Survey of Jewish Opinion do not represent a radical retreat from tribalism among American Jews. Given the right circumstances, American Jews have no compunction about expressing tribalist sentiment. In fact, their increased integration into white America has often made tribalism more compelling, as long as it does not conflict with the roles Jews wish to play in the wider world. Yet, as these tensions have continued to grow during the 1990s and the first years of the twenty-first century, there are suggestions that an increasing number of Jews are becoming frustrated with the constraints of acceptance in white America and are expressing a sense of alienation and disengagement from whiteness.

One indication of this trend is the appearance of *Heeb*, a magazine heralding the birth of a new, lively subculture among young Jews who take great pleasure in distancing themselves from the white mainstream of which they are unquestionably a part.[91] Since its debut in 2002, *Heeb* has taken aim at any aspect of Jewish culture thought to be characterized by obedient conformity to the values of white America. The clothing designer Ralph Lauren, maker of the exclusive Polo label, for example, was unmasked as Ralph Lifschitz in a parody of his trademark advertisements.[92] The magazine regularly celebrates Jewish physical distinctiveness, with articles on the "Jewfro" hairstyle and a photo exposé on the "crazy curls, shapely schnozzes and hefty hips" of the "Jewess."[93]

In addition to such pieces, *Heeb* abounds with articles and features linking Jews with African Americans, including a piece on the role of Jews in hip-hop and a satirical advertisement in which an African American man proclaims a piece of Streit's Matzoh to be a "big ass cracker!"[94] The "Nell Carter Memorial Page" in the spring 2003 issue honored the Presbyterian-born diva who became Jewish in 1983. The writeup on Carter expressed glee that Jews have "lucked out and gotten some of the best black celebrities as converts."[95] While *Heeb* treats both Jewish and black culture with a heavy dose of stereotype, the point of the magazine is to use over-the-top imagery to disturb the easy labeling of Jews as undifferentiated whites. And *Heeb* has not been alone in this quest. In 2003, writer-director Jonathan Kesselman presented the first "Jewxsploitation" film, *The Hebrew Hammer*, which used similar comic hyperbole to explicitly link Jews with African Americans. Drawing on the popular blaxploitation genre of the 1970s, the film follows the adventures of a tough Jewish action hero who speaks with "a mix of Black Panther argot and Yiddish" and "struts through the 'chood' instilling Jewish pride in its youth."[96]

While *Heeb* and *The Hebrew Hammer* are particularly vivid illustrations of how some Jews have become disenchanted with their role as privileged whites, this trend has also become apparent in more subtle ways, like the retreat of some American Jews from their classical liberal position on affirmative action. In 2003, when students sued the University of Michigan in the largest affirmative action case since *Bakke*, Jewish organizations took a decidedly lower profile in voicing their opinions, and only one of the major organizations, the Anti-Defamation League, continued to oppose educational admissions policies that took race into account. The American Jewish Committee, which in 1977 filed a brief in support of Allan Bakke, this time submitted one in support of the university, citing the "imperative to produce educated citizens and professionals who reflect the diversity of our society." This is a sharp turn in policy for Jewish organizations, because it is the first time they have accepted the notion that racism is endemic in American society, a revelation that signifies the growing uneasiness among Jews concerning their privileged status. Explaining the shift in attitude, attorney Alan Dershowitz ventured that, whereas in 1977 American Jews were still raw from their own experiences with discriminatory quotas imposed on them by WASPs, today Jews were conscious of—and likely unnerved by—the fact that "we are the WASPs."[97]

Viewed alongside the frustration of Jews who wish to be counted and legitimized by the government bureaucracy as something other than white, and the discomfort of those who object to the way African Americans often paint them as part of the white power structure, trends such as these suggest a growing disaffection among American Jews from the lures of a white identity and underscore the emotional costs whiteness has carried for them. Granted, one cannot view these developments apart from a larger social and historical context in which Jews have both sought and benefited from the privileges of whiteness. But these feelings among Jews do tell us something about the pain and resentment that has resulted from a system that often predicated full acceptance in white America on the abandonment of cultural distinctiveness and the disavowal of deeply held group ties, once expressed in the language of "race." For Jews who want to assert a particularist identity in today's America, the benefits of whiteness are increasingly questionable. Despite all of the economic and social benefits whiteness has conferred upon them, these Jews do not feel the kind of freedom whiteness is *supposed* to offer—the freedom to be utterly unselfconscious about one's cultural or ethnic background. In fact, many Jews at the turn of the twenty-first century seem particularly conscious of the way that being seen as white delegitimizes their claim to difference as Jews.

25. Jewish is cool, 2002. This satirical ad from *Heeb Magazine* uses a stereotypical image to associate Jewishness with the perceived assertiveness and independence of black popular culture. The tendency of young Jews to draw on black culture in fashioning Jewish identity since the 1960s suggests an increasing impatience with the constraints of whiteness.

With this said, it should be made clear that American Jews are by no means on the verge of renouncing their status as white. Even if whiteness has come into increasing conflict with their self-conception as a group apart, it has remained integral to most Jews' self-understanding and is critical to their ongoing desire for success and acceptance in an America defined by race. It is no coincidence that the only Jews who have explicitly advocated a Jewish disengagement from whiteness are political progressives like Michael Lerner, editor of *Tikkun*, and the radical Jewish activist Melanie Kaye/Kantrowitz, who implores Jews to reassert Jewishness as part of a larger break with the "dominant and privileged few—white, Christian, and rich." As Kaye/Kantrowitz admits, however, most American Jews, even those involved in liberal causes, are too invested in American life and are too fearful of transgressing its standards to totally reject the black-white paradigm.[98]

Observable trends among American Jews seem to support this judgment. The fact that more than 50 percent of American Jews feel the need to denounce opposition to intermarriage as "racist," for example, reveals the strength of pressure that is still acting on American Jewry to affirm their ties to the non-Jewish, mainly white world. So does the fact that so many contemporary Jewish leaders and intellectuals advocate a Jewish religious revival, rather than an ethnic or "tribalist" revival, as the key to Jewish continuity. In many respects, these spokespersons resemble Jewish leaders of the early twentieth century, who tried to bridge the gap between Jewishness and whiteness by asserting a religious self-definition, even though most Jews continued to think of themselves primarily as a "race." Conservative rabbi and scholar Arthur Hertzberg, for example, argued in his 1989 history of American Jewry that without a spiritual revival, "American Jewish history will soon end, and become part of American memory as a whole."[99] Elliott Abrams made a similar point in his popular treatise *Faith or Fear* (1997). Ethnicity "can and does strengthen ties to the Jewish community," he argued, "but alone—absent a commitment as well to Judaism—it cannot sustain them." According to Abrams, religion offers the only true guarantee of Jewish survival, since ethnic "substitutes for Judaism are false idols and following them is a path to ruin."[100] These sentiments were echoed the same year by Alan Dershowitz, who warned American Jews that "Judaism must become less tribal, less ethnocentric, less exclusive, less closed off, less defensive, less xenophobic, less clannish. . . . Tribalism might be easy to justify when others treat us like a tribe, as they long have. But it becomes anachronistic—and antagonistic—to behave like a tribe when others treat us like part of the mainstream."[101] While such pleas speak to the intense conflict many Jews perceive between "tribalism" and white American identity, however, it is unlikely that they will energize a community largely uninterested in active religious participation to refashion themselves as a purely denominational group. Moreover, a 2001 survey by the American Jewish Committee revealed that a plurality of American Jews—40 percent—said that "being a part of the Jewish people" was the most important aspect of their identity. A much smaller percentage, only 14 percent, gave religious observance as their answer.[102]

If Jews will ever be able to avoid the tensions between acceptance and group assertion that they have felt since the late nineteenth century, a necessary prerequisite is the ultimate dissolution of the dominant culture of which Jews have long strived to be a part. As long as whiteness, with its demand for a modicum of group homogeneity, remains the social ideal for American Jews, there seems little hope for a tribalist revival. Yet the possibility for a dramatic change in these circumstances may not be as distant as many might think. Some scholars predict that within fifty years, the ethno-racial landscape of the United States will be drastically different. Whites will be a minority, and Asians and Latinos will increasingly compete with African Americans, who will no longer be the archetypal "outsider" group in the United States.[103] In such a context, without a stable, monolithic "other" against which to define itself, whiteness could lose its power and attractiveness. In a truly more pluralistic, multicultural setting, in which there was little pressure to fit within a dominant grouping, the door could be opened to a reinvigorated group identity among Jews. This shift may take more than a mere demographic change, however, to be realized. California already has a white minority, yet white elites still maintain social and cultural hegemony, suggesting that a similar pattern may continue to prevail nationwide for the foreseeable future. Even if whites were to slip from power, Jews may not be able to totally disassociate themselves so easily from their former status, especially if groups like African Americans wish to preserve their paradigmatic role as a minority. In the meantime, for most American Jews, the continued power of the black-white dichotomy leaves them to struggle, as they have long done, with conflicting impulses for inclusion and distinctiveness.

NOTES

ABBREVIATIONS USED IN NOTES

AH	*American Hebrew* (New York, NY)
AI	*American Israelite* (Cincinnati, OH)
AJA	American Jewish Archives, Cincinnati, OH
AJA	*American Jewish Archives*
AJH	*American Jewish History*
AJHQ	*American Jewish Historical Quarterly*
BBN	*B'nai B'rith News* (Chicago, IL)
CFLPS	Chicago Foreign Language Press Survey, compiled by the Chicago Public Library Omnibus Project, Work Projects Administration of Illinois, 1942 (microfilm, Chicago Historical Society)
NYT	*New York Times*
PAJHS	*Publications of the American Jewish Historical Society*
RA	*Reform Advocate* (Chicago, IL)
YCCAR	*Yearbook of the Central Conference of American Rabbis*

INTRODUCTION

1. James Baldwin, "Negroes Are Anti-Semitic Because They're Anti-White," in *Black Anti-Semitism and Jewish Racism*, ed. Nat Hentoff (New York: Richard Baron, 1968), 10.

2. General histories of the multiple ways in which "race" was used in the United States during the nineteenth and early twentieth centuries include Thomas F. Gossett, *Race: The History of an Idea in America* (Dallas: Southern Methodist University Press, 1963); and Reginald Horsman, *Race and Manifest Destiny: The Origins of American Racial Anglo-Saxonism* (Cambridge: Harvard University Press, 1981). For efforts to fit various groups into the mold of black and white, see Gary Gerstle, *American Crucible: Race and Nation in the Twentieth Century* (Princeton: Princton University Press, 2001), 27–8, 50–3, 203–4; Alexander Saxton, *Indispensable Enemy: Labor and the Anti-Chinese Movement in California* (Berkeley and Los Angeles: University of California Press, 1971), 19–20; Gary Okihiro, *Margins and Mainstreams: Asians in American History and Culture* (Seattle: University of Washington Press, 1994), 31–63; John Higham, *Strangers in the Land: Patterns of American Nativism, 1860–1925* (New York: Atheneum, 1963), 173; Ronald Takaki, *Iron Cages: Race and Culture in Nineteenth-Century America* (New York: Oxford University Press, 1990), 219–20; and George J. Sanchez, "Reading Reginald Denny: The Politics of Whiteness in the Late Twentieth Century," *American Quarterly* 47 (Sept. 1995): 388–94. For a broader view of various uses of "race" in the West, see Ivan Hannaford, *Race: The History of an Idea in the West* (Washington, DC: Woodrow Wilson Center Press, 1996); and George M. Frederickson, *Racism: A Short History* (Princeton: Princeton University Press, 2002).

3. For studies of Jewish mobility, see Steven Hertzberg, *Strangers within the Gate City: The Jews of Atlanta, 1845–1915* (Philadelphia: Jewish Publication Society of America, 1978), 139–54; William Toll, *The Making of an Ethnic Middle Class: Portland Jewry over Four Generations* (Albany: State University of New York Press, 1982); Thomas Kessner, *The Golden Door: Italian and Jewish Immigrant Mobility in New York City, 1880–1915* (New York: Oxford University Press, 1977); Joel Perlmann, *Ethnic Differences: Schooling and Social Structure among the Irish, Italians, Jews, and Blacks in an American City, 1880–1935* (Cambridge: Cambridge University Press, 1988).

4. See Michael Alexander, *Jazz Age Jews* (Princeton: Princeton University Press, 2001), 1, 3–6.

5. Representative works include: Hasia Diner, *The Jews of the United States, 1654–2000* (Berkeley and Los Angeles: University of California Press, 2004); Diner, *In the Almost Promised Land: American Jews and Blacks, 1915–1935* (Westport, CT: Greenwood Press, 1977); Jonathan D. Sarna, *American Judaism: A History* (New Haven: Yale University Press, 2004); Deborah Dash Moore, *At Home in America: Second Generation New York Jews* (New York: Columbia University Press, 1981); Henry Feingold, ed. *The Jewish People in America*, 5 vols. (Baltimore: Johns Hopkins University Press, 1992); Jenna Weissman Joselit, *The Wonders of America: Reinventing Jewish Culture, 1880–1950* (New York: Hill and Wang, 1994).

6. On the tendency of American Jewish historians—and modern Jewish historians more generally—to emphasize continuity and the successful transformation of Jewish identity, see Todd M. Endelman, "The Legitimization of the Diaspora Experience in Recent Jewish Historiography," *Modern Judaism* 11 (1991): 195–209; and Tony Michels, "Writing Socialism Back into American Jewish History," paper delivered before the Association for Jewish Studies, Dec. 17, 1996. I thank Professor Michels for sharing this paper with me.

7. David R. Roediger, *The Wages of Whiteness: Race and the Making of the American Working Class* (London: Verso, 1991); Noel Ignatiev, *How the Irish Became White* (New York: Routledge, 1995); Michael Rogin, *Blackface/White Noise: Jewish Immigrants in the Hollywood Melting Pot* (Berkeley and Los Angeles: University of California Press, 1996); Matthew Frye Jacobson, *Whiteness of a Different Color: European Immigrants and the Alchemy of Race* (Cambridge: Harvard University Press, 1998); Karen Brodkin, *How Jews Became White Folks And What That Says about Race in America* (New Brunswick, NJ: Rutgers University Press, 1998). Thomas Guglielmo, in *White on Arrival: Italians, Race, Color, and Power in Chicago, 1890–1945* (New York: Oxford University Press, 2003), details the tendency of Italian immigrants to see themselves as a distinct race, but does not argue that this self-understanding had much of an enduring impact on their emerging white identity. Among the whiteness historians who discuss Jews, only Brodkin suggests that they developed a "whiteness of their own" that differed from the formulations of other groups and the dominant culture. Yet her conception of Jewish difference, which stresses the low economic status of immigrant Jews, is drawn too directly from a black-white understanding of race.

8. Cultural theorist Stuart Hall describes identity as something that is "constantly in the process of change and transformation," "multiply constructed," and characterized by "antagonistic discourses, practices and positions." See Hall, "Who Needs Identity?" in *Questions of Cultural Identity*, ed. Stuart Hall and Paul du Gay (London: Sage, 1996), 3–4.

9. One of the strongest assertions of this view is George Lipsitz, *The Possessive Investment in Whiteness: How White People Profit from Identity Politics* (Philadelphia: Temple University Press, 1998). For a critical view of this interpretation, see Eric Arneson, "Whiteness and the Historians' Imagination," *International Labor and Working-Class History* 60 (Fall 2001): 6, 9–13.

10. David Roediger, "Whiteness and Ethnicity in the History of 'White Ethnics' in the United States," in *Toward the Abolition of Whiteness: Essays on Race, Politics and Working Class History* (London: Verso, 1994), 185.

CHAPTER 1

1. Solomon Schindler, "Why Am I a Jew?" *Jewish Messenger*, Jan. 21, 1887, 5.

2. The major exceptions include Michael R. Marrus, *The Politics of Assimilation: The French Jewish Community at the Time of the Dreyfus Affair* (Oxford: Clarendon Press, 1971), 10–27; and John M. Efron, *Defenders of the Race: Jewish Doctors and Race Science in Fin-de-Siècle Europe* (New Haven: Yale University Press, 1994). Briefer mention of this trend is made in Naomi W. Cohen, *Encounter with Emancipation: The German Jews in the United States, 1830–1914* (Philadelphia: Jewish Publication Society of America, 1984), 272–5; David Feldman, *Englishmen and Jews: Social Relations and Political Culture, 1840–1914* (New Haven: Yale University Press, 1994), 122–6; and Jacob Katz, "Misreadings of Anti-Semitism," *Commentary* 76 (July 1983): 41–2.

3. See Cohen, *Encounter with Emancipation*, chaps. 3 and 4. Some scholars have argued that Central European Jewish immigrants of this period identified strongly with German culture after their arrival in the United States, leading to what Avraham Barkai has termed "Americanization delayed." See his *Branching Out: German-Jewish Immigration to the United States, 1820–1914* (New York: Holmes and Meier, 1994), 152–90; and Michael A. Meyer, "German-Jewish Identity in Nineteenth-Century America," in *Toward Modernity: The European Jewish Model*, ed. Jacob Katz (New Brunswick, NJ: Rutgers University Press, 1987), 247–67. My own view concurs with those of Leon Jick and Hasia Diner, who have emphasized that attachment to German culture was exhibited mainly by rabbis and intellectuals, while a strong desire for Americanization characterized the bulk of immigrants. See Leon Jick, *The Americanization of the Synagogue, 1820–1870* (Hanover, NH: Brandeis University Press, 1992) 143–6, 155–6, 175, 190–1; Hasia Diner, *A Time for Gathering: The Second Migration, 1820–1880* (Baltimore: Johns Hopkins University Press, 1992), 163–5.

4. Isaac Mayer Wise quoted in Jick, *Americanization of the Synagogue*, 173.

5. Morris A. Gutstein, *A Priceless Heritage: The Epic Growth of Nineteenth Century Chicago Jewry* (New York: Bloch Publishing Company, 1953), 47–50. For a similar pattern in Atlanta, see Steven Hertzberg, *Strangers within the Gate*

City: The Jews of Atlanta, 1845–1915 (Philadelphia: Jewish Publication Society of America, 1978), 50–1.

6. Deborah Dash Moore, *B'nai B'rith and the Challenge of Ethnic Leadership* (Albany: State University of New York Press, 1981), 1–34.

7. Rudolph Glanz, *Studies in Judaica Americana* (New York: Ktav Pubishing House, 1970), 173–6, 203–55. Glanz exaggerates the high degree of social interaction between non-Jewish Germans and Central European Jews in America. For a corrective see Barkai, *Branching Out*, 175–90; and Diner, *A Time for Gathering*, 107, 165.

8. Hertzberg, *Strangers within the Gate City*, 51.

9. Max Vorspan and Lloyd P. Gartner, *History of the Jews of Los Angeles* (Philadelphia: Jewish Publication Society of America, 1970), 81–2.

10. Ibid., 67.

11. John Higham, *Send These to Me: Immigrants in Urban America*, rev. ed. (Baltimore: Johns Hopkins University Press, 1984), 123–30. On the anxiety over class instability in Victorian America, see David Scobey, "Anatomy of the Promenade: The Politics of Bourgeois Sociability in Nineteenth-Century New York," *Social History* 17 (May 1992): 203–27.

12. *AH*, Nov. 4, 1889, 37.

13. On Adler, see Benny Kraut, *From Reform Judaism to Ethical Culture: The Religious Evolution of Felix Adler* (Cincinnati: Hebrew Union College Press, 1979).

14. Bernhard Felsenthal, "The Society for Ethical Culture," *Jewish Advance*, Jan. 24, 1879, 4.

15. *AH*, Jan. 7, 1881, 86; Mar. 13, 1884, 66.

16. Karla Goldman, "The Ambivalence of Reform Judaism: Kaufmann Kohler and the Ideal Jewish Woman," *AJH* 79 (Summer 1990): 477–99; Paula E. Hyman, *Gender and Assimilation in Modern Jewish History: The Roles and Representations of Women* (Seattle: University of Washington Press, 1995), 10–49.

17. *AI*, Nov. 5, 1880, 146.

18. *London Jewish World*, April 2, 1875, quoted in Rudolph Glanz, *The Jewish Woman in America: Two Female Immigrant Generations, 1820–1929* (New York: Ktav Publishing House, 1976), 2:97.

19. *NYT*, May 31, 1878, 1.

20. Yosef Hayim Yerushalmi, *Assimilation and Racial Anti-Semitism: The Iberian and the German Models* (New York: Leo Baeck Institute, 1982).

21. Maurice Olender, *The Languages of Paradise: Race, Religion, and Philology in the Nineteenth Century*, trans. Arthur Goldhammer (Cambridge: Harvard University Press, 1992); Efron, *Defenders of the Race*, 13–57; Sander Gilman, *The Jew's Body* (London: Routledge, 1990).

22. Reginald Horsman, *Race and Manifest Destiny: The Origins of American Racial Anglo-Saxonism* (Cambridge: Harvard University Press, 1981); Ronald Takaki, *Iron Cages: Race and Culture in Nineteenth-Century America* (New York: Oxford University Press, 1990); Thomas F. Gossett, *Race: The History of an Idea in America*, new ed. (New York: Oxford University Press, 1997); George M. Fredrickson, *The Black Image in the White Mind: The Debate on Afro-American Character and Destiny, 1817–1914* (New York: Harper and Row, 1971). For a

comparison of European and American racial systems, see Fredrickson, *Racism: A Short History* (Princeton: Princeton University Press, 2002).

23. Matthew Frye Jacobson, *Whiteness of a Different Color: European Immigrants and the Alchemy of Race* (Cambridge: Harvard University Press, 1998), 39–52.

24. Josiah Clark Nott and George R. Gliddon, *Types of Mankind* (Philadelphia: Lippincott, Grambo and Co., 1854), 117–8. See also Nott, "The Physical History of the Jewish Race," *Southern Quarterly* 1 (July 1850): 426–51.

25. Jews used the term "nation" during the colonial period to distinguish between Jews of different geographical (i.e., Portuguese or German) origins as well as to refer to the Jewish collective. See Eli Faber, *A Time for Planting: The First Migration, 1654–1820* (Baltimore: Johns Hopkins University Press, 1992), 60–61, 136. On the history of the term, see Guido Zernatto, "Nation: The History of a Word," *Review of Politics* 6 (1944): 351–66.

26. Jonathan D. Sarna, "The Jews in British America," in *The Jews and the Expansion of Europe to the West, 1450–1800*, ed. Paolo Bernardini and Norman Fiering (New York: Berghahn Books, 2001), 529.

27. *AH*, Oct. 13, 1882, 102; Isaac Mayer Wise quoted in James G. Heller, *Isaac M. Wise: His Life, Work and Thought* (Cincinnati: Union of American Hebrew Congregations, 1965), 599.

28. Higham, *Send These to Me*, 99–101; Louise Mayo, *The Ambivalent Image: Nineteenth-Century America's Perception of the Jew* (Rutherford, NJ: Fairgleigh Dickinson University Press, 1988); Jonathan D. Sarna, "The 'Mythical Jew' and the 'Jew Next Door' in Nineteenth-Century America," in *Anti-Semitism in American History*, ed. David A. Gerber (Urbana: University of Illinois Press, 1986), 57–78.

29. See, for example, the famous lecture delivered across the country in the 1870s by Zebulon Vance, "The Scattered Nation" in *Library of Southern Literature*, ed. Edwin Anderson Alderman and Joel Chandler Harris (Atlanta and New Orleans: Martin and Hoyt Company, 1907), 12:5560–74; and the speeches of Benjamin F. Butler and Henry Ward Beecher in Herbert N. Eaton, *An Hour with the American Hebrew* (New York: Jesse Haney and Co., 1879), 27–32, 51–76. For the 1890s, see Oscar Handlin, "American Views of the Jew at the Opening of the Twentieth Century," *PAJHS* 40 (1950–51): 323–44.

30. See David Roediger, "Irish-American Workers and White Racial Formation in the Antebellum United States," in *The Wages of Whiteness: Race and the Making of the American Working Class* (London: Verso, 1991), 133–63; and Noel Ignatiev, *How The Irish Became White* (New York: Routledge, 1995).

31. General surveys of antebellum Jews and the slavery question include Bertram W. Korn, *American Jewry and the Civil War* (Philadelphia: Jewish Publication Society of America, 1951), 15–31; Korn, "Jews and Negro Slavery in the Old South, 1789–1865," *PAJHS* 50 (Mar. 1961): 151–201; and Jonathan Silverman, "'The Law of the Land Is the Law': Antebellum Jews, Slavery, and the Old South," in *Struggles in the Promised Land: Toward a History of Black-Jewish Relations in the United States*, ed. Jack Salzman and Cornell West (New York: Oxford University Press, 1997), 73–86. For works arguing that antebellum Jews supported slavery as a means of assuring their own status, see Clive Webb, *Fight against Fear: Southern Jews and Black Civil Rights* (Athens: University of Georgia Press, 2001), 7–10;

Gary P. Zola, *Isaac Harby of Charleston, 1788–1828: Jewish Reformer and Intellectual* (Tuscaloosa: University of Alabama Press, 1994), 95–8; and Mark I. Greenberg, "Becoming Southern: The Jews of Savannah, Georgia, 1830–70," *AJH* 86 (March 1998): 60–3. In 1863, Jewish leaders invoked Jewish whiteness as a means of responding to General Ulysses S. Grant's attempted expulsion of the Jews from the Military Department of Tennessee. See [Isaac Leeser], "Are Israelites Slaves?" *Occident and American Jewish Advocate* 20 (Feb. 1863): 490–501; and [Isaac Mayer Wise], "Letter from the Editor," *AI*, Jan. 16, 1863, 218.

32. *Minnesota Star Democrat* quoted in the *Asmonean*, May 23, 1851, 36.

33. Nott, "Physical History," 428.

34. Madison Marsh, "Jews and Christians," *Medical and Surgical Reporter* 30 (1874): 344. See also George Fitzhugh, "Our Trip to the Country—Virginia," *De Bow's Review* 3 (Jan. 1867): 168.

35. William Levy, "A Jew Views Black Education: Texas—1890," in *Western States Jewish Historical Quarterly* 8 (July 1976): 351–60, reprinted from *Sabbath Visitor* (Cincinnati), Sept. 1 and 15, 1890. Max J. Kohler's history of Jews in the abolitionist movement, written in 1897, seems to betray a desire of Jews during this period to identify themselves as sympathizers with the plight of African Americans. See Max J. Kohler, "Jews and the American Anti-Slavery Movement," *PAJHS* 5 (1897): 137–55; 9 (1901): 45–56. See also the sentiments expressed toward the end of the nineteenth century by Abram Isaacs, editor of the *Jewish Messenger*, in Philip Foner, "Black-Jewish Relations in the Opening Years of the Twentieth Century," *Phylon* 36 (Winter 1975): 361–2.

36. Cyrus L. Sulzburger, "A Word to Mr. Montefiore," *AH*, April 18, 1884, 148.

37. *AH*, March 14, 1884, 66. This sentiment infused the racial discourse of the period, but was most directly articulated by those who spoke of the Jews' special mission to spread ethical monotheism. See, for example, David Einhorn, "Noch ein Wort über gemischte Ehen," *Jewish Times*, Jan. 28, 1870, 10–13; Kaufmann Kohler, "I Am a Jew," *Jewish Messenger*, Nov. 1, 1878, 6; Clara Block in *National Council of Jewish Women: Proceedings of the First Convention, November 15–19, 1896* (Philadelphia: Jewish Publication Society of America, 1897), 358.

38. *AH*, March 14, 1884, 66.

39. Jacob H. Schiff quoted in Paul Ritterband and Harold S. Wechsler, *Jewish Learning in American Universities* (Bloomington: University of Indiana Press, 1994), 101.

40. Max J. Kohler, preface to Charles P. Daly, *The Settlement of the Jews in North America* (New York: P. Cowen, 1893), vi.

41. Naomi W. Cohen, "American Jewish Reactions to Anti-Semitism in Western Europe, 1875–1900," *Proceedings of the American Academy for Jewish Research* 45 (1978): 40; Bernhard Felsenthal, "Who Is a Jew?" *Menorah* 8 (June 1890): 297–8.

42. Emma Lazarus, "Was the Earl of Beaconsfield a Representative Jew?" *Century* 23 (April 1882): 939–42; Bette Roth Young, *Emma Lazarus in Her World: Life and Letters* (Philadelphia: Jewish Publication Society of American, 1995), 53–5.

43. Friedrich Kohlbenheyer, "Jewish Blood," *American Jewess* 2 (April 1896): 451–3; (July 1896): 511.

44. *AH*, March 14, 1884, 66.

45. Leo N. Levi, *Memorial Volume* (Chicago: Hamburger Printing Co., 1905), 264.

46. Ada Robeck, "In the Bonds of Religion," *American Jewess* 1 (July 1895): 184–7.

47. Quoted in Kenneth Libo and Irving Howe, *We Lived There Too* (New York: St. Martin's/Marek, 1984), 240.

48. Kraut, *From Reform Judaism to Ethical Culture*, 125, 132; *AH*, April 18, 1884, 148; *RA*, March 21, 1896, 95.

49. *AH*, March 6, 1896, 509.

50. For a fuller discussion of the relationship between gender and Jewish racial identity during this period, see my article, "Between Race and Religion: Jewish Women and Self-Definition in Late Nineteenth Century America," in *Women in American Judaism: Historical Perspectives*, ed. Pamela S. Nadell and Jonathan D. Sarna (Hanover, NH: Brandeis University Press, 2001), 182–200.

51. Diner, *A Time for Gathering*, 162–3; Goldman, "Ambivalence of Reform Judaism," 477–99; Hyman, *Gender and Assimilation*, 10–49.

52. Kohler quoted in Goldman, "Ambivalence of Reform Judaism," 480.

53. Gustav Gottheil, "The Jewess as She Was and Is," *Ladies Home Journal* 15 (Dec. 1897): 21.

54. Abram Isaacs, "The Jewess in Authorship," *Ladies Home Journal* 9 (Oct. 1892): 17.

55. Carrie Wise, "Book Reviews," *American Jewess* 2 (Nov. 1895): 112–4.

56. Mrs. Julius C. Abel, "Characteristics of the Semitic Nations," *American Jewess* 1 (July 1895): 181–3.

57. "Race Characteristics," *American Jewess* 3 (Aug. 1896): 578.

58. See Hannah Greenebaum Solomon, *Fabric of My Life* (New York: Bloch Publishing Company, 1948), 80.

59. *National Council of Jewish Women: Proceedings of the First Convention*, 251.

60. Ibid., 358.

61. Ibid., 206.

62. Selma C. Berrol, *Julia Richman: A Notable Woman* (Philadelphia: Balch Institute Press, 1993), 109.

63. "The Jewess at Summer Resorts," *American Jewess* 1 (June 1895): 140.

64. Mary M. Cohen, "Hebrew Women," *Good Company* 3 (July 1879): 623.

65. David Einhorn, quoted in David Philipson, "Kaufmann Kohler as Reformer," in *Studies in Jewish Literature Issued in Honor of Professor Kaufmann Kohler*, ed. Philipson, David Newmark, and Julian Morgenstern (Berlin: G. Reimer, 1913), 17. See also Einhorn, "Noch ein Wort über gemischte Ehen," 10–13. At the time of his statement about mixed marriages, Einhorn was attacked by Samuel Hirsch, the former chief rabbi of Luxemburg, who had taken up a rabbinical post in Philadelphia. See Hirsch, "Der Nagel zum Sarge der winzigen jüdischen Race," *Jewish Times*, Jan. 22, 1870, 10–11.

66. Kaufmann Kohler, "Race und Religion," *Illinois Staatszeitung*, Sept. 10, 1878.

67. Kohler, "I Am a Jew," 6. For Kohler's strongly racial view of Jewish identity during this period, see also "Something about the Proselyte Question," *Jewish Advance*, Aug. 23, 1878, 4–5; Aug. 30, 1878, 4–5; "Abraham, the Prototype of the Jewish Race," *Jewish Advance*, Feb. 7, 1879, 4–5; "The Jewish Nationality," *AH*, May 14, 1880, 147–8; and "Die Semitenfrage," *Populär wissenschaftliche Monatsblätter* 3 (May 1883): 97–103.

68. Emil G. Hirsch, "Zur Mischehen-Frage," *Zeitgeist*, May 13, 1880, 154–5. For similar views see Adolph Moses, "Das physiologische Judenthum," *Zeitgeist*, Sept. 30, 1880, 318–20; and "Semitismus," *Zeitgeist*, Oct. 27, 1881, 352–3.

69. *AH*, March 25, 1881, 64.

70. Meyer, "German-Jewish Identity," 262–3.

71. Bernhard Felsenthal, *Zur Proselytenfrage in Judenthum* (Chicago: E. Rubovitz, 1878); "Religion und Race," *Illinois Staatszeitung*, Sept. 11, 1878; "Society for Ethical Culture," *Jewish Advance*, Jan. 3, 1879, 4; Jan. 10, 1879, 4; Jan. 17, 1879, 4; Jan. 24, 1879, 4.

72. Bernhard Felsenthal, "Erwiderung," *Jewish Advance*, Feb. 14, 1879, 7; Feb. 21, 1879, 7; "Weiteres über die Frage: Ob Race, ob Religionsgenossenschaft," *Jewish Advance*, March 7, 1879, 7; "Who Is a Jew?" *Menorah* 8 (June 1890): 296–304; "Where Do We Stand?" (1895), in *Bernhard Felsenthal: Teacher in Israel*, ed. Emma Felsenthal (New York: Oxford University Press, 1924), 228–40.

73. Wise quoted in Heller, *Isaac Mayer Wise*, 599.

74. Isaac Mayer Wise, "A Sketch of Judaism in America," *American Jews Annual* 1 (1885): 37; *AI*, May 6, 1881, 350.

75. *AI*, Dec. 5, 1879, 4; Mar. 18, 1881, 300; Mar. 9, 1883, 300; May 22, 1885, 4; Nov. 3, 1898, 4–5; Feb. 16, 1899, 4.

76. Walter Jacob, ed., *The Changing World of Reform Judaism: The Pittsburgh Platform in Retrospect* (Pittsburgh: Temple Rodeph Shalom, 1985), 101, 108.

77. Kaufmann Kohler, "The Spiritual Forces of Judaism," *YCCAR* 4 (1894): 137. Kohler and Hirsch were both influenced by the theories of "ethnic psychology" which had been propounded by scholars Moritz Lazarus and Herman Steinthal in Germany. See "Professor Moritz Lazarus," *AH*, Sept. 21, 1894, 612–16; Naomi W. Cohen, "The Challenges of Darwinism and Biblical Criticism to American Judaism," *Modern Judaism* 4 (1984): 129–30.

78. Emil G. Hirsch, "Why Am I a Jew?" *RA*, Dec. 14, 1895, 723–4. See also his "The Philosophy of the Reform Movement in American Judaism," *YCCAR* 5 (1895): 102–4, 107–8.

79. David Strassler, "The Changing Definitions of the 'Jewish People' Concept in the Religious-Social Thought of American Reform Judaism during the Period of the Mass Immigration from East Europe, 1880–1914," Ph. D. Dissertation, Hebrew University, 1980, 22–33. The wording of the Pittsburgh Platform, which disclaimed the *nationality* of Jews and not their racial identity, may itself have indicated the ambivalence of its framers.

80. Adolph Moses, *Yahvism and Other Discourses*, ed. Hyman G. Enelow (Louisville, KY: Council of Jewish Women, 1903), 1–10, 216–39. See also Moses, "A Glimpse at the Past and Future of Judaism," *American Jewess* 3 (Sept. 1896): 628–31; (Nov. 1896): 63–6. For the sentiments of another rabbi who consistently

opposed the racial definition, see David Philipson, *My Life as an American Jew* (Cincinnati: John G. Kidd and Son, 1941), 124.

81. See C. Vann Woodward, *The Strange Career of Jim Crow*, 3d rev. ed. (New York: Oxford University Press, 1974); *Origins of the New South, 1877–1913* (Baton Rouge: Louisiana State University Press, 1971), 324–6; John Higham, *Strangers in the Land: Patterns of American Nativism, 1860–1925* (New Brunswick, NJ: Rutgers University Press, 1963), 165–75; Robert H. Wiebe, *The Search for Order, 1877–1920* (New York: Hill and Wang, 1967), esp. 58–9.

CHAPTER 2

1. Paul Antonie Distler, "The Rise and Fall of the Racial Comics in American Vaudeville," Ph. D. Dissertation, Tulane University, 1963; Rudolph Glanz, *The Jew in American Wit and Early Graphic Humor* (New York: Ktav Publishing House, 1973); John Appel and Selma Appel, "Anti-Semitism in American Caricature," *Society* 24 (Nov./Dec. 1986): 78–83.

2. Irving Weingarten, "The Image of the Jew in the American Periodical Press, 1881–1921," Ph. D. Dissertation, New York University, 1979; Rudolph Glanz, "Jewish Social Conditions as Seen by the Muckrakers," *Studies in Judaica Americana* (New York: Ktav Publishing House, 1970), 384–407.

3. Jacob R. Marcus, *To Count a People: American Jewish Population Data, 1585–1984* (Lanham, MD: University Press of America, 1990), 240.

4. Moses Rischin, *The Promised City: New York Jews, 1870–1914* (Cambridge: Harvard University Press, 1964), 94, places the Jewish population for that year at 1.4 million or 28 percent of the total. For the Jewish population statistics of the smaller urban centers, see Marcus, *To Count a People*, 57, 87, 92, 194.

5. On the link between antisemitism and antimodernism in the United States, see T. J. Jackson Lears, *No Place of Grace: Antimodernism and the Transformation of American Culture, 1880–1920* (Chicago: University of Chicago Press, 1981), 108, 115–16, 133, 137, 180, 262, 275, 280, 287, 309.

6. Todd M. Endelman, "Comparative Perspectives on Modern Anti-Semitism in the West," in *History and Hate: The Dimensions of Antisemitism*, ed. David Berger (Philadelphia: Jewish Publication Society of America, 1986), 105–9; Shulamit Volkov, *The Rise of Popular Antimodernism in Germany: The Urban Master Artisans, 1873–1896* (Princeton: Princeton University Press, 1978).

7. Carl Smith, *Urban Disorder and the Shape of Belief: The Great Chicago Fire, the Haymarket Bomb and the Model Town of Pullman* (Chicago: University of Chicago Press, 1995); George Cotkin, *Reluctant Modernism: American Thought and Culture, 1880–1900* (New York: Twayne Publishers, 1992), 109–11.

8. On the sometimes disorienting changes during this period, see Robert H. Wiebe, *The Search for Order, 1877–1920* (New York: Hill and Wang, 1967); Alfred D. Chandler, *The Visible Hand: The Managerial Revolution in American Business* (Cambridge: Harvard University Press, Belknap Press, 1977); Alan Trachtenberg, *The Incorporation of America: Culture and Society in the Gilded Age* (New York: Hill and Wang, 1982); Timothy Gilfoyle, *City of Eros: New York City, Prostitution and the Commercialization of Sex, 1790–1920* (New York:

Norton, 1992), 179–315; Tom Lutz, *American Nervousness, 1903: An Anecdotal History* (Ithaca, NY: Cornell University Press, 1991); Lears, *No Place of Grace*.

9. On this point, see John Higham, *Send These To Me: Immigrants in Urban America*, rev. ed. (Baltimore: Johns Hopkins University Press, 1984), 109.

10. The predominance of male images probably has to do with the fact that Jewish men had greater interaction with the non-Jewish public than did Jewish women, allowing them to serve more effectively as a symbol for larger societal concerns.

11. Several historians have argued that the American view of the Jew during the nineteenth and early twentieth centuries was ambivalent, rather than wholly negative. See Higham, *Send These to Me*, 101; Louise Mayo, *The Ambivalent Image: Nineteenth-Century American Perceptions of the Jew* (Rutherford, NJ: Fairleigh Dickinson University Press, 1988); Jonathan D. Sarna, "The 'Mythical Jew' and the 'Jew Next Door' in Nineteenth-Century America," in *Anti-Semitism in American History*, ed. David A. Gerber (Urbana: University of Illinois Press, 1986), 57–78; Oscar Handlin, "American Views of the Jew at the Opening of the Twentieth Century," *PAJHS* 40 (1950–51): 323–44. Major histories of antisemitism in the United States, however, do not echo this view. Leonard Dinnerstein has argued that an "antisemitic society" had emerged in the United States by 1900, but does not measure this trend against the positive images of Jews common during this period. See Dinnerstein, *Antisemitism in America* (New York: Oxford University Press, 1994), chaps. 3 and 4. Rather than trying to neatly categorize period views of the Jew as either "antisemitic" or "philosemitic," I have sought to present a broader "racial discourse" in which the Jew was seen as different, but in which positive and negative images were often intertwined. For an application of this approach to the case of England during the same period, see Brian Cheyette, *Constructions of 'the Jew' in English Literature and Society: Racial Representations, 1875–1945* (Cambridge: Cambridge University Press, 1993).

12. John R. Commons, *Races and Immigrants in America* (New York: Macmillan Co., 1907), 146–8.

13. "The Jew in American Life," reprinted from the *New York Journal of Commerce and Commercial Bullletin* in *The Two Hundred and Fiftieth Anniversary of Jewish Settlement of the Jews in the United States* (New York: New York Co-operative Society, 1906), 224.

14. Jacob A. Riis, *The Battle with the Slum* (Montclair, NJ: Patterson Smith, 1969), 192–3.

15. Commons, *Races and Immigrants*, 146–8.

16. Jacob Riis, *How the Other Half Lives: Studies among the Tenements of New York* (New York: Hill and Wang, 1957), 79.

17. *Puck*, Dec. 14, 1898, 26.

18. *Frank Leslie's Illustrated Weekly*, Feb. 18, 1897, 102–3; *Puck*, April 17, 1901, Oct. 20, 1901; Appel and Appel, "Anti-Semitism in American Caricature," 81; Andrew R. Heinze, *Adapting to Abundance: Jewish Immigrants, Mass Consumption, and the Search for American Identity* (New York: Columbia University Press, 1990), 205.

19. Theodore A. Bingham, "Foreign Criminals in New York," *North American Review* 188 (1908): 383–94; George Kibbe Turner, "The City of Chicago: A

NOTES TO PAGES 40-43 **251**

Study of the Great Immoralities," *McClure's Magazine* 28 (April 1907): 575–92; Turner, "The Daughters of the Poor," *McClure's Magazine* 34 (Nov. 1909): 45–61. On Jewish involvement in prostitution during this period and the response of the organized Jewish community, see Edward J. Bristow, *Prostitution and Prejudice: The Jewish Fight against White Slavery, 1870–1939* (New York: Schocken Books, 1982).

20. "Chat With Dave Warfield," *New York Sun*, Nov. 12, 1901, and "The Evolution of Warfield's Jew," *Broadway Magazine* (Nov. 1903): 212–13, both in David Warfield Clipping File, Billy Rose Theater Collection, New York Public Library for the Performing Arts, Lincoln Center, New York (hereafter Billy Rose Theater Collection); and "Famous Old Play to be Filmed," n.d., in Joe Welch Clipping File, Billy Rose Theater Collection.

21. Mark Twain, *Concerning the Jews* (Philadelphia: Running Press, 1995), 14. On the virtue of the Jewish home and Jewish women, see also the *New York Evening Post*, quoted in *Two Hundred and Fiftieth Anniversary of Jewish Settlement*, 214; and Turner, "Daughters of the Poor," 47.

22. Wiebe, *The Search for Order*, 58. On the concept of "civilization" during this period, see Gail Bederman, *Manliness and Civilization: Race and Gender in American Culture, 1875–1920* (Chicago: University of Chicago Press, 1995).

23. *World's Work* 6 (1903): 3612.

24. Ibid., 3716.

25. Riis, *How the Other Half Lives*, 112.

26. Frederick Bushee quoted in *"Kike!" A Documentary History of Anti-Semitism in America*, ed. Michael Selzer (New York: World Publishing, 1972), 64.

27. Turner, "The City of Chicago," 587.

28. Ibid., 587, 590.

29. "The Leo Frank Case," *Watson's Magazine* 20 (Jan. 1915): 143.

30. Watson quoted in C. Vann Woodward, *Tom Watson: Agrarian Rebel* (Oxford: Oxford University Press, 1963), 443. General treatments of the Leo Frank Case include Leonard Dinnerstein, *The Leo Frank Case* (Athens: University of Georgia Press, 1968); and Steve Oney, *And the Dead Shall Rise: The Murder of Mary Phagan and the Lynching of Leo Frank* (New York: Pantheon, 2003). For an account that places discussions of Frank within the context of southern racial and gender identity, see Jeffrey Melnick, *Black-Jewish Relations on Trial: Leo Frank and Jim Conley in the New South* (Jackson: University Press of Mississippi, 2000). Also helpful are Eugene Levy, "Is the Jew a White Man? Press Reaction to the Leo Frank Case, 1913–1915" *Phylon* 35 (1974): 212–22; and Nancy MacLean, "The Leo Frank Case Reconsidered: Gender and Sexual Politics in the Making of Reactionary Populism," *Journal of American History* 78 (Dec. 1991): 917–48.

31. Arthur T. Abernethy, *The Jew a Negro: Being a Study of the Jewish Ancestry from an Impartial Standpoint* (Moravian Falls, NC: Dixie Publishing Company, 1910), 105. On Abernethy's career, see *Dictionary of North Carolina Biography*, ed. William S. Powell (Chapel Hill: University of North Carolina Press, 1979), 1:4.

32. Abernethy, *The Jew a Negro*, 110.

33. William Z. Ripley, *The Races of Europe* (New York: D. Appleton and Co., 1899), 386; Woodward, *Tom Watson*, 438.

34. Abernethy, *The Jew a Negro*, 109.

35. Charles E. Woodruff, *Effects of Tropical Light on White Men* (New York: Rebman Co., 1905); Woodruff, "The Complexion of the Jews," *American Journal of Insanity* 62 (1905): 327–33.

36. Ripley, *Races of Europe*, 103–30, 246–80. See also, John Higham, *Strangers in the Land: Patterns of American Nativism, 1860–1925* (New Brunswick, NJ: Rutgers University Press, 1955), 154–5.

37. Ripley, *Races of Europe*, 386, 390, 394.

38. Sidney Reid, "So You're a Jew," *Independent* 65 (Nov. 1908): 1212.

39. Thomas Dixon, Jr., "Booker T. Washington and the Negro," *Saturday Evening Post*, Aug. 19, 1905, 2.

40. Thomas Dixon, Jr., *The Traitor: A Story of the Fall of the Invisible Empire* (New York: Doubleday, Page & Company, 1907), 105–10, 159, 328. For Dixon's attitudes toward Jews more generally, see Raymond A. Cook, *Thomas Dixon* (New York: Twayne, 1974), 63.

41. Madison C. Peters, *Justice to the Jew: The Story of What He Has Done for the World* (New York: Trow Press, 1909), xi, 35.

42. "Address by Mayor McClellan," in *Two Hundred and Fiftieth Anniversary of Jewish Settlement*, 26–7.

43. N[athaniel]. S. Shaler, *The Neighbor: The Natural History of Human Contacts* (Boston: Houghton, Mifflin and Company, 1904), 117–8.

44. Ibid., 328–30.

45. William Howard Taft, quoted in Simon Wolf, *The Presidents I Have Known, from 1860–1918* (Washington, DC: Byron S. Adams, 1918), 348–51.

46. Theodore Roosevelt to Editor of the National Encyclopedia Company, May 15, 1901, quoted in Michael N. Dobkowski, *The Tarnished Dream: The Basis of American Anti-Semitism* (Westport, CT: Greenwood Press, 1979), 154.

47. On this general theme, see Gary Gerstle, *American Crucible: Race and Nation in the Twentieth Century* (Princeton: Princeton University Press, 2001), chap. 1. The names of several Jewish Rough Riders can be found in the muster rolls published in Theodore Roosevelt, *The Rough Riders* (New York: C. Scribner's, 1899), 239–69.

48. J. Lebowich, "Theodore Roosevelt and the Jews," *Menorah* 37 (Oct. 1904): 189–94; Theodore Roosevelt to James Andrew Drain, June 27, 1911, in *The Letters of Theodore Roosevelt*, ed. Elting E. Morison (Cambridge: Harvard University Press, 1954), 7:299–300. On Straus's career, see Naomi Cohen, *A Dual Heritage: The Public Career of Oscar S. Straus* (Philadelphia: Jewish Publication Society of America, 1969); and Oscar S. Straus, *Under Four Administrations from Cleveland to Taft* (Boston: Hougton Mifflin Co, 1922).

49. See the dedication page in Israel Zangwill, *The Melting Pot: A Drama in Four Acts* (London: Heinemann, 1915). On Roosevelt and the Jews, see Thomas G. Dyer, *Theodore Roosevelt and the Idea of Race* (Baton Rouge: Louisiana State University Press, 1980), 124, 131.

50. Abernethy, *The Jew a Negro*, 110.

51. Tom Watson quoted in Melnick, *Black-Jewish Relations on Trial*, 67.

52. On this point, see John Dollard, *Caste and Class in a Southern Town*, 2d ed. (New York: Harper, 1949), 129–30.

53. J. G. Wilson, "The Crossing of the Races," *Popular Science Monthly* (1908): 493–5.

54. *World's Work* 6 (1903): 2592–3.

55. Higham, *Send These to Me*, 130–6.

CHAPTER 3

1. On Jewish attitudes toward slavery, see Bertram W. Korn, *American Jewry and the Civil War* (Philadelphia: Jewish Publication Society of America, 1951), 15–31; Korn, "Jews and Negro Slavery in the Old South, 1789–1865," *PAJHS* 50 (March 1961): 151–201; Max J. Kohler, "The Jews and the American Anti-Slavery Movement," *PAJHS* 5 (1897): 137–55; 9 (1901): 45–51; Jonathan Silverman, "'The Law of the Land Is the Law': Antebellum Jews, Slavery, and the Old South," in *Struggles in the Promised Land: Toward a History of Black-Jewish Relations in the United States*, ed. Jack Salzman and Cornell West (New York: Oxford University Press, 1997), 73–86.

2. On this point, see Korn, "Jews and Negro Slavery in the Old South," 200; Naomi W. Cohen, *Encounter with Emancipation: The German Jews in the United States, 1830–1914* (Philadelphia: Jewish Publication Society of America, 1984), 22.

3. See, for example, the speech of Confederate veteran William Levy before students of a black school in Texas, in which he directly compares black and Jewish history. William Levy, "A Jew Views Black Education: Texas—1890," in *Western States Jewish Historical Quarterly* 8 (July 1976): 351–60.

4. Herbert Elzas, *The Jews of South Carolina from the Earliest Times to the Present Day* (New York: J. P. Lippincot Co., 1905), 250–1. On Wade Hampton, see C. Vann Woodward, *Origins of the New South, 1877–1913* (Baton Rouge: Louisiana State University Press, 1971), 79–80, 321.

5. Myron Berman, *Richmond's Jewry, 1769–1976: Shabbat in Shockoe* (Charlottesville: University Press of Virginia, 1979), 235.

6. Leo E. Turitz and Evelyn Turitz, *Jews in Early Mississippi, 1840–1900* (Jackson: University Press of Mississippi, n.d.), 100; Margaret England Armbrester, *Samuel Ullman and "Youth": The Life, the Legacy* (Tuscaloosa: University of Alabama Press, 1993), 39.

7. See Joel Williamson, *Crucible of Race: Black-White Relations in the American South since Emancipation* (New York: Oxford University Press, 1984), 113–5.

8. *Jewish South* (Richmond), Sept. 29, 1893, 4.

9. Arnold Shankman, "Friend or Foe? Southern Blacks View the Jew, 1880–1935," in *Turn to the South: Essays on Southern Jewry*, ed. Nathan M. Kaganoff and Melvin I. Urofsky (Charlottesville: University Press of Virginia, 1979), 191 n. 49. For another case, see Maurice Fishberg, *The Jews: A Study of Race and Environment* (New York: Scribner's, 1911), 120.

10. William F. Holmes, "Whitecapping: Anti-Semitism in the Populist Era," *AJHQ* 63 (1973–74): 244–61.

11. Heller quoted in Bobbie Malone, *Rabbi Max Heller: Reformer, Zionist, Southerner, 1860–1929* (Tuscaloosa: University of Alabama Press, 1997), 48.

12. For a partial list of southern Jewish officeholders during this period, see Raymond Arsenault, "Charles Jacobson of Arkansas: A Jewish Politician in the Land of the Razorbacks, 1891–1915," in Kaganoff and Urofsky, *Turn to the South*, 179 n. 6.

13. Tillman quoted in Leonora E. Berson, *The Negroes and the Jews* (New York: Random House, 1971), 28.

14. Steven Hertzberg, *Strangers within the Gate City: The Jews of Atlanta, 1845–1915* (Philadelphia: Jewish Publication Society of America, 1978), 157–8, 160–2.

15. *Jewish South*, Sept. 8, 1893, 3. The exclusion of Jews from political office during this period seems to have been especially common in the larger urban centers. For a similar trend in New Orleans, see Malone, *Rabbi Max Heller*, 49.

16. Hertzberg, *Strangers within the Gate City*, 121, 171; Malone, *Rabbi Max Heller*, 37–8.

17. *Jewish Comment*, May 31, 1907, 122, quoted in Jeffrey Gurock, "The 1913 New York State Civil Rights Act," *AJS Review* 1 (1976): 98.

18. *Jewish South*, Sept. 29, 1893, 4.

19. *Jewish Sentiment* (Atlanta), Nov. 25, 1898, 1.

20. *Jewish South*, Nov. 25, 1898, 6–7.

21. "A Poor Parallel," *Modern View* (St. Louis), May 4, 1906, 2.

22. Thomas Dixon, Jr., "Booker T. Washington and the Negro," *Saturday Evening Post*, Aug. 19, 1905, 1–2.

23. "An Impudent Nigger," *Jewish Ledger* (New Orleans), Sept. 22, 1905, 12.

24. Quoted in Williamson, *Crucible of Race*, 193. On Tillman, see Stephen Kantrowitz, *Ben Tillman and the Reconstruction of White Supremacy* (Chapel Hill: University of North Carolina Press, 2000).

25. Gurock, "The 1913 New York State Civil Rights Act," 96.

26. Max Heller, "Regulating the Summer Hotel," *AI*, May 30, 1907, 4.

27. *Jewish South*, Sept. 22, 1893, 4.

28. *Jewish Sentiment*, Oct. 28, 1898, 1. For similar articles, see Dec. 31, 1897, 1; March 11, 1898, 1; Apr. 22, 1898; June 10, 1898, 1; June 24, 1898, 1, 6; Nov. 4, 1898, 1; Nov. 18, 1898, 1; Nov. 25, 1898, 1; March 19, 1899, 4; April 30, 1899, 3; May 19, 1899, 3–4; Aug. 11, 1899, 3; Aug. 18, 1899, 3; Nov. 10, 1899.

29. Arsenault, "Charles Jacobson of Arkansas," 60, 72–3.

30. *Baltimore Sun*, Oct. 18, 1903, 14; Oct. 22, 1903, 12.

31. *Afro-American* (Baltimore), Nov. 7 and Dec. 2, 1907; Margaret Law Callcott, *The Negro in Maryland Politics, 1870–1912* (Baltimore: Johns Hopkins University Press, 1969), 124–29. Rayner had opposed a disenfranchisement measure in 1905 because he feared it could threaten the voting rights of some white immigrants. This momentary opposition has led some Jewish historians to portray him improperly as a champion of black rights. See, for example, Joshua Bloch, "Isidor Rayner (1850–1912)" *PAJHS* 40 (March 1951): 291–2.

32. *Jewish Ledger*, Aug. 10, 1906, 20; Sept. 28, 1906, 16.

33. *Jewish Sentiment*, Mar. 18, 1898, 13.

34. This claim was first made in print by Rabbi David Marx, "History of the Jews of Atlanta," *RA*, Nov. 4, 1911. See also Janice O. Rothschild, *As But a Day* (Atlanta: Hebrew Benevolent Congregation, 1967), 33. This founding myth was so often repeated among Atlanta Jews in the period before World War II that it was memorialized in Alfred Uhry's Tony Award-winning play, *The Last Night of Ballyhoo* (New York: Theater Communications Group, 1997), 11.

35. Philip Foner, "Black-Jewish Relations in the Opening Years of the Twentieth Century," *Phylon* 36 (Winter 1975): 366.

36. Minutes of Hebrew Benevolent Congregation, Oct. 14, 1901, 507, Cuba Archives, William Breman Jewish Heritage Museum, Atlanta.

37. Julius Lester, *Lovesong: Becoming a Jew* (New York: Arcade Publishing, 1988), 8–12.

38. Jack E. Davis, *Race against Time: Culture and Separation in Natchez since 1930* (Baton Rouge: Louisiana State University Press, 2001), 93–4.

39. "Resolution of Sympathy from Colored Citizens," *Alexandria Town Talk*, Jan. 28, 1910, reprinted in Martin I. Hinchin, *Four Score and Eleven: A History of the Jews of Rapides Parish, 1828–1919* (Alexandria, LA: Privately published, 1984), app. 108–9.

40. Louis R. Harlan, "Booker T. Washington's Discovery of Jews," in *Region, Race, and Reconstruction: Essays in Honor of C. Vann Woodward*, ed. J. Morgan Kousser and James M. McPherson (New York: Oxford University Press, 1982), 271, 274.

41. Ibid., 274.

42. Carolyn Gray Le Master, *A Corner of the Tapestry: A History of the Jewish Experience in Arkansas, 1820s–1990s* (Tuscaloosa: University of Alabama Press, 1994), 56; Byron L. Scherwin, "Portrait of a Romantic Rebel: Bernard C. Ehrenreich (1876–1955)," in Kaganoff and Urofsky, *Turn to the South*, 8; Harold S. Wechsler, "Rabbi Bernard C. Ehrenreich: A Northern Progressive Goes South," in *Jews of the South: Selected Essays from the Southern Jewish Historical Society*, ed. Samuel Proctor and Louis Schmier (Macon, GA: Mercer University Press, 1984), 56–7.

43. Alfred Geiger Moses to Booker T. Washington, October 8, 1901, in *The Booker T. Washington Papers*, ed. Louis Harlan (Urbana: University of Illinois Press, 1974), 6:236–8.

44. Turitz and Turitz, *Jews of Early Mississippi*, 17.

45. Malone, *Rabbi Max Heller*, 103–5.

46. Max Heller, "A Departure in Jewish Philanthropy," *AI*, Jan. 12, 1911, 4.

47. Rothschild, *As But a Day*, 50; Williamson, *Crucible of Race*, 221–2.

48. Max Heller, "A National Problem," *AI*, March 17, 1904, 4.

49. Quoted in Hertzberg, *Strangers within the Gate City*, 213.

50. Because the back files of the *Exponent* are missing for this period, evidence of the paper's stance on antiblack violence and its willingness to compare blacks and Jews comes from the indignant responses of Southern Jewish journals. See *Jewish Sentiment*, Nov. 25, 1898, 1; and *Jewish South*, Nov. 25, 1898, 6–7.

51. See Foner, "Black-Jewish Relations," 361.

52. *AH*, Aug. 17, 1900, 367; Aug. 24, 1900, 396.

53. *Public* (Chicago), Aug. 22, 1903, 307–8.

54. Louis Marshall to Rabbi Henry Cohen, Dec. 9, 1914; and Marshall to Edgar H. Farrar, Dec. 18, 1914, both in box 1583, Louis Marshall Papers, AJA (hereafter cited as Marshall Papers).

55. Louis Marshall to Milton Klein, Sept. 9, 1913, box 1582, Marshall Papers.

56. Eugene Levy, "Is the Jew a White Man? Press Reaction to the Leo Frank Case, 1913–1915" *Phylon* 35 (June 1974): 219.

57. Morgenstern quoted in Gurock, "The 1913 New York State Civil Rights Act," 99.

58. Deborah Dash Moore, *B'nai B'rith and the Challenge of Ethnic Leadership* (Albany: State University of New York Press, 1981), 109–11.

59. *The Standard Club's First Hundred Years* (Chicago: Standard Club of Chicago, 1969), 38–40. On p. 39, the editors of this commemorative volume scratched out the word "coon" on the program from the 1902 show.

60. YMHA *Monthly Bulletin* 5 (April 1904): 3.

61. YMHA *Monthly Bulletin* 3 (April 1902): 8; 6 (April 1905): 3; 12 (Feb. 1911): 26; (March 1911): 14, 20; 13 (Jan. 1912): 9; (Nov. 1912): 18; 14 (Feb. 1913): 17; 15 (Feb. 1914): 39; (March 1914): 10; 17 (March–April 1916): 21; 18 (Feb. 1917): 11; (March 1917): 2. For a minstrel show held in Los Angeles under the auspices of the local B'nai B'rith lodge, see *B'nai B'rith Messenger* (Los Angeles), March 10, 1911, 1; March 24, 1911, 1; April 7, 1911, 1; April 27, 1911, 1; May 12, 1911, 1.

62. *New York Age*, Nov. 26, 1908; Sept. 2, 1909, quoted in Steven Bloom, "Interactions between Blacks and Jews in New York City, 1900–1930, as Reflected in the Black Press," Ph.D. dissertation, New York University, 1973, 165–6.

63. Gilbert Osofsky, *Harlem: The Making of a Ghetto* (New York: Harper Torchbooks, 1971), 121.

64. Philip Bregstone, *The Jews of Chicago: A Cultural History* (Chicago: Privately published, 1933), 148–9.

65. Thomas Lee Philpott, *The Slum and the Ghetto: Immigrants, Blacks and Reformers in Chicago, 1880–1930* (Belmont, CA: Wadsworth Publishing Co., 1991), 167–8.

66. *Chicago Tribune*, Oct. 21, 1919.

67. *AH*, Sept. 11, 1903, 525.

68. *Jewish Criterion* (Pittsburgh), Aug. 20, 1915. See also the *Jewish Sentinel* (Chicago), April 12, 1918, for a condemnation of lynching in Illinois.

69. *Jewish Sentinel*, March 10, 1916, 8.

70. Nina Mjagkij, "A Peculiar Alliance: Julius Rosenwald, the YMCA, and African-Americans, 1910–1933," *AJA* 44 (1992): 587; Dorothy Fuld to Booker T. Washington, 1909 (n.d.), reel 303, Booker T. Washington Papers, Library of Congress, Washington, DC (hereafter cited as Washington Papers).

71. Annie Joseph Levi to Booker T. Washington, Jan. 29, 1905, reel 258, Washington Papers.

72. Felix Adler, "The Conduct of Life, Third Lecture: The Negro Problem as a Test of the Supreme Moral Rule," Nov. 25, 1906, Felix Adler Papers, Archives of the New York Society for Ethical Culture, New York. On Adler's interest in African American issues, see Benny Kraut, *From Reform Judaism to Ethical Culture: The Religious Evolution of Felix Adler* (Cincinnati: Hebrew Union College

Press, 1979), 16–17, 231 n. 55; Howard B. Radest, *Toward Common Ground: The Story of the Ethical Societies in the United* States (Garden City, NY: Fieldston Press, 1969), 93–4, 170–1; Horace L. Friess, *Felix Adler and Ethical Culture: Memories and Studies*, ed. Fannia Weingartner (New York: Columbia University Press, 1981), 194–7.

73. B. Joyce Ross, *J. E. Spingarn and the Rise of the NAACP, 1911–1939* (New York, 1972); Nancy J. Weiss, "Long Distance Runners of the Civil Rights Movement: The Contribution of Jews to the NAACP and the National Urban League in the Early Twentieth Century," in Salzman and West, *Struggles in the Promised Land*, 123–52; Hasia Diner, *In the Almost Promised Land: American Jews and Blacks, 1915–1933* (Westport, CT: Greenwood Press, 1977), 19–24.

74. Joseph Krauskopf, "The American Negro," in *Sunday Discourses before the Reform Congregation Keneseth Israel, Series XXIX, 1915–1916* (Philadelphia: Oscar Klonower, 1916), 145–54; Egal Feldman, "The Social Gospel and the Jews," *AJHQ* 58 (March 1969): 308–329; Leonard J. Mervis, "The Social Justice Movement and the American Reform Rabbi," *AJA* 7 (June 1955): 171–230.

75. *Jewish Criterion*, Jan. 13, 1905, 8; Jan. 20, 1905, 1; Booker T. Washington, "The Success of Negro Education," *The Reform Pulpit: Sunday Lectures Delivered before Congregation Rodeph Shalom, Pittsburg, Pa.*, ed. Leonard J. Levy (Pittsburgh: Congregation Rodeph Shalom, 1904–5), 4:3–20; *Crisis* 6 (June 1913): 86. For a southern Jewish criticism of Levy, see *Jewish Ledger*, Sept. 22, 1905, 12.

76. Stephen S. Wise, "Abolition and Fifty Years After," *Crisis* 5 (Feb. 1913): 188–9.

77. Joseph Krauskopf, quoted in *Crisis* 6 (June 1913): 86.

78. On Jewish philanthropic support of black causes during this period, see Weiss, "Long Distance Runners of the Civil Rights Movement," 135–7, 139–43; Diner, *In the Almost Promised Land*, 125, 185–7.

79. On the social role of philanthropy during the Progressive Era, see Kathleen D. McCarthy, *Noblesse Oblige: Charity and Cultural Philanthropy in Chicago, 1849–1929* (Chicago: University of Chicago Press, 1982), 99–122.

80. Rosenwald quoted in Mjagkij, "A Peculiar Alliance," 587.

81. Jacob H. Schiff, *Jacob H. Schiff: His Life and Letters*, ed. Cyrus Adler (Garden City, NY: Doubleday, Doran, 1928), 1:314–8; Naomi W. Cohen, *Jacob H. Schiff: A Study in American Jewish Leadership* (Hanover, NH: Brandeis University Press, 1999), 71; Harlan, "Booker T. Washington's Discovery of Jews," 271–3; Ron Chernow, *The Warburgs* (New York: Vintage Books, 1993), 306; Mjagkij, "A Peculiar Alliance," 585–605; Edwin R. Embree and Julia Waxman, *Investment in People: The Story of the Julius Rosenwald Fund* (New York: Harper and Brothers, 1949); Morris Robert Werner, *Julius Rosenwald: The Life of a Practical Humanitarian* (New York: Harper and Brothers, 1939).

82. Bloom, "Interactions between Blacks and Jews," 35; Mjagkij, "A Peculiar Alliance," 589.

83. Mjagkij, "A Peculiar Alliance," 591–2.

84. Harold Brackman, "The Ebb and Flow of Conflict: A History of Black-Jewish Relations through 1900," Ph.D. dissertation, University of California at Los Angeles, 1977, 465–67. As long as Booker T. Washington was alive, Jacob H.

Schiff and several other Jewish philanthropists remained somewhat hesitant to support the efforts of African American leaders who disagreed with the Tuskeege educator. See the interchange between Schiff and W.E.B. DuBois in *The Correspondence of W.E.B. DuBois*, ed. Herbert Aptheker (Amherst: University of Massachussets Press, 1973), 108–9.

85. Brackman, "The Ebb and Flow of Conflict," 467.

86. See Jeffrey Gurock, *When Harlem Was Jewish, 1870–1930* (New York: Columbia University Press, 1979), 147.

87. *AH*, Dec. 16, 1910, 188.

88. Philpott, *The Slum and the Ghetto*, 381 n. 12.

89. Amy Vorhaus to Booker T. Washington, July 9, 1915, reel 88, Washington Papers.

90. Charles Waddell Chesnutt to Booker T. Washington, Oct. 31, 1903, in Harlan, *Papers of Booker T. Washington*, 7:320–2.

91. *List of Books in the Library of the Harmonie Club of New York and Addendum* (New York: Harmonie Club, 1905).

92. *New York Age*, Jan 4, 1906, quoted in Osofsky, *Harlem*, 37.

93. *Jewish Sentinel*, Aug. 8, 1919.

94. On feelings of racial "inbetweenness" among various Southern and Eastern European immigrant groups, see James R. Barrett and David Roediger, "Inbetween Peoples: Race, Nationality and the 'New Immigrant' Working Class," *Journal of American Ethnic History* 16 (Sept. 1997): 3–44. On job and housing competition between immigrants and blacks, see Joseph Parot, "Ethnic versus Black Metropolis: The Origins of Polish-Black Housing Tensions in Chicago," *Polish-American Studies* 29 (Spring–Autumn 1972): 5–33; Thaddeus Radzialowski, "The Competition for Jobs and Racial Stereotypes: Poles and Blacks in Chicago," *Polish-American Studies* 33 (1976): 5–18; James R. Barrett, *Work and Community in the Jungle: Chicago's Packinghouse Workers, 1894–1922* (Urbana: University of Illinois Press, 1987), 224; and Rudolph Glanz, *Jew and Italian: Historic Group Relations and the New Immigration, 1881–1924* (New York, 1971), 29. On the sources of Jewish mobility, see Thomas Kessner, *The Golden Door: Italian and Jewish Immigrant Mobility in New York City, 1880–1915* (New York: Oxford University Press, 1977).

95. On the entry of blacks into the garment industry after 1917, see Sterling D. Spero and Abram L. Harris, *The Black Worker: The Negro and the Labor Movement* (New York: Columbia University Press, 1931), 338–40.

96. Mary White Ovington, *Half A Man: The Negro in New York* (New York: Longmans, Green and Co., 1910); Brackman, "The Ebb and Flow of Conflict," 448.

97. On this point, see Hasia Diner, "Between Words and Deeds: Jews and Blacks in America, 1880–1935," in Salzman and West, *Struggles in the Promised Land*, 98.

98. See Arnold Shankman, "Friend or Foe? Southern Blacks View the Jew, 1880–1935," in Kaganoff and Urofsky, *Turn to the South*, 109.

99. Taped interview with Dr. Maurice Klawans, Aug. 29, 1990, Jewish Museum of Maryland, Baltimore.

100. Louis Schmier, "'For Him the "Schwartzers" Couldn't Do Enough': A Jewish Peddler and His Black Customers Look at Each Other," *AJH* 73 (1983–4): 39–55.

101. Shankman, "Friend or Foe?" 109.

102. Hertzberg, *Strangers within the Gate City*, 184–88.

103. Baruch Charney-Vladek, "Vi azoy lebn di iden in di South?" (How do Jews live in the South?), *Forverts*, March 22, 1911, 5.

104. Gurock, *When Harlem Was Jewish*, 148.

105. Ibid.

106. James Grossman, *Land of Hope: Chicago, Black Southerners and the Great Migration* (Chicago: University of Chicago Press, 1989), 162, 321–2, n. 2.

107. Jane Addams, *Twenty Years at Hull-House* (New York: Macmillan Company, 1910), 255–6.

108. *Allgemeine Zeitung des Judenthums* (Berlin), Sept. 22, 1905, app. 4.

109. Isaac Metzker, ed., *A Bintel Brief: Sixty Years of Letters from the Lower East Side to the Jewish Daily Forward* (New York: Schocken Books, 1971), 95–97.

110. *AH*, Aug. 9, 1912, 404; *Forverts*, Aug. 5, 1912, 8; *Yidishes tageblat*, Aug. 5, 1912, 1; *NYT*, June 7, 1930, 17. A similar marriage in 1886 drew comment in the European Hebrew press. See *Ha-melits*, Nov. 28 (Dec. 10), 1886, 2033.

111. Hertzberg, *Strangers within the Gate City*, 190–1.

112. S. Niger Charney, "America in the Works of I. M. Dick (1814–1893)," *YIVO Annual of Jewish Social Science* 9 (1954): 68–70.

113. "Di negern," (The negroes), *Amerikaner*, Oct. 4, 1904, 14.

114. Fred Somkin, "Zion's Harp by the East River: Jewish-American Popular Songs in Columbus's Golden Land, 1890–1914," in *Perspectives in American History*, N.S., 2 (1985): 189 n. 18. Somkin reports that a search of over five hundred sets of Yiddish theater lyrics from the period turned up only one reference to African Americans.

115. On the frequent comparison of "wage slavery" to chattel slavery by socialists and labor unionists during this period, see Barry H. Goldberg, "Beyond Free Labor: Labor, Socialism and the Idea of Wage Slavery, 1890–1920," Ph. D. dissertation, Columbia University, 1979.

116. David Edelshtat, *Folks-gedikhte* (People's poems) (New York: Yehuda Katsenelenbogen, 1895), 79, 213–4; Edelshtat, "Di undankbare negerin," (The ungrateful Negress) *Fraye arbeter shtime*, June 12, 1891, 5; *Yidishes tageblat*, Feb. 22, 1892, 1; Clara Lemlich, "Why Waistmakers Strike," *New York Evening Journal*, Nov. 26, 1909; Hadassa Kosak, *Cultures of Opposition: Jewish Immigrant Workers, New York City, 1881–1905* (Albany: State University of New York Press, 2000), 112.

117. *Forverts*, Aug. 17, 1900, 1. See also the article of Aug. 16, 1900, 1.

118. *Forverts*, July 7, 1903, 1.

119. *Yidishes tageblat*, May 11, 1906, 8 (English Department). For similar sentiments, see "Di negern un di iden" (The Negroes and the Jews), *Forverts*, Aug. 16, 1908, 4.

120. "Jews and Negroes, A Comparison," *Yidisher kurier*, Aug. 5, 1912. See also "The War of Colors," *Yidisher kurier*, May 31, 1917; and "Due to Prejudice," *Yidisher kurier*, April 22, 1914; all in CFLPS.

121. Philip Krants, *Di kulturgeshikhte* (The history of culture) (New York: International Library Publishing Co., 1903), 2:325; 3:86–95, 306.

122. Ab[raham]. Cahan, *Bleter fun mayn lebn* (Pages from my life) (New York: Forverts Association, 1926), 131–3.

123. Hillquit quoted in B. Gornberg [Boris Frumkin], "Emigration and Immigration: A Report to the International Socialist Congress in Stuttgart, 1907," in *On Jews, America and Immigration: A Socialist Perspective*, trans. and ed. Uri D. Herscher and Stanley F. Chyet (Cincinnati: American Jewish Archives, 1980), 43.

124. See Norma Fain Pratt, *Morris Hillquit: A Political History of an American Jewish Socialist* (Westport, CT: Greenwood Press, 1987), 92–6.

125. Quoted in Bloom, "Interactions between Blacks and Jews," 167–70.

126. Abraham Bisno, *Abraham Bisno: Union Pioneer* (Madison: University of Wisconsin Press, 1967), 47.

127. Rubin quoted in Hertzberg, *Strangers within the Gate City*, 191.

128. *Forverts*, Aug. 17, 1908, 1; Aug. 19, 1908, 1.

129. Seth Scheiner, *Negro Mecca: A History of the Negro in New York City, 1865–1920* (New York: New York University Press, 1965), 133.

130. Louis Marshall to Henry Fleischman, April 26, 1907, in *Louis Marshall: Champion of Liberty, Selected Papers and Addresses*, ed. Charles Reznikoff (Philadelphia: Jewish Publication Society of America, 1957), 1:425–6.

131. Morris Winchevsky, "Perets in Amerike," *Di tsukunft* 20 (June 1915): 539.

CHAPTER 4

Part of this chapter was previously published as "Contesting the Categories: Jews and Government Racial Classification in the United States," *Jewish History* 19 (2005): 79–107, and is republished here with the kind permission of Springer Science and Business Media.

1. Jonathan D. Sarna, *A Great Awakening: The Transformation that Shaped Twentieth Century American Judaism and Its Implications for Today* (New York: Council for Initiatives in Jewish Education, 1995). Sarna dates the Jewish "revival" of this period from the late 1870s and sees it continuing through the turn of the century. See also Sarna, *JPS: The Americanization of Jewish Culture, 1888–1988* (Philadelphia: Jewish Publication Society of America, 1989), 13–16; and Shuly Rubin Schwartz, *The Emergence of Jewish Scholarship in America: The Publication of the Jewish Encyclopedia* (Cincinatti: Hebrew Union College Press, 1991), 11–15.

2. *AI*, April 7, 1898, 4.

3. *AI*, April 20, 1899, 4. For other articles forwarding similar views, see Jan. 26, 1899, 4; and Feb. 16, 1899, 4.

4. *RA*, March 21, 1896, 95; June 27, 1896, 380–3; Dec. 14, 1901, 399–401; *UAHC Proceedings* (1903): 5042–51; *NYT*, April 27, 1909, 4.

5. *RA*, Feb. 19, 1898, 5; Simon Wolf, *The American Jew as Patriot, Soldier and Citizen* (Philadelphia: Levytype Company, 1895), 8.

6. Cyrus Adler, ed., *Jacob H. Schiff: His Life and Letters* (Garden City, NY: Doubleday, Doran and Co., 1929), 2:72.

7. Louis Marshall to Editors, *Jewish Daily News*, Feb. 7, 1906, in *Louis Marshall: Champion on Liberty, Selected Papers and Addresses*, ed. Charles Reznikoff (Philadelphia: Jewish Publication Society of America, 1957), 2:797–8.

8. Louis Marshall to Charles H. Shapiro, Feb. 14, 1911, quoted in Jerold S. Auerbach, *Rabbis and Lawyers: The Journey from Torah to Constitution* (Bloomington: Indiana University Press, 1990), 115.

9. S[igmund]. Hecht, "Nationality, Race, or Religion," *B'nai B'rith Messenger* (Los Angeles), March 11, 1910, 9.

10. *AI*, Jan. 26, 1899, 4; April 20, 1899, 4.

11. Deborah Dash Moore, *B'nai B'rith and the Challenge of Ethnic Leadership* (Albany: State University of New York Press, 1981), 104, 112.

12. *Variety*, Jan. 30, 1909, in Joe Welch clipping file, Billy Rose Theater Collection, New York Public Library for the Performing Arts, Lincoln Center, New York (hereafter cited as Billy Rose Theater Collection); Harley Erdman, *Staging the Jew: The Performance of an American Ethnicity, 1860–1920* (New Brunswick, NJ: Rutgers University Press, 1997), 149–52; Paul Antonie Distler, "The Rise and Fall of the Racial Comics in American Vaudeville," Ph. D. dissertation, Tulane University, 1963, 188–91.

13. See Rudolph Glanz, "Some Remarks on Jewish Labor and American Public Opinion in the pre–World War I Era," *YIVO Annual of Jewish Social Science* 16 (1976): 179–80; Naomi W. Cohen, *Encounter with Emancipation: The German Jews in the United States, 1830–1914* (Philadelphia: Jewish Publication Society of America, 1984), 330.

14. See Naomi W. Cohen, "The Reaction of Reform Judaism in America to Political Zionism (1897–1922)," *PAJHS* 40 (1950–51): 361–94.

15. Kohler quoted in Michael A. Meyer, *Response to Modernity: A History of the Reform Movement in Judaism* (New York: Oxford University Press, 1988), 52.

16. Quoted in Bobbie Malone, *Rabbi Max Heller: Reformer, Zionist, Southerner, 1860–1929* (Tuscaloosa: University of Alabama Press, 1997), 119.

17. Maurice Fishberg, *Di gefahr fun di yidishe natsionalistishe bavegung* (The danger of the Jewish nationalist movement) (New York: Max N. Meisel, 1906), 74–5.

18. Yonathan Shapiro, *Leadership of the American Zionist Organization, 1897–1930* (Urbana: University of Illinois Press, 1971), 29–36.

19. Richard Gottheil, "The Aims of Zionism" (1898), in *The Zionist Idea*, ed. Arthur Hertzberg (New York: Atheneum, 1986), 496–500. See also Louis Lipsky, "An Outline and an Argument: On Zionist Principles," *Maccabaean* 16 (March 1909): 96.

20. These early Reform Zionists require much greater scholarly examination. They have been deemphasized by most scholars of American Zionism who, like Melvin Urofsky, have focused on the leadership of Louis Brandeis or, like Evyatar Friesel, have concentrated on the "cultural" Zionists led by Israel Friedlaender. See Urofsky, *American Zionism: From Herzl to the Holocaust* (Lincoln: University of Nebraska Press, 1975); and Friesel, *Ha-tenua ha-tsiyonit ba-artsot ha-brit, 1898–1914* (The Zionist movement in the United States, 1898–1914) (Tel Aviv: Ha-kibbutz Ha-meuchad Publishing House, 1970). One of the most helpful recent studies of an early Reform Zionist is Malone, *Rabbi Max Heller*. On the elder

Gottheil, see Richard J. H. Gottheil, *The Life of Gustav Gottheil: Memoir of a Priest in Israel* (Williamsport, PA: Bayard Press, 1936).

21. Cohen, *Encounter with Emancipation*, 286–7; Marianne R. Sanua, *"Here's to Our Fraternity": One Hundred Years of Zeta Beta Tau, 1898–1998* (Hanover, NH: Zeta Beta Tau Foundation, 1998), 10.

22. Gottheil, "The Aims of Zionism," 499. For similar sentiments from another Zionist leader, see Max Heller, quoted in Malone, *Rabbi Max Heller*, 113.

23. Representative articles include: Bernhard Felsenthal, "The Fundamental Principles of Judaism," trans. Adele Szold, *Maccabaean* 1 (Nov. 1901): 66–8; (Dec. 1901): 108–11; Felsenthal, "Are the Jews a Race or a Denomination?" *Maccabaean* 7 (June 1905): 240–2; "Race Consciousness and National Consciousness," *Maccabaean* 18 (April 1910): 131; " 'Juden Heraus': Dr. Fishberg Pronounces the Doom of the Jew," *Maccabaean* 19 (Jan. 1911): 257–9; A. S. Waldstein, "A Study of the Jew," *Maccabaean* 21 (Aug. 1911): 41–3; (Sept. 1911): 69, 76–80; Ignaz Zollschan, "The Jewish Race Problem," *Maccabaean* 21 (Feb. 1912): 210–6, 230–1; Meyer Waxman, "The Ethnic Character of the Jews," *Maccabaean* 22 (Dec. 1912): 190–4. See also the discussion of the American tour of European Jewish racial theorist Ignaz Zollschan in *Maccabaean* 23 (Dec. 1913): 355–6; 24 (Jan. 1914): 5, 29; (Feb. 1914): 64; (Mar.1914): 94.

24. David Philipson, "Judaism—Race, Nationality or Religion?" *Jewish Exponent* (Philadelphia), Jan. 7, 1910, 8.

25. Israel Friedlaender, "Race and Religion," in *Past and Present: A Collection of Jewish Essays* (Cincinnati: Ark Publishing Co., 1919), 431.

26. Alexander quoted in Hertzberg, *Strangers within the Gate City*, 126.

27. Adler, *Jacob H. Schiff*, 2:72–3, 129–31, 167. For another example, see Evyatar Friesel, "Jacob H. Schiff Becomes a Zionist: A Chapter in American-Jewish Self-Definition, 1907–1917," *Studies in Zionism* 5 (April 1982): 69.

28. *UAHC Proceedings* (1903): 5050.

29. Kaufmann Kohler, *Jewish Theology: Systematically and Historically Considered* (New York: Macmillan Co., 1918), 7.

30. See Dana Evan Kaplan, "W. E. Todd's Attempt to Convert to Judaism and Study for the Reform Rabbinate in 1896," *AJH* 83 (Dec. 1995): 429–44.

31. Louis Marshall to Benjamin Marcus, March 8, 1912, in Reznikoff, *Louis Marshall*, 2:809–10. See also the discussion in Cohen, *Encounter with Emancipation*, 330–1.

32. New Orleans *Times-Democrat* [Sept.?] 6, 1902, clipping in David Warfield file, Billy Rose Theater Collection.

33. *AH*, Aug. 25, 1911, 486. See also *Jewish Encyclopedia* (New York: Funk and Wagnalls, 1906), 1:xi–xii; Schwartz, *The Emergence of Jewish Scholarship in America*, 109.

34. Friedlaender, "Race and Religion," 437.

35. Louis D. Brandeis, "The Jewish Problem—How to Solve It," in Jacob De Haas, *Louis D. Brandeis: A Biographical Sketch* (New York: Bloch Publishing Company, 1929), 178–9. See also, Richard Gottheil, *Zionism* (Philadelphia: Jewish Publication Society of America, 1914), 33; and Mordecai Kaplan, "Judaism and Nationality," *Maccabaean* 17 (Aug. 1909): 60–1.

36. Caspar Levias, "The Justification of Zionism," *HUC Journal* 3 (April 1899): 173–4.

37. Max L. Margolis, "What Are We?" *BBN* (March–April 1910): 3.

38. Helpful in understanding the often overlapping concerns and goals of Zionist and "assimilationist" or "liberal" Jewish leaders, although in a very different context, is Steven M. Poppel, *Zionism in Germany, 1897–1933: The Shaping of a Jewish Identity* (Philadelphia: Jewish Publication Society of America, 1977).

39. Isaac B. Berkson, *Theories of Americanization: A Critical Study, with Special Reference to the Jewish Group* (New York: Columbia University Teachers College, 1920), 100.

40. Avrom Liessin in *Forverts*, May 8, 1909, translated as "Senator Guggenheim and the Jewish Immigrants," *Forward*, May 16, 1997 (100th Anniversary Issue), 13.

41. B[ernard]. G. R[ichards]., "The Non-Jewish Definition of the Jew," *AH*, Dec. 25, 1908, 209. See also Maurice H. Harris, "The Non-Religious Definition of 'Jew' and Its Menace," *AH*, Dec. 18, 1908, 178–79; "The Term Jew," *AH*, Dec. 18, 1908, 186–7; J. Fuchs, "Nicht Gedacht Soll Ihrer Werden," *AH*, Dec. 25, 1908, 208.

42. *Yidisher kurier*, June 20, 1906, CFLPS. For similar sentiments, see the articles published on Nov. 24, 1908 and July 15, 1914.

43. See Bernard H. Bloom, "Yiddish-Speaking Socialists in America, 1892–1905," *AJA* 12 (1960): 34–68.

44. Philip Krantz, *Di kultur-geshikhte* (History of culture) (New York: International Publishing Co., 1903), 3:94.

45. Philip Krantz, *Vos heyst natsyon?* (What is a nation?) (New York: International Bibliothek, 1903), 11–12.

46. Morris Winchevsky, "Mayn natsyonaler ani-mamin" (My national declaration of faith), *Gezamelte verk* (New York: Frayhayt Publishing Co., 1927), 7:221–2.

47. Bernard G. Richards, "Yidn gegn der yidisher rase" (Jews against the Jewish race), in *Dos yidishe folk*, Jan. 14, 1910, 5; Ab[raham] Goldberg, "Der yidisher kerper" (The Jewish body), May 6, 1910, 2–3.

48. For historical surveys of intermarriage as an issue in Jewish communal discussion, see Moshe Davis, "Mixed Marriage in Western Jewry: Historical Background to the Jewish Response," *Jewish Journal of Sociology* 10 (1968): 177–220; Alan Levenson, "Reform Attitudes, in the Past, toward Intermarriage," *Judaism* 38 (1989): 320–32; Jenna Weissman Joselit, *The Wonders of America: Reinventing Jewish Culture, 1880–1950* (New York: Hill and Wang, 1994), 43–54.

49. Julius Drachsler, *Democracy and Assimilation: The Blending of Immigrant Heritages in America* (New York: Macmillan Co., 1920), 102, 121–2; Drachsler, *Intermarriage in New York City: A Statistical Study of the Amalgamation of European Peoples* (New York: Columbia University, 1921), 43–5. Maurice Fishberg, *The Jews: A Study of Race and Environment* (New York: Walter Scott Publishing Co., 1911), 203–4, gives somewhat exaggerated figures for intermarriage in the United States, designed perhaps to support his thesis that Jews were on the path to absorption in American society. Figures from Cincinnati put the rate there at 4.5 percent in 1916–18. See Jonathan D. Sarna and Nancy H. Klein, *The Jews*

of Cincinnati (Cincinnati: Center for Study of the American Jewish Experience, Hebrew Union College–Jewish Institute of Religion, 1989), 7, 20 n. 28.

50. Esther J. Ruskay, "Intermarriage," in *Hearth and Home Essays* (Philadelphia: Jewish Publication Society of America, 1902), 58.

51. *Hebrew Standard* (New York), April 14, 1905, 8; April 21, 1905, 8.

52. On "The House Next Door," a popular intermarriage drama of the period, see *AH*, April 9, 1909, 607; and April 16, 1909, 634. For a survey of Jewish intermarriage plots on the American stage during this period, see Erdman, *Staging the Jew*, 118–43.

53. See the unfavorable review in *NYT*, Sept. 7, 1909, 9. On the symbolic importance of the play, see Werner Sollors, *Beyond Ethnicity: Consent and Descent in American Culture* (New York: Oxford University Press, 1986), 66–75.

54. Samuel Sale, "Intermarriage," *RA*, Jan. 30, 1909, 717.

55. George Fox, "Intermarriage as It Affects the Relation between the I.O.B.B. and the Temple," *BBN* 2 (Dec. 1909): 4. For another defense of intermarriage, see Emanuel A. Hirsch, " 'The Melting Pot': Will the Jews Become Merged in It and Disappear?" *AI*, March 4, 1909, 1.

56. G[otthard]. Deutsch, " 'The Melting Pot': The Question of Intermarriage in Zangwill's Play," *AI*, March 25, 1909, 1. Tobias Schanfarber, "Zangwill's 'Melting Pot': Another View of the Englishman's Latest Play," *AI*, Oct. 29, 1908, 1. Bernard G. Richards, "Zangwill's New Play, 'The Melting Pot,'" *AH*, Oct. 9, 1908, 557–8; S[amuel]. Schulman, "Judaism and Intermarriage with Christians," *AH*, Nov. 20, 1908, 59–61; "Mixed Marriages," *AH*, Nov. 27, 1908, 101; *AH*, Dec. 11, 1908, 161; and J[udah]. L. Magnes, "The Melting Pot," *AH*, Oct. 22, 1909, 619–20.

57. *AH*, March 19, 1909, 528.

58. *AI*, Feb. 17, 1910, 4.

59. See "Mixed Marriages," *AH*, Nov. 27, 1908, 101.

60. Mendel Silber, "Intermarriage," *YCCAR* 18 (1908): 273.

61. Emil G. Hirsch, "Intermarriage," *RA*, Nov. 21, 1908, 381–4; *AI*, Nov. 26, 1908, 1, 4. There was some dispute as to whether this statement by Hirsch was meant to encourage intermarriage or not. See *BBN* 1 (Dec. 1909): 4.

62. *Yidisher kurier*, Nov. 24, 1908, CFLPS; *Maccabaean* 8 (April 1905): 160–1; (May 1905): 215–6.

63. See the advertisement in the *Jewish Exponent*, Jan. 21, 1910, 12.

64. For comments on Einhorn's legacy at the conference, see *AH*, Nov. 12, 1909, 36–7, 49; Dec. 3, 1909, 131; Dec. 10, 1909, 154. See also Emil G. Hirsch's rejection of Einhorn's racialism in "Intermarriage," 383.

65. Ephraim Feldman, "Intermarriage Historically Considered," *YCCAR* 19 (1909): 271–307; S[amuel]. Schulman, "Mixed Marriages in the Relation to the Jewish Religion," *YCCAR* 19 (1909): 308–35.

66. *AH*, Nov. 19, 1909, 74.

67. *Jewish Exponent*, Feb. 4, 1910, 4. For an official description of Jews as a subgroup of the "Caucasian" race, see U.S. Immigration Commission, *Dictionary of Races and Peoples* (Washington, DC: Government Printing Office, 1911), 73.

68. *RA*, Oct. 30, 1909.

69. Ibid.

70. Cyrus Adler to Mayer Sulzburger, Dec. 7, 1909 and Dec. 14, 1909 in Adler, *Collected Letters*, ed. Ira Robinson (Philadelphia: Jewish Publication Society of America), 176–7.

71. *American Jewish Yearbook* 12 (1910–11): 350; "The Hebrew and the Census," *AH*, Dec. 10, 1909, 160–1; *BBN* 1 (May 1909): 2; Naomi W. Cohen, *Not Free to Desist: The American Jewish Committee, 1906–1966* (Philadelphia: Jewish Publication Society of America, 1972), 47.

72. Louis Marshall to Sen. Simon Guggenheim, May 10, 1910, box 1579, folder 5, Louis Marshall papers, AJA.

73. *American Jewish Yearbook*, 13 (1911–12): 303–4.

74. See Esther L. Panitz, "In Defense of the Jewish Immigrant (1891–1924)," *AJHQ* 55 (Sept. 1965): 89–97. For a survey of the contentious issue of immigrant classification, see Nathan Goldberg, "Forty-Five Years of Controversy: Should Jewish Immigrants Be Classified as Jews?" in *The Classification of Jewish Immigrants and Its Implications* (New York: Yiddish Scientific Institute—YIVO, 1945), 90–105.

75. On Wolf, see Esther L. Panitz, *Simon Wolf: Private Conscience and Public Image* (Rutherford, NJ: Fairleigh Dickinson University Press, 1987).

76. Wolf to Frank P. Sargent, July 6, 1903, in file on the Racial Classification of Jewish Immigrants, small collection 5328, AJA (hereafter cited as Racial Classification file, AJA).

77. Ibid.

78. *UAHC Proceedings* (1903): 5046–50.

79. *AH*, Nov. 13, 1903, 822–3.

80. *NYT*, Apr. 27, 1909, 4.

81. A copy of Kohler's brief, "Memorandum in Opposition to Classification of Immigrants as 'Hebrews,'" can be found in the Racial Classification file, AJA.

82. A typescript copy of the original hearing transcript is in box 29, folder 6, Union of American Hebrew Congregations Records, AJA (hereafter cited as UAHC Records). It was published in the *Jewish Exponent*, Jan 28, 1910, 1, 8; and the *Maccabaean* (Jan. 1910): 16–29.

83. For correspondence and internal memos reflecting the commission's thinking on this issue, see the Racial Classification file, AJA.

84. Letter of Rabbi Rudolph Coffee, *Jewish Exponent*, Feb. 11, 1910.

85. Bernard G. Richards, "Jews against the Jewish Race," *Hebrew Standard*, Jan. 7, 1910.

86. *Yidishes Tageblat*, Jan. 4, 1910, 1; Panitz, "In Defense of the Jewish Immigrant," 92.

87. *Jewish Exponent*, Feb. 4, 1910, 4.

88. Simon Wolf to Max Heller, April 16, 1909, box 29, folder 6, UAHC Records; Wolf to Heller, Feb. 11, 1910, box 6, folder 9, Max Heller Papers, AJA.

89. Daniel G. Brinton and Morris Jastrow, *The Cradle of the Semites* (Philadelphia, 1890).

90. William Z. Ripley, *The Races of Europe* (New York: D. Appleton and Company, 1899), 368–400.

91. Ibid., 390.

92. The popular belief during this period that Jews were of Semitic origin is made clear in the writings of two rabbis who tried to dispel such a notion. See Martin A. Meyer, "Are the Jews Semites?" *Emanu-El* (San Francisco), Sept. 10, 1909, 5–8; and Samuel Sale, "Intermarriage," *RA*, Jan. 30, 1909, 717.

93. *Public*, Aug. 15, 1903; Aug. 22, 1903, 307–8.

94. *AH*, Apr. 27, 1911, 740. Waldstein, who later changed his name to Walston, had written in the 1890s about the need for Jews to eliminate their "racial traits" and "tribal bonds" if they wanted to be accepted by non-Jewish society. See his anonymous treatise, *The Jewish Question and the Mission of the Jews* (London: Gay and Bird, 1894); and the discussion in Cohen, *Encounter with Emancipation*, 274–5.

95. See George Zepin, *The Falashas: A Report Concerning the Advisability of Establishing a School for Hebrew among the Falashas of Abyssinia* (Cincinnati: Union of American Hebrew Congregations, 1912). Zepin was charged with evaluating Faitlovich's proposal that Ethiopian Jews be taught Hebrew as a means of bringing them back into the Jewish fold. He concluded that such a plan was impractical, arguing that the experience of African Americans had proven the lack of ability among blacks for scholarly attainments.

96. Meyer, "Are the Jews Semites?" 5–8.

97. Sale, "Intermarriage," 717.

98. Meyer, "Are the Jews Semites?" 5.

99. Even Emil G. Hirsch, a fierce opponent of Jewish racial self-definition during these years, lauded Semitic accomplishments in an article in the *Jewish Encyclopedia* and raised no objection to the notion that the Jews were descendants of the Semites. See *Jewish Encyclopedia*, s.v. "Semites."

100. Cyrus Adler to Mayer Sulzburger, Dec. 14, 1909, in Adler, *Collected Letters* 1:176.

101. The one major exception was his *Changes in the Bodily form of Descendants of Immigrants* (New York: Columbia University Press, 1912), which dealt with Jewish and Italian immigrants, although here, too, one sees Boas's tendency not to focus exclusively on Jews. For reasons described below, this study did not significantly help advance Jews' claims to whiteness. On Boas's stance toward Jewishness, see Leonard Glick, "'Types Distinct from Our Own': Franz Boas on Jewish Identity and Assimilation," *American Anthropologist* 84 (1982): 545–65. Later, in the 1930s and early 1940s, Boas worked more closely with Jewish groups in the effort to counter Nazi racial theories. See Elazar Barkan, *The Retreat of Scientific Racism: Changing Concepts of Race in Britain and the United States between the World Wars* (Cambridge: Cambridge University Press, 1992), chaps. 2 and 6.

102. Boas's most important work of this period was *The Mind of Primitive Man* (New York: Macmillan, 1911).

103. For Fishberg's biography, see Y. Slonim, "Ayner fun di fier milyon," *Der tog*, April 30, 1925, 5; Zalman Reyzen, *Leksikon fun Yidisher literatur, prese un filologye* (Lexicon of Yiddish literature, press and philology), s.v. "Fishberg, Moris"; *Universal Jewish Encyclopedia*, s.v. "Fishberg, Maurice"; and my article in *American National Biography*, s.v. "Fishberg, Maurice."

104. See, for example, "The Comparative Pathology of the Jews," *New York Medical Journal*, March 30, 1901, 537–43; April 6, 1901, 576–82; "The Relative Infrequency of Tuberculosis Among Jews," *American Medicine*, Nov. 2, 1901, 695–99; and "Health and Sanitation of the Immigrant Jewish Population of New York," *Menorah* 33 (1902): 37–46, 73–82, 168–80. For an overview of Fishberg's writings on Jewish health, see Alan Kraut, *Silent Travelers: Germs, Genes and the "Immigrant Menace"* (New York: Basic Books, 1994), 136–65.

105. Dorothy Levinson, *Montefiore: The Hospital as Social Instrument, 1884–1984* (New York: Farrar, Straus and Giroux, 1985), 97; Levinson, "Moments at Montefiore: Anarchism, Zionism and Tuberculosis," *Montefiore Medicine* 5 (1983): 26.

106. Maurice Fishberg, "Physical Anthropology of the Jews. I—the Cephalic Index," *American Anthropologist* 4 (1902): 701.

107. Ibid., 704–5. Fishberg also describes the Jews as a distinct race in his contributions to the *Jewish Encyclopedia*. See Schwartz, *The Emergence of Jewish Scholarship*, 110–2.

108. Ripley, *Races of Europe*, 388.

109. Maurice Fishberg, "Physical Anthropology of the Jews. II—Pigmentation," *American Anthropologist* 5 (1903): 89–106.

110. Maurice Fishberg, "North African Jews" in *Boas Anniversary Volume* (New York: G. E. Stechert and Co., 1906), 55–63; "Materials for the Physical Anthropology of the Eastern European Jews," *Memoirs of the American Anthropological and Ethnological Societies* 1 (1905–7): 1–146; *Science* 17 (1903): 470.

111. Fishberg, *The Jews*, 25, 179–80.

112. Maurice Fishberg, "Assimilation" in *Menorah Journal* 6 (1920): 26–7.

113. Fishberg, *The Jews*, vii.

114. "'Juden Heraus': Dr. Fishberg Pronounces the Doom of the Jew," *Maccabaean* 19 (Jan. 1911): 257–9; A. S. Waldstein, "A Study of the Jew," *Maccabaean* 21 (Aug. 1911): 41–3; (Sept. 1911): 69, 76–80; Meyer Waxman, "The Ethnic Character of the Jews," *Maccabaean* 22 (Dec. 1912): 190–4.

115. *Emanu-El*, Dec. 23, 1910, 2–3. See also the *Jewish Comment* (Baltimore), Jan. 20, 1911; and Abram Lipsky, "Are the Jews a 'Pure Race'?" *Popular Science Monthly* 81 (1912): 70–7.

116. *Jewish Sentinel* (Chicago), March 4, 1911, 7, 21. For similar sentiments, see *AH*, Aug. 25, 1911, 486.

117. Margolis, "What Are We?" 3.

118. "Our Race Question," *Jewish Criterion* (Pittsburgh), Dec. 2, 1910, 13.

CHAPTER 5

1. Harold E. Stearns, "A Gentile's Picture of the Jew," *Menorah Journal* 2 (Oct. 1916): 228.

2. Judah L. Magnes, "Jewry at the End of the War: A Review," *Nation*, May 4, 1921, 647.

3. *Forum* 75 (March 1926): 321–2.

4. See Ann Douglas, *Terrible Honesty: Mongrel Manhattan in the 1920s* (New York: Farrar, Straus and Giroux, 1995); William E. Leuchtenberg, *The Perils of*

Prosperity, 1914–1932 (Chicago: University of Chicago Press, 1958); Lynn Dumenil, *The Modern Temper: American Culture and Society in the 1920s* (New York: Hill and Wang, 1995). On earlier expressions of American antimodernism, see Jackson Lears, *No Place of Grace: Antimodernism and the Transformation of American Culture, 1880–1920* (Chicago: University of Chicago Press, 1981).

5. Nell Irvin Painter, *Standing at Armageddon: The United States, 1877–1919* (New York: W. W. Norton, 1987), 344–80; Warren Sussman, "Culture and Civilization: The Nineteen Twenties," in *Culture as History: The Transformation of American Society in the Twentieth Century* (New York: Pantheon, 1984), 105–21.

6. On the widespread concern about the process of "modernization" in interwar America, see Alan Brinkley, "Historians and the Interwar Years," in *Liberalism and Its Discontents* (Cambridge: Harvard University Press, 1998), 118–9.

7. Lawrence Levine, "Progress and Nostalgia: The Self Image of the Nineteen Twenties," in *The Unpredictable Past: Explorations in American Cultural History* (New York: Oxford University Press, 1993), 189–205; Lizabeth Cohen, *Making a New Deal: Industrial Workers in Chicago, 1919–1939* (Cambridge: Cambridge University Press, 1990), 99–158; Roland Marchand, *Advertising the American Dream: Making Way for Modernity, 1920–1940* (Berkeley and Los Angeles: University of California Press, 1985); and Robert Rydell, *World of Fairs: The Century of Progress Exhibitions* (Chicago: University of Chicago Press, 1993).

8. Works documenting the success of Jews in creating their own niche in American culture during this period are too numerous to mention, but the following will give some sense of the breadth of the phenomenon: Neil Gabler, *An Empire of Their Own: How the Jews Invented Hollywood* (New York: Crown Publisher, 1988); Andrea Most, *Making Americans: Jews and the Broadway Musical* (Cambridge: Harvard University Press, 2004); Steven Fraser, *Labor Will Rule: Sidney Hillman and the Rise of American Labor* (New York: Free Press, 1991); Stephen J. Whitfield, *In Search of an American Jewish Culture* (Hanover, NH: Brandeis University Press, 1999); Kenneth A. Kantor, *The Jews on Tin Pan Alley: The Jewish Contribution to American Popular Music, 1830–1940* (New York: Ktav Publishing House, 1982); Peter Levine, *Ellis Island to Ebbets Field: Sport and the American Jewish Experience* (New York: Oxford University Press, 1992).

9. Henry Feingold, *A Time for Searching: Entering the Mainstream* (Baltimore: Johns Hopkins University Press, 1992), 7; Leonard Dinnerstein, *Antisemitism in America* (New York: Oxford University Press, 1994, 80).

10. Dinnerstein, *Antisemitism in America*, 98.

11. See Kenneth T. Jackson, *The Ku Klux Klan in the City, 1915–1930* (New York: Oxford University Press, 1967), xi–xv.

12. For an overview of American antisemitism during this era, see Dinnerstein, *Antisemitism in America*, 78–127. On Henry Ford, see Leo P. Ribuffo, "Henry Ford and the *International Jew*," *AJH* 69 (June 1980): 437–77; and Neil Baldwin, *Henry Ford and the Jews: The Mass Production of Hate* (New York: Public Affairs, 2001).

13. Donald S. Strong, *Organized Antisemitism in America: The Rise of Group Prejudice During the Depression Decade, 1930–1940* (Washington, DC: American Council on Public Affairs, 1941); A. Scott Berg, *Lindbergh* (New York: Putnam, 1999), 385–6, 425–9.

14. Ronald H. Bayor, *Neighbors in Conflict: The Irish, Germans, Jews and Italians of New York City, 1929–1941* (Urbana: University of Illinois Press, 1988), 87–108, 112–4, 150–62; Donald Warren, *Radio Priest: Charles Coughlin, The Father of Hate Radio* (New York: Free Press, 1996), 129–60.

15. See Albert S. Lindemann, *Esau's Tears: Modern Antisemitism and the Rise of the Jews* (Cambridge: Cambridge University Press, 1997), 383.

16. See Robert P. Ingalls, *Herbert Lehman and New York's Little New Deal* (New York: New York University Press, 1975); and Edward Mazur, "Jewish Chicago: From Diversity to Community," in *The Ethnic Frontier: Essays in the History of Group Survival in Chicago and the Midwest*, ed. Melvin H. Holli and Peter d'A. Jones (Grand Rapids, MI: William B. Eerdmans Publishing Company, 1977), 285–91.

17. See Baldwin, *Henry Ford and the Jews*, 150–1.

18. See Benny Kraut, "A Wary Collaboration: Jews, Catholics and the Protestant Goodwill Movement," in *Between the Times: The Travail of the Protestant Establishment, 1900–1960*, ed. William R. Hutchison (Cambridge: Cambridge University Press, 1989), 193–230, esp. 197; Kraut, "Towards the Establishment of the National Conference of Christians and Jews: The Tenuous Road to Religious Goodwill in the 1920s," *AJH* 77 (March 1988): 388–412; Lance Sussman, "Toward 'Better Understanding': The Rise of the Interfaith Movement in America and the Role of Rabbi Isaac Landman," *AJA* 34 (April 1982): 35–51.

19. Judith E. Endelman, *The Jewish Community of Indianapolis, 1849 to the Present* (Bloomington: Indiana University Press, 1984), 124–6.

20. John McGreevy, *Parish Boundaries: The Catholic Encounter with Race in the Twentieth-Century Urban North* (Chicago: University of Chicago Press, 1996), 48–53; Bayor, *Neighbors in Conflict*, 104–7.

21. Albert Lee, *Henry Ford and the Jews* (New York: Stein and Day, 1980), 34.

22. Berg, *Lindbergh*, 163–5, 427, 429.

23. Dinnerstein, *Antisemitism in America*, 97; Eleanor Perlstein Weinbaum, *Shalom America: The Perlstein Success Story* (San Antonio, TX: Naylor Press, 1969), 85.

24. See, for example, Norman Angell, "Essentials of the Better Spirit," in *Christian and Jew: A Symposium for Better Understanding*, ed. Isaac Landman (New York: Horace Liveright, 1929), 55; and John W. Herring's statement in the *Jewish Tribune*, Sept. 2, 1927, 18.

25. Lothrop Stoddard, *The Rising Tide of Color against White World Supremacy* (New York: Charles Scribner's Sons, 1920); Madison Grant, *The Passing of the Great Race* (New York: Charles Scribner's Sons, 1916).

26. See Gilbert Osofsky, *Harlem: The Making of a Ghetto; Negro New York, 1890–1930* New York: Harper Torchbooks, 1971), 179–87; Lewis Erenberg, *Steppin' Out: New York Nightlife and the Transformation of American Culture, 1890–1930* (Chicago: University of Chicago Press, 1981), 252–9; and Douglas, *Terrible Honesty*, 98–107.

27. On the ethos of "terrible honesty," see Douglas, *Terrible Honesty*, 31–72.

28. *The International Jew: The World's Foremost Problem* (Dearborn: Dearborn Independent, 1920–22), 2:7–29.

29. Ibid., 4:109–19, 179–91.

30. Ibid., 241.

31. Ibid. 3:64–74.

32. Ibid. 4:26–9.

33. On the term "kike" and other epithets for Jews during this period, see H. L. Mencken, *The American Language: An Inquiry into the Development of English in the United States*, suppl. I (New York: A. A. Knopf, 1945), 614; and Eric Partridge, "Nicknames for Jews," in *Words at War, Words at Peace: Essays on Language in General and Particular Words* (London: Frederick Muller, 1948), 10–14.

34. See Feingold, *A Time for Searching*, 20–1; Marcia Graham Synnott, *The Half-Opened Door: Discrimination and Admissions at Harvard, Yale, and Princeton, 1900–1970* (Westport, CT: Greenwood Press, 1979), 76, 82, 101; *NYT*, Jan. 15, 1923, 17. In actuality, Jews excelled at many college sports, particularly basketball. See Dan Oren, *Joining the Club: A History of Jews and Yale* (New Haven: Yale University Press, 1985), 78–80.

35. Quoted in Synnott, *The Half-Opened Door*, 82.

36. The poster is located in box 66, folder 1, Louis Marshall Papers, AJA.

37. See Robin D. G. Kelley, *Hammer and Hoe: Alabama Communists during the Great Depression* (Chapel Hill: University of North Carolina Press, 1990), 25–6, 48, 61–3, 29; Joel Williamson, *The Crucible of Race: Black-White Relations in the American South since Emancipation* (New York: Oxford University Press, 1984), 473–4.

38. Arnold Shankman, "Friend or Foe? Southern Blacks View the Jew, 1880–1935," in *Turn to the South: Essays on Southern Jewry*, ed. Nathan M. Kaganoff and Melvin I. Urofsky (Charlottesville: University Press of Virginia, 1979), 117–8.

39. James Goodman, *Stories of Scottsboro* (New York: Vintage Books, 1994), 133, 201–2.

40. Strong, *Organized Antisemitism*, 125–6, 151, 164–6. On True, see also Porter Niles, "Pogrom in September," *New Masses*, Aug. 18, 1936; and Michael Hale, "Fifteen Leading Jews Marked for Death," *New Masses*, Aug. 25, 1936.

41. Meyer Levin, *The Old Bunch* (New York: Viking Press, 1937), 801.

42. Chicago Commission on Race Relations, *The Negro in Chicago: A Study of Race Relations and a Race Riot* (Chicago: University of Chicago Press, 1922), 125, 220–1.

43. James T. Farrell, *Studs Lonigan* (Urbana: University of Illinois Press, 1993), 375.

44. Ibid., 434, 455.

45. *NYT*, Jan. 27, 1922, 3; July 13, 1923, 16.

46. Lothrop Stoddard, "The Pedigree of Judah," *Forum* 75 (March 1926): 326.

47. Ibid., 329.

48. Burton J. Hendrick, *The Jews in America* (Garden City: Doubleday, Page and Co., 1923), esp. 92–133.

49. John M. Efron, *Defenders of the Race: Jewish Doctors and Race Science in Fin-de-Siécle Europe* (New Haven: Yale University Press, 1994), 106–7; Maurice Fishberg, *The Jews: A Study of Race and Environment* (New York: Walter Scott, 1911), 114, 191–4.

50. See Todd M. Endelman, "Comparative Perspectives on Modern Anti-Semitism in the West," in *History and Hate: The Dimensions of Anti-Semitism*, ed. David Berger (Philadelphia: Jewish Publication Society of America), 109.

51. Stoddard, "The Pedigree of Judah," 329.

52. Hendrick, *The Jews in America*, 169–71.

53. *International Jew* 4:3–4, 231–3.

54. *NYT*, June 17, 1922, 1, 3; Jan. 16, 1923, 23.

55. On Harvard's policy toward African Americans, see *NYT*, Jan. 12, 1923, 5; and Synnott, *The Half-Opened Door*, 47–53, 80–84.

56. See, for example, Hendrick, *The Jews in America*, 171.

57. Lindbergh, quoted in Berg, *Lindbergh*, 386.

58. See the statement of the "eminent Christian liberal" John W. Herring, *Jewish Tribune*, Sept. 2, 1927, 18.

59. Kraut, "Towards the Establishment," 396–7, 400. This sense of a "problem" in need of a solution pervades the essays collected in Landman, *Christian and Jew*.

60. Angell, "Essentials of the Better Spirit," 55.

61. S. Parkes Cadman, "Unity not Uniformity," in Landman, *Christian and Jew*, 147.

62. Spargo, *The Jew and American Ideals* (New York: Harper Brothers, 1921), 76, 110, 113, 120.

63. Elmer Davis, "Neither Jew Nor Greek," in Landman, *Christian and Jew*, 79–80.

64. Heywood Broun and George Britt, *Christians Only: A Study in Prejudice* (New York: Da Capo Press, 1974), 304–33. Similar sentiments were expressed in Walter Hurt, *The Truth about the Jews, Told by a Gentile* (Chicago: Horton and Company, 1922), 65–7, 79, 127, 310–6, 332.

65. *NYT*, May 22, 1926, 14; Thomas Scripps, "The Movie Jew as an Image of Assimilationism, 1903–1927," *Journal of Popular Film* 4 (1975): 200–2; Riv-Ellen Prell, *Fighting to Become Americans: Jews, Gender and the Anxiety of Assimilation* (Boston: Beacon Press, 1999), 69–77.

66. Prell, *Fighting to Become Americans*, 72.

67. *NYT*, Dec. 20, 1930, 20.

68. Norman Hapgood, "The Jews and American Democracy," *Menorah Journal* 2 (Oct. 1916): 201–5; Randolph S. Bourne, "The Jew and Trans-National America," *Menorah Journal* 2 (Dec. 1916): 277–84; John Dewey, "The Principle of Nationality," *Menorah Journal* 3 (Oct. 1917): 203–8. For a history of pluralist theories, see John Higham, "Ethnic Pluralism in Modern American Thought," in *Send These to Me: Immigrants in Urban America* (Baltimore: Johns Hopkins University Press, 1984), 198–232.

69. John Haynes Holmes, *Through Gentile Eyes: A Plea for Tolerance and Goodwill* (New York: Jewish Opinion Publishing Corporation, 1938), 22. On Holmes's background and his relationship with the Jewish community, see Carl Hermann Voss, *Rabbi and Minister: The Friendship of Stephen S. Wise and John Haynes Holmes* (Cleveland: World Publishing Company, 1964).

70. Rachel David-Du Bois and Emma Schweppe, eds., *The Jews in American Life* (New York: Thomas Nelson and Sons, 1935). On Davis-Du Bois and her

other work with the Jewish community, see Stuart Svonkin, *Jews against Prejudice: American Jews and the Fight for Civil Liberties* (New York: Columbia University Press, 1997), 63.

71. On Clinchy, see Benny Kraut, "A Wary Collaboration," 200; and Everett R. Clinchy, *All in the Name of God* (New York: John Day, 1934). Herberg's views were articulated in his classic *Protestant-Catholic-Jew: An Essay in American Religious Sociology* (Garden City, NY: Doubleday, 1955).

72. Hooten quoted in Elazar Barkan, *The Retreat of Scientific Racism: Changing Concepts of Race in Britain and the United States between the World Wars* (Cambridge: Cambridge University Press, 1992), 313.

73. Danforth quoted ibid., 315.

CHAPTER 6

1. I. J. Schwartz, *Kentucky*, trans. Gertrude W. Dubrovsky (Tuscaloosa: University of Alabama Press, 1990), 90.

2. On the public school as an agency of acculturation, see Deborah Dash Moore, *At Home in America: New York's Second Generation Jews* (New York: Columbia University Press, 1981), 89–121.

3. Hermann Hagedorn, *You Are the Hope of the World: An Appeal to the Boys and Girls of America* (New York: Macmillan Co., 1917), 33–4, 54, 90.

4. Grace A. Turkington, *My Country: A Textbook for Civics and Patriotism for Young Americans* (Boston: Ginn and Company, 1918), 36–41. See also Roscoe Lewis Ashley, *The New Civics: A Textbook for Secondary Schools* (New York: Macmillan Co., 1918), 45–6, 350–1.

5. On "Colonial Day," see Mame Warren, *Then Again: Annapolis, 1900–1965* (Annapolis, MD: Time Exposures Limited, 1990), 70–1; *Colonial Day, Annapolis—May 15: Official Program* (Annapolis, MD: n.p., 1928); taped interview with Faye Snyder Lieberman, Sept. 27, 1990, Jewish Museum of Maryland, Baltimore.

6. On the importance of historical pageantry in forging American national identity during this period, see David Glassberg, *American Historical Pageantry: The Uses of Tradition in the Early Twentieth Century* (Chapel Hill: University of North Carolina Press, 1990); Barry Schwartz, *Abraham Lincoln and the Forge of National Identity* (Chicago: University of Chicago Press, 2000), 195–7.

7. See Elizabeth Ewen, *Immigrant Women in the Land of Dollars: Life and Culture on the Lower East Side, 1890–1925* (New York: Monthly Review Press, 1985), 209–10; Andrew Heinze, *Adapting to Abundance: Jewish Immigrants, Mass Consumption, and the Search for American Identity* (New York: Columbia University Press, 1990), 204–5.

8. Morris Winchevsky, "Perets in Amerike," *Di tsukunft* 20 (June 1915): 539; Peter Levine, *Ellis Island to Ebbets Field: Sport and the American Jewish Experience* (New York: Oxford University Press, 1992), 144–69, 183–8.

9. Melvin Patrick Ely, *The Adventures of Amos 'n' Andy: A Social History of An American Phenomenon* (New York: Free Press, 1991), 141, 282 n. 23.

10. Neil Gabler, *An Empire of Their Own: How the Jews Invented Hollywood* (New York: Crown Publishers, 1988), 90–1.

11. Bruno Lasker, *Race Attitudes in Children* (New York: Henry Holt and Co., 1929), 189–225.

12. *Forverts*, Sept. 6, 1927, 2 (Flit Insect Repellant); Nov. 1, 1927, 7 (Aunt Jemima); Nov. 6, 1927, arts section (Duz Soap); *Morgn zhurnal*, Feb. 22, 1929, 3 (Aunt Jemima); March 5, 1929, 2 (Gold Dust Twins); Jan. 17, 1929, 3 (Old Gold with Eddie Cantor); Jan. 24, 1929, 9 (Lucky Strikes with Al Jolson). On the growth of black imagery in national advertising and marketing in the twentieth century, see Grace Elizabeth Hale, *Making Whiteness: The Culture of Segregation in the South, 1890–1940* (New York: Pantheon Books, 1998); and Marilyn Kern-Foxworth, *Aunt Jemima, Uncle Ben and Rastus: Blacks in Advertising Yesterday, Today and Tomorrow* (Westport, CT: Greenwood Press, 1994).

13. Chicago Commission on Race Relations, *The Negro in Chicago: A Study of Race Relations and a Race Riot* (Chicago: University of Chicago Press, 1922), 231.

14. Barney Balaban and Sam Katz, *The Fundamental Principles of Balaban & Katz Theatre Management* (Chicago: Balaban & Katz Corporation, 1926), cited in Lizabeth Cohen, *Making a New Deal: Industrial Workers in Chicago* (Cambridge: Cambridge University Press, 1990), 125.

15. Deborah Dash Moore, "On the Fringes of the City: Jewish Neighborhoods in Three Boroughs," in *The Landscape of Modernity*, ed. David Ward and Oliver Zunz (New York: Russell Sage Foundation, 1992), 253.

16. Henry Roth, *From Bondage*, vol. 3 of *Mercy of a Rude Stream* (New York: Picador, 1996), 236.

17. For the very different experience of Slavic workers, see James Barrett, *Work and Community in the Jungle: Chicago's Packinghouse Workers, 1894–1922* (Urbana: University of Illinois Press, 1987), 188–231.

18. See Will Herberg, "The Old Timers and The Newcomers: Ethnic Group Relations in a Needle Trades Union," *Journal of Social Issues* 9 (1953): 12–19; Cohen, *Making a New Deal*, 18–20; St. Clair Drake and Horace R. Cayton, *Black Metropolis: A Study of Negro Life in a Northern City*, rev. edition (Chicago: University of Chicago Press, 1993), 222–23.

19. Sterling D. Spero and Abram L. Harris, *The Black Worker: The Negro and the Labor Movement* (New York: Columbia University Press, 1931), 338–40. On racial divisions in the garment industry and African Americans' mistrust of the unions, see Meyer Levin, *The Old Bunch* (New York: Viking Press, 1937), 610; James R. Grossman, *Land of Hope: Chicago, Black Southerners and the Great Migration* (Chicago: University of Chicago Press, 1989), 208–45.

20. On Jewish businesses in African American neighborhoods in the North, see Steven Bloom, "Interactions between Blacks and Jews in New York City, 1900–1930, As Reflected in the Black Press," Ph. D. dissertation, New York University, 1973, 174–99; and Marshall Field Stevenson, "Points of Departure, Acts of Resolve: Black-Jewish Relations in Detroit, 1937–1962," Ph. D. dissertation, University of Michigan, 1988, 66–7.

21. Richard Wright, *Black Boy (American Hunger): A Record of Childhood and Youth* (New York: Harper Perennial, 1993), 309–17.

22. On Jews as victims of the Chicago Race Riot of 1919, see the extensive daily coverage in the *Yidisher kurier* between July 20 and July 31, 1919.

23. In the wake of the 1919 riots, Jews on Chicago's South Side organized an association to protect them against further attacks from local African Americans. See the Chicago *Forverts*, Aug. 9, 1919; and *Yidisher kurier*, Aug. 13, 1919, both in CFLPS.

24. See Ruth Schuster, "The German Refugee Grocer in Atlanta," typescript, Cuba Archives, William Breman Jewish Heritage Museum, Atlanta; and Monna Troub, "Anti-Semitism among Negroes," typescript, Edward Burgess Papers, Joseph Regenstein Library Special Collections, University of Chicago.

25. See Moore, *At Home in America*, 30–3.

26. See John T. McGreevy, *Parish Boundaries: The Catholic Encounter with Race in the Twentieth-Century Urban North* (Chicago: University of Chicago Press, 1996), 48–9; Ronald H. Bayor, *Neighbors in Conflict: The Irish, Germans, Jews and Italians of New York City, 1929–1941* (Urbana: University of Illinois Press, 1988), 155–6, 160–2; Frederick Thrasher, *The Gang*, 2d ed. (Chicago: University of Chicago Press, 1936), 174, 200, 214–5.

27. See, for example, Hasia Diner, *In the Almost Promised Land: American Jews and Blacks, 1915–1935* (Westport, CT: Greenwood Press, 1977); David Levering Lewis, "Parallels and Divergences: Assimilationist Strategies of Afro-American and Jewish Elites from 1910 to the Early 1930s," *Journal of American History* 71 (1984): 543–64; Murray Friedman, *What Went Wrong? The Creation and Collapse of the Black-Jewish Alliance* (New York: Free Press, 1993); Mark K. Bauman and Berkley Kalin, eds., *The Quiet Voices: Southern Rabbis and Black Civil Rights, 1880s to 1990s* (Tuscaloosa: University of Alabama Press, 1997). In recent years, however, a more complex view of the period has begun to emerge. See Diner, "Between Words and Deeds: Jews and Blacks in America, 1880–1935," in *Struggles in the Promised Land: Toward a History of Black-Jewish Relations in the United States*, ed. Jack Salzman and Cornel West (New York: Oxford University Press, 1997), 87–106; and Jeffrey Melnick, *A Right to Sing the Blues: African Americans, Jews and American Popular Song* (Cambridge: Harvard University Press, 1999).

28. B. Joyce Ross, *J. E. Spingarn and the Rise of the NAACP, 1911–1939* (New York, 1972); Marshall Van Deusen, *J. E. Spingarn* (New York: Twayne Publishers, 1971); Susanne Klingenstein, *Jews in the American Academy, 1900–1940: The Dynamics of Intellectual Assimilation* (New Haven: Yale University Press, 1991), 104–11.

29. Marshall Hyatt, "Franz Boas and the Struggle for Black Equality: The Dynamics of Ethnicity," *Perspectives in American History*, N.S. 2 (1985): 269–95.

30. Marshall became a director of the NAACP in 1923. As an expert in constitutional law, he advised the organization regarding several civil rights cases. See Louis Marshall, *Louis Marshall: Champion of Liberty*, ed. Charles Reznikoff (Philadelphia: Jewish Publication Society of America, 1957), 1:426–65.

31. For a particularly stinging attack on Rosenwald, albeit from an earlier period, see the remarks of the governor of South Carolina reprinted in *Crisis* 6 (July 1913): 119–20.

32. Harry Rogoff, *An East Side Epic: The Life and Work of Meyer London* (New York: Vanguard Press, 1930), 249–52; Emanuel Celler, *You Never Leave Brooklyn* (New York: John Day Company, 1953).

33. My interpretation here differs somewhat from that of Hasia Diner, who sees Jewishness as a more critical factor than socialism in shaping the labor leaders' approach to African Americans. See Diner, *In the Almost Promised Land*, 224–5.

34. David Pierce, "Is the Jew a Friend of the Negro?" *Crisis* 30 (Aug. 1925): 184.

35. *RA*, Aug. 16, 1919, 29–30.

36. Bloom, "Interactions between Blacks and Jews," 258.

37. *NYT*, May 7, 1919, 15.

38. Leonard J. Mervis, "The Social Justice Movement and the American Reform Rabbi," *AJA* 7 (Jun. 1955): 194–5.

39. For a rare statement on blacks by an American Orthodox rabbi, see Bernard Drachman, *The Unfailing Light: Memoirs of an American Rabbi* (New York: Rabbinical Council of America, 1948), 361.

40. Mark K. Bauman and Arnold Shankman, "The Rabbi as Ethnic Broker: The Case of David Marx," *Journal of American Ethnic History* 2 (Spring 1983): 51–52; Mark K. Bauman, "Centripetal and Centrifugal Forces facing the People of Many Communities: Atlanta Jewry from the Frank Case to the Great Depression," *Atlanta Historical Journal* 23 (Fall 1979): 45–6.

41. Jacquelyn Dowd Hall, *Revolt against Chivalry: Jessie Daniel Ames and the Women's Campaign against Lynching* (New York: Columbia University Press, 1993), 178; Clive Webb, *Fight against Fear: Southern Jews and Black Civil Rights* (Athens: University of Georgia Press, 2001), 148–50.

42. Berkley Kalin, "A Plea For Tolerance: Fineshriber in Memphis," in Bauman and Kalin, *The Quiet Voices*, 56–7.

43. *Southern Israelite* (Atlanta), Nov. 15, 1935, 2; Feb. 14, 1936, 3.

44. *Southern Israelite*, July 1925, 2.

45. *Southern Israelite*, March 2, 1928, 2; Oct. 26, 1928.

46. See Diner, *In the Almost Promised Land*, 199–235.

47. *Justice*, Feb. 13, 1925, 2. For a similar election, see also Aug. 28,1925, 1–2.

48. *Justice*, August 1, 1935, 16.

49. Edith Kine, "The Garment Union Comes to the Black Worker," *Opportunity* 12 (April 1934): 108.

50. Spero and Harris, *The Black Worker*, 337–9; Grossman, *Land of Hope*, 210, 230; Joseph Brandes, "From Sweatshop to Stability: Jewish Labor between Two World Wars," *YIVO Annual of Jewish Social Science* 16 (1976): 38.

51. "A Plea for Our Negro Workers," *Justice*, Feb. 29, 1924, 7. See also "A Letter from a Negro Worker," *Justice*, March 7, 1924, 12.

52. Charles Lionel Franklin, *The Negro Labor Unionist of New York* (New York: Columbia University Press, 1936), 305–6, 312.

53. On racial transition within the garment industry, see Herberg, "Old Timers and Newcomers," 12–19.

54. Louis Wirth, *The Ghetto* (Chicago: University of Chicago Press, 1928), 230–1.

55. Chicago Commission of Race Relations, *The Negro in Chicago*, 456.

56. *Bronzviller idishe post*, July 16, 1927; *New York Amsterdam News*, July 13, 1927; July 20, 1927; *New York Age*, July 3, 1926.

57. Bloom, "Interactions between Blacks and Jews," 171, 173–4; A. N. Roth to "Dear Neighbor," Dec. 17, 1927, part 5, reel 2, frames 93–4, Papers of the NAACP (microfilm, Robert Woodruff Library, Emory University; hereafter cited as Papers of the NAACP).

58. Thomas Lee Philpott, *The Slum and the Ghetto: Immigrants, Blacks, and Reformers in Chicago, 1880–1930* (Belmont, CA: Wadsworth Publishing Co., 1991), 189, 197.

59. Bloom, "Interactions between Blacks and Jews," 173–4; *NYT*, July 13, 1923, 16.

60. On this point, see Bloom, "Interactions between Blacks and Jews," 165–70.

61. Open letter from A. N. Roth, Dec. 10, 1927, pt. 5, reel 2, frame 91, Papers of the NAACP.

62. Levin, *The Old Bunch*, 508.

63. In recent studies of Jews and neighborhood change, economic and structural factors are stressed more than cultural or historical factors in explaining Jews' tendency to move. See McGreevy, *Parish Boundaries*, 18–20; and Gerald Gamm, *Urban Exodus: Why the Jews Left Boston and the Catholics Stayed* (Cambridge: Harvard University Press, 1999).

64. See Cohen, *Making a New Deal*, 99–147; Levine, *Ellis Island to Ebbets Field*; Gabler, *An Empire of Their Own*; Stephen J. Whitfield, *In Search of American Jewish Culture* (Hanover, NH: Brandeis University Press, 1999).

65. *Forverts*, Nov. 17, 1927, 10. On the Yiddish press's coverage of black issues, see the extensive review in Diner, *In the Almost Promised Land*, 28–88.

66. A number of Weinstein's poems on African American themes are reproduced in *American Yiddish Poetry: A Bilingual Anthology*, ed. Benjamin Harshav and Barbara Harshav (Berkeley and Los Angeles: University of California Press, 1986), 636–49.

67. Joseph Opatoshu, *Lintsheray un andere dertsaylungen* (Lynching and other stories) (Vilna: B. Kletskin, 1927).

68. Isaac E. Rontch, "The Negro in Yiddish Fiction," in *Canadian Jewish Outlook Anthology*, ed. Henry M. Rosenthal and S. Cathy Berson (Vancouver: New Star Books, 1988), 201–3. For a more complete survey of this literature, see Rontch's discussion in *Amerike in der Yidisher literature* (America in Yiddish literature) (New York: Y. E. Rontch Book Committee, 1945), 203–55.

69. *Forverts*, quoted in Diner, *In the Almost Promised Land*, 69.

70. Ronald Sanders, "The American Popular Song," in *Next Year in Jerusalem: Portraits of the Jew in the Twentieth Century*, ed. Douglas Villiers (New York: Viking Press, 1976), 197–216. For varying perspectives on Jews and blackface, see Michael Rogin, *Blackface/White Noise: Jewish Immigrants in the Hollywood Melting Pot* (Berkeley and Los Angeles: University of California Press, 1996); and Hasia Diner, "Trading Faces," *Common Quest* (Summer 1997): 40–4.

71. Sanders, "American Popular Song," 198–9.

72. Berlin quoted in Ann Douglas, *Terrible Honesty: Mongrel Manhattan in the 1920s* (New York: Farrar, Straus and Giroux, 1995), 359.

73. Roback quoted in Diner, *In the Almost Promised Land*, 112.

74. On Jews in boxing, see Levine, *Ellis Island to Ebbets Field*, 144–69. On the African American experience, see Gail Bederman, *Manliness and Civilization: A Cultural History of Gender and Race in the United States, 1880–1917*, chap. 1; Thomas R. Hietala, *The Fight of the Century: Jack Johnson, Joe Louis and the Struggle for Racial Equality* (Armonk, NY: M. E. Sharpe, 2002).

75. Harold U. Ribalow, *The Jew in American Sports* (New York: Bloch Publishing Co., 1955), 172–3.

76. Bloom, "Interactions between Blacks and Jews," 233.

77. Kate Simon, *A Wider World: Portraits in an Adolescence* (New York: Harper and Row, 1986), 66–70.

78. Levin, *The Old Bunch*, 57, 263–6.

79. *JPC Progress* 14 (Aug. 1931): 4; 16 (Nov. 1935): 2–3, Jewish Progressive Club Records, Cuba Archives, William Breman Jewish Heritage Museum, Atlanta (hereafter cited as Jewish Progressive Club Records). For examples of jokes from the *B'nai B'rith Magazine*, see Diner, *In the Almost Promised Land*, 92–93.

80. Diner, *In the Almost Promised Land*, 93. See also the short story by Walter Hart Blumenthal, "The Jungle," *AH*, April 18, 1924, 682, 711, 713, 726.

81. *JPC Progress* 2 (March 10, 1924), 1; (April 10, 1924), 1; (Sept. 1924): 1; (Oct. 1924), 1; (Nov. 1924), 1, 4, Jewish Progressive Club Records.

82. *CHI Observer* (Jan. 1917): 8.

83. Jewish People's Institute Scrapbooks, Group B, vol. 3 (1931–4), 21, Jewish Community Centers of Chicago Records, Chicago Historical Society; *JPC Progress* 16 (June 1935): 4, Jewish Progressive Club Records.

84. On feelings of insecurity among Depression-era Jews, see Beth Wenger, *New York Jews in the Great Depression: Uncertain Promise* (New Haven: Yale University Press, 1996), esp. 197–201.

85. Jacob J. Weinstein, "The Jew and the Negro: A Comparative Study in Race Prejudice," *Crisis* 41 (June 1934): 178–9; (July 1934): 197–8. See also Stephen S. Wise, "Parallel between Hitlerism and the Persecution of Negroes in America," *Crisis* 41 (May 1934): 127–9; Harold Preece, "Fascism and the Negro," *Crisis* 41 (Dec. 1934): 355–6; and David H. Pierce, "Fascism and the Negro," *Crisis* 42 (April 1935): 107, 114. For a survey of fascist groups in America and their activities during this period, see Donald Strong, *Organized Anti-Semitism in America: The Rise of Group Prejudice during the Depression Decade, 1930–1940* (Washington, DC: American Council on Public Affairs, 1941).

86. Diner, *In the Almost Promised Land*, 220.

87. Irving Howe, *A Margin of Hope: An Intellectual Autobiography* (San Diego: Harcourt Brace Jovanovich, 1982), 24.

88. Melech Epstein, *The Jew and Communism: The Story of Early Communist Victories and Ultimate Defeats in the Jewish Community, U.S.A., 1919–1941* (New York: Trade Union Sponsoring Committee, 1959), 245–6; Mark Naison, *Communists in Harlem during the Depression* (New York: Grove Press, 1983), esp. 321–8; Ruth Jacknow Markowitz, *My Daughter the Teacher: Jewish Teachers in the New York City Schools* (New Brunswick, NJ: Rutgers University Press, 1993), 163–72; Levin, *The Old Bunch*, 790–805.

89. *AH*, Feb. 23, 1934, 290.

90. See Diner, *In the Almost Promised Land*, 42–3, 99, 114.

91. See Weinstein, "The Jew and the Negro," 178.

92. Alfred Kazin, *A Walker in the City* (San Diego: Harcourt, Brace and Company, 1979), 141.

93. The survey of Jewish merchants in Chicago's Black Belt completed by Monna Troub during World War II indicates that at least some of them were forced by the Depression to move their businesses to the black neighborhood. See Troub, "Anti-Semitism among Negroes." Carl Ruthven Offord's novel of Depression-era Harlem, *The White Face* (New York: Robert M. McBride and Company, 1943), provides a vivid portrait of the growing animosity between Jewish merchants and black customers. For an example of a near race riot resulting from these tensions, see *NYT*, July 20,1930. For background information on black-Jewish tensions in Harlem during the Depression, see Cheryl Lynn Greenberg, *"Or Does It Explode?": Black Harlem in the Great Depression* (New York: Oxford University Press, 1991), esp. chap. 5; and Robert G. Weisbord and Arthur Stein, "Negro Perceptions of Jews between the World Wars," *Judaism* 18 (Fall 1969): 428–47.

94. Ella Baker and Marvel Cooke, "The Bronx Slave Market," *Crisis* 42 (Nov. 1935): 330–1, 340.

95. Ibid. On the New York "slave markets," see also *NYT*, May 19, 1938, 23; Dec. 1, 1939, 24; and Offord, *The White Face*, 68–71.

96. Drake and Cayton, *Black Metropolis*, 245–6.

97. Gold, quoted in Bloom, "Interactions between Blacks and Jews," 300.

98. Diner, *In The Almost Promised Land*, 53–4, 80.

99. Kim Chernin, *In My Mother's House: A Daughter's Story* (New York: Harper and Row, 1983), 88, 100.

100. See, for example, Kazin, *A Walker in the City*, 141–2.

101. *Frayhayt*, Nov. 9, 1932. For other similar trials, see also the issues of Feb. 7 and Feb. 9, 1932. For background on these trials, see Melech Epstein, *The Jew and Communism*, 246–8.

102. Edward L. Israel, "Jew Hatred among Negroes," *Crisis* 43 (Feb. 1936): 39.

103. *YCCAR* 43 (1933): 58–9; Mervis, "The Social Justice Movement," 195–6; Cowett, "Morris Newfield," 39–49.

104. Simon, *A Wider World*, 124.

105. Offord, *The White Face*, 74; Drake and Cayton, *Black Metropolis*, 244.

106. *Forverts*, March 20–22, 1935; Greenberg, *"Or Does it Explode?"* 126–7, 211–4; Diner, *In the Almost Promised Land*, 79–81; Drake and Cayton, *Black Metropolis*, 432. A rare copy of *Dynamite*, Aug. 27, 1938, an antisemitic paper published by African Americans in Chicago, can be found box 389, folder 8, Claude A. Barnett Papers, Chicago Historical Society.

CHAPTER 7

1. Maurice Stern to Louis Marshall, July 12, 1922, box 5, folder 2, Louis Marshall Papers, AJA (hereafter cited as Marshall Papers).

2. *Yidisher kurier*, Sept. 19, 1921, CFLPS.

3. *Forverts* (Chicago edition), Jan. 4, 1925, CFLPS.

4. Louis Marshall to Isaac Landman, Dec. 19, 1918; and Marshall to Mayer Sulzburger, Dec. 21, 1918, in *Louis Marshall: Champion of Liberty*, ed. Charles Reznikoff (Philadelphia: Jewish Publication Society of America, 1957), 2:536–8. Philipson's use of race was discussed in "Race and Nationality," *Yidisher kurier*, Nov. 24, 1920, CFLPS. Marshall's use of the term "ethnical" refers to a biological or racial understanding of Jewishness, and should not be confused with the new cultural definition of Jewishness that was first proposed about this time, and which is discussed below. During the nineteenth and early twentieth centuries, the terms "ethnic" and "ethnical" were used interchangeably with "race," and were invariably biological in their meaning. As I argue here, only in the 1920s was the term "ethnic group" coined to describe a cultural, rather than racial, understanding of group difference.

5. Cyrus Adler, quoted in Naomi W. Cohen, *Not Free to Desist: A History of the American Jewish Committee* (Philadelphia: Jewish Publication Society of America, 1972), 143–4.

6. On this shift, see Naomi W. Cohen, *Jews in Christian America: The Pursuit of Religious Equality* (New York: Oxford University Press, 1992), 94–100.

7. Milton Waldman, *The Disinherited* (New York: Longmans, Green and Co., 1929).

8. Anzia Yezierska, *Salome of the Tenements* (Urbana: University of Illinois Press, 1995), esp. 132, 177.

9. Leah Morton, *I Am a Woman and a Jew* (New York: J. H. Sears and Co., 1926), 358–60. For a nonfiction account of failed intermarriage that invokes racial logic, see the pamphlet by Rebecca E. Mack, *You Are a Jew and a Jew You Are!* (Jersey City, NJ: Privately published, 1933), esp. 25–6, 38.

10. For book reviews, see the *Jewish Woman* 7 (April 1927): 41; 8 (Jan.–March 1928): 42.

11. National Council of Jewish Women, *Anti-Semitism: A Study Outline* (New York: National Council of Jewish Women, 1934). For further use of racial language within the NCJW, see Nannie A. Reis, "Council 'Thou Shall Nots,' " *Jewish Woman* 9 (April–June 1929): 6–7; Adele Szold Seltzer, "What Women Read," *Jewish Woman* 5 (June 1925): 4–5.

12. *Southern Israelite* (Atlanta), Jan. 17, 1928, 9.

13. Irwin Edman, "Race and Culture," *Menorah Journal* 10 (Nov.–Dec. 1924): 426.

14. On the Massena and Rosenbluth cases, see Henry Feingold, *A Time for Searching: Entering the Mainstream, 1920–1945* (Baltimore: Johns Hopkins University Press, 1992), 5–6.

15. Yonathan Shapiro, *Leadership of the American Zionist Organization, 1897–1930* (Urbana: University of Illinois Press, 1971), 228–30.

16. Michael Berkowitz, *Western Jewry and the Zionist Project, 1914–1933* (Cambridge: Cambridge University Press, 1997), 71.

17. Shapiro, *Leadership of the American Zionist Organization*, 228–9; Lipsky quoted in Berkowitz, *Western Jewry*, 71. On Louis Lipsky, see Deborah E. Lipstadt, *The Zionist Career of Louis Lipsky, 1900–1921* (New York: Arno Press, 1982).

18. Maurice Samuel, *You Gentiles* (New York: Harcourt, Brace and Company, 1924), 23–4. Similar works by Samuel include *I, The Jew* (New York: Harcourt, Brace and Co., 1927) and *Jews on Approval* (New York: Liveright, 1932).

19. Ludwig Lewisohn, *Up Stream: An American Chronicle* (New York: Boni and Liveright, 1922), 143.

20. Ibid., 286, 290; Lewisohn, *Mid-channel: An American Chronicle* (New York: Harper and Row, 1929), 99. For similar sentiments, see Lewisohn, *The Island Within* (New York: Harper and Row, 1928), 228, 263. On Lewisohn, see Ralph Melnick, *The Life and Work of Ludwig Lewisohn*, 2 vols. (Detroit: Wayne State University Press, 1998); and Judd L. Teller, *Strangers and Natives: The Evolution of the American Jew from 1921 to the Present* (New York: Delacorte Press, 1968), 58–9.

21. Bertha Wallerstein, "The Jewish Babbitt," *Nation*, May 28, 1924, 603–4.

22. Walter Lippmann to Walter J. Henderson, Oct. 27, 1922, in *Public Philosopher: Selected Letters of Walter Lippmann*, ed. John Morton Blum (New York: Ticknor and Fields, 1985), 149–50.

23. *Jewish Tribune*, Dec. 16, 1927, 26, 55.

24. Samuel Ornitz, *Haunch, Paunch and Jowl* (New York: Boni and Liveright, 1923), 191–202.

25. Maurice Fishberg, "Intermarriage between Jews and Christians," in *Eugenics in Race and State: Scientific Papers of the Second International Congress of Eugenics* (Baltimore: Williams and Wilkins Co., 1923), 2:125–33.

26. For a description of the trend, see Louis Weitzenkorn, "A Jew among the Fords," *Nation*, May 4, 1921, 652–3; "Are You Jew-Conscious?" *Forverts* (Chicago ed.), Aug. 22, 1926, CFLPS; *AH*, Nov. 16, 1923, 4.

27. Gdal Saleski, *Famous Musicians of a Wandering Race* (New York: Bloch Publishing Company, 1927); Mac Davis, *They All Are Jews: From Moses to Einstein* (New York: Jordan Publishing Company, 1937).

28. *Jewish Tribune*, Feb. 3, 1928, 10, 21.

29. Davis, *They All Are Jews*, 7.

30. David Ewen, "A Master of Symphonic Jazz," *Jewish Tribune*, Oct. 7, 1927, 16.

31. See Marianne R. Sanua, *"Here's to Our Fraternity": One Hundred Years of Zeta Beta Tau, 1898–1998* (Hanover, NH: Zeta Beta Tau Foundation, 1998), 70–2.

32. *AH*, Dec. 18, 1925, 202.

33. Max Baer quoted in Peter Levine, *Ellis Island to Ebbets Field: Sport and the American Jewish Experience* (New York: Oxford University Press, 1992), 182.

34. *Forverts* (Chicago ed.), Jan. 4, 1925, CFLPS; *AH*, April 18, 1924, 687.

35. Julian Morgenstern, "American Judaism Faces the Future," *AH*, Sept. 22, 1922, 502.

36. On the popular interest in psychology during the period, see John C. Burnham, *Paths into American Culture: Psychology, Medicine and Morals* (Philadelphia: Temple University Press, 1988), chap. 5.

37. Shapiro, *Leadership of the American Zionist Organization*, 229; Samuel, *You Gentiles*, 19–20, 31–2.

38. Max Margolis, "The Truth about the Jew," *BBN* 15 (June 1924): 308.

39. "Semitism," *BBN* 15 (May 1924): 276–7.

40. *Yidisher kurier*, Sept. 19, 1921, CFLPS.

41. Louis Marshall to "a Judge in Iowa," June 15, 1922, in Reznikoff, *Louis Marshall: Champion of Liberty*, 1:400.

42. Louis Marshall to Henry Ford, July 5, 1927, in Reznikoff, *Louis Marshall: Champion of Liberty*, 379–80.

43. Quoted in Teller, *Strangers and Natives*, 94.

44. Louis Marshall to Rabbi Leo Franklin, July 31, 1927; and Marshall to Henry Abrahams, Aug 16, 1927, both in box 1599, Marshall Papers.

45. See Landman's editorial preface to "Who's Who Among American Jews—1925," *AH*, Dec. 4, 1925, 99.

46. See Landman's preface to *Universal Jewish Encyclopedia* (New York: Universal Jewish Encyclopedia, Inc., 1939), 1:[ix–xi].

47. Lance J. Sussman, "'Toward Better Understanding': The Rise of the Interfaith Movement in America and the Role of Rabbi Isaac Landman," *AJA* 34 (April 1982): 51 n. 20; Isaac Landman, "When Jews and Non-Jews Do Not Meet," *American Hebrew*, Sept. 22, 1922, 494, 504.

48. On the phenomenon of Jewish self-hatred, see Sander Gilman, *Jewish Self-Hatred: Anti-Semitism and the Hidden Language of the Jews* (Baltimore: Johns Hopkins University Press, 1986); Joachim Doron, "Classic Zionism and Modern Anti-Semitism: Parallels and Influences (1883–1914)," *Studies in Zionism* 8 (Autumn 1983): 169–204.

49. Marianne R. Sanua, *Going Greek: Jewish College Fraternities in the United States, 1895–1945* (Detroit: Wayne State University Press, 2003), 154, 156.

50. Riv-Ellen Prell, *Fighting to Become Americans: Jews, Gender, and the Anxiety of Assimilation*, (Boston: Beacon Press, 1999), esp. chap. 3; Sanua, *Going Greek*, 145–6, 157, 257–8. On the relationship between assimilation and gender politics in America, see also Paula Hyman, *Gender and Assimilation in Modern Jewish History: The Roles and Representation of Women* (Seattle: University of Washington Press, 1995), 157–60.

51. *Southern Israelite*, March 29, 1929, 25–6.

52. Linder quoted in Sanua, *Going Greek*, 148–9.

53. On plastic surgery and its popularity among Jews during this period, see Elizabeth Haiken, *Venus Envy: A History of Cosmetic Surgery* (Baltimore: Johns Hopkins University Press, 1997). On Brice, see Barbara W. Grossman, *Funny Woman: The Life and Times of Fanny Brice* (Bloomington: Indiana University Press, 1991), 138, 146–65.

54. On Kallen and his thinking on Jewish identity, see Sarah Schmidt, *Horace M. Kallen: Prophet of American Zionism* (Brooklyn, NY: Carlson Publishing, 1995); and William Toll, "Horace M. Kallen: Pluralism and American Jewish Identity," *AJH* 85 (March 1997): 57–74.

55. For Kallen's racial understanding of Jewishness, see his "The Ethics of Zionism," *Maccabaean* 11 (1906): 61–71; "The Eugenic Aspect of the Jewish Problem," *American Jewish Chronicle*, March 29, 1918, 558–9, 598; April 5, 1918, 630–31, 633; April 12, 1918, 655, 658; and *Culture and Democracy in the United States: Studies in the Group Psychology of the American Peoples* (New York: Boni and Liveright, 1924), 226. See also Kallen's 1913 speech before the Intercollegiate

282 NOTES TO PAGES 179-182

Menorah Association, reprinted in *The Menorah Movement: For the Study and Advancement of Jewish Culture and Ideals* (Intercollegiate Menorah Association: Ann Arbor, MI, 1914), 81–6.

56. Kallen, "The Ethics of Zionism," 65–7; Schmidt, *Horace M. Kallen*, 22–3; John Higham, *Send These to Me: Immigrants in Urban America* (Baltimore: Johns Hopkins University Press, 1975), 207.

57. Kallen, "The Ethics of Zionism," 67–8.

58. Kallen, *Culture and Democracy*, 226 n. 1. On the place of African Americans in Kallen's cultural pluralism, see Higham, *Send These to Me*, 210; and George Hutchinson, *The Harlem Renaissance in Black and White* (Cambridge: Harvard University Press, Belknap Press, 1995), 90.

59. On Boas's contribution to the "culture concept," see George W. Stocking, Jr., *Race, Culture, and Evolution: Essays in the History of Anthropology* (Chicago: University of Chicago Press, 1982), 195–233. For Boas's views on Jewishness, see "Are the Jews a Race?" *World Tomorrow*, Jan. 1923, 5–6; and Leonard B. Glick, "Types Distinct from Our Own: Franz Boas on Jewish Identity and Assimilation," *American Anthropologist* 84 (1982): 545–65. On the Boas school and the discrediting of scientific racism, see Elazar Barkan, *The Retreat of Scientific Racism: Changing Concepts of Race in Britain and the United States between the World Wars* (Cambridge: Cambridge University Press, 1992).

60. Julius Drachsler, *Democracy and Assimilation: The Blending of Cultural Heritages in America* (New York: Macmillan, 1920).

61. On Drachsler, see *NYT*, July 23, 1927, 13.

62. See Julius Drachsler, *Intermarriage in New York City: A Statistical Study of the Amalgamation of European Peoples* (New York: Columbia University Press, 1921), 7, 13, 17–19. Although this study was issued as a companion volume to Drachsler's *Democracy and Assimilation* and was published one year later, it was actually an earlier work based on his research in the prewar marriage records of New York City.

63. Drachsler, *Democracy and Assimilation*, 93.

64. Ibid., 163–5, 234–8. See also Julius Drachsler, *The Cultural Contributions of the Immigrant and a Policy of Incorporation* (Milwaukee: National Conference of Jewish Social Service, 1921), 9.

65. Isaac B. Berkson, *Theories of Americanization: A Critical Study, with Special Reference to the Jewish Group* (New York: Teachers College of Columbia University, 1920), 77, 83–5, 89, 97–118. For Friedlaender's use of racial terminology, see his "Race and Religion," in *Past and Present: A Collection of Jewish Essays* (Cincinnati: Ark Publishing Co., 1919), 431.

66. Berkson, *Theories of Americanization*, 61, 83–4.

67. Ibid., 51

68. Ibid., 102.

69. For Kallen's evolving understanding of racial and ethnic difference, see Toll, "Horace M. Kallen," 69–71. For an example of the journal's initial orientation toward racial Jewishness, see Charles W. Eliot, "The Potency of the Jewish Race," *Menorah Journal* 1 (1915): 141–4.

70. Intercollegiate Menorah Association, *The Jew in the Modern World: A Syllabus* (New York: Menorah Press, 1921), 26.

71. A. L. Kroeber, "Are the Jews a Race?" *Menorah Journal* 3 (1917): 290; Maurice Fishberg, "Assimilation," *Menorah Journal* 6 (1920): 25–37; Alexander Goldenweiser, "Concerning Racial Differences," *Menorah Journal* 8 (1922): 309–16; Irwin Edman, "Race and Culture," *Menorah Journal* 10 (1924): 421–7; Edward Sapir, "Racial Superiority," *Menorah Journal* 10 (1924): 206. For the larger context of the *Menorah Journal*'s shift from race to culture, see Seth Korelitz, "The Menorah Idea: From Religion to Culture, from Race to Ethnicity," *AJH* 85 (March 1997): 75–100.

72. Mordecai M. Kaplan, *Judaism as a Civilization* (New York: Macmillan, 1934), 178.

73. On Kaplan, see Mel Scult, *Judaism Faces the Twentieth Century: A Biography of Mordecai M. Kaplan* (Detroit: Wayne State University Press, 1993); Jeffrey S. Gurock and Jacob J. Schacter, *A Modern Heretic and a Traditional Community: Mordecai M. Kaplan, Orthodoxy, and American Judaism* (New York: Columbia University Press, 1997); Arnold M. Eisen, *The Chosen People in America: A Study in Jewish Religious Ideology* (Bloomington: Indiana University Press, 1983), 48–9, 73–98.

74. Mordecai M. Kaplan, "Judaism and Nationality" *Maccabaean* 17 (Aug. 1909): 60–1; [Mordecai M. Kaplan], *The Jewish Center* (New York: Privately published, 1918), unpaginated pamphlet.

75. Korelitz, "The Menorah Idea," 92–4.

76. Kaplan, *Judaism as a Civilization*, 231.

77. Ibid.

78. Joseph Tenenbaum, *Races, Nations, and Jews* (New York: Bloch Publishing Company, 1934), 36.

79. Alexander A. Goldenweiser, "Race and Culture in the Modern World," *Proceedings of the National Conference of Jewish Social Service at the Annual Session Held in Washington, D.C., May 13–16, 1923* (New York: National Conference of Jewish Social Service, 1924), 303–26.

80. George E. Sokolsky, *We Jews* (Garden City, NY: Doubleday, Doran and Company, 1935), 35–6.

81. David Goldblatt, *Is the Jewish Race Pure?* (New York: Goldblatt Publishing Co., 1933). On Goldblatt's background, see Samuel Niger and Jacob Shatsky, eds., *Leksikon fun der nayer Yidisher literature* (Biographical dictionary of modern Yiddish literature) (New York: Congress for Jewish Culture, 1956–1981), 2:37–9.

82. Stephen S. Wise, "Parallel between Hitlerism and the Persecution of the Negro in America," *Crisis* 41 (May 1934): 127.

83. *Aryan and Semite: With Particular Reference to Nazi Racial Dogmas* (Cincinnati: B'nai B'rith, 1934).

84. *American Jewish World*, Nov. 1, 1935, 14.

85. Bertram Jonas, "If Broadway Went Aryan," *American Jewish World*, Jan. 17, 1936, 5.

86. *Nation*, May 17, 1933, 557. Rice was responding to an essay by Ludwig Lewisohn, "Germany's Lowest Depths," which also appeared in the *Nation*, May 3, 1933, 493.

87. Feingold, *A Time for Searching*, 236.

88. Julian Morgenstern, "The Jewish Problem," *AH*, Oct. 12, 1934, 419–20, 430. See also Stephen S. Wise, *Challenging Years* (New York: G. T. Putnam's Sons, 1949), 246–66, 312.

89. *AH*, March 30 1934, 422.

90. *AH*, June 16, 1933, 93.

91. Cyrus Adler, "Teutons, Aryans and Semites," *American Hebrew*, March 23, 1934, 371. Adler was denounced as a coward by the Chicago *Yidisher kurier*, which accused him of "compromising with conscience and tampering with truth." See "The Question of Race," *Yidisher kurier* (English section), Sept. 17, 1935, 8.

CHAPTER 8

1. On Jewish participation in the Roosevelt administration, see Henry Feingold, *A Time for Searching: Entering the Mainstream* (Baltimore: Johns Hopkins University Press, 1992), 215–20.

2. On Wise's relationship with Roosevelt, see Stephen S. Wise, *The Challenging Years: The Autobiography of Stephen Wise* (New York: G. P. Putnam's Sons, 1949), 216–32. On Hillman, see Steve Fraser, *Labor Will Rule: Sidney Hillman and the Rise of American Labor* (New York: Free Press, 1991).

3. Gary Gerstle, *American Crucible: Race and Nation in the Twentieth Century* (Princeton: Princeton University Press, 2001), 138.

4. Roosevelt, quoted ibid.

5. Harvard Sitkoff, *A New Deal for Blacks: The Emergence of Civil Rights and a National Issue* (Oxford: Oxford University Press, 1978), 1:118–21.

6. Edward S. Shapiro, "Antisemitism Mississippi Style," in *Antisemitism in American History*, ed. David A. Gerber (Urbana: University of Illinois Press, 1986), 129–51.

7. Ibid., 138.

8. Leonard Dinnerstein, *Antisemitism in America* (New York: Oxford University Press, 1994), 128–49.

9. Ibid., 132–4.

10. For the larger context of these developments, see Philip Gleason, "Americans All: World War II and the Shaping of American Identity," *Review of Politics* 43 (Oct. 1981): 483–518. On the OWI, see Stuart Svonkin, *Jews against Prejudice: American Jews and the Fight for Civil Liberties* (New York: Columbia University Press, 1997), 42.

11. Marian L. Smith, "Race, Nationality, and Reality: INS Administration of Racial Provisions in U.S. Immigration and Nationality Law since 1898," *Prologue: Quarterly of the National Archives and Records Administration* 34 (Summer 2002): 99–100; *YIVO bleter* 23 (March–April 1944): 282–3; *The Classification of Jewish Immigrants and Its Implications: A Survey of Opinion* (New York: Yiddish Scientific Institute—YIVO, 1945), 7.

12. Gerstle, *American Crucible*, 204.

13. On wartime racial views of the Japanese, see John Dower, *War without Mercy: Race and Power in the Pacific War* (New York: Pantheon Book, 1986).

14. "Resolutions and Manifestoes of Scientists," in Ruth Benedict, *Race: Politics and Science* (New York: Viking Press, 1945), 195–6.

15. Gerstle, *American Crucible*, 192; Ruth Benedict, *The Races of Mankind* (New York: Public Affairs Committee, 1943); Ashley Montagu, *Man's Most Dangerous Myth: The Fallacy of Race* (New York: Columbia University Press, 1942); W. Lloyd Warner and Leo Srole, *The Social Systems of American Ethnic Groups* (New Haven: Yale University Press, 1945), 285.

16. The perception of Jews as a race continued to decline in surveys taken later in the postwar period. See Charles Herbert Stember, *Jews in the Mind of America* (New York: Basic Books, 1966), 49–53.

17. Gary Gerstle, *Working-Class Americanism: The Politics of Labor in a Textile City, 1914–1960* (Cambridge: Cambridge University Press, 1989), 289–95.

18. On this point, see Gleason "Americans All," 504–5.

19. Letter from Manny Krupin, April 22, 1944 in *Jewish Youth at War: Letters from American Soldiers*, ed. Isaac E. Rontch (New York: Marstin Press, 1945), 107–8.

20. Hakohen [pseud.], "My Experience and Observations as a Jew in World War II," 17, Record Group 110 (Memoirs of American-Jewish Soldiers), box 1, folder 17, YIVO Institute for Jewish Research, New York.

21. Morris ("Babe") Palansky to "Dear Mothers," Oct. 25, 1943, in Rontch, *Jewish Youth at War*, 283–4.

22. Quoted in Cheryl Lynn Greenberg, "Black and Jewish Responses to Japanese Internment," *Journal of American Ethnic History* 14 (Winter 1995): 7.

23. *Jewish Examiner* (Brooklyn), Jan. 29, 1943, 4.

24. *American Jewish Times* (Greensboro, NC) 11 (Oct. 1945): 1.

25. On this trend, see Svonkin, *Jews against Prejudice*, chap. 1.

26. Steinbrink, quoted ibid., 19.

27. See Max D. Danish, *The Story of the ILGWU* (New York: International Ladies' Garment Workers' Union, 1947), 53.

28. See Deborah Dash Moore, *GI Jews: How World War II Changed a Generation* (Cambridge: Harvard University Press, 2004), 119; Alex J. Goldman, *Giants of Faith: Great American Rabbis* (New York: Citadel Press, 1964), 319–20.

29. *Jewish Examiner*, Dec. 10, 1943, 4.

30. The quotations are from Michael E. Staub, *Torn at the Roots: The Crisis of Jewish Liberalism in Postwar America* (New York: Columbia University Press, 2002), 25–6. My interpretation of these statements differs substantially from that of Staub, who sees them as making direct linkages between Jewish and black suffering. Of the several examples of "Nazi analogies" Staub presents from Jewish periodicals of the period, however, only one of them specifically mentions the word "Jew."

31. Lawrence W. Levine, *The Opening of the American Mind: Canons, Culture and History* (Boston: Beacon Press, 1996), 137. See also Nat Hentoff, *Boston Boy* (New York: Alfred A. Knopf, 1986), 59–61; Leonard Garment, *Crazy Rythym* (New York: Time Books, 1997), 20–2; and Justin Martin, *Greenspan: The Man behind the Money* (Cambridge, MA: Perseus Publishing, 2000), 11–22.

32. See Peter Levine, *Ellis Island to Ebbets Field: Sport and the American Jewish Experience* (New York: Oxford University Press, 1992), 237, 282.

33. *AH*, Feb 18, 1948, quoted in Levine, *Ellis Island to Ebbets Field*, 241.

34. See Harold U. Ribalow, *The Jew in American Sports* (New York: Bloch Publishing Company, 1948), 136.

35. *American Hebrew*, June 14, 1946, quoted in Levine, *Ellis Island to Ebbets Field*, 188.

36. Moore, *GI Jews*, 72–3.

37. Janice Rothschild Blumberg, *One Voice: Rabbi Jacob Rothschild and the Troubled South* (Macon, GA: Mercer University Press, 1985); Melissa Faye Greene, *The Temple Bombing* (Reading, MA: Addison-Wesley, 1996); Gary Zola, "At What Price Amos? Perry Nussbaum's Career in Jackson, Mississippi," in *The Quiet Voices: Southern Rabbis and Black Civil Rights, 1880s to 1990s*, ed. Mark K. Bauman and Berkley Kalin (Tuscaloosa: University of Alabama Press, 1997), 230–57; Clive Webb, *Fight against Fear: Southern Jews and Black Civil Rights* (Athens: University of Georgia Press), 117–22, 129–43; John K. Cauthen, *Speaker Blatt: His Challenges Were Greater* (Columbia: University of South Carolina Press, 1978).

38. Webb, *Fight against Fear*, 114.

39. Bauman and Kalin, *The Quiet Voices;* Webb, *Fight against Fear*; Marc Dollinger, *Quest for Inclusion: Jews and Liberalism in Modern America* (Princeton: Princeton University Press, 2000), 166–73.

40. See Dollinger, *Quest for Inclusion*, 173–90.

41. "The Changing of North Lawndale and the Jewish People's Institute of the Jewish Community Centers of Chicago," box 27, Assorted Community Studies folder, Jewish Community Centers of Chicago Collection, Chicago Historical Society.

42. Ibid.

43. Clement E. Vose, *Caucasians Only: The Supreme Court, the NAACP, and the Restrictive Covenant Cases* (Berkeley and Los Angeles: University of California Press, 1959), 194; Herbert J. Gans, *The Levittowners: Ways of Life and Politics in a New Suburban Community* (New York: Columbia University Press, 1967), 371–84 (esp. 372), 404 n. 6.

44. For a discussion of the contradictions often inherent in postwar Jewish liberalism, see Dollinger, *Quest for Inclusion*.

45. Lee J. Levinger, *Antisemitism, Yesterday and Tomorrow* (New York: Macmillan, 1936), 229.

46. James Waterman Wise and Lee J. Levinger, *Mr. Smith Meets Mr. Cohen* (New York: Reynal and Hitchcock, 1940), 138–9.

47. Milton Steinberg, *A Partisan Guide to the Jewish Problem* (Indianapolis: Bobbs-Merrill Co., 1945), 145–53.

48. Roland B. Gittelsohn, *Modern Jewish Problems* (Cincinnati: Union of American Hebrew Congregations, 1943), 16–21.

49. Levinger, *Antisemitism: Yesterday and Tomorrow*, 220–32.

50. Gittelsohn, *Modern Jewish Problems*, 16–7.

51. "Three Questions Jews Must Answer," in *Facts about Fictions Concerning the Jew* (Chicago: Anti-Defamation League of B'nai B'rith, 1939).

52. *The Classification of Jewish Immigrants*, 16, 21, 51.

53. Mac Davis, *Jews Fight Too!* (New York: Hebrew Publishing Company, 1945); Ralph Nunberg, *The Fighting Jew* (New York: Creative Age Press, 1945); Morris N. Kertzer, *With an H on my Dog Tag* (New York: Behrman House, 1947).

54. Sigmund Livingston, *Must Men Hate?* (New York: Harper and Brothers Publishers, 1944), 147, 185–6, 231–2, 240–325.

55. Mac Davis, *Jews at a Glance* (New York: Hebrew Publishing Company, 1956), xi.

56. Gleason "Americans All," 504–5.

57. Moore, *GI Jews*, 118–55, esp. 123.

58. Will Herberg, *Protestant-Catholic-Jew: An Essay in American Religious Sociology* (Garden City, NY: Doubleday, 1955), n 51.

59. Most of these trends remained in force into the 1960s. See Judith R. Kramer and Seymour Leventman, *Children of the Gilded Ghetto* (New Haven: Yale University Press, 1961), 105, 152–3, 178–9, 180–1; Marshall Sklare and Joseph Greenblum, *Jewish Identity on the Suburban Frontier: A Study of Group Survival in the Open Society* (New York: Basic Books, 1967), 200, 252, 268, 269–90.

60. Stephen J. Whitfield, *In Search of American Jewish Culture* (Hanover, NH: Brandeis University Press, 1999), 168–96; Deborah Dash Moore, *To The Golden Cities: Pursuing the American Jewish Dream in Miami and Los Angeles* (Cambridge: Harvard University Press, 1994), chap. 8.

EPILOGUE

Part of this epilogue was previously published as "Contesting the Categories: Jews and Government Racial Classification in the United States," Jewish History 19 (2005): 79–107, and is republished here with the kind permission of Springer Science and Business Media. The epigraph is from Adam Sandler, "The Chanukah Song," on *What the Hell Happened to Me!* (Warner Bros. compact disc, 1996).

1. *Harry B. Kelman Academy News* (Cherry Hill, NJ), March 1998, 6 (on the Web at *http://www.kellmanacademy.org/kesher/mar98.pdf*); Jennifer Fishbein-Gold, "Playing Sweetheart to West Point Cadets—at Least for a Night," *Forward*, Dec. 31, 1999.

2. Lisa Keys, "Adam Sandler's Chanukah Flick Serves up Judaism by the Gross," *Forward*, Nov. 22, 2002.

3. J. Hoberman, "Antichirst Superstar: What the Devil Made Adam Sandler Do," *Village Voice*, Nov. 15–20, 2000.

4. Cesar G. Soriano, "Sandler Puts a New Spin on 'Chanukah,'" *USA Today*, Nov. 26, 2002.

5. Hoberman, "Antichirst Superstar."

6. Ibid.

7. Soriano, "Sandler Puts a New Spin on 'Chanukah.'"

8. Adam Sandler, "The Chanukah Song, Part Three," on *Adam Sandler's Eight Crazy Nights* (Sony compact disc, 2002).

9. On Carew, see Justin Shubow, "Playing Who's a Jew? And Other Virtual Games," *Forward*, Nov. 5, 1999.

10. See, for example, Elliott Abrams, *Faith or Fear: How Jews Can Survive in a Christian America* (New York: Free Press, 1997); Alan M. Dershowitz, *The Vanishing American Jew: In Search of Jewish Identity for the Next Century* (New York: Simon and Schuster, 1997); and Bernard Susser and Charles S. Liebman, *Choosing Survival: Strategies for a Jewish Future* (New York: Oxford University Press, 1999).

11. Stephen J. Whitfield, *In Search of American Jewish Culture* (Hanover, NH: Brandeis University Press, 1999), 168–96. For a critical view, see Peter Novick, *The Holocaust in American Life* (Boston: Houghton Mifflin Company, 1999).

12. Abraham Joshua Heschel, *The Insecurity of Freedom* (New York: Farrar, Straus and Giroux), chaps. 5 and 6; Arthur Lelyveld, "Negro and Jewish Relationships," *Congress Bi-weekly* 33 (1966): 9. On other Jews who linked their Jewishness with civil rights activism during these years, see Michael E. Staub, *Torn at the Roots: The Crisis of Jewish Liberalism in Postwar America* (New York: Columbia University Press, 2002), 45–62. On the larger group of civil rights activists who did not stress their Jewish connections, see Debra L. Schultz, *Going South: Jewish Women in the Civil Rights Movement* (New York: New York University Press, 2001).

13. Marc Dollinger, "'Is it Good for the Jews?': Liberalism and the Challenges of the 1960s," *"Jewishness" and the World of "Difference" in the United States*, ed. Marc Lee Raphael (Williamsburg, VA: College of William and Mary, 2001), 8–25.

14. Nat Hentoff, introduction to *Black Antisemitism and Jewish Racism* (New York: Richard Baron, 1969), ix.

15. See Riv-Ellen Prell, *Prayer and Community: The Havurah in American Judaism* (Detroit: Wayne State University Press, 1989).

16. Richard Siegel, Michael Strassfeld, and Sharon Strassfeld, eds., *The First Jewish Catalog* (Philadelphia: Jewish Publication Society of America, 1973).

17. M. J. Roseberg, "Uncle Tom and Other Jews," *Jewish Radicalism*, ed. Jack Nusan Porter and Peter Dreier (New York: Grove Press, 1973), 7, 10.

18. On the ethnic revival, see Nathan Glazer and Daniel Patrick Moynihan, *Beyond the Melting Pot: The Negroes, Puerto Ricans, Jews, Italians, and Irish of New York City* (Cambridge: MIT Press, 1970); Matthew Jacobson, "Ethnic Jewishness in a 'Nation of Immigrants,' 1963–2000," in Raphael, *"Jewishness" and the World of "Difference,"* 26–49.

19. Jacobson, "Ethnic Jewishness," 35, 38; Irving Howe, *World of Our Fathers* (New York: Harcourt Brace Jovanovich, 1976).

20. Janet L. Dolgin, *Jewish Identity and the JDL* (Princeton: Princeton University Press, 1977), 159.

21. See Stuart Svonkin, *Jews against Prejudice: American Jews and the Fight for Civil Liberties* (New York; Columbia University Press, 1997), chap. 8.

22. See Norman Podhoretz, "My Negro Problem—and Ours," *Commentary* 35 (Feb. 1963): 93–101; Staub, *Torn at the Roots*, 70–5.

23. Jacobson, "Ethnic Jewishness," 42–7.

24. See, for example, Jonathan Rieder, *Canarsie: The Jews and Italians of Brooklyn against Liberalism* (Cambridge: Harvard University Press, 1985).

25. Dollinger, *Quest for Inclusion*, 191.

26. Quoted in William W. Orbach, *The American Movement to Aid Soviet Jews* (Amherst: University of Massachusetts Press, 1979), 5.

27. Dollinger, *Quest for Inclusion*, 220.

28. Dolgin, *Jewish Identity and the JDL*, 37–8, 160.

29. Jeffrey Melnick, *A Right to Sing the Blues: African Americans, Jews and American Popular Song* (Cambridge: Harvard University Press, 1999), 1–15.

30. Hasia Diner, *In the Almost Promised Land: American Jews and Blacks*, 2d ed. (Baltimore: Johns Hopkins University Press, 1995), xiii.

31. Jane Anna Gordon, *Why They Couldn't Wait: A Critique of the Black-Jewish Conflict over Community Control in Ocean Hill–Brownsville, 1967–1971* (New York: RoutledgeFalmer, 2001), esp. chap. 3. Gordon conveys the Jewish misunderstanding of black needs well, but does not match this with an explanation of the way African Americans read Jewish actions through their own needs.

32. James Baldwin, "Negroes Are Anti-Semitic Because They're Anti-white," in Hentoff, *Black Anti-Semitism and Jewish Racism*, 6.

33. Ibid., 7.

34. Ibid., 9.

35. Harold Cruse, *The Crisis of the Negro Intellectual* (New York: William Morrow and Co., 1967), 147–70, 476–97.

36. Harold Cruse, "My Jewish Problem, and Ours," in Hentoff, *Black Anti-Semitism and Jewish Racism*, 184.

37. See Stephen Steinberg, *The Ethnic Myth: Race, Ethnicity and Class in America* (Boston: Beacon Press, 1981), 249–52.

38. On Farrakhan and Jeffries, see Leonard Dinnerstein, *Antisemitism in America* (New York: Oxford University Press, 1994), 220–22; and Arthur J. Magida, *Prophet of Rage: A Life of Louis Farrakhan and His Nation* (New York: Basic Books, 1996).

39. See George J. Sanchez, "Reading Reginald Denny: The Politics of Whiteness in the Late Twentieth Century," *American Quarterly* 47 (Sept. 1995): 393.

40. David Hollinger, *Post-ethnic America: Beyond Multiculturalism* (New York: Basic Books, 1995), chap. 2.

41. Sanchez, "Reading Reginald Denny," 392–3.

42. For a general discussion of this trend, see the conversation between Cornel West and Michael Lerner in *Jews and Blacks: Let the Healing Begin* (New York: G. P. Putnam's Sons, 1995), 62–79. See also the essays in David Biale, Michael Galchinsky, and Susannah Heschel, *Insider/Outsider: American Jews and Multiculturalism* (Berkeley and Los Angeles: University of California Press, 1998); and Marla Brettschneider, *The Narrow Bridge: Jewish Views on Multiculturalism* (New Brunswick, NJ: Rutgers University Press, 1996).

43. Joyce Purnick, "125th Street: What Jackson Didn't Say," *NYT*, Dec. 21, 1995, B1.

44. "Radio Excerpts in Harlem Store Dispute," *NYT*, Dec. 14, 1995, B4.

45. Ibid.

46. On the ethnic and racial mix of employees at Freddy's, see Joe Sexton, "Death on 125th Street: The Victims," *NYT*, Dec. 9, 1995, A31.

47. Hooks quoted in Jonathan Kaufman, *Broken Alliance: The Turbulent Times between Blacks and Jews in America* (New York: Touchstone, 1988), 292.

48. Transcript from *Nightline* episode "Stephen Spielberg and *Amistad*: Who Owns History?" Dec. 17, 1997, 9, Transcription Company, Burbank, CA.

49. Spike Lee quoted in *NYT*, March 28, 1994, C11.

50. Courtland Milloy, "'Amistad' through a Different Lens," *Washington Post*, Dec. 14, 1997, B1.

51. Steven M. Cohen and Arnold M. Eisen, *The Jew Within: Self, Family and Community in America* (Bloomington: Indiana University Press, 2000), chap. 5.

52. Ibid., 107

53. Susan A. Glenn, "In the Blood? Consent, Descent, and the Ironies of Jewish Identity," *Jewish Social Studies* 8 (Spring 2002): 140.

54. For an examination of the legal issues in the *Shaare Tefila* case, see Joseph Avanzato, "Section 1982 and Discrimination against Jews: *Shaare Tefila Congregation v. Cobb*," *American University Law Review* 37 (1987): 225–57.

55. *United States v. Lemrick Nelson*, 277 F.3d 164 (U.S. Court of Appeals Second Circuit, 2002).

56. Quoted in Naomi Cohen, "*Shaare Tefila Congregation v. Cobb*: A New Departure in American Jewish Defense?" *Jewish History* 3 (Spring 1988): 100.

57. Nacha Cattan, "Victim's Kin Expected Crown Height's Ruling," *Forward*, Jan. 11, 2002. Nelson was subsequently retried and found guilty of the civil rights violation, even though the jury held that the violation was not the cause of Rosenbaum's death. See *NYT*, May 15, 2003, A1.

58. See the H-Ethnic postings by Robert Tabak, March 17, 2000, and March 23, 2000. These postings are searchable from the H-Net Discussion Logs Search Web page, *http://www2.h-net.msu.edu/logsearch/*.

59. Ibid.

60. H-Ethnic posting by Sharon Vance, March 16, 2000.

61. "Some Other Race" (editorial), *Forward*, March 17, 2000.

62. David Holzel, "Do Not Adjust Your Color: How Did Jews Become White All of a Sudden?" *Atlanta Jewish Times*, Aug. 11, 1995. See also Michael Lerner, "Jews Are Not White," *Village Voice*, May 18, 1993, 33–4.

63. Harlan Spector, "Genetic Screening Finding Acceptance among Jews," *Cleveland Plain Dealer*, May 19, 2003; Sheryl Gay Stolberg, "Jewish Concern Grows as Scientists Deepen Studies of Ashkenazic Genes," *NYT*, April 22, 1998.

64. The original study was published as "Y Chromosomes of Jewish Priests," *Nature* 385 (Jan. 2, 1997): 32.

65. Hillel Halkin, "Wandering Jews—and Their Genes," *Commentary* 110 (Sept. 2000): 55.

66. Maurice Fishberg, *The Jews: A Study of Race and Environment* (New York: Scribner's, 1911), 179–94. In a more recent study on Ashkenazic Jews who identify as Levites, a broader tribal grouping that includes the *kohanim*, Hammer and Skorecki had a harder time substantiating the tradition of descent from the ancient Israelites. In more than half of the sample population, they found a genetic marker pointing to a common ancestor who lived in Central Asia about one thousand years ago. Interestingly, these findings have not received the widespread publicity enjoyed by the team's earlier studies. See *NYT*, Sept. 27, 2003, 2A.

67. Stolberg, "Jewish Concern Grows."

68. Ibid.

69. *Cleveland Plain Dealer*, May 19, 2003, A1.

70. David Olson, *Mapping Human History: Genes, Race and Our Common Origins* (Boston: Houghton Mifflin, 2002), 117–18.

71. Zoloth-Dorfman quoted in John Travis, "The Priests' Chromosome? DNA Analysis Supports the Biblical Story of the Jewish Priesthood," *Science News* 154 (Oct. 3, 1998): 218.

72. "Finding Genetic Traces of Jewish Priesthood," *NYT*, Jan. 7, 1997, C6.

73. On the desire for testing, see ibid.; and Travis, "The Priests' Chromosome?" 219. For Greenspan's genealogical testing service, see *Family Tree DNA*, *http://www.familytreedna.com*.

74. *The Tribe: The Cohen-Levi Family Heritage*, *http://www.cohen-levi.org*.

75. Stolberg, "Jewish Concern Grows."

76. Ibid.

77. Ibid.

78. Robert Pollack, "The Fallacy of Biological Judaism," *Forward*, March 7, 2003.

79. Karen H. Rothenberg, "Genetic Research and the Role of the Community: A Case Study of Jewish Attitudes," paper presented at the First Community Consultation on the Responsible Collection and Use of Samples for Genetic Research, National Institute of General Medical Sciences (NIGMS), National Institutes of Health, September 25–26, 2000. See also Rothenberg and Amy B. Rutkin, "Toward A Framework of Mutualism: The Jewish Community in Genetics Research," *Community Genetics* 1 (1998): 148–53.

80. Barry A. Kosmin, Sidney Goldstein, Joseph Waksberg, Nava Lerer, Ariella Keysar, and Jeffrey Schenker, *Highlights of the CJF 1990 National Jewish Population Survey* (New York: Council for Jewish Federations, 1991).

81. Mik Moore, "Sex, Miscegenation, and the Intermarriage Debate," *New Voices* 6 (Nov. 1997), available on the Web at *http://www.shmoozenet.com/jsps/stories/miscegination.shtml*.

82. Philip Weiss, "What Would a Jewish Veep Say about Intermarriage?" *New York Observer*, May 1, 2000, 1.

83. Binyamin L. Kolkovsky, "Lieberman: Intermarriage Is Kosher," *Jewish World Review*, Sept. 19, 2000.

84. Ibid.

85. Eric Fingerhut, "Stereotypes Persist in Portrayals of TV's Jews, New Report Says," *Washington Jewish Week*, Sept. 15, 2000.

86. See David Zurawik, *The Jews of Prime Time* (Hanover, NH: Brandeis University Press, 2003), chaps. 3, 5, and 6.

87. Fingerhut, "Stereotpes Persist." This tendency is also prevalent in film. See Joseph Greenblum, "Does Hollywood Still Glorify Jewish Intermarriage? The Case of the *Jazz Singer*," *AJH* 83 (Dec. 1995): 445–69.

88. Cohen and Eisen, *The Jew Within*, 108.

89. Ibid., 133.

90. Lisa Schiffman, *Generation J* (New York: HarperCollins, 1999), 17. On the attachment to Jewishness among those who intermarry, see also Ellen Jaffe McCain, *Embracing the Stranger: Intermarriage and the Future of the American Jewish Community* (New York: Basic Books, 1995), chap. 6.

91. On this new subculture more generally, see Joanna Smith Rakoff, "The New Super Jews," *Time Out New York*, Dec. 4–11, 2003.

92. *Heeb* 6 (Summer 2004): 81.

93. "Jewess," *Heeb* 3 (Spring 2003): 40–51.

94. Matthew Cowan, "All about the Benjamins," *Heeb* 4 (Fall 2003): 38–43. For the Streit's ad, see *Heeb* 3 (Spring 2003):1.

95. "The Nell Carter Memorial Page," *Heeb* 3 (Spring 2003): 26.

96. Raven Snook, "Undercover Brocha: The Hebrew Hammer Swings into Action" *Heeb* 4 (Fall 2003): 67–8. See also David Rooney, "The Hebrew Hammer," *Variety* 389 (Feb. 3–11, 2003): 37–8.

97. Charles Lane, "Critics of Affirmative Action Temper their Opposition," *Washington Post*, Dec. 22, 2002, A17.

98. Lerner, "Jews Are Not White"; Melanie Kaye/Kantrowitz, "Jews in the U.S.: The Rising Costs of Whiteness," in *Names We Call Home: Autobiography on Racial Identity*, ed. Becky Thompson and Sangeeta Tyagi (New York: Routledge, 1996), 126–7.

99. Arthur Hertzberg, *The Jews in America: Four Centuries of an Uneasy Encounter* (New York: Simon and Schuster, 1989), 386–8.

100. Abrams, *Faith or Fear*, 163–4.

101. Dershowitz, *The Vanishing American Jew*, 321.

102. *2001 Annual Survey of American Jewish Opinion* (New York: American Jewish Committee, 2001).

103. Dale Maharidge, *The Coming White Minority: California, Multiculturalism, and America's Future* (New York: Vintage Books, 1999), 3.

INDEX

Abbot, Lyman, 69

Abernethy, Arthur T., 46, 48; *The Jew a Negro,* 43–4

Abie's Irish Rose (Nichols), 134

Abrams, Elliott, *Faith or Fear,* 238

acculturation: of Central European Jewish immigrants, 12, 243n3; of Eastern European Jewish immigrants, 138, 140–5. *See also* assimilation of Jews; social integration of Jews

Addams, Jane, 78

Adler, Cyrus, 88–9, 103, 110, 185–6

Adler, Felix, 14, 28, 70

affirmative action, Jewish stance on, 219–20, 236

Africa, theory of Jewish origins in, 44–6, 108–9, 111–2, 130, 179

African Americans, 120, 125, 128, 139–40, 142; commercial relations with Jews, 49, 52–3, 59–60, 76–8, 144–5, 159–60, 164; during World War II era, 192, 195, 207; as emotional surrogates for Jews, 6, 154–5, 198–9; in garment industry, 76, 144, 150–1, 158, 196–7; Jewish approach to, 3, 18, 51–85, 138–9, 145–64, 194–201, 245–6n31; Jews compare themselves to, 5, 18, 55, 61, 64, 79–81, 151, 157–9, 162, 197, 211–2, 215–6; Jews compared to, 42–4, 64–5, 130; Jews distance themselves from, 3, 55–6, 64–8, 114, 150–2, 154–7, 159–62, 182–3, 245–6n31; Jews identify with, 3, 51, 69–72, 154–6, 197, 246n35; in pluralist theories, 179, 182–3, 206–7, 221; as primary racial outsiders in the United States, 1, 4, 17, 41, 47, 50, 72, 239; tensions between Jews and, 5–6, 72, 164, 215–23

Agudath Israel of America, 233

Alabama, 145, 159. *See also specific locations*

Alexander, Henry, 93

Alexandria, LA, 59

Alliance Israélite Universelle, 112

Altschul, Adolph, 59

Amalgamated Clothing Workers of America, 150, 190

America First Committee, 191

American Anthropological Society, 193

American Civil Liberties Union, 157

American Hebrew: compares African Americans and Jews, 159; criticizes "race consciousness," 185; on intermarriage, 14–5, 21–2; on Jewish peoplehood, 14; on Jewish racial classification, 105; lauds Jewish racial characteristics, 19–20, 172, 174, 176–7; on New York race riot, 64–5; supports African American rights, 69, 199

American Israelite, 15, 29, 88

American Jewess, 21, 23–4, 26

American Jewish Committee, 147, 165, 186; civil rights work, 196, 200, 215; and Jewish racial classification, 105, 107, 110; and "racial" discrimination against Jews, 168, 176, 226; stance on affirmative action, 219, 236; surveys on Jewish identity, 234, 239. *See also* Survey of Jewish Opinion

American Jewish Congress, 167, 183; civil rights work, 196, 200, 215; and "racial" discrimination against Jews, 226; stance on affirmative action, 219, 236

American Jewish Historical Society, 20

American Jewish Joint Distribution Committee, 167

American Jewish Times, 196

American Jewish World, 184

American Revolution, 16

Amerikaner, 79

Amistad, 222–3

Amos 'n' Andy, 140

Amter, Israel, 162

Angell, Norman, 133

Annapolis, MD, 139–41

anthropology, and study of Jews, 110–4, 131, 136, 193. *See also* racial science

Anti-Defamation League of B'nai B'rith, 67, 168, 205; civil rights work, 196, 215; fights racial images of Jews, 90; opposes racial definition of Jews, 203–4;

Anti-Defamation League (*cont'd*)
and "racial" discrimination against
Jews, 226; stance on affirmative action,
219, 236. *See also* B'nai B'rith
antisemitism: among African Americans,
164, 220, 222; difficulty of disentangling
from philosemitism, 37, 124, 131–5,
250n11; in interwar period, 122–3, 126–
31, 134–5, 137–9, 146, 158–9, 169,
175–7, 184–5, 191; in Progressive Era,
37–40, 42–5; in World War II era, 191,
194. *See also* image of the Jew in American culture; philosemitism; social
discrimination
Antler, Joyce, 233
Arabs, in theories of Jewish origins,
45, 109
Arbeter tsaytung, 81–2
Arkansas, 58. *See also specific locations*
Aryan-Semite dichotomy, 16–17, 19, 89,
184, 193. *See also* Semites
Asian Americans, 1, 192, 206, 221, 239.
See also Chinese immigrants; Japanese
immigrants
"Asiatic," Jews described as, 103–4, 131
assimilation of Jews, 224; Jewish advocacy
of, 114, 171–2, 180, 266n94; Jewish
fears of, 14–5, 90; non-Jewish advocacy
of, 5, 47–50, 87, 89, 99, 100, 102, 131–
5, 194, 206, 233–4. *See also* acculturation; intermarriage, Jewish; social integration of Jews
Association of Southern Women for the Prevention of Lynching, 149
athletics: Jewish participation in, 174, 177,
184–5; Jews accused of avoiding, 38–9,
127; Jews as fans of black athletes, 198–
9. *See also* boxing
Atlanta, GA: discrimination against Jews
in, 54; Jewish social life in, 13; Jews and
African Americans in, 57–8, 61, 77–8,
156–7, 199; and Leo Frank Case, 43,
62; views on Jewish racial identity in,
93, 149, 169, 177
Atlanta Jewish Times, 227
Atlanta University, 58
Atlantic City, NJ, 54
Ausubel, Nathan, *Pictorial History of the
Jewish People*, 205
Austria, status of Jews in, 37
Axman, Sophie, 25

Baer, Max (Maxie), 174, 185
Bakke, Allen, 219, 236
Balaban and Katz (movie chain), 142
Balch Institute for Ethnic Studies
(Philadelphia), 226
Baldwin, James, 1, 218–20
Balfour Declaration (1917), 167
Baltimore, 36, 55, 162–3, 230
Baptists, 59–60, 134
Bayme, Stephen, 233–4
Benedict, Ruth, *Races of Mankind*, 193
Berkson, Isaac B., 96, 181, 183, 202; *Theo-
ries of Americanization*, 181
Berlin, Irving, 155
Bernhardt, Sarah, 94
Bierhoff, Harry, 130, 152
Bilbo, Theodore, 191, 196
Birmingham, AL, 53, 84
Birnbaum, Jacob, 216
Birth of a Nation, 74, 140
Bisno, Abraham, 82
blackface, 154–5. *See also* minstrel shows
black-white dichotomy: acculturating Jews
adapt to, 139–45; African American as-
sertion of, 218, 221–3; efforts to fit Jews
into, 36, 41–8, 119; emphasis on, in
American culture, 17, 31, 216, 221; as
ideology, 3–4, 17, 41–2, 63; Jews' uncer-
tain place in 1–2, 31, 36, 120, 125–37;
problematic nature for Jews 1–3, 87,
190, 212, 225–7, 239; as source of stabil-
ity for American whites, 1–2, 31, 36, 41
black nationalism, 213, 215–6, 218, 221
Black Panthers, 216
Blatt, Sol, 200
Bloch, Charles, 199
Block, Clara, 25
Blumenbach, Johann, 131
Blumstein, L. M., 68
B'nai B'rith, 13, 21, 23, 25, 47, 100, 105,
184, 200, 256n61. *See also* Anti-Defama-
tion League
B'nai B'rith Magazine, 156
B'nai B'rith News, 175
Boas, Franz, 110, 113–4, 136, 147, 180–1,
183, 193
Bob Jones University, 233
Bohemian immigrants, 144
Boston, 11, 36, 42, 230
Bottingsheim, Seymour, 61
Bourne, Randolph, 135

Clinchy, Everett R., 136
Cohen, Frank, 55, 57
Cohen, Mary, 26
Cohen, Stephen M., 223–4, 234
Cohens and the Kellys, The, 134
Cohens and Kellys in Africa, The, 134–5
Color Purple, The, 222
Colorado, 105
Colored American, 64
Columbia University, 91–2, 147, 168–9, 180, 182, 230
Columbus, Christopher, 46–7
Committee for Racial Cooperation (Atlanta), 149
Commons, John, 38
communism, 120; Jews accused of, 122, 128
Communist Party (American), 128, 159, 161–2
communists, Jewish, 128, 158–2, 164
Concordia Association (Atlanta), 13
Congregation Keneseth Israel (Philadelphia), 70
Conley, Jim, 65–6
Connecticut, 191
conservatism, racial, among Jews, 215
Conservative Jews, 148, 203, 226. *See also* Jewish Theological Seminary of America
consumer culture, racial imagery in, 140, 142–3
conversion to Judaism: by African Americans, 79, 211, 235; opposition to on racial grounds, 21, 27–9, 93
Coughlin, Charles E., 123–4, 191–2
Cowen, Philip, 64, 105
crime: and Jewish perceptions of African Americans, 79, 145; Jewish involvement in, 35; Jews accused of, 39–40, 42. *See also* prostitution
Crisis of the Negro Intellectual, The (Cruse), 219
Crown Heights riots, 225
Cruse, Harold, 218–20; *Crisis of the Negro Intellectual*, 219
culture, as basis of group definition, 136. *See also* ethnicity
cultural pluralism, 135–6, 179–81, 183. *See also* religious pluralism

Dana-Farber Cancer Institute (Boston), 230
Danforth, C. H., 136

Davis, Elmer, 134
Davis, Jeff, 58
Davis, Mac: *Jews at a Glance*, 206; *They All Are Jews*, 172–3
Davis-Du Bois, Rachel, 136
Dearborn Independent, 122–3, 126, 132
Defenders of the Christian Faith, 191
Democracy and Assimilation (Drachsler), 180
Democratic Party, 195, 233
Dershowitz, Alan, 236, 238
Detroit, 124, 144
Dewey, John, 135, 168
Dharma and Greg, 233
Dick, Isaac Mayer, 79
Dictionary of Races and Peoples, 106
Dies, Martin J., 191
Dillingham, William Paul, 105
Diner, Hasia, 159, 217
Dinnerstein, Leonard, 191
disenfranchisement of African Americans: Jewish support of, 58, 84; Jewish opposition to, 69
Disinherited, The (Waldman), 168
Disraeli, Benjamin, 20, 94, 107
Dixon, Thomas, 46, 49, 56, 74; *The Clansman*, 58, 74; *The Traitor*, 46, 49
Dollinger, Marc, 212
domestic servants, African American, 142, 161, 163–4
Douglas, Kirk, 209–10
Downtown Ethical Society (New York), 70
Drachsler, Julius, 180–1, 183, 202; *Democracy and Assimilation*, 180
Drake, St. Clair, 161, 164
drama, depictions of Jews in, 35, 40, 94. *See also* image of the Jew in American culture; popular culture
Dreyfus, Alfred, 64
Du Bois, W.E.B., 58, 78, 258n84
Dubinsky, David, 158

Eagle, Joshua, 210
Eastern Europe, status of Jews in, 3, 56, 145, 161
Eastern European Jews in the United States, 2, 31, 40, 60, 63, 121; acculturation into black-white racial system, 138, 140–5; aloofness from racial thought, 95–6; ambivalence about whiteness, 146–7; approach to African Americans, 52, 75–85, 162; assume leadership of

Germany: boycott of goods from, 185; status of Jews in, 28, 37, 131, 158, 184–5. *See also* Nazis
Gershwin, George, 174
Gerstle, Gary, 194
Gilbert, Melissa, 210
Gittelsohn, Roland B., 203
Glenn, Susan, 224
Gliddon, George, *Races of Mankind*, 16
Gold, Michael, 161
Goldberg, Abraham, 97
Goldblatt, David, 184–5, 203
Goldenweiser, Alexander, 183
Goldfogle, Henry, 103–4
Goldstein, Benjamin, 162–3
Goode, Alexander, 197
"goodwill" movement. *See* Christian-Jewish relations; philosemitism
Gottheil, Gustav, 23, 91–2
Gottheil, Richard J.H., 91–2
government racial classification of Jews, 102–8, 192, 224–7
Grant, Madison, 125, 136, 183
Grant, Ulysses S., 246n31
Great Depression, 190; ambivalence about Jewish racial self-definition during, 184–6, 189; Jewish approach to African Americans during, 157–64; as period of increased antisemitism, 123, 128, 157, 166, 184, 189
Great Society, 216, 225
Greensboro, NC, 196
Greenspan, Bennett, 229
Gries, Moses, 74
Griffith, D.W., 74, 140
Groper, William, 160
Guggenheim, Simon, 96, 105, 126
Gurock, Jeffrey, 78
Guyanese immigrants, 221

Haas, Caroline, 58
Hadassah, 156–7
Hagedorn, Hermann, *You Are the Hope of the World*, 139
Hall, Frank, 150
Hall, Stuart, 243n8
Halkin, Hillel, 228
Hammer, Michael, 228–30
Hampton, Wade, 53
Harari, Fred, 221–2
Harlem, 96; African American-Jewish residential proximity in, 78, 143–4; African

American-Jewish tensions in, 84, 218, 221–2, 278n93; anti-black restrictionist movements in, 68, 82, 152; Jewish activism in, 158–9, 161; Jewish interest in African American culture of, 153, 155–6; Jews as landlords in, 130, 152; riot of 1935, 164
Harmonie Club (New York), 74
Harrison, Earl H., 192
Harvard University, 20, 47, 136, 174, 179; discrimination against Jews at, 122, 127–8, 132, 161, 165, 171
Haunch, Paunch and Jowl (Ornitz), 171
Havurat Shalom (Somerville, MA), 214
Hawn, Goldie, 209
"Hebrew" as racial designation, 1, 30, 35, 89, 133, 230; used by U.S. government, 96, 102, 104, 106, 192, 204. *See also* government racial classification of Jews
Hebrew Benevolent Congregation (Atlanta), 58, 61
Hebrew Hammer, 235–6
Hebrew Standard, 98
Hebrew Union College, 29–30, 66, 94–5, 102, 175
Hecht, Simon, 89–90
Heeb magazine, 235–7
Heller, Max, 54, 57, 61, 66
Hendrick, Burton, 130
Hentoff, Nat, 213
Herberg, Will, 136; *Protestant-Catholic-Jew*, 206
Hertzberg, Arthur, 238
H-Ethnic listserv, 227
Heschel, Abraham Joshua, 212
Hillman, Sidney, 190
Hillquit, Morris, 82
Hirsch, Emil G.: asserts racial definition of Jews, 29–30; compares race riots and pogroms, 148; on intermarriage, 101; opposes racial definition of Jews, 28, 88; on Semites, 266n99
Hirsch, Samuel, 247n65
Hoberman, J., 210
Hollinger, David, 221
Holmes, John Haynes, 136
Holocaust, 207, 211, 223, 230
Holzel, David, 227
Home Missions Council, 133
Hooks, Benjamin, 222
Hooten, Ernest, 136
Horner, Henry, 123

Races of Mankind (Nott and Gliddon), 16
racial science, 44–6, 83, 108–14. *See also*
anthropology
radicals. *See* socialists; communists
Rankin, John, 191, 196
Rayner, Isidor, 54, 58
Reconstruction, 52, 58
Reconstructionist Jews, 226
Reform Advocate, 103
Reform Jews: on intermarriage and conversion, 21, 101–2, 175; on Jewish particularism, 11, 27–8, 92, 94, 96, 109–10,
114–5, 167, 176–7, 185, 202–3, 226,
248n79; support of African American
civil rights, 70–1, 148, 162–3. *See also*
Central Conference of American Rabbis;
Hebrew Union College; Union of Ameri-
can Hebrew Congregations
Reimer, Abraham, 84
religious pluralism, 136, 206–7
residential patterns, Jewish, 2; flight from
changing neighborhoods, 72, 74, 142–4,
152–3; housing conditions, 35, 38, 42;
proximity to African Americans, 76–78,
143–5, 159–62, 200; segregation of
Jews, 146
Response magazine, 214
Rhoda, 233
Rice, Elmer, 185
Richards, Bernard, 96–7
Richman, Julia, 25–26
Richmond, 53–5, 57, 77
Richmond Times, 53, 55
Riegelman, Harold, 174
Riis, Jacob, 38, 42
Ripley, William Z., 111; *Races of Europe*,
44–6, 108
Roback, Abraham, 155
Robeck, Ada, 21
Robinson, Jackie, 199
Roediger, David, 5
Rontch, Isaac, 154
Roosevelt, Franklin D., 189–93
Roosevelt, Theodore, 38, 48–9, 87, 99,
123, 189
Rosenbaum, Yankel, 225–6
Rosenberg, M. J., 214
Rosenbluth, Robert, 169
Rosenfield, Adolph B., 68
Rosenwald, Julius, 69, 71–3, 148
Ross, Barney, 199
Roth, David Lee, 209–10

Roth, Henry, *From Bondage*, 143–4
Rothschild, Jacob, 199
Rough Riders, 48
Rubin, Charles, 82
Ruskay, Esther J., 98

Sachs, Howard, 199
St. Louis, 22, 28, 55, 69, 99
Sale, Samuel, 99, 109
Saleski, Gdal, *Famous Musicians of a
Wandering Race*, 172
Salome of the Tenements (Yezierska), 168
Samuel, Maurice, 170–2, 175, 203; *You
Gentiles*, 170
San Francisco, 109, 114
San Francisco State University, 229
San Juan Hill (district of New York), 76
Sanders, Ronald, 154–5
Sandler, Adam, "The Chanukah Song,"
209–11
Sanua, Marianne, 177
Sargent, Frank P., 104
Saturday Night Live, 209
Savannah, 77
Schanfarber, Tobias, 74, 100, 101
Schiff, Jacob H.: endorses *The Melting Pot*,
101; and Maurice Fishberg, 91, 111;
opposes racial definition of Jews, 88–9,
93; on Semites, 20; supports African
American causes, 71–2, 257–8n84
Schiff, Sidney, 151
Schiffman, Lisa, 234
Schindler, Solomon, 11
Schindler's List, 223
Schmeling, Max, 185
Schoen, Max, 204
School for Jewish Communal Work (New
York), 180
schools. *See* public schools
Schulman, Samuel, 102
Schwartz, I. J., 138–9, 164
Schwartz, Ulysses S., 68
Schweppe, Emma, 136
Scottsboro Case, 128, 159, 163
segregation of African Americans, 55, 78,
142; Jewish opposition to, 69, 72, 149,
191, 197; Jewish support of, 58, 61, 68,
72, 149–50, 199–200. *See also* housing
restrictions
Seinfeld, Jerry, 210
self-definition of Jews: cultural (*see* eth-
nicity); national, 11, 17, 27, 167; racial,

3, 11–31, 86, 91–8, 100–2, 104–5, 107–11, 114–5, 165, 204–6 (*see also* "tribalism"); religious, 11–12, 28, 89, 100, 102, 104, 105, 108, 165, 168, 238–9

Seligman, Edwin R.A., 70

Seligman, Herbert, 147

Seligman, Isaac N., 71

Selikovitch, George, 103

Selma, AL, 216

Semites, 20, 44, 108–10, 111, 171, 179. *See also* Aryan-Semite dichotomy.

Sephardic Jews, 130–1

sexuality, stereotypes about Jewish, 42–3, 48–9

Shaare Tefila Congregation (Silver Spring, MD), 225

Shaare Tefila Congregation v. Cobb, 225

Shaarei Shomayim Congregation (Mobile, AL), 60

Shafran, Avi, 233

Shaler, Nathaniel S., 47–9, 87; *The Neighbor,* 47

Shapiro, Yonathan, 170

Sharpton, Al, 222

Shatner, William, 210

Sherman, Allen, 210

Sherman, TX, 18

Shore, Dinah, 209–10

Sid Jacobson Jewish Community Center (Long Island), 209

Silber, Mendel, 100

Silver Shirts, 191

Silver Spring, MD, 225

Simon, Kate, 155–6, 163

Simpson, O. J., 211

Sinai Temple (Chicago), 148

Singer, Al, 155

Singing Fool, 142

Sissle, Noble, 156

Six-Day War, 214

Skorecki, Karl, 228–30

Slaton, John, 43

slavery, 139; Jewish attitudes toward, 18, 79, 153, 245n31

Slavic immigrants, 76, 105, 273n17. *See also* Polish immigrants

"slumming," 155–6

Smith, Jack, 156

Smith College, 180

social dimension of Jewishness, 94, 96, 166–7, 206–8; clubs and lodges as focus for, 12–13; in-group marriage, 2, 12,

49–50, 174, 182, 207. *See also* outsider identity of Jews; peoplehood; self-definition of Jews

social discrimination against Jews, 13–14, 54, 57, 146, 161, 177. *See also* antisemitism; quotas against Jews in colleges and universities

social integration of Jews, 1, 5, 12–3, 19, 21–2, 190, 194, 197–201, 205, 208, 211, 223–4; as determinant of empathy for African Americans, 70, 197–201. *See also* acculturation; assimilation of Jews

Social Gospel, 70–1

socialists, Jewish, 81–2, 84, 96–7, 148, 150, 158–60, 162, 167

Socialist Party (American), 82, 159

Society for Ethical Culture. *See* Ethical Culture movement

Sokolsky, George, 183

Solis-Cohen, Solomon, 65

Somerville, MA, 214

Sonneschein, Solomon H., 28, 30

South: Jewish approach to African Americans in, 18, 52–62, 149–50, 82, 84, 199–200; racial context compared to that in North, 57, 62–3; rise of racial radicalism in, 31, 53; status of Jews in, 46, 52–55, 128. *See also specific locations*

South Carolina, 52, 54, 56, 199–200

Southern Israelite, 149, 169, 177

Soviet Jewry, movement to aid, 213–4, 216

Spain, Clarence, 78

Spanish-American War, 38, 88

Spargo, John, 123, 133–4; *The Jew and American Ideals,* 134

Spielberg, Stephen, 222–3

Spingarn, Arthur, 147

Spingarn, Joel Elias, 70, 147

sports. *See* athletics

Springfield, IL, race riot, 82, 84

Srole, Leo, 193

Stein, Mary, 78

Steinberg, Milton, *Partisan Guide to the Jewish Problem,* 203

Steinthal, Herman, 248n77

Stern, Howard, 210

Stern, Marc, 226

Stern, Maurice, 165

Stoddard, Lothrop, 125, 130–1

Stokes, John Phelps, 98, 168

Standard Club (Chicago), 67

Stanford University, 136